JUL 1 4 2017
MAIN

iOS in Practice

iOS in Practice

BEAR CAHILL

MANNING
SHELTER ISLAND

OLDHAM COUNTY PUBLIC LIBRARY
308 YAGER AVENUE
LAGRANGE, KY 40031

For online information and ordering of this and other Manning books, please visit www.manning.com. The publisher offers discounts on this book when ordered in quantity. For more information, please contact

Special Sales Department
Manning Publications Co.
20 Baldwin Road
PO Box 261
Shelter Island, NY 11964
Email: orders@manning.com

©2013 by Manning Publications Co. All rights reserved.

No part of this publication may be reproduced, stored in a retrieval system, or transmitted, in any form or by means electronic, mechanical, photocopying, or otherwise, without prior written permission of the publisher.

Many of the designations used by manufacturers and sellers to distinguish their products are claimed as trademarks. Where those designations appear in the book, and Manning Publications was aware of a trademark claim, the designations have been printed in initial caps or all caps.

♾ Recognizing the importance of preserving what has been written, it is Manning's policy to have the books we publish printed on acid-free paper, and we exert our best efforts to that end. Recognizing also our responsibility to conserve the resources of our planet, Manning books are printed on paper that is at least 15 percent recycled and processed without the use of elemental chlorine.

Manning Publications Co.
20 Baldwin Road
PO Box 261
Shelter Island, NY 11964

Development editor: Scott Meyers
Technical proofreader: James Hatheway
Copyeditors: Linda Kern, Benjamin Berg
Proofreaders: Katie Tennant, Alyson Brener
Typesetter: Dottie Marsico
Cover designer: Marija Tudor

ISBN 9781617291265
Printed in the United States of America
1 2 3 4 5 6 7 8 9 10 – MAL – 17 16 15 14 13 12

To Kelly Ripa, who brightens my wife's day,
who in turn brightens mine

brief contents

contents

preface

My professional coding career has gone from large to small in a variety of ways. I started on 3279 terminals at IBM, and with each professional move (from Ericsson to Travelocity and others) I went to smaller machines and smaller companies. Now I work on computers you can fit in your pocket and at a company of one: me.

When I first started working in mobile development, I used J2ME on various phones, including Blackberries. When I got the chance to work on an iPhone, I purchased my first MacBook and loved it! It wasn't until sometime later that I realized that I had gotten in at the beginning of the mobile wave. Solving problems alone, and often under non-disclosure agreements, I learned a lot, and as each new version of the OS came out, it got easier and better. The platform quickly became more sophisticated, and so did the user.

Then Manning approached me to talk about a book on iOS development, and I was surprised how clear and formed my opinions were about what should be included. I had learned a lot on my own—from frameworks to widgets to the UI to MVC and more—and I felt that emphasis was often placed on the wrong areas. I also felt that the sample code provided by Apple was underemphasized. I believe that project-based learning is the best—at least it is for me—and seeing how the different parts of a project come together is not only useful but necessary to make sense of the project and put it into context.

I was flattered that Manning asked me to write this book and I hope it will help you to learn iOS development—and to put it into practice.

acknowledgments

First I'd like to thank everyone at Manning, starting with my editors, Scott Meyers, Troy Mott, and Jeff Bleiel, and then going on to publisher Marjan Bace and all the others who helped along the way, including Nick Chase, Linda Kern, Benjamin Berg, Katie Tennant, Alyson Brener, and Janet Vail, for their support and hard work.

I'd like to thank the following reviewers for reading my manuscript at various stages of its development and providing invaluable feedback: Jonas Bandi, Jeremy Villeneuve, Mekka Okereke, Amos Bannister, Stephen Aument, Bryan "Groucho" Duke, Serban Porumbescu, Clint Tredway, Mike Stok, Arif Shaikh, Jonathan Hohle, Gavin Whyte, Subhasis Ghosh, Mark Janssen, Barry Tolnas, and Christopher Haupt. I would also like to thank James Hatheway for his technical review of the final manuscript shortly before it went into production.

I'd also like to thank Eric Silverthorn, David Barnard, and Mekka Okereke for giving me so much help and work early on to get me started.

I'd like to thank Steve Jobs and everyone at Apple for creating this market and for everything that surrounds what I get to do every day.

To O.A.R. and Seryn, thanks for providing the soundtrack to my writing of this book and my coding in general.

Amy, my wife, deserves a lot of thanks for putting up with me during this time (and all other times). Thanks to her and my sons for so much love.

And I thank God for all of the above—and everything else!

about this book

This book is organized into two parts. Part one talks about iOS development in general. How to get started, the frameworks provided by Apple, the Provisioning Portal, the IDE, and several core concepts are introduced in this first part of the book. The second part includes techniques for putting iOS development into practice. The chapters in part 2 contain projects that are developed using multiple techniques. By the end of the chapter (or two chapters in one case), you'll go through the development of an app from beginning to end.

The apps developed in the chapters can be found for free in the AppStore so you can see how they wound up. But if you go through the chapters and follow along (or download the source code), you will be able to see see how the app is coded and run it yourself.

My suggestion is to follow along with the development of each project in each chapter. Downloading the source code is helpful, but try typing out the lines of code from the book, if you have time. This will help you to experience the process and you will see how Xcode handles things like code-completion, navigation, UI design, and so on. That hands-on experience is invaluable.

I expect you're reading this book because you want to learn about different aspects of iOS development and are just starting out. However, this is not an Objective-C programming book. It's assumed that you already know a bit of Objective-C, are learning it concurrently, or are willing to glean what you can from diving right in. Regardless of your level of experience, I recommend that you digest each line of code in order to understand the details of all aspects of iOS development.

Roadmap

Part 1 covers the groundwork needed to get started in iOS development. In chapter 1, you'll get to develop your first Hello World app, but we'll also cover some of the core areas and concepts of iOS development. Chapter 2 covers the development environment, including Xcode for editing the code and user interface along with other concepts and tools.

Chapter 3 begins part 2 with your first real app project: PicDecor. In this chapter you'll learn about view controllers and displaying images as well as how to interface with sending email. You'll see how to design the UI, and how to connect it to the code you're writing.

Chapter 4 builds on what you learned in chapter 3 about view controllers by showing you table view controllers and how to access the address book.

Chapter 5 continues with access to images through the photo album and the camera and how to manipulate those images. Also, in chapter 5 you'll see how to display a map and the user's location and store data for later retrieval and display.

The Settings Bundle is the official way to have a user manage app settings and is covered in chapter 6. Also covered are playing MP3s and detecting motion (particularly shaking) of the device. Chapter 7 goes further in playing audio, allowing the user to make playlists and play them via the iPad framework. This includes covering CoreData for database design and for storing app data.

Push notifications and in-app purchase both use external server interaction for their functionality and are covered in chapter 8 for our Rock, Paper, Scissors game. Chapter 9 continues the game with GameCenter interaction including leaderboards and achievements.

Chapter 10 could be called the "iChapter" as it covers using the iTunes API to search music, designing for the iPad, and advertising using iAds.

Finally, chapter 11 covers the more recent additions to iOS. Specifically, it covers the collection view, Social Framework, reminders, and UI state restoration.

Code conventions

There are many Objective-C code examples in this book edited with Xcode. Source code in listings and text is in a `fixed-width font like this` to separate it from ordinary text.

Writing code for a book is challenging compared with writing code that isn't going to be published for the world to see. Restrictions on line length, readability, and conciseness encouraged decisions I might not have made otherwise. You will find that I may have added a method to a class that might not make the most sense, or named some variables in less-than-perfect ways. Please concentrate on the content over form in those cases.

As all aspects of mobile, websites, documentation, tools, and so on change regularly, some images in the book may not match what you see online and elsewhere. However, the concepts are likely to remain, and the variance you might see shouldn't cause confusion.

Source code downloads

You will need a few things to benefit from the information presented in this book, starting with an Apple computer. Then you will need to download Xcode and the accompanying documentation, including public/open source libraries, as well as the source code for the examples in the book. The chapters will then direct you on what to do, one step at a time.

You will find the source code for the working examples in this book available for download from the publisher's website at www.manning.com/iOSinPractice.

You can also find some of the apps developed in this book in the Apple App Store.

About the title

The title of this book communicates its two core aspects—it covers iOS development both in general and in practice. Learning happens best through examples and exercises, as opposed to learning about theories or concepts in isolation. So I've included numerous hands-on techniques and examples to get you started in iOS development.

About the author

Bear Cahill has worked in iOS development at Brainwash Inc. since 2008 and through the development of several dozen apps. Prior to that, Bear worked at IBM, Ericsson, and Travelocity, among other companies.

From REXX to BASIC to C++ to Java to Objective-C, along with several other languages, Bear has worked on a variety of platforms and technologies. He now focuses on independent work, using friends to handle related server, Android, and other work.

Bear enjoys spending time with his wife and two sons around downtown Denton, Texas. He has too many hobbies past and future to list here, so we'll just say he's never been sky diving, scuba diving, or stage diving. No diving allowed!

Author Online

The purchase of *iOS in Practice* includes free access to a private forum run by Manning Publications where you can make comments about the book, ask technical questions, and receive help from the author and other users. You can access and subscribe to the forum at www.manning.com/iOSinPractice. This page provides information on how to get on the forum after you're registered, what kind of help is available, and the rules of conduct in the forum.

Manning's commitment to our readers is to provide a venue where a meaningful dialogue among individual readers and between readers and the author can take place. It's not a commitment to any specific amount of participation on the part of the author, whose contribution to the book's forum remains voluntary (and unpaid). We suggest you try asking the author some challenging questions, lest his interest stray!

The Author Online forum and the archives of previous discussions will be accessible from the publisher's website as long as the book is in print.

about the cover illustration

The figure on the cover of *iOS in Practice* is captioned “A man from Kastela, near Split, Dalmatia, Croatia.” The illustration is taken from a reproduction of an album of traditional Croatian costumes from the mid-nineteenth century by Nikola Arsenovic, published by the Ethnographic Museum in Split, Croatia, in 2003. The illustrations were obtained from a helpful librarian at the Ethnographic Museum in Split, itself situated in the Roman core of the medieval center of the town: the ruins of Emperor Diocletian’s retirement palace from around AD 304. The book includes finely colored illustrations of figures from different regions of Croatia, accompanied by descriptions of the costumes and of everyday life.

Kastela is a series of seven towns located on the Adriatic coast in central Dalmatia. Once an ancient Greek port, a stopover point for the Roman army, and a summer place for Croatian kings, Kastela today is a popular tourist resort. Along its long sandy beach there are many terraces and lookout points, surrounded by pine and tamaris trees. The figure on the cover is wearing black woolen trousers and a jacket over a white linen shirt. His costume is richly trimmed with the colorful embroidery that is typical for this region. He wears a red cap on his head and in his hand he holds a long pipe.

Dress codes and lifestyles have changed over the last 200 years, and the diversity by region, so rich at the time, has faded away. It’s now hard to tell apart the inhabitants of different continents, let alone of different hamlets or towns separated by only a few miles. Perhaps we have traded cultural diversity for a more varied personal life—certainly for a more varied and fast-paced technological life.

Manning celebrates the inventiveness and initiative of the computer business with book covers based on the rich diversity of regional life of two centuries ago, brought back to life by illustrations from old books and collections like this one.

Part 1

Getting started

Before I cover the iOS apps created in each chapter, there's some groundwork to lay. Apple manages the AppStore and app development quite closely. I believe this is for the protection of Apple, the developers, and the users. However, there's a good bit of work and learning that needs to be done to get things rolling. Early in chapter 1, you'll get to develop your first Hello World app, but I'll also cover some of the core areas and concepts of iOS development. Chapter 2 will cover more about the development environment, including Xcode for editing the code and user interface, and other concepts and tools.

1 Getting started with iOS development

This chapter covers

- Xcode and Objective-C
- Getting to know Xcode
- A Hello World example

I've been developing professionally for over 20 years in about every language and platform, but I believe iOS development is some of the most exciting, fun, gratifying, and challenging work I've ever done. I love iOS development.

Not only is it appealing from a developer's standpoint, it's also the leading mobile platform. This means that there's lots to do, with lots of growth and changes, and plenty of support out there from Apple, forums, other developers, books, conferences, and so on.

With the growth of iOS and other mobile platforms, tablets, which nicely bridge traditional computers and smart phones, are now a huge market. These mobile devices allow for more opportunities for development, and iOS lets you develop for both platforms simultaneously.

In this chapter, we develop an iOS application (or *app*). We need to go over a few topics, including setting up the development environment, but by the end of the chapter, you'll have your first app. Let's go!

1.1 The iOS development environment

Xcode is the primary tool for developing iOS (and OS X) applications. It's free from Apple and helps with a variety of development-related tasks including user interface (UI) design/development, revision control, and more.

The primary language that iOS is developed in is called *Objective-C*. Objective-C is a descendent of C, which means that all C code will compile and run in Objective-C. But, unlike C, Objective-C is object-oriented. If you know C++, Java, or other object-oriented languages, you'll have no problem understanding this language. Keep in mind that the purpose of this book isn't to teach you Objective-C, so if you find you're having a hard time with the language, you may want to take some time and use other resources to research Objective-C.

Apple also provides a rich set of frameworks. Some are required for any app and are automatically included. The rest are optional, depending on your preferences, and can greatly add to your project. When iOS first came out, displaying a map of a location was difficult and labor intensive. Adding pinned locations to the map was even more complex. When MapKit was introduced, adding a map and displaying the user's location became practically effortless.

WebKit, StoreKit, MediaPlayer, Social, and CoreData are a few more frameworks that bring ease of functionality when added to your projects. Many open source and/or third-party frameworks are available to keep you from having to reinvent the wheel for common—but complicated—functionality.

iOS development also relies heavily on the *Model-View-Controller (MVC)* architecture pattern. MVC is the separation of your development into three aspects: model, view, and controller. The *model* is the data layer (for example, the database in a project). The *view* is the UI that the user interacts with. The *controller* is between the view and the model, and it translates the user interaction to logic and accesses data as necessary.

As you can see, Xcode does a lot to facilitate what you need to do as a developer as well as enables you to do it in a fashion best suited for iOS projects. Let's look into the details of getting, installing, and becoming familiar with Xcode, and then you'll develop your first app.

1.2 Using Xcode

As stated in the previous section, Xcode is the primary development tool for iOS projects. In this section, we look at how to get Xcode from Apple and tour the various parts of Xcode to simplify iOS development.

1.2.1 Getting Xcode

Using the App Store from Apple, you can search for Xcode and quickly find it. It's free, so just click on the FREE button to begin the install (see figure 1.1). It's a large download and might take a while, but the download process is pretty easy. Xcode and related apps will then be installed in /Developer/Applications and key apps will be added to the Developer folder in Launchpad.

Figure 1.1 Xcode in the App Store

You may also go to http://developer.apple.com and download Xcode if you'd like to go the more manual route. There you'll also see information about joining the various developer programs such as Safari, iOS, and Mac.

In most cases, the developer programs cost money to join, but they also allow access to advance/beta releases, developer forums, and other resources. If you intend to do much iOS development, I highly recommend joining. If you intend to release any apps, you have to join.

Now that you have Xcode installed, let's look at the various aspects of it.

1.2.2 Tour of Xcode

Xcode can handle all of the major aspects of project development for iOS projects. It can manage the organization of code, linking frameworks, UI design, editing, projects (such as regular and pro versions of the same code base for separate apps), building, testing, and submission to Apple for review. In this chapter, we look at some of the basics to get started with Xcode. In later chapters, we explore more details and areas of Xcode.

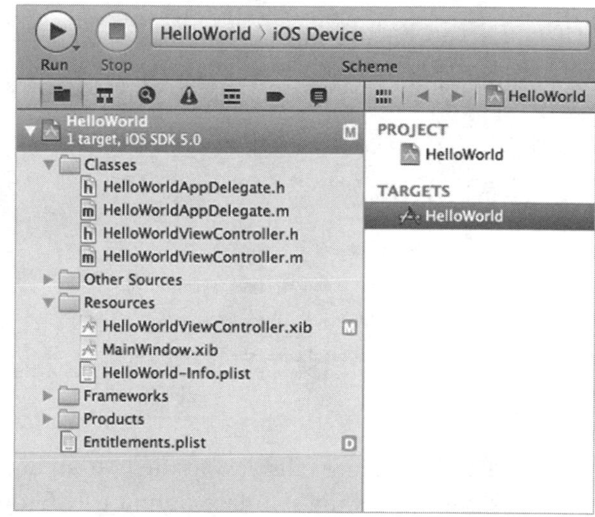

Figure 1.2 Navigator in Xcode

Given that Xcode helps in so many ways, it makes sense that there are a lot of areas, panes, views, and such included in it. The Navigator on the left displays the various files, frameworks, projects, and related items included in your project (see figure 1.2). This allows you to select files to edit or control in various ways.

The Utilities area, displayed by the right button above View on the top right, shows various aspects and settings of a selected item such as a file (see figure 1.3). Here you can see how a given item relates to other items, set various attributes, and more. This is particularly helpful when using the Interface Builder (IB) UI editor to set attributes on visual items.

The Editor is probably the most familiar-looking item in Xcode because all development needs a way to edit code (see figure 1.4). But the Editor serves as the editor not only for code, but also the UI and data (such as database design for CoreData), which you'll see throughout the projects in this book.

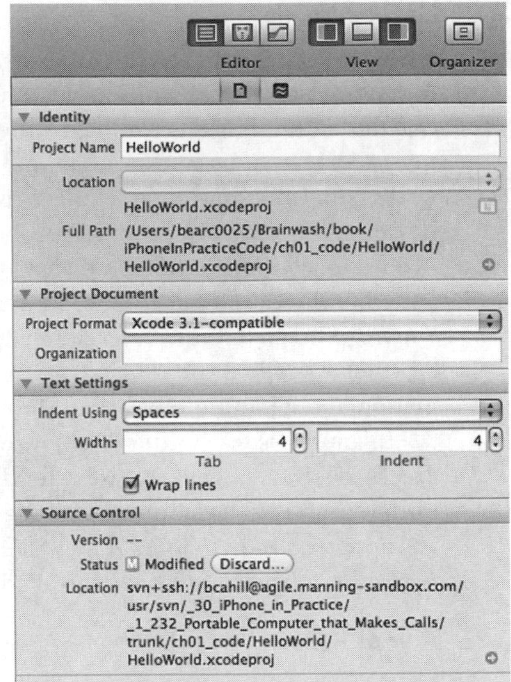

Figure 1.3 Utilities in Xcode for HWViewController.m

```
HelloWorld 〉 HelloWorld 〉 HWViewController.m 〉 No Selection
//
//  HWViewController.m
//  HelloWorld
//
//  Created by Bear Cahill on 11/30/11.
//  Copyright (c) 2011 __MyCompanyName__. All rights reserved.
//

#import "HWViewController.h"

@implementation HWViewController

- (void)didReceiveMemoryWarning
{
    [super didReceiveMemoryWarning];
    // Release any cached data, images, etc that aren't in use.
}
```

Figure 1.4 Xcode Editor with HWViewController.m selected

The Debug area displays at the bottom and can be split to display the Console on the right for viewing standard output (see figure 1.5). Both of these can be helpful for displaying variable values and output during testing.

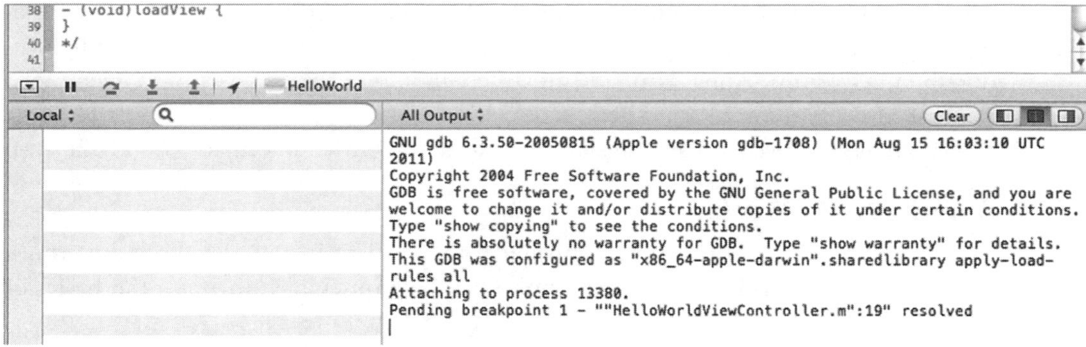

Figure 1.5 Debug view and console during Hello World execution

The Toolbar is located at the top of the window and is helpful for displaying various areas, starting/stopping test runs, and selecting what scheme to use for building (see figure 1.6).

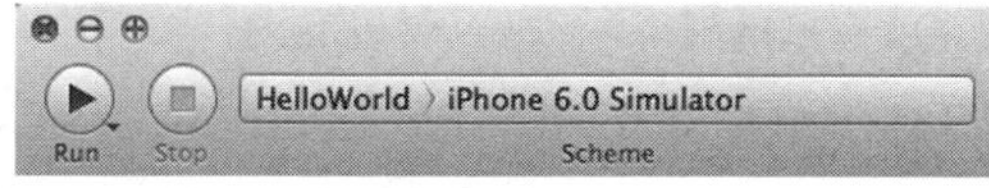

Figure 1.6 Xcode toolbar at the top of the window

The Organizer, which is displayed in the Window menu, is used for a variety of aspects of development. It displays framework and other help documentation, facilitates submitting your binary to the AppStore for review, organizes your various devices, and more (see figure 1.7). It can help you keep track of your provisioning profiles as well as give you access to your crash reports on your devices (not that your apps will crash—other people need this).

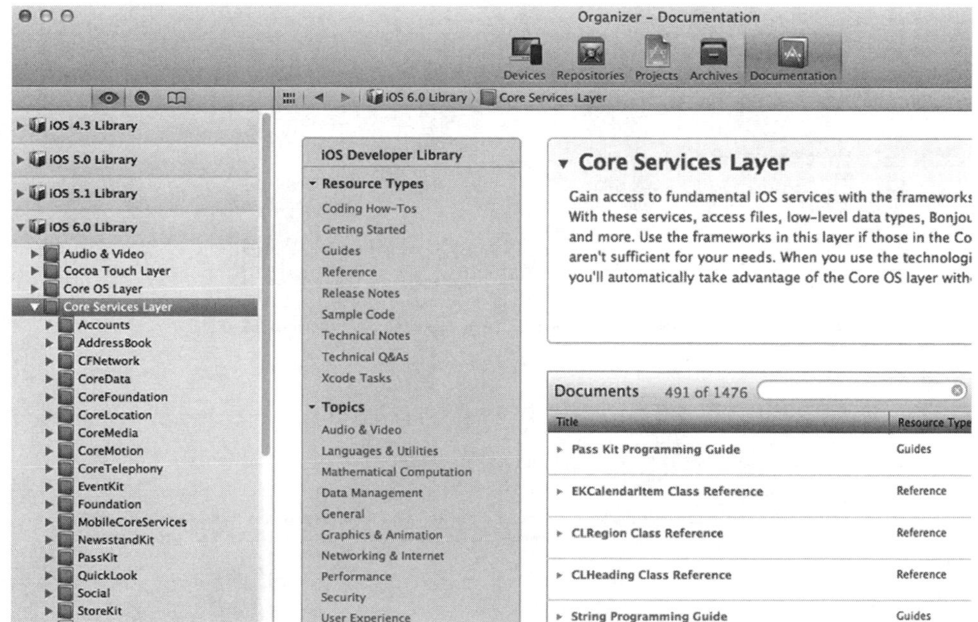

Figure 1.7 Xcode Organizer displaying framework documentation

The Organizer can be particularly helpful in bringing up context-related documentation by using command-click on text in your code. Also, it gives you access to helpful documents like the "Apple Human Interface Guidelines" and "Learning Objective-C: A Primer." Both are recommended reading.

Now that you have your bearings with Xcode and its environment, let's build that app!

1.3 A quick Hello World app

As a way to explore Xcode more and get your feet wet in iOS development, you'll create a basic app. It won't do much, but it will be a quick pass through the basics of creating an app.

First, you'll create a new project that includes several steps to specify necessary aspects of your project. Then you'll create the UI for your app and run it.

1.3.1 Creating a New Project

Start Xcode and, when prompted, select Create a New Project (see figure 1.8).

You'll be presented with various options for a template for your project. Be sure that Application is selected under iOS on the top left. The appropriate options will be displayed on the right. Select Single View Application (see figure 1.9) and click Next on the bottom right.

Figure 1.8 Create a new project with Xcode.

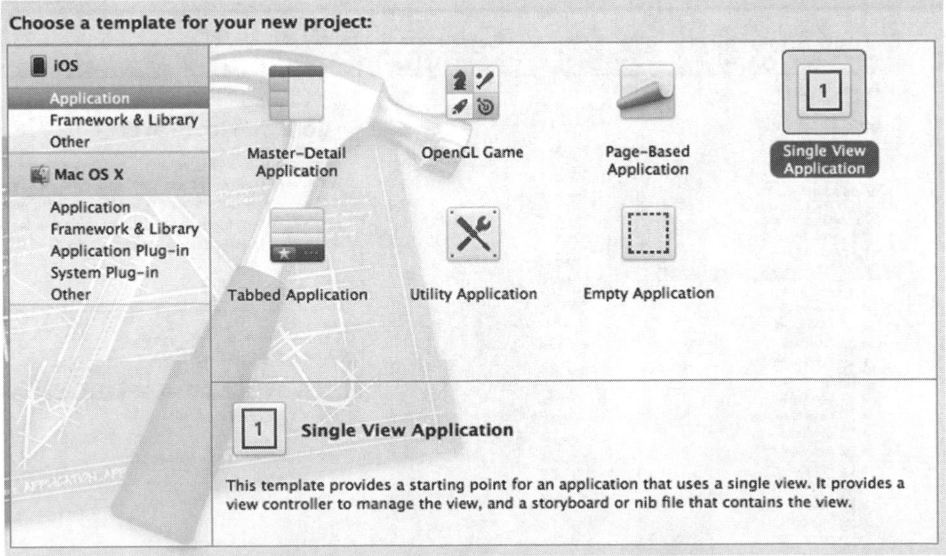

Figure 1.9 Single View Application template for new project

You'll then be prompted to name your product as well as set the company identifier, which is typically a reverse DNS value. You'll also specify a class prefix (for the naming convention) and specify the device family (such as iPhone). Finally, select Storyboard for UI design, reference counting for memory management, and unit tests (see figure 1.10).

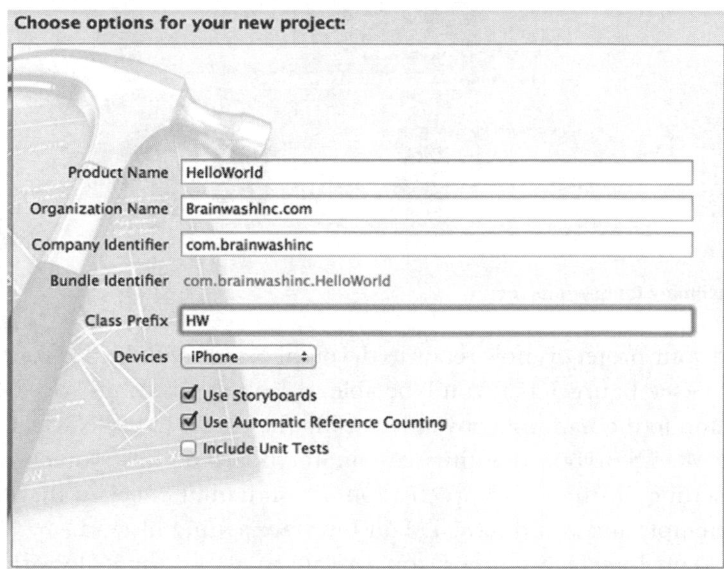

Figure 1.10 Xcode options for a new project

Click Next and you'll be presented with a Finder window to specify the location of the project (see figure 1.11). You can also create a local git repository for your project during this step (see the bottom of figure 1.11).

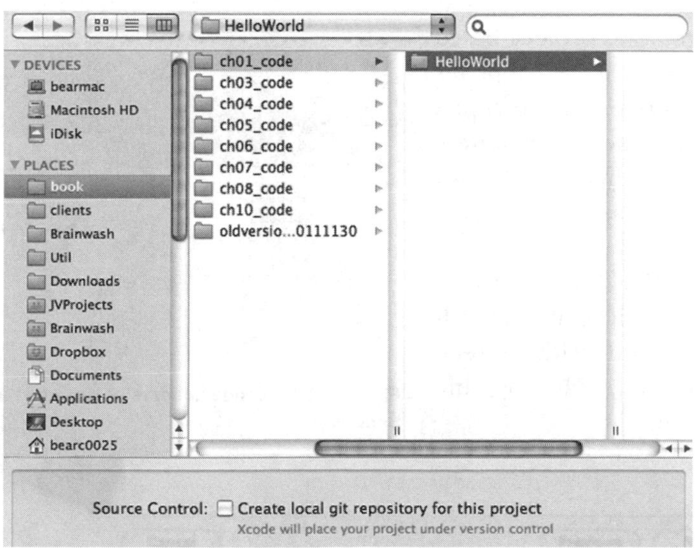

Figure 1.11 Specify the location of a new project.

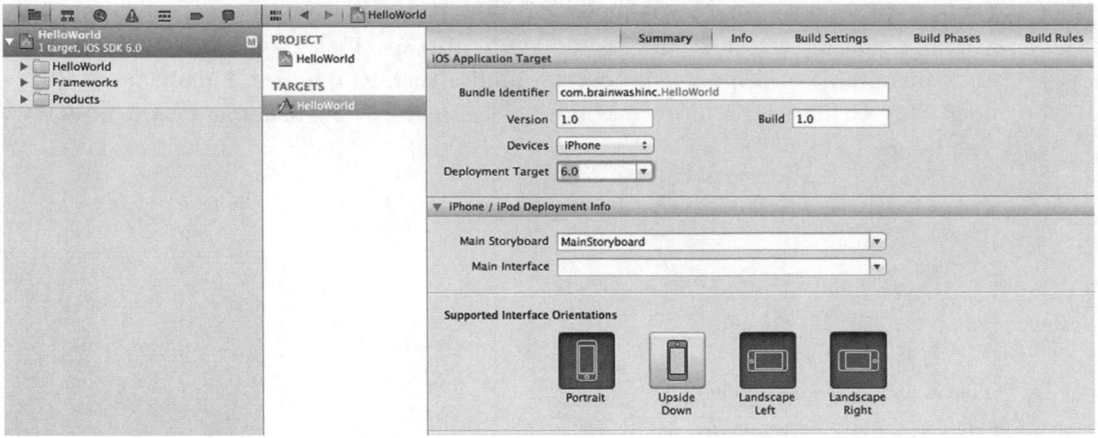

Figure 1.12 Xcode Target summary for new project

Click Create and your project is now ready to develop! Xcode will display your default Target's summary (see figure 1.12). You'll be able to see the selections you made. Pay particular attention to the naming convention using the prefix in the Navigator.

Note also the Main Storyboard setting of MainStoryboard because you chose to use the Storyboard setting during your app creation. If you hadn't checked that box, this setting would be empty and you'd have a Main Interface setting instead.

The default Main Interface settings would relate to a UI design file with the file extension of xib. Instead, you have a .storyboard file in your project. Most of the projects in this book use XIB files for UI design, but you'll use Storyboard here. Now let's look at the file and the UI of your first app.

1.3.2 Editing the user interface

Before you change your project based on the template, let's run it. Yep, it's already in a state where you can compile and run it. Make sure the iPhone Simulator is selected in the scheme pull-down menu on the top left (see figure 1.13) and click Run.

Xcode will compile, link, and execute the code using the iOS Simulator. It will only display a blank white screen because your app doesn't do anything yet. Let's change that!

Figure 1.13 Xcode scheme selected as an iPhone Simulator

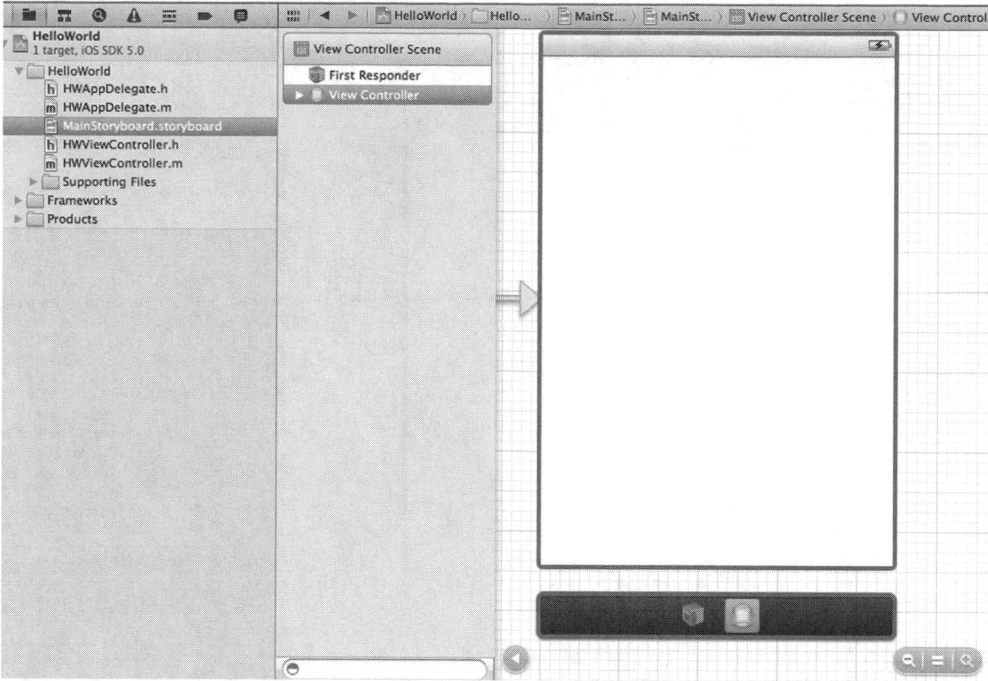

Figure 1.14 Storyboard file displayed in the Editor

Click on the Storyboard file in your project (for example, MainStoryboard.storyboard); the UI contents will be displayed in the Editor, which, in this case, is Interface Builder for the user interface (see figure 1.14). That white rectangle is the view controller you saw displayed when you ran the project in the simulator.

Note the HWViewController.h/.m files in the Navigator. Note the items in the list on the left in the Editor (see figure 1.14). The one listed as View Controller is an instance of your `HWViewController` class. Therefore, changes to it in the Editor will affect how your app runs.

Be sure that Utilities is visible (right button above View on the top right of Xcode) and note that there's a list of items at the bottom (see figure 1.15).

That list on the bottom right contains other UI items that can be dropped onto your UI. Scroll down the list until you see Label. Drag it into the Editor and drop it in the big white area of your view controller.

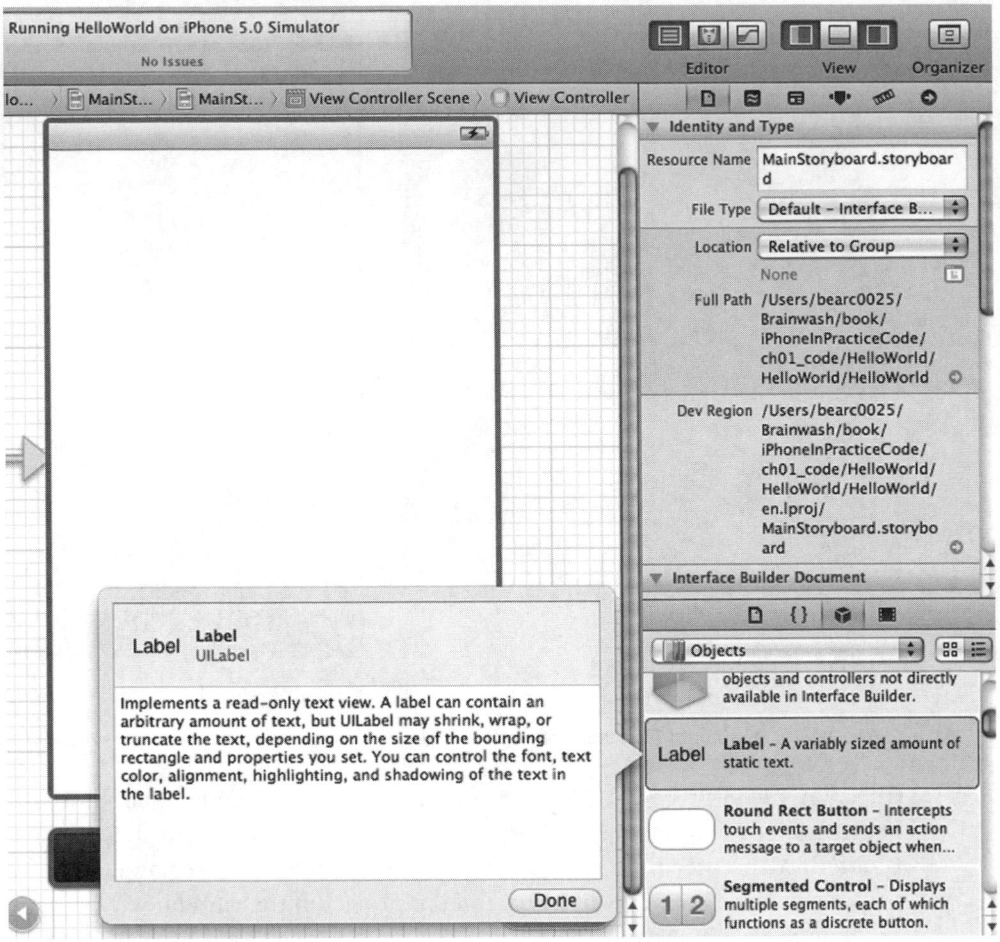

Figure 1.15 Utilities displayed for Storyboard file

Double-click on the newly dropped label and type `Hello World` (see figure 1.16). Now run your app again and … congrats! You have a functioning app! Check out figure 1.17 to see what your app's label should look like.

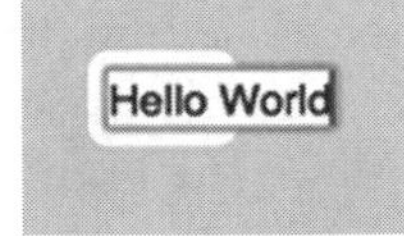

Figure 1.16 Adding a label to the project UI

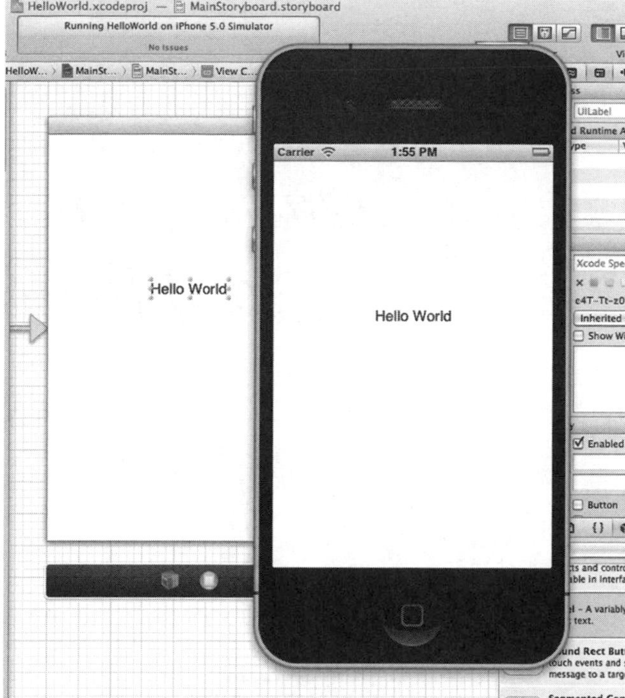

Figure 1.17 Hello World app running in iOS Simulator

Now run your app again and … congrats (see figure 1.17)!

1.4 Summary

Great job! Your first app is done! Not so painful, right? Now you're an iOS developer (although I don't expect you to make much money from the app you created)!

In this chapter, you learned about Xcode, including how to get it and its various parts, areas, views, editors, and so on. Based on that knowledge, we quickly moved into developing a Hello World app to get a taste of iOS development.

But that's only the start. I'm sure you've seen the amazing things that iOS apps can do, so you know there's so much more possible than what you've done so far. In the next chapter, you'll take the next step of including user interaction in your Hello World app. There's no limit to what you can do, so let's dive in!

2 Creating an iOS application

This chapter covers

- Implementation and header files
- Working with buttons
- Actions and outlets

At the end of the last chapter, you created your first iOS app. But it's a stretch to say you "developed" an app. Xcode did the majority of the work—you just added a label and typed "Hello World." You didn't include any user interaction or even write any code.

In this chapter, you'll add to your current Hello World app to make it do some basic things that will move it from an Xcode template closer to a legitimate app.

First, let's look at the types of source code files (.h and .m). Then you'll see how to tap into that process to get user actions and then act on them. Finally, I'll briefly talk about notifications as a way to notify any observing objects of something.

2.1 Source code files

Objective-C, like other object-oriented languages, has classes that typically encapsulate data and the actions that manipulate that data.

> **FROM "LEARNING OBJECTIVE-C: A PRIMER"** The specification of a class in Objective-C requires two distinct pieces: the interface and the implementation. The interface portion contains the class declaration and defines the instance variables and methods associated with the class. The interface is usually in a .h file. The implementation portion contains the code for the methods of the class. The implementation is usually in a .m file.

If you're not familiar with Objective-C, I'd recommend "Learning Objective-C: A Primer" (see http://mng.bz/65W2). You don't need to master Objective-C in order to learn a lot from this book, but you'll be able to learn more easily if Objective-C particulars aren't getting in the way.

In your project, you can see that there are two classes: `HWAppDelegate` and `HWViewController` (see figure 2.1); note the HW prefixing the filenames based on your setting when you created the project. Each of these classes has its interface files (.h) and their implementation files (.m). In both cases, the interface files (more commonly called *header files*) don't have much in them.

Figure 2.1 Source code files in the Hello World project

The most interesting thing in each of these cases is what comes after the class name (see the following code snippet). The item after the colon (:) specifies the parent class that this class inherits from. In the case of your `HWViewController`, the class inherits from the `UIViewController`.

```
@interface HWAppDelegate : UIResponder <UIApplicationDelegate>
```

Your `HWAppDelegate` inherits from the `UIResponder`. But what's more important is what's between the less-than (<) and greater-than (>) symbols: `<UIApplicationDelegate>`. That denotes that the class implements the interface specified in that file. Command-click on `UIApplicationDelegate` to see the definition of that interface (see figure 2.2).

Inheritance is a basic part of object-oriented development and I recommend that you research that subject more if you're not comfortable with it. Implementing interfaces will come up a lot in iOS development, and we'll discuss it more in this chapter.

For now, make a note of it. Next you'll add a button to your UI and continue with your app.

```
@protocol UIApplicationDelegate<NSObject>

@optional

- (void)applicationDidFinishLaunching:(UIApplication *)application;
- (BOOL)application:(UIApplication *)application didFinishLaunchingWithOptions:(NSDictionary *)
    launchOptions __OSX_AVAILABLE_STARTING(__MAC_NA,__IPHONE_3_0);

- (void)applicationDidBecomeActive:(UIApplication *)application;
- (void)applicationWillResignActive:(UIApplication *)application;
- (BOOL)application:(UIApplication *)application handleOpenURL:(NSURL *)url;  // Will be deprecated
    at some point, please replace with application:openURL:sourceApplication:annotation:
- (BOOL)application:(UIApplication *)application openURL:(NSURL *)url sourceApplication:(NSString *
    )sourceApplication annotation:(id)annotation __OSX_AVAILABLE_STARTING(__MAC_NA,__IPHONE_4_2);
    // no equiv. notification. return NO if the application can't open for some reason

- (void)applicationDidReceiveMemoryWarning:(UIApplication *)application;      // try to clean up as
    much memory as possible. next step is to terminate app
- (void)applicationWillTerminate:(UIApplication *)application;
- (void)applicationSignificantTimeChange:(UIApplication *)application;        // midnight, carrier
    time update, daylight savings time change

- (void)application:(UIApplication *)application willChangeStatusBarOrientation:
    (UIInterfaceOrientation)newStatusBarOrientation duration:(NSTimeInterval)duration;
- (void)application:(UIApplication *)application didChangeStatusBarOrientation:
    (UIInterfaceOrientation)oldStatusBarOrientation;

- (void)application:(UIApplication *)application willChangeStatusBarFrame:(CGRect)newStatusBarFrame
```

Figure 2.2 `UIApplicationDelegate` definition

2.2 Adding a button to your app

Back in your Hello World project, click on the Storyboard file to display your UI.

Like you did with the label, display the Utilities and scroll down the items list on the bottom right to find the Round Rect Button (see figure 2.3).

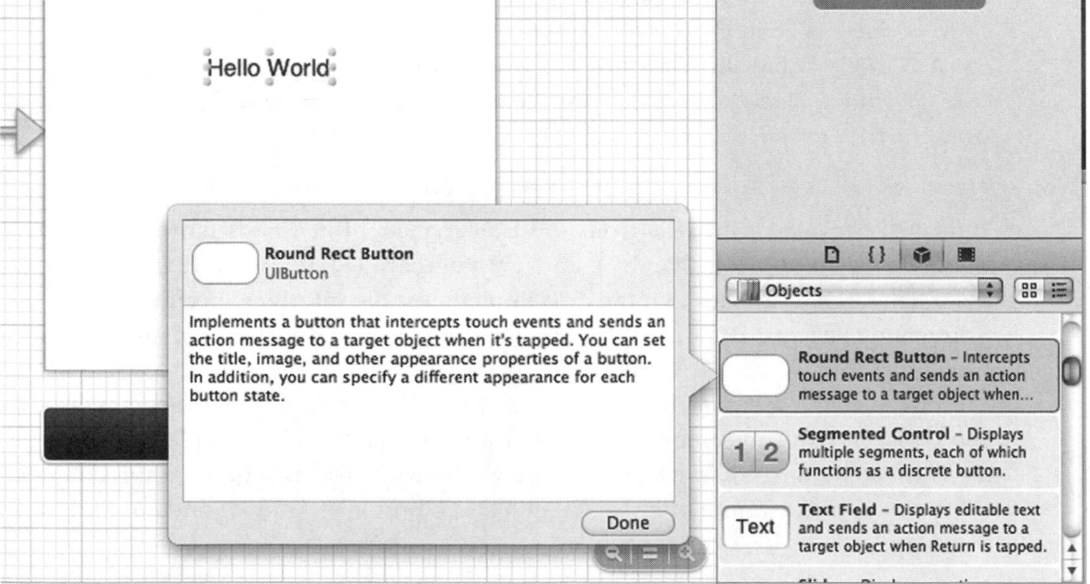

Figure 2.3 Storyboard utilities with Round Rect Button selected

Drag and drop the button to your UI design below the Hello World label you created. Double-click on the button and type `Hide` (see figure 2.4).

Figure 2.4 Adding a Hide button to Hello World

If you run the project now, it'll display the button. You can even click/tap it, but it doesn't do anything. That's because you haven't developed anything for it to do. Let's do that now.

2.3 Connecting your button to an action

The goal of adding some items to the UI for the user to interact with is getting that action to the code where you can add some logic.

This goes back to the MVC pattern. The UI is the view for the user to see and interact with. For your app, you need to capture that user's tap on the button to call some code and act on it.

In iOS development, you do that by assigning an *action* for the button to call when tapped. The UI editor, IB, can create this relationship and even stub out the code for you.

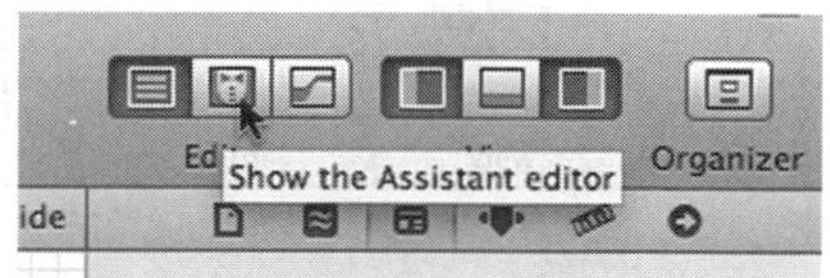

Figure 2.5 Displaying the Assistant for the UI editor

Click on the Storyboard file to display it in the Editor. Next, click on the Assistant toggle (the tuxedo icon) to use that (see figure 2.5).

Now you see the Storyboard file on the left and the HWViewController.h file on the right (see figure 2.6). If for some reason you need to change the file displayed on the right, use the hierarchy menu just above the file in the Editor.

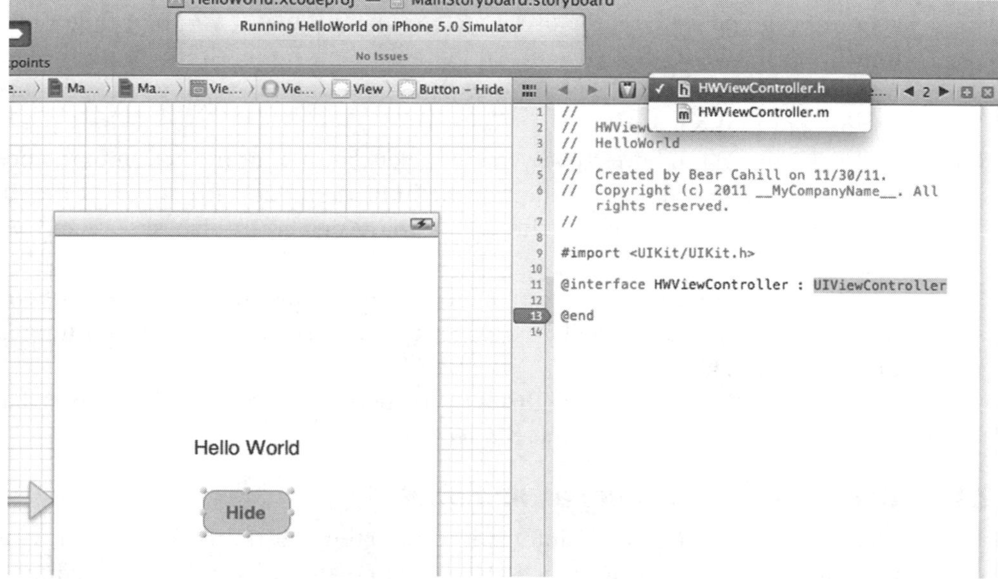

Figure 2.6 Storyboard and HWViewController.h file with Assistant

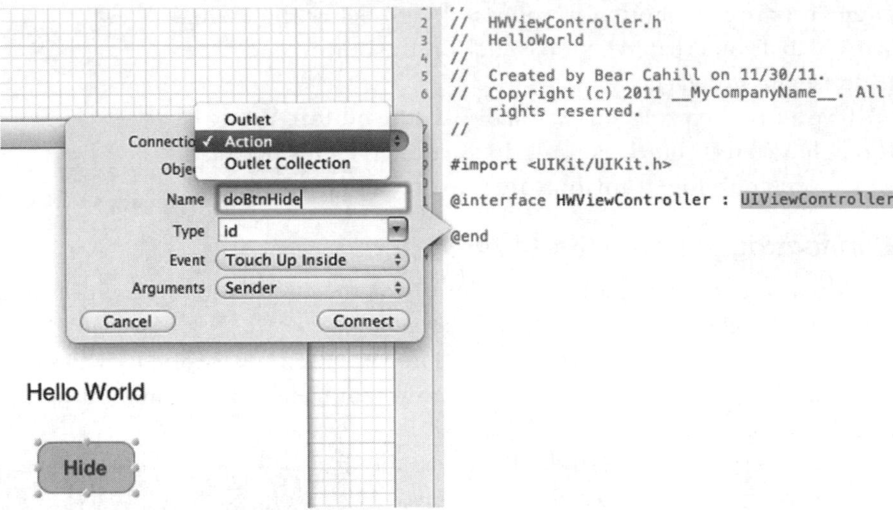

Figure 2.7 Creating an action for the Hide button using IB

Control-drag the connection line from the button in the UI on the left to the header file on the right just above `@end` and release. A pop-up allows you to specify the connection being created (see figure 2.7).

The pop-up allows you to specify from the drop-down menu that the connection is an action. Type in the name of the action method you'd like to create. For buttons I usually start with `doBtn` and then something appropriate.

Note the other settings. The Type is set to id; this specifies the type of item that the action will accept in the signature. The Event is Touch Up Inside, which means this action should be called if the user touches the button and *lifts* their finger off the button (for example, it's not an action if they *slide* their finger off the button). Finally, the Argument is Sender, which, in this case, is the button, so you get a reference to the button sent to this action.

Click Connect to have Xcode create the declaration of the action in the header file and a stub of the implementation in the implementation file. Look at the .h and .m files and you'll see almost the same thing in both places: `(IBAction)doBtnHide:(id)sender`.

The only difference is the empty block in the implementation. Now when the button is tapped, this action will be called, but it's currently empty, so nothing happens. Let's change that.

An alternative way of doing this is to create the `IBAction` declaration first and then select it as the end point for the connection.

2.4 Connecting your label as an outlet

Like you connect UI items' interactions to actions in the code, you can connect UI items to *outlets* in the code. This allows you to create UI items in the UI editor but have a reference to them in the code.

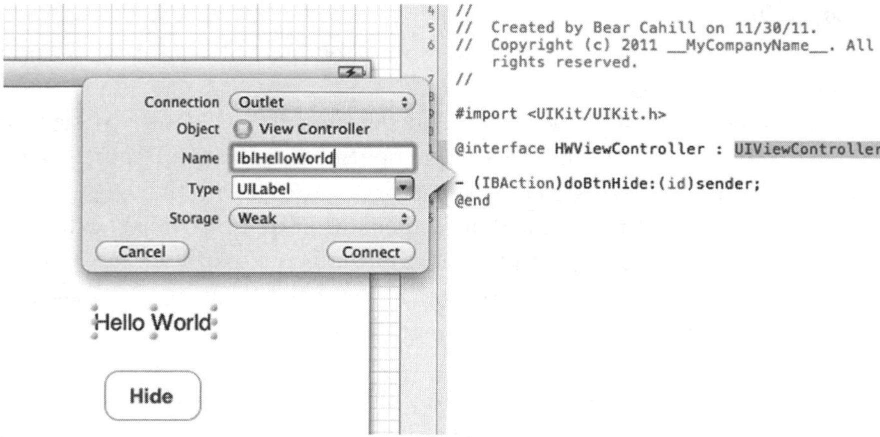

Figure 2.8 Connect your label to an outlet in `HWViewController`.

To create an outlet connection in the code to your label, you do something similar to the way you created the action. Open the Storyboard file, display the Assistant, and Control-drag from the label to the header file (see figure 2.8). You can leave all of the settings as the defaults and type in a name for the variable: `lblHelloWorld`.

Now you have an action connected to your button and a reference to the label. What should you have the Hide button do when it's tapped?

Like with the action, an alternative way of doing this is to create the `IBOutlet` declaration first and then select it as the end point for the connection.

2.5 Implementing your button action

You can now implement your `doBtnHide:` to do what you'd like. The obvious action to perform would be to hide something. Because you also have an outlet defined as a reference to the Hello World label, let's hide that.

The only code you need to add to the method is `[lblHelloWorld setHidden:YES];` and you're done. Run that and hide the label (see figure 2.9).

Figure 2.9 The Hello World label hidden by tapping the Hide button

It might be nice to have it show the label again if it's tapped again. That's easy enough with `[lblHelloWorld setHidden:![lblHelloWorld isHidden]];`. It sets the button to the opposite of whatever its current hidden setting is. But I don't like the fact that the button always says *Hide*. Toggle that based on the hidden setting also:

```
[sender setTitle:[lblHelloWorld isHidden]
    ? @"Show" : @"Hide" forState:UIControlStateNormal];
```

2.6 Delegation

There's one concept that will come up more later, but I also want to mention it here. It's the concept of *delegation.*

I mentioned that interfaces specified between the (<) and (>) symbols in the header specify interfaces that class implements. In the case of your `HWAppDelegate` class, it implements the `UIApplicationDelegate` interface.

Delegation is similar to the action connection in that one object calls methods on another object as needed. A simple example of this is a text field. If, when typing in a text field, the user taps the Return key, the text field asks its delegate if it should return. It asks this by calling this method on its delegate: `textFieldShouldReturn:(UITextField*)textField;`.

That method returns a Boolean as to whether the text field should include a newline in the text. In most cases, the action would treat this as finishing the input and would then save, submit, send, or whatever else it needs to do with the user's input.

In the case of your app, the `HWAppDelegate` class is the delegate for the app, so most lifecycle–related methods, like `applicationWillTerminate:`, are called on it.

This concept is used often in iOS development and is another way the MVC pattern is employed.

2.7 Summary

Now you've taken your Hello World app a bit further. You didn't do a lot, but you used a lot of the key ideas, concepts, and practices used in the development of most apps. Using the UI editor, you can drop an image view, switch, text field, or any number of controls onto your interface. And by using the Utilities view, you can set the attributes the way you'd like them.

By creating action and outlet connections to your various UI items, you can allow the user to interact with them and perform tasks based on the interactions.

In the rest of the book, you'll take on a different project from start to finish in each chapter and will explore many more UI items and functionalities provided in various frameworks. The basic steps you learned from the development of your first app will carry forward in your development of a good portion of all the projects.

Part 2

Putting iOS into practice

Chapter 3 begins part 2 with your first real app project: PicDecor. In this chapter you'll learn about view controllers and displaying images, as well as how to interface with sending email. You'll see how to design the UI and how to connect it to the code you're writing. Chapter 4 builds on what you learned in chapter 3 about view controllers by showing you table view controllers and how to access the address book. Chapter 5 continues by discussing access to images through the photo album and the camera and how to manipulate those images. Also, in chapter 5 you'll see how to display a map and the user's location and store data for retrieving and displaying later. The Settings bundle is the official way to allow a user to manage settings for apps and is covered in chapter 6. Also covered are playing MP3s and detecting motion (particularly shaking the device). Chapter 7 goes further into playing audio with allowing the user to make playlists and play them via the iPad framework. This includes covering CoreData for database design and for storing app data. Push Notifications and In-App Purchase both include using external server interaction for their functionality and are covered in chapter 8 for a Rock, Paper, Scissors game. Chapter 9 continues the game with GameCenter interaction including leaderboards and achievements. Chapter 10 could be called *the iChapter* because it covers iTunes' API to search music, iPad design, and iAds for advertising.

3 Using view controllers and images in PicDecor

This chapter covers

- UI design concepts
- View controllers
- Working with the camera
- Creating and displaying images

Let's move on to the real reason for what you've learned so far: development. In each of the following chapters, we'll take a project that examines and utilizes a variety of SDK aspects. Each of the projects is an app currently available in the iTunes App Store for you to examine freely.

For this chapter, I developed PicDecor, an app that allows users to upload an image from their photo albums or take a picture using their camera and decorate it with various, small stock images in the app. Once completed, the image can be saved and/or emailed from within the app. Though the actual outcome is silly, the functionality is applicable for many other uses. The app can be found in the App Store here: http://itunes.com/apps/picdecor. The steps in this chapter are exactly the same steps I took as I developed the app, except that I added the artwork and an About page to the app before submitting it to the App Store.

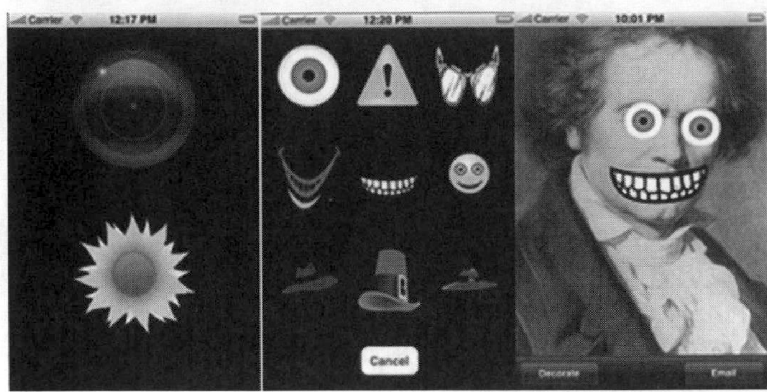

Figure 3.1 PicDecor displays: image source selection, stock images, decorated image

To get an idea of PicDecor's interface, see figure 3.1. The first page allows the user to select the image source—camera or photo album. After the user selects the image, they can choose from a selection of stock images to add to the images. With their finger, they can move the added images around their picture.

In this chapter, you'll see how PicDecor is both designed and coded in Xcode. As part of the UI and code work, you'll learn about view controllers, image views, image manipulation, delegation in the view controller, and messaging (for example, in app email). Learning these processes will help you in almost any app you'll ever develop. You'll know what your options are and can decide when to use them. Also, you'll learn about lesser-used functionality, like access to the camera and photo album.

First, you'll start designing the UI. You'll need to keep an open mind during the UI design to see how you might build it in a more useful, less obvious fashion.

Then, you'll move into the code and prepare the corresponding classes to the UI elements you've designed. Declaring classes and methods in the code a certain way allows you to wire up the code to the visually designed UI with IB.

From there you can begin to connect the UI to the code to relate user interaction to the respective functionality. In some cases, the UI drives the functionality or vice versa. Sometimes it's a mixture of the two. Based on that, you might decide whether to design the UI first or the code.

PicDecor is a smaller project, so you can refine the UI design as you develop without much, if any, cost to the speed of development.

Because you'll start with designing your interface, let's look at how that's done with the UI editor, IB, in Xcode.

3.1 UI design concepts

When deciding how your UI should look and operate, it's important to consider more than appearance. In some cases multiple items can accomplish the same task by using different techniques. Depending on your app, audience, functionality, and other aspects, different design decisions make more or less sense. There's more to consider than the size, shape, placement, and color of buttons or lists.

You may prefer to design your UI on paper, a whiteboard, or IB. They all have their strengths. Regardless of how your reach your design decisions, be sure to consider more than just function and form.

As previously mentioned, IB in Xcode is a great tool for designing your UI. Not only does it provide the standard Apple widgets, but if you decide to later programmatically implement your UI, IB gives you the coordinates, sizes, colors, and more that you can use in the code.

Because your interface is fairly straightforward and will use all built-in widgets, it makes sense to use Xcode to lay it out. This allows you to see how it will actually look in execution. Not only that, but once you have the layout as you like it, there's no need to translate that from paper.

Xcode helps by providing great building blocks for your UI. Let's look at that, but also consider some ways that an app can be customized and made unique.

3.1.1 Building blocks that can be customized

All of the items in the Apple Library can be customized in different ways. The majority of them grew out of other, more basic items and can be altered in related ways. For example, `UIImageView`, `UITableView`, and `UIWebView` are all `UIViews` and can be sized as necessary.

> **UIVIEW (FROM APPLE CLASS REFERENCE DOCS)**
> `UIView` provides a structure for drawing and handling events. A `UIView` object claims a rectangular region of its enclosing superview (its parent in the view hierarchy) and is responsible for all drawing in that region, as well as receiving events that occur in the region.

In the IB Attributes window, the selected class's attributes are displayed, including their parent classes. For a `UITableView`, you'll see the attributes for the table view on the top. Each subsequent parent class's attributes appear below the previous class. In figure 3.2, you can see that the scroll view attributes appear under the table view attributes. The last item is the `UIView`'s attributes.

As you change the attributes in the Attributes Inspector, you may see visible changes in the UI displayed (and vice versa for changing the item visibly). Other aspects of UI design besides size and appearance need also to be taken into consideration. For example, what else makes an interface appealing to the user?

Figure 3.2 Attributes Inspector displays hierarchy of a class's attributes

3.1.2 *Product definition statement*

The best UI is subject to the project for which it's designed. Often the project dictates that the UI be solely functional. Many of Apple's apps use fairly sparse, largely functional UI designs. It isn't that they don't look good or do a great job, but there usually aren't spinning knobs, customized table views, or distracting background images.

Before you even begin to design your UI, you need to determine your product definition statement (PDS). Who is your audience? It's iPhone/iPod Touch users, of course, but what is unique about the users of this particular app? They have images they want to manipulate and share.

What features should you provide? You want to deliver the means to make simple additions to images and email them to others. Based on those two things, you should have a decent PDS.

Now, let's define your PDS so that you sharpen your focus on what the app is, what it does, and who its target users are. Let's say that you want it to be a *simple, fun image decorator for people who want to share pictures.*

Given that PDS, what would be a clear and intuitive design for the UI? First, you need a way to allow the user to pick an image to decorate. The first thought might be to provide a button on the front page to tap and select the image source and then the image. But why not go right into the image source selection? The user knows they'll need to get an image either via the camera or photo album. Also, on subsequent executions of the app, they'll appreciate the fewer steps required for them to get where they want to go.

From there, the Apple image picker or camera functionality is controlled by the various controls. When the image has been selected and loaded into the app, you need to provide the means for adding decorations and emailing the result. A toolbar at the bottom might be nice for this. You can have two buttons—Decorate and Send.

Because you're using a stock set of images to decorate the image, you need a mechanism for the user to select a decoration. To simplify this task, you'll use buttons with the stock images on them. The user taps a button with the desired image and it's added to their initial picture.

Finally, emailing the image will use the default email message controller, so that UI is a given.

3.1.3 *Thinking outside the box*

As developers, we often think straightforward (at least to us) in our design. It is function over form every time. But we understand and appreciate an impressive and appealing design. Apple has consistently provided ways to create enriched interfaces while maintaining performance and functionality.

Though the idea of creating three seemingly simple views makes three designs pop into your head, are they *interesting* designs? Is there a way to keep these designs functional, but make them interesting? If your first thought for the image source selection view was two buttons, Camera and Photo Albums, then you're like me: function over form.

But what if you instead put two images on the view—a camera and a photo album? It's just as obvious what the user is selecting, yet it's custom and appealing. It takes a person from using their iPhone into using PicDecor. The iPhone feel carries over, and now you've added to it.

While you want to build upon what Apple gives you, you also want to set your app apart. The intangible enjoyment of the interface creates the experience that can make or break the user's acceptance of the app. Apple has built a lot upon their interface concepts and we can learn much by thinking like they do.

3.1.4 Think Apple

In many cases, Apple creates an interface that's intuitive and creative. But in some cases, the interface isn't immediately obvious. Prior to Lion, the only way to resize a window in Mac OS was to use the bottom-right corner.

But once you do it, you know it forever. There's no need to point it out again and again. You want the UI to be intuitive, but you don't need to spoon-feed your users. When you first started using your iPhone, did you read the manual? What manual? How did you figure out how to delete an app? Take a picture? View your photo album?

The point is, pick your audience and cater to them. Don't try to cater to everyone. Don't try to please everyone and in doing so cater to the 5 percent who want everything while abandoning the 95 percent who want a simple app. And by all means, don't create a feature bucket. Stick to your PDS.

Now that you've made your basic UI decisions, let's look at how you'll create the UI.

3.2 Creating view controllers and other widgets

For your PicDecor project, you have three views—image source selection, image editing, and decoration selection. A view controller handles displaying a view that may contain other views including image views, buttons, and pretty much every other viewable control. You need to create the various view controllers, associate views to them, and lay out the UI on these views. In this section, you'll lay out all of these view controllers, views, and controls.

UIVIEWCONTROLLER Provides view management functionality for toolbars, navigation bars, and app views. The `UIViewController` class also supports modal views and rotating views when device orientation changes.

TECHNIQUE 1 Designing a view controller with IB

Most projects use view controllers. When you're first getting started, it's the best way to go. In fact, the majority of Apple project templates create a default view controller of some kind for you. Let's look at how to do that and what you get.

PROBLEM

You need to create a view controller for your project to allow the user to select which image source they'd like to use—camera or photo album.

SOLUTION

First, you'll create a new project in Xcode. The project is created with a default XIB file. Second, using the UI editor, you'll add the necessary buttons for user selection and, finally, set the background color of the view to black.

DISCUSSION

For your image source selection, I mentioned using two standard buttons—function over form. But in brainstorming through some more unique options, I mentioned using two big icons for the user to tap on. You need something for a camera and something for a photo album. Taking a page from Apple, you can use a camera lens and a sunflower, respectively.

This not only makes sense and looks good, but borrows from the concepts the user is already familiar with in reality and within the iPhone.

To start, create a new project in Xcode. Choose a Single View Application (see figure 3.3). After choosing the view-based project, the subsequent steps ask for a location and name of the project. You'll use PicDecor for the name.

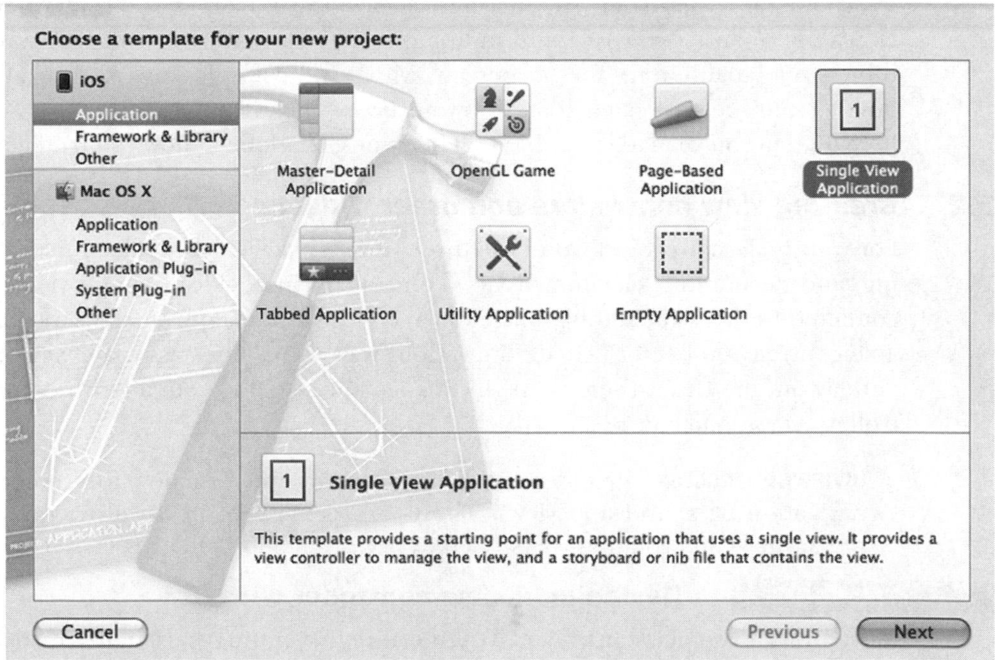

Figure 3.3 Create a new, view-based project in Xcode.

Figure 3.4 Expanding the Resources group to locate the PicDecorViewController.xib file

In the PicDecor project in Xcode, expand the Resources group and click on the PicDecorViewController.xib file to open it (see figure 3.4).

Figure 3.5 Default view for a new project run in the simulator

Interface Builder displays a blank view which is your app's current UI. Similarly, if you run the app in the simulator (Command-r), you'll see the blank view (see figure 3.5).

Because you want to start the app with the image source selection, add a couple of buttons and a label. In the Object Library, drag a Round Rect Button onto your view (see figure 3.6).

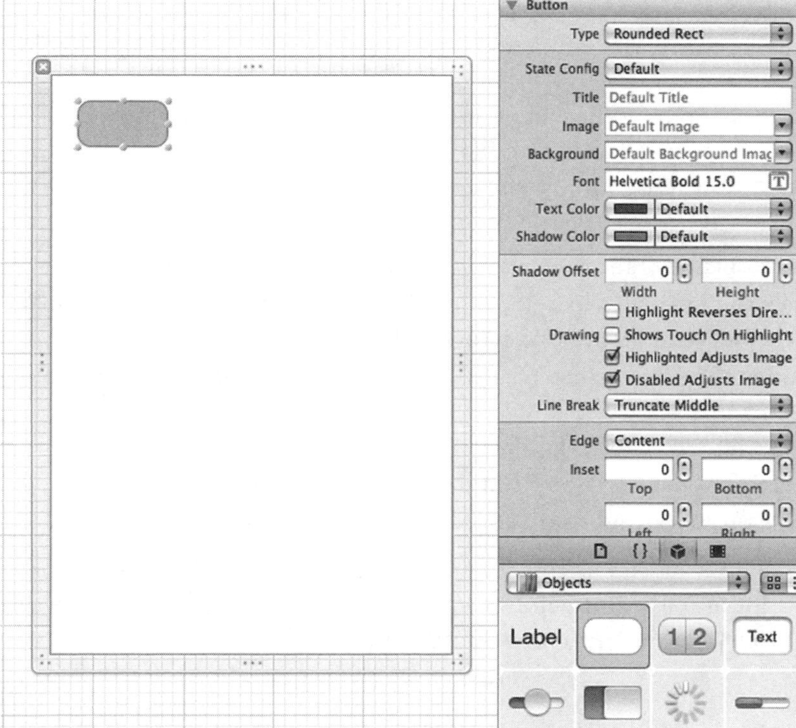

Figure 3.6 Dropping a Round Rect Button onto the view

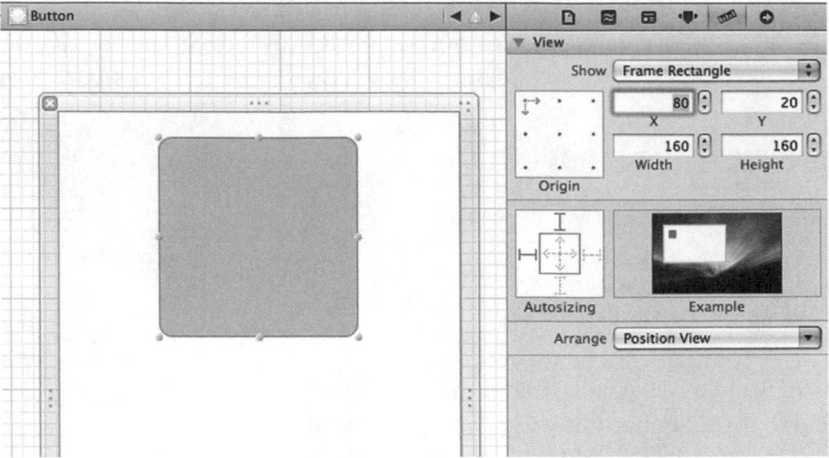

Figure 3.7 Setting the X, Y, Width, and Height for a selected button

You want your button to be a custom size, so you can either click on the button to display the points for dragging and resizing, or you can resize using the Size Inspector. Let's use the Size Inspector and set the dimensions in the size values.

Click on the button to select the item if it's not already selected. From the Tools menu, select Size Inspector (or click the ruler icon on the top of the Inspector window). Change the X, Y, Width, and Height values to 80, 20, 160, and 160, respectively (see figure 3.7).

Insert a second button (or copy and paste the first one) into the view. Use the same size values except set Y to 230 (see figure 3.8). Later you'll set the images for these buttons, but for now you'll leave them as-is.

Finally, set the view's background color to black using the following steps:

1. Click outside of the buttons in the gray, background view area.
2. View the attributes by selecting Attributes Inspector from the Tools menu (or the slider icon on the Inspector window).
3. Under the View group of attributes, click on the Background color, and the Colors tool will display.
4. If not already selected, select the Color Palettes icon (middle icon) at the top and the Apple selection from the drop-down menu.
5. Click on Black, and your view should appear black (see figure 3.9).

You can see how this view is coming together, and with just the addition of the images it makes a lot of sense. But before you get too far into polishing this view, let's lay out the other views, starting with the editing view.

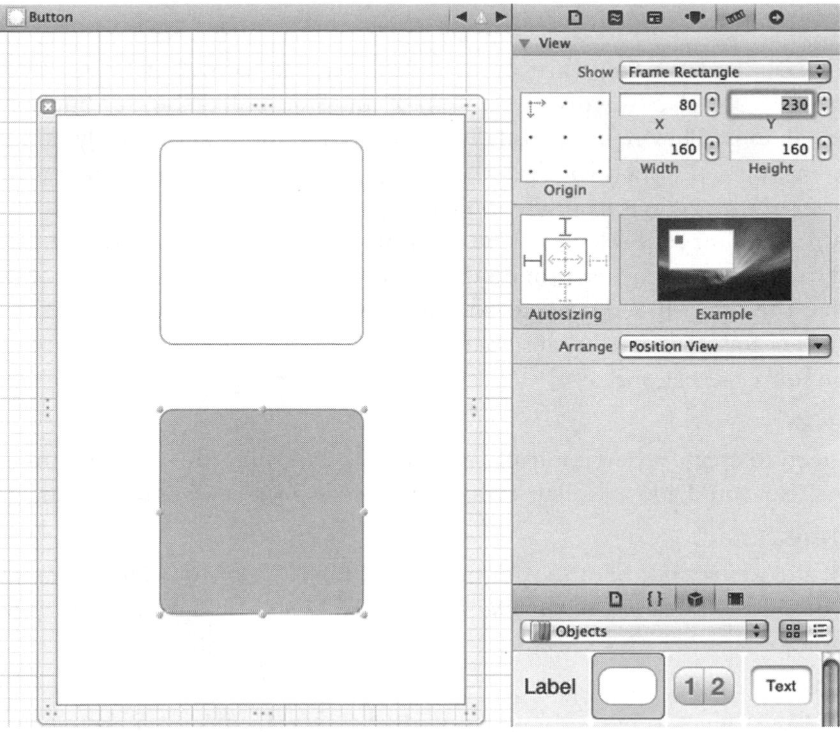

Figure 3.8 Copy and paste the first button to create a second button at Y location 230.

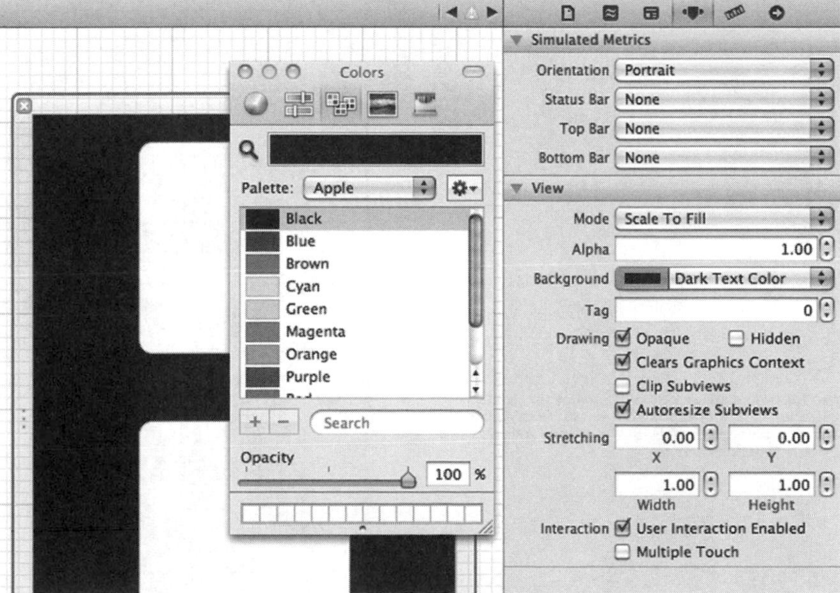

Figure 3.9 Setting the view's background color to black

TECHNIQUE 2 Adding an ImageView and toolbar to a view

`ImageViews` and `Toolbars` are two common widgets provided by Apple's SDK. Of course, the `UIImageView` displays an image and the toolbar houses buttons for user-driven actions. They're both easily used by the developer and quickly understood by the user. You can display your selected image in the image view and allow the user to act upon it with actions from the toolbar.

After the image is selected from the photo album or taken with the camera, you need to display it to the user for editing. The image editing view is basic, because most of what the user will see is based on selections and interaction. You need a new view controller for this view because the project's root view controller is handling the image source selection.

PROBLEM

You need to create a view controller with a view to display the image the user can decorate. Also, you'll add a toolbar with buttons to decorate and email the image.

SOLUTION

You'll add a view controller to your project's XIB file. Then you can add an image view, toolbar, and buttons to your new view controller. Also, you'll set the text and colors as necessary.

DISCUSSION

Select Controllers from the Library and drag a View Controller into the XIB file (see figure 3.10).

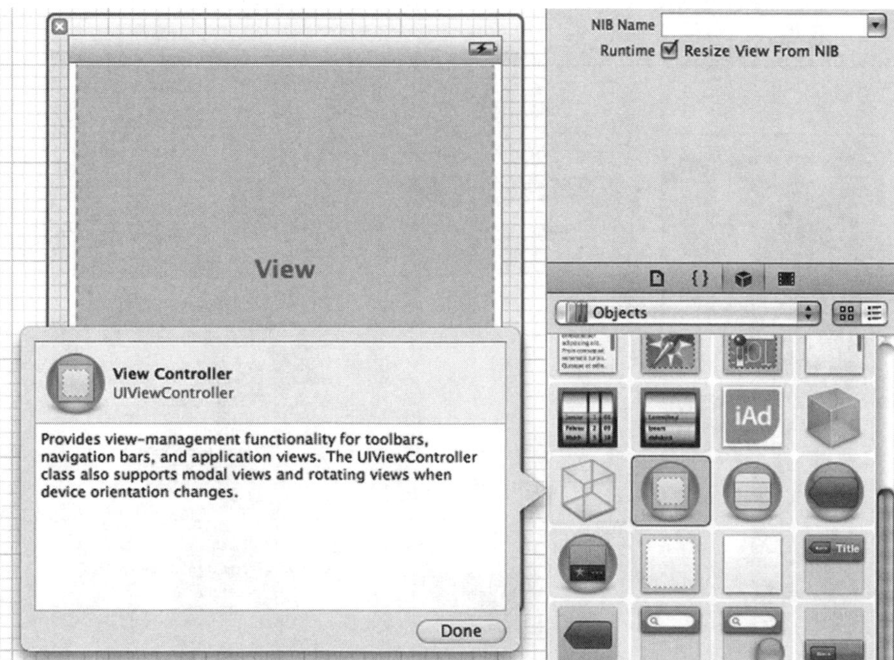

Figure 3.10 Adding a View Controller to the XIB file/project

The displayed window has the word View in the middle. This is where the view will go. You haven't told the controller what view to use. Because many objects are views (for example, table, image, button, label, and text views), you have a choice to make. The obvious choice is an image view because you'll be editing an image.

From the Object Library, drag an Image View into the controller's window. It automatically sizes the view to fit the full screen (see figure 3.11).

You also need a toolbar to house your buttons. Select Windows and Bars in the Library and drag a toolbar on top of the image view you just added (see figure 3.12). What happened?

IB replaced the view controller's view, which was the image view, with the toolbar. A view controller only has one view, so it removed the image view for the new view—the toolbar. But you want both on there. How can you design your interface to contain both (or more) items?

Delete the toolbar by selecting it and typing Command-x. Instead of dropping an image view on the controller window, drop a view. Now for the toolbar and image view: drop the toolbar, placing it on the lower end of the view. Finally, drop an image

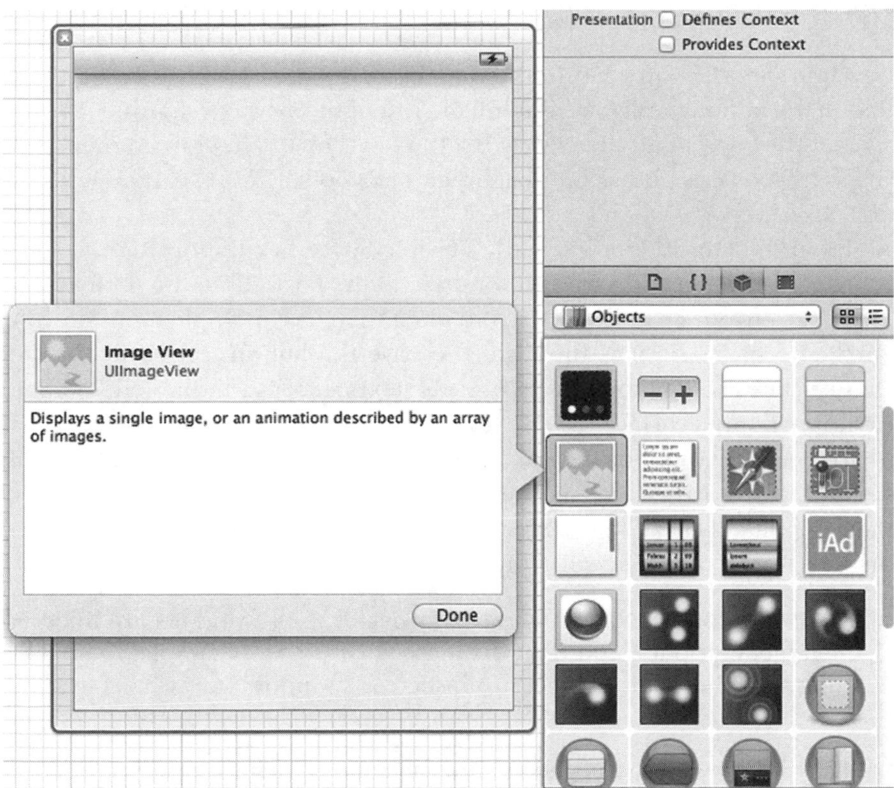

Figure 3.11 An Image View added to the view of a view controller

Figure 3.12 Adding a toolbar to a view controller replaces the image view

Figure 3.13 Dropping the image view in the view after the toolbar to auto-size

view into the white area left in the view. You drop the image view after the toolbar so that IB will automatically size it to fill the rest of the view (see figure 3.13).

Now the view controller's view is a `UIView`. The `UIView` can contain multiple subviews. In your case, it has an image view and toolbar. A `UIToolbar` is also a subclass of `UIView`.

From the Object Library, add a Flexible Space Bar Button Item to the center of your toolbar. Then add a Bar Button Item to the far right in the toolbar. The flexible space bar provides consistent spacing when there are multiple items on your toolbar. For PicDecor, it provides the means to have the buttons on either end of the bar. Double-click each button and type in the text `Decorate` in the left and `Email` in the right (see figure 3.14).

To keep the width of the bar buttons equal, select each one and set the width to 100 in the Size Inspector. Another way to do this is to select one of the buttons and then Command-click the other item. When both items are selected, set the width in the Size Inspector, which will be applied to both buttons.

> **SIZE INSPECTOR WINDOW TITLE** The Inspector tools' windows are titled using the item description and then the inspector type. For example, in the case of sizing a bar button item, the Size Inspector's window title is Bar Button Item Size.

Later, you'll wire up the image view to the code as well as specify the actions for the buttons. For now, you can be satisfied that you have the basic UI laid out and that it looks good. But, in keeping with your black background from the first view, select the toolbar (either click on it, tab around the view controller, or select it from the XIB file

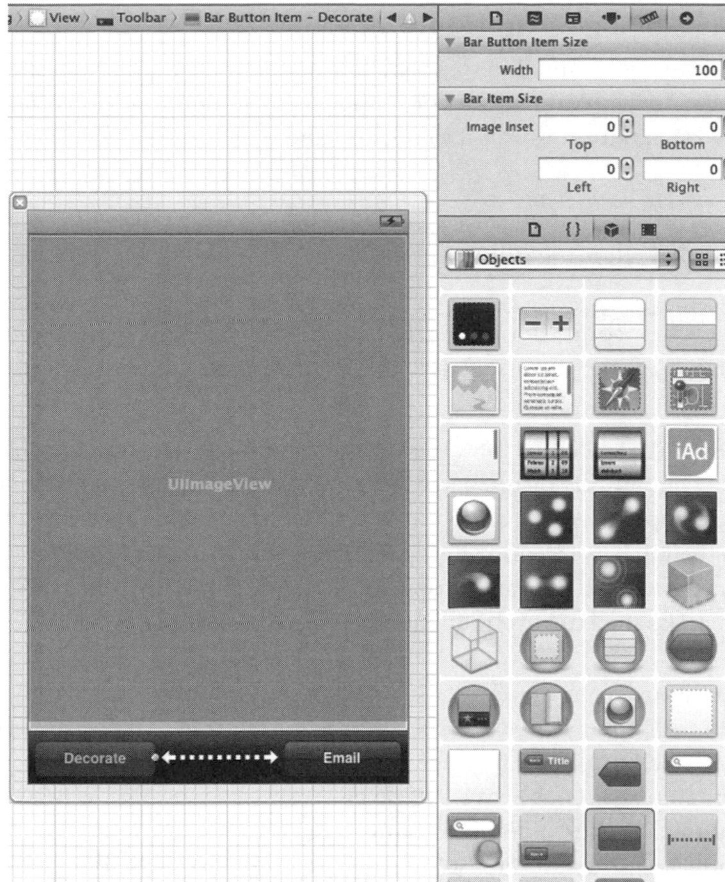

Figure 3.14 Two buttons separated by a Flexible Space Bar Button Item

window) and set its Style to Black Opaque in the attributes (see figure 3.15). This affects the buttons automatically and your app is getting a style of its own.

Now that you've created and designed your image source selection and image editing views, you can define the decoration selection view. You'll use a technique similar to when you created the image source selection view with buttons on the view. This will provide a consistent look and feel between all of your pages and a cohesiveness to your app.

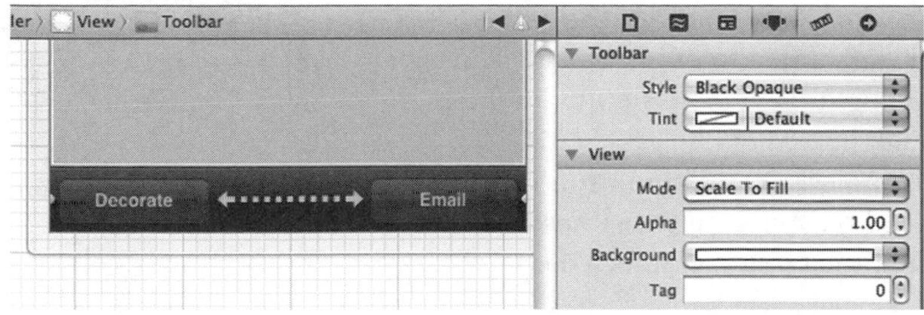

Figure 3.15 Setting the toolbar style to Black Opaque

TECHNIQUE 3 Adding buttons to a view

Buttons are the most common UI device for allowing the user to interact with the app. Whether it's a standard-looking button or it appears as something less obvious (such as an image or text), a button is useful to the app and easy for the developer to add.

PROBLEM

You need to create a view that allows the user to tap on various decoration images to add them to the image they're editing.

SOLUTION

You'll create a new view controller. For image selection, you'll add several buttons and later (in technique 5) make the associated images the images to use for decoration.

DISCUSSION

Like your image source selection view, the decoration image selection view should be quick to design. The buttons on the view will each display the associated image that, when the button is tapped, will be added to decorate the main image. Drop a new view controller from the Objects & Controllers group into your XIB file. From the Windows & Bars group in the Object Library, drop a view on the new controller. In the Attributes Inspector, make the background black like you did with the image source selection view.

Next, drop a button from the Inputs & Values group into the view. You'll use nine stock images that will fit nicely if you use a 3 x 3 grid of buttons. The width of the view is 320, and with three buttons with a nice buffer between them of 20 pixels, that leaves 240 pixels for the three buttons' widths. So set the buttons X, Y, Width, and Height at 20, 20, 80, and 80, respectively.

Copy the three buttons and make a second row with Y equaling 150. Then make a third row at 280. Finally, add a button at the bottom in the center. Double-click on it and type `Cancel` (see figure 3.16).

You've checked out your interface and it seems fairly solid. Depending on where you think this app might go as it grows, you might have made different interface decisions. For example, if you wanted to grow your stock image gallery, you might use a table view to let the user scroll through dozens of choices.

For this project, let's assume you're content with learning how your interface translates to the code and how the two are connected.

Figure 3.16 Button grid with a Cancel button

Again, this is a skeleton that you'll put some flesh on later. For now, you want to validate that your initial design ideas work out. It appears that they do. You'll come back to the UI editor after you build up your classes in Xcode.

Now that you've laid out the dimensions, locations, sizes, and some attributes, it's time to get the code involved. Soon you'll tell IB how these views you've created relate to the code and what to do with the user's interactions.

3.3 Developing actions and outlets

In this section you'll run the app for the first time in the iPhone Simulator. You still have some work to do, but your app will come together, which is nice to see.

In some cases, you can use a control dropped in your XIB file the same as you can in IB. You can set some attributes and other aspects and that's enough. For example, let's say you want to display a single image in an image view. You can drop an image view in your XIB file and set the image to a file in your project and you're done.

Similarly, in many cases you can add buttons without involving any code. Drop the button in a view; set the text, color, and background image, specify the method to call, and you're done.

But in other cases you'll need to do some work in the code. Often, that means subclassing the item's class, and then telling IB that the item you dropped in the XIB is really an instance of your new class.

A common example of this is to subclass `UIViewController` and tell IB that the appropriate view controller is an instance of the defined class. At that point, the Inspector analyzes the class and gives you access to any custom outlets and actions defined in the header file. For example, if you specify a `UIButton` as an outlet and a method as an action, IB will let you relate the button to one you dropped in your XIB. Also, you can then specify that the given action method is called when the button is tapped.

But, if you define the UI first with the UI editor, you can let Xcode declare the actions and outlets for you by Control-dragging the item to the header file, as you'll see.

In PicDecor, you'll use standard UI objects like `UIButton` for your outlets. Because you won't need any customization for the buttons, you'll take the route that doesn't require subclassing or other work. In this section, we'll look at how you specify the applicable outlets and actions for PicDecor.

TECHNIQUE 4 Declaring actions and outlets in Xcode

Actions are what the methods are called when something in the UI is acted upon. *Outlets* are UI items the code needs to know about. It's pretty clear why you'd need actions—how else would the code know to do something unless the UI is tied to it? Outlets are sometimes unnecessary, but if you want to change the attributes of the widget, you need a reference to it.

Interface Builder allows you to Control-drag UI items or their associated actions into header files for declaration. But, if you already have them declared in the header, IB is aware of them and can facilitate relating the two.

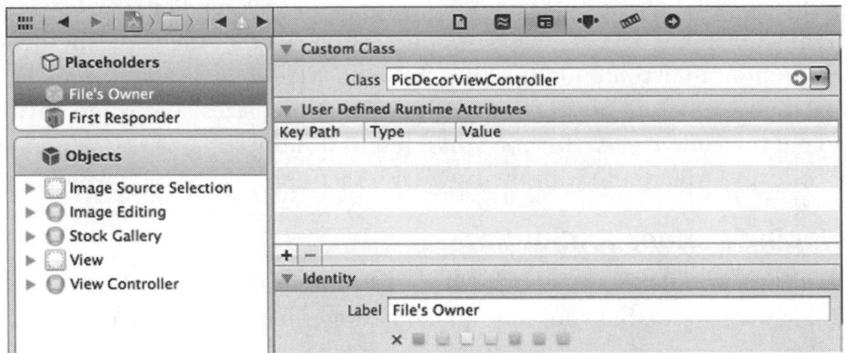

Figure 3.17 File's Owner is an instance of `PicDecorViewController` from the PicDecor project

PROBLEM

You need to be able to associate various UI items to instances in the code. Also, you need to wire up actions from the UI to method calls in the code.

SOLUTION

In your header files, you'll declare the various actions and outlets to be wired up with IB.

DISCUSSION

Click on the XIB element titled File's Owner. Note that in the Identity Inspector, the class type is `PicDecorViewController` (see figure 3.17). Note that I expanded the file listing by using the right-arrow icon at the bottom of the window.

Now, look at the PicDecorViewController.h file (see figure 3.18). It's basically empty. But your view design of this class's view has a black background and two big buttons on it. The code doesn't need to know about the background view's color. And you really don't need to know about the buttons. But you *do* need to know when those buttons are tapped.

In declaring the actions in Xcode, you have two actions: one for each button. Let's call them `doCameraBtn` and `doPhotoAlbumBtn`. Define them in the header (see the following code snippet). You specify the return type of `IBAction`. This lets IB know

PicDecor > C... > PicDecorViewController.h > @interface PicDecorVie

```
//
//  PicDecorViewController.h
//  PicDecor
//
//  Created by Bear Cahill on 12/20/09.
//  Copyright Brainwash Inc. 2009. All rights reserved.
//

#import <UIKit/UIKit.h>

@interface PicDecorViewController : UIViewController  {
}

@end
```

Figure 3.18 Default version of PicDecorView-Controller.h in Xcode

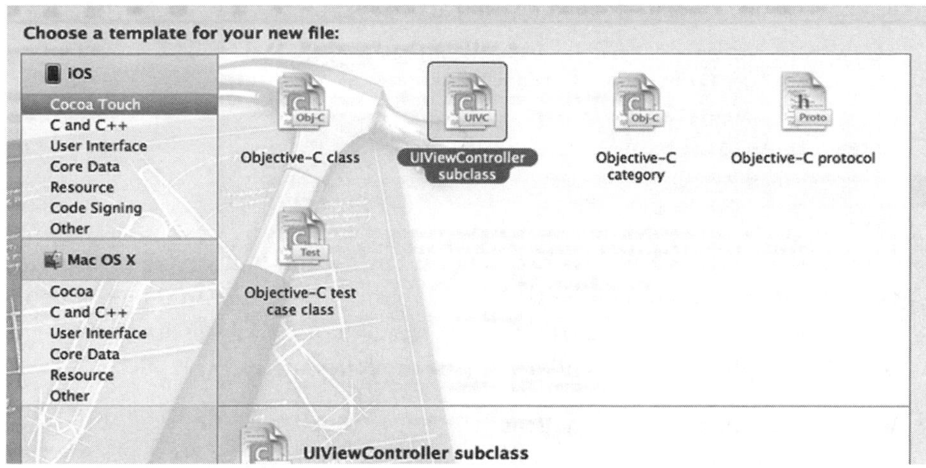

Figure 3.19 Creating a new view controller subclass in Xcode

that they are declared to be accessible. There's no real return type that you're interested in because you aren't calling these methods directly in the code. You can call these methods directly in the code, but treat them like a return type of `void`:

```
-(IBAction)doCameraBtn:(id)sender;
-(IBAction)doPhotoAlbumBtn:(id)sender;
```

These methods send one parameter: `id`. This is a reference to the sender class, which in this case is the button being tapped. You can use this reference as you would any other `UIButton` reference. You can change the title, color, location, or whatever you like.

Let's now turn to declaring your view controllers in the code that will relate to what you've done in IB. Xcode gave you the first controller and its view, but you'll have to create and declare all additional classes. For PicDecor, you have two other view controllers. To create these in Xcode, right-click on Classes and select Add > New File…. On the resulting window, select Cocoa Touch class on the left and `UIViewController` subclass on the right (see figure 3.19).

Click Next, name the class `VCImageEditing`, and it will be automatically added. Repeat the process for the `VCDecorations` class, and now you've created your view controller classes (see figure 3.20).

The `VCImageEditing` class has one outlet (for the image view) and two actions (for the Decorate and Email buttons). Declare these in the header file (see the following listing).

Figure 3.20 Created view controller files listed in Xcode

VCImageEditing.h defining the outlet and actions

```
@interface VCImageEditing : UIViewController {
    IBOutlet UIImageView *ivEditingImage;
}

-(IBAction)doDecorateBtn:(id)sender;
-(IBAction)doEmailBtn:(id)sender;

@end
```

The `VCDecorations` class has two actions. One action handles all of the Stock Image buttons and the other handles the Cancel button. Because you'll be passed the button to the method, you can determine what image to use by accessing it through the button. Declare these in the header file (see the following listing).

VCDecorations.h defining the actions

```
@interface VCDecorations : UIViewController {
}

-(IBAction)doImageBtn:(id)sender;
-(IBAction)doCancelBtn:(id)sender;

@end
```

Let's now relate the view controllers. The image source selection controller needs to know about the image editing view controller in order to display it when the time comes. Similarly, the image editing view controller needs to know about the decorations controller. These are also outlets to be defined in the headers (see the following listing). This means that the header must import the image editing controller .h file.

PicDecorViewController full header file

```
#import "VCImageEditing.h"

@interface PicDecorViewController : UIViewController {

    IBOutlet VCImageEditing *vcImageEditing;

}

-(IBAction)doCameraBtn:(id)sender;
-(IBAction)doPhotoAlbumBtn:(id)sender;

@end
```

In the VCImageEditing.h file, import the VCDecorations.h file and declare an `IBOutlet` of that type.

Now that the code is declared (though not implemented), you're ready to connect the applicable pieces in the UI to your classes. You've defined the buttons and image view in the UI and you've declared the corresponding actions and outlets in the code. Time to relate them in IB.

TECHNIQUE 5 Connecting actions and outlets to code

As stated in the previous technique, there are two ways to associate outlets and actions from IB to the code. If the outlets and actions are declared in the header file, IB makes them available to wire up to UI widgets. The other way is to Control-drag UI widgets or their events into the header file to declare as outlets or actions, respectively.

PROBLEM

You need to connect the actions and outlets you created in the code to UI events and items defined with IB.

SOLUTION

You can inspect the code for declared actions and outlets. You'll associate the applicable UI items to the declarations in the code.

DISCUSSION

Select File's Owner in the XIB file. Then select the Connections Inspector (the circle with a white arrow icon) and you'll see the outlets listed (see figure 3.21). Drag the hollow dot from the circle on the right of each outlet to the appropriate button on the view, as in the figure. A pop-up list lets you select which action by the user will trigger calling the action method. Select Touch Up Inside. This means that the method will be called only when the user touches the button and lifts their finger while still within the boundaries of the button.

Running the app now and pressing these buttons would cause a crash because you haven't yet implemented the methods.

Similar to the `PicDecorViewController`, you need to tell IB that your image editing controller is an instance of your `VCImageEditing` class and that your decorations view controller is a `VCDecorations` object (see figure 3.22). Also, it's helpful to set the Name value to help keep the classes straight in the XIB window.

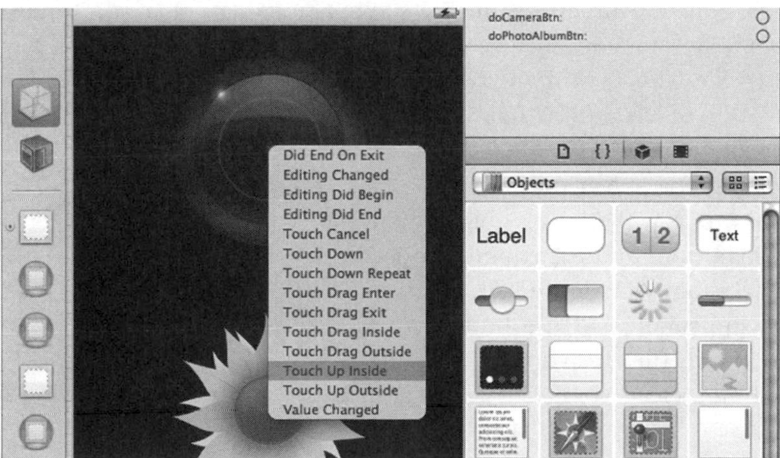

Figure 3.21 Wiring the actions from PicDecorViewController.h to the buttons

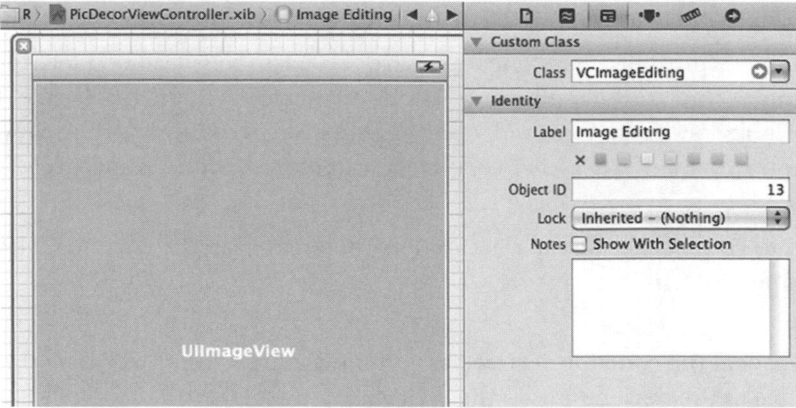

Figure 3.22 Specifying the class and name for the image editing view controller

Click on the `VCImageEditing` instance and select Connections Inspector. Drag the hollow dot next to the `ivEditingImage` outlet you defined to the image view you dropped on the control earlier (see figure 3.23). Similarly, drag the connection dots from the actions/methods to the applicable buttons on the toolbar. Toolbar buttons don't have the variety of actions that regular buttons do, so there's no pop-up list to pick from.

Now pick the `VCDecorations` item and set its class to `VCDecorations`. View the connections and connect the `doCancelBtn` action to the Cancel button in the view (again, pick Touch Up Inside from the pop-up list). Drag the hollow dot by the `doImageBtn` action to the top-left button (selecting Touch Up Inside). Now the dot is filled in like normal. Drag the filled-in dot to the second button and select Touch Up Inside again. Now the action specifies that it's related to multiple items. Repeat this for all of the image buttons (see figure 3.24).

The next step is to finalize your view's appearance. For this, you'll need images. I'm using public domain images found online. Drop these files into your project under the Resources group in Xcode (see figure 3.25). Be sure to click Copy Items into Destination Group's Folder.

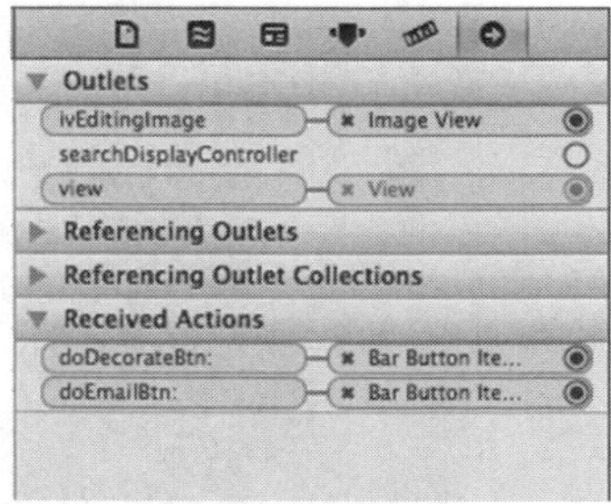

Figure 3.23 Connecting the outlet and actions for `VCImageEditing`

In the UI editor, select the image source selection view (the one with the two big buttons) and select the top button. In the Attributes Inspector, set the Type to Custom (see figure 3.26). This removes the current appearance of the button so that it's blank/clear. From the drop-down list by the Background setting, select your lens image (such as lens.png).

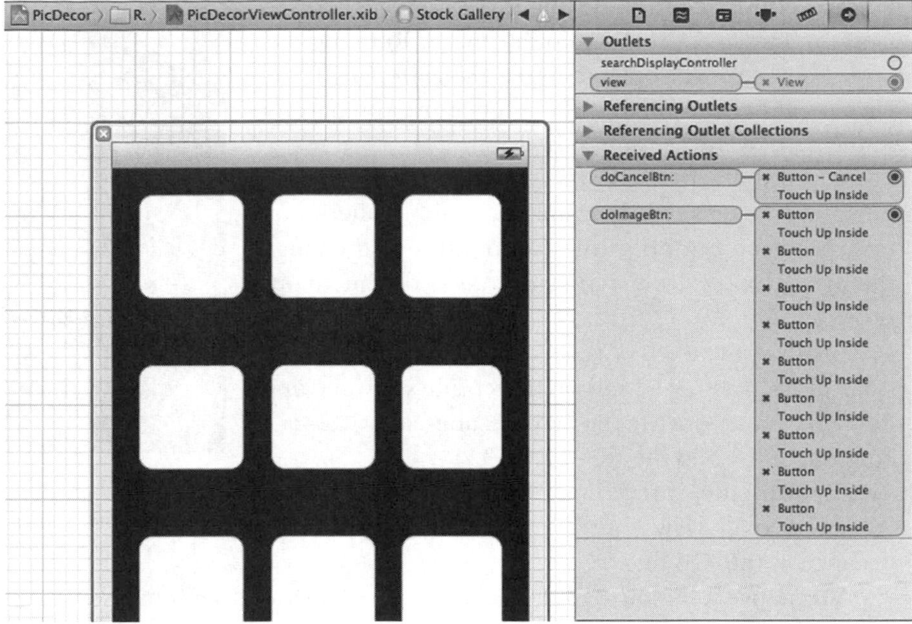

Figure 3.24 `VCDecorations` **action wired to all of the image buttons**

Figure 3.25 Dropping image files into the Resources group of your project in Xcode

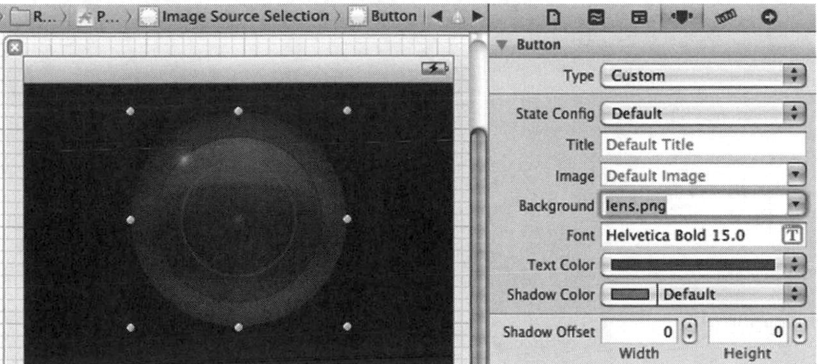

Figure 3.26 Setting the camera button's type and background image

For the bottom button, do the same—set the Type to Custom and select the sunflower image. Running the app shows you the outcome (see figure 3.27). If you click on either button, it will crash because you haven't implemented the action methods yet.

Figure 3.27 Image source selection view in the simulator

As you did with the image selection controller buttons, find images for the nine decoration gallery buttons. Set each button to the Custom type and change the Background to the images you drop into your project.

Finally, you need to relate the view controllers to each other. In the UI editor, select File's Owner and drag its `vcImageEditing` connection to `VCImageEditing` in the XIB file (see figure 3.28).

Repeat the preceding steps to connect the `VCDecorations` view controller to the image editing instance in the XIB file.

Alternatively, if you hadn't declared the outlets and actions in the header file, you could have just dropped the items in Interface Builder and Control-dragged the widgets (see figure 3.29) and events (see figure 3.30) into the header file. The XIB and header file can be side by side by turning on the Assistant under the View > Editor menu.

Your UI is designed and wired up to the code. This is a process you'll do countless times going forward with iOS development. Before long, you'll be so comfortable doing this that everything you've done here will take you 5 minutes. But this is just the tip of the iceberg, and the real power comes in the code and everything behind the UI. The UI is everything to the user, and its importance can't be overstated. But what goes on behind the scenes is often the rest of the iceberg.

Figure 3.28 Connecting `vcImageEditing` in File's Owner to the `VCImageEditing` instance

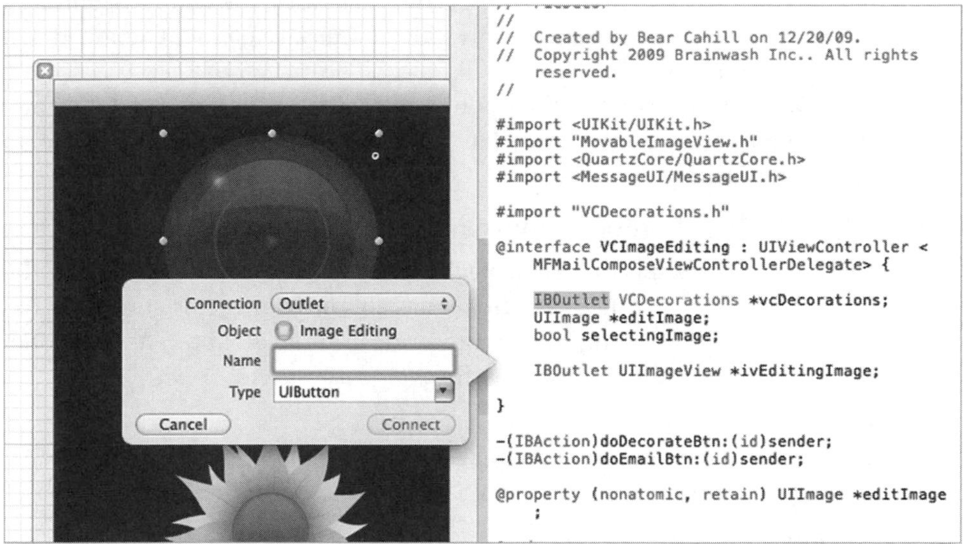

Figure 3.29 Control-drag UI widget from IB to header to declare the outlet

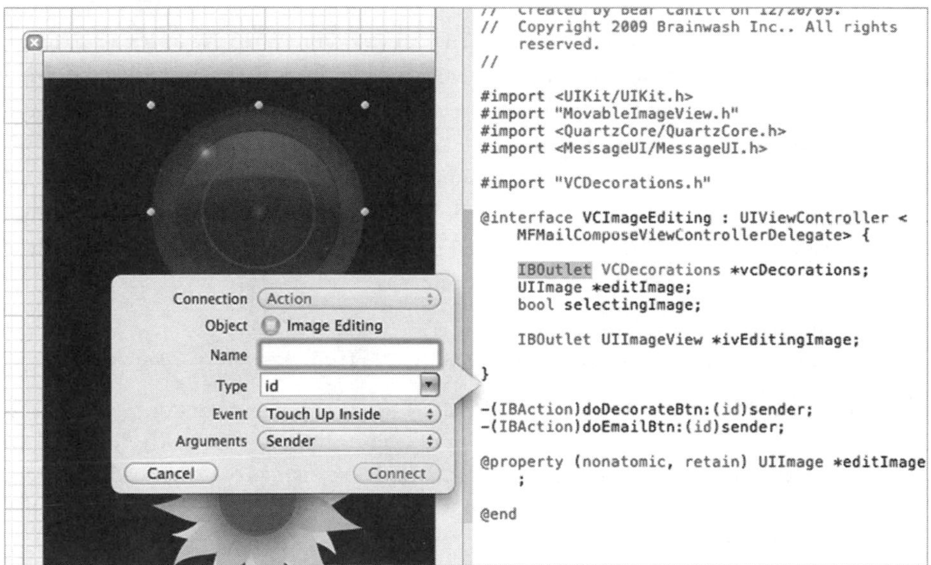

Figure 3.30 Control-drag UI widget from IB to header to declare the action

3.4 Using the camera/photo album

Now that you've declared the actions and connected them to the UI, you need to implement these methods. In some cases, a tap on a button will load a new view controller or display a choice to a user. In other cases, the action begins a process or connects to a server. Most actions start with an interface element action kicking off the related method.

PicDecor has several actions, but none are too complicated. Because you've already made your connections, let's dive into the implementations of the image selection buttons.

TECHNIQUE 6 Adding camera/photo album access

Whenever an app wants to access images, there's a single controller to use. It has a setting for accessing the camera or the photo album. Adding this controller to your app and displaying it isn't a huge effort, but it adds a lot to an app. The controller needs a delegate to call various methods to process the user's selections.

PROBLEM

To allow the user to decorate an image, you need to present them with ways to select an image to decorate.

SOLUTION

You'll allow the user to select their image source as either the camera or photo album. You'll implement the button actions to present the image picker in the correct state.

DISCUSSION

Your first defined controller is the `PicDecorViewController`, so let's start there. You'll implement the two actions for the buttons dealing with selecting an image. Each method will instantiate and display their instance of the `UIImagePickerController` to allow the user to select an image.

The `UIImagePickerController` needs to notify the app when an image is selected. To do that you'll set the controller's delegate to your object—self. Knowing that, you can update the `PicDecorViewController` header to declare that it implements the `UIImagePickerControllerDelegate` protocol:

```
@interface PicDecorViewController : UIViewController
    <UIImagePickerControllerDelegate, UINavigationControllerDelegate> {
```

UIIMAGEPICKERCONTROLLER DELEGATE The `UIImagePickerController`'s `setDelegate` method requires an object that implements both the `UIImagePickerControllerDelegate` and the `UINavigationControllerDelegate` interface. But the `UINavigationControllerDelegate` interface has no required methods.

To implement the methods, copy the declarations from the .h file into the .m file below the `@implementation PicDecorViewController` line of code. The only difference is that the `doCameraBtn` method will specify that the source is the camera (see the following listing).

PicDecorViewController implementing the actions

```
-(IBAction)doCameraBtn:(id)sender;                         <-- Copied from .h file
{
    UIImagePickerController *ipController =
        [[UIImagePickerController alloc] init];             Check for
    if ([[[UIDevice currentDevice] model]                   simulator
          rangeOfString:@"Sim"].location == NSNotFound)
    [ipController setSourceType:UIImagePickerControllerSourceTypeCamera];
    [ipController setDelegate:self];                        Image picker
    [self presentModalViewController:ipController animated:YES];  delegate
}
-(IBAction)doPhotoAlbumBtn:(id)sender;                      Copied from
{                                                           .h file
    UIImagePickerController *ipController =
        [[UIImagePickerController alloc] init];             Image picker
    [ipController setDelegate:self];                        delegate
    [self presentModalViewController:ipController animated:YES];
}
```

Because the simulator doesn't implement a camera simulator, there's an extra line to check the device model for `Sim`. If that isn't found, it sets the type to camera. Otherwise, it will use the photo album like the other method.

The image editing controller needs to be told what image was selected. This is done by declaring a `UIImage` member, `editImage`, and making it a property (see the following listing). Don't forget the synthesize and dealloc aspects of the `editImage` addition in the .m file.

VCImageEditing full header file

```
#import "VCDecorations.h"

@interface VCImageEditing : UIViewController {

    UIImage *editImage;                          <-- Image to edit

    IBOutlet UIImageView *ivEditingImage;

}

-(IBAction)doDecorateBtn:(id)sender;
-(IBAction)doEmailBtn:(id)sender;

@property (nonatomic, retain) UIImage *editImage;

@end
```

Based on the `UIImagePickerControllerDelegate` interface, `PicDecorViewController` can implement the method to handle the image selection (see the following listing). In your case, it gets the selected image and passes it to the editing image controller. Then it displays the editing image controller (after dismissing the image picker controller).

PicDecorViewController implementation of the image selection method

```
- (void)imagePickerController:(UIImagePickerController *)picker
    didFinishPickingMediaWithInfo:(NSDictionary *)info
{
    [self dismissModalViewControllerAnimated:NO];
    UIImage *i =
           [info objectForKey:UIImagePickerControllerOriginalImage];
    [vcImageEditing setEditImage:i];
    [self presentModalViewController:vcImageEditing animated:YES];
}
```

PicDecorViewController now handles the two button actions as well as hands the selected image off to the editing image controller to be displayed. Next, you need to implement the actions for the editing image controller.

TECHNIQUE 7 Presenting a view controller modally

Whether it's an About page, Settings view, a list to select items from, or many other options, it's often helpful to present a view controller to the user for some side interaction that may not be in the same flow as the rest of the app. In the case of your app, you want to display to the user the various decoration image options for them to select one.

PROBLEM

Your image editing controller needs to display the image decoration options when the Decorate button is pressed.

SOLUTION

You'll implement the doImageBtn: action you declared earlier and have it present the decorations controller modally.

DISCUSSION

Later in this chapter, we'll go into detail about how to email and specifically how to attach the image to the email. Here let's focus on the action for selecting a decoration image. VCImageEditing needs a reference to the VCDecorations instance and you use a flag to specify when an image is being selected: selectingImage (see the following listing). The main function of the doDecorationsBtn method is just to display the decorations controller.

VCImageEditing full header file and doDecorateBtn action implementation

```
#import "VCDecorations.h"

@interface VCImageEditing : UIViewController {

    UIImage *editImage;
    IBOutlet VCDecorations *vcDecorations;
    bool selectingImage;

    IBOutlet UIImageView *ivEditingImage;

}

-(IBAction)doDecorateBtn:(id)sender;
-(IBAction)doEmailBtn:(id)sender;
```

```
@property (nonatomic, retain) UIImage *editImage;

@end

-(IBAction)doDecorateBtn:(id)sender;
{
    selectingImage = YES;
    [self presentModalViewController:vcDecorations animated:YES];
}
```

Presenting a view controller modally like this will slide the view up from the bottom of the display. This a great technique for prompting the user for input that doesn't imply a hierarchy or deviation from their current navigation. Once the user interaction is complete, the view should be dismissed in a reverse slide. Let's look at dismissing the view controller.

TECHNIQUE 8 Dismissing a modally displayed view controller

Just as important as displaying a view controller modally is removing the same view controller after it's been used. This might be after the user taps a Done button, makes their appropriate selection, or some other action.

PROBLEM

The decorations view controller needs to store the selected image. That simply involves setting a variable. But it also needs to dismiss itself from being displayed modally from the parent.

SOLUTION

You'll store the image selected and also access the parent view controller to dismiss the view controller.

DISCUSSION

The decorations view controller needs a member to store the selected button's image in for access later by the calling image editing controller (see the following listing).

VCDecorations.h declares `selectedImage` as a `UIImage` instance

```
@interface VCDecorations : UIViewController {

    UIImage *selectedImage;
}

@property (nonatomic, retain) UIImage *selectedImage;

-(IBAction)doImageBtn:(id)sender;
-(IBAction)doCancelBtn:(id)sender;

@end
```

Implementing the action methods is similar to the previous classes. Copy the declarations into the .m file first. The Cancel button simply calls the dismiss method on the parent controller to remove itself (see the following listing). The Image button method stores the selected button's background image as the selected image for access later.

VCDecorations.m full implementation

```
@implementation VCDecorations

@synthesize selectedImage;

-(IBAction)doImageBtn:(id)sender;
{
    [selectedImage release];
    selectedImage =
        [sender backgroundImageForState:UIControlStateNormal];
    [self dismissModalViewControllerAnimated:YES];
}

-(IBAction)doCancelBtn:(id)sender;
{
    [self dismissModalViewControllerAnimated:YES];
}

@end
```

How does the image editing controller get access to the selected image? `VCDecorations` stored the image and `VCEditingImage` has a reference to the decorations view controller (that is, `vcDecorations`). But how does `VCEditingImage` know that an image was selected? There are a few ways to accomplish this. The `VCDecorations` class could send out a general notification. Any classes observing that notification would then know the state. `VCDecorations` could define a delegate interface that `VCEditingImage` could implement. Then `VCDecorations` could have a delegate property that `VCEditingImage` could set as itself. After the image is selected, the decorations controller could call a method on its delegate (the editing image controller) with the selected image.

For this size app those methods feel a bit heavy-handed. You know when you're intending to get an image and can just set a flag. You can set the `selectingImage` flag to Yes in `VCEditingImage` when the Decorations button is pressed. You use standard delegation methods on the view controller to manipulate the flag and retrieve the selected image. Let's look at those now.

3.5 Displaying and handling images

Some standard delegation methods on view controllers are commonly used to initialize certain aspects of the controller's view. These methods allow you to run various operations in just the right time. Three key ones are `viewDidLoad`, `viewWillAppear`, and `viewDidAppear`.

These methods can be helpful not only in updating the UI just after it loads, appears, or will appear, but also what functionality to run at those times.

PicDecor takes advantage of these method calls to know when to display the selected images and decorations. Let's look at how the view controller delegation methods work in PicDecor.

3.5.1 Interact with the process as it goes

The `viewDidLoad` method is called just after the view loads. This is often during startup of the app, so be careful about performance-intensive operations. It's good for things that only need to be done once per execution.

Just before the view is displayed, `viewWillAppear` is called. This is a good time to update/reset any UI states. You might want to remove the keyboard or initialize your input fields to their defaults.

Just after the view appears, `viewDidAppear` is called. This can be a good time to animate something the user will see or do some processing during which the user needs feedback.

In all three of these cases, the super (or parent) version of the same method should be called and any parameters must be passed. This should be done before any custom code is executed in your overriding method.

TECHNIQUE 9 Displaying selected images

As stated before, an image view is a common widget in UIs. The iOS SDK makes it easy to add them to a project and also easy to display an image. When an image view is on the UI, setting its image is all that's necessary to display an image. Other settings can make it display various ways, but the core functionality is setting the image.

PROBLEM

You need to handle two possibilities: the user selects an image to edit, either from the camera or photo album, and the user selects decoration images.

SOLUTION

You'll detect when an image was selected to edit and display it in the main image view area. Also, you'll detect when the user selects a decoration image and add that to the top of the image being edited. The user needs to be able to move the decoration images. You'll create a special class to handle the movement by touch.

DISCUSSION

You can use the `viewWillAppear` method on `VCEditingImage` to handle the selected camera/photo album image. The app uses the image property in the image selection controller, `vcDecorations`, to create the displayed image view.

Also, you can use the `viewWillAppear` method to be notified when your `VCEditingImage` controller's view will be displayed. This only happens two times: when `PicDecorViewController` displays it and when `VCDecorations` is removed. You set the `selectingImage` flag to Yes when you display `VCDecorations`. When it's removed, you can determine if you were selecting an image.

In `viewWillAppear`, you check for the `selectingImage` flag. If it's `true`, you simply access its `selectedImage` member, create an image view with it, and add it to the main view. Be sure to set the `selectingImage` flag back to No (see the following listing).

VCImageEditingviewWillAppear accessing selected image

```
-(void)viewWillAppear:(BOOL)animated
{
    [super viewWillAppear:animated];

    if (editImage != nil)
    {
        [ivEditingImage setImage:editImage];
        [self.view sendSubviewToBack:ivEditingImage];      <- Put image in back
     }

    if (selectingImage)
    {
        MovableImageView *iv =
            [[MovableImageView alloc]
              initWithImage:[vcDecorations selectedImage]];
        [iv setUserInteractionEnabled:YES];                 <- Must allow interaction
         [self.view addSubview:iv];
    }

    selectingImage = NO;
}
```

Note that the image view created is an instance of `MovableImageView`. This is a custom class (and must be imported in the header) that allows for the decorations to be moved around with the user's finger. The class descends from `ImageView` and simply intercepts the touch events to move the image around (see the following listing).

MovableImageView implementation intercepting touch events to move images by touch

```
#import "MovableImageView.h"
@implementation MovableImageView

- (void)touchesBegan:(NSSet *)touches withEvent:(UIEvent *)event
{
    [super touchesBegan:touches withEvent:event];          <- Pass these through
 }

-(void)touchesEnded:(NSSet*)touches withEvent:(UIEvent *)event
{
    [super touchesEnded:touches withEvent:event];          <-
 }

- (void)touchesMoved:(NSSet *)touches withEvent:(UIEvent *)event
{
    [super touchesMoved:touches withEvent:event];

    float deltaX = [[touches anyObject] locationInView:self].x    <- Move distance
         - [[touches anyObject] previousLocationInView:self].x;
    float deltaY = [[touches anyObject] locationInView:self].y
        - [[touches anyObject] previousLocationInView:self].y;

    self.transform = CGAffineTransformTranslate(self.transform,
        deltaX, deltaY);
}

@end
```

Now if you run the app you can select the input source (it will only use the photo album in the simulator), choose an image, and add a decoration (see figure 3.31). If you don't have any images in your simulators photo album, open Safari in the simulator and hold your finger down on an image to save it into your photo album.

Figure 3.31 PicDecor with a selected image and added decoration images

TECHNIQUE 10 Detecting a device without a camera

Not all iOS devices have cameras. It may be important to know, at runtime, if you're app can function with or without a camera. From there, you might give the user various messages or options, or default to certain actions.

PROBLEM

Because you don't want to allow a device without a camera to select the camera option, you need to skip this step for noncamera devices (such as older iPods and iPads).

SOLUTION

You'll use the built-in method for detecting if the camera is available. If not, you can default to the photo album.

DISCUSSION

This is another good use for the delegation methods. You can implement `viewDidAppear` in the first controller to bypass itself if the user has no camera (see the following listing). You define a static `BOOL` at the top of the file called `startedUp`. In `viewDidAppear`, if `startedUp` is set to No (which it will be the first time around), it checks for camera availability. If the camera isn't available, it programmatically calls the `doPhotoAlbumBtn` method. It passes `nil` in as the sender, which is fine because you're not manipulating that parameter in the method.

Auto-select `PhotoAlbum` if no camera

```
-(void)viewDidAppear:(BOOL)animated
{
    [super viewDidAppear:animated];

    if (!startedUp)
        if (![UIImagePickerController
       isSourceTypeAvailable:UIImagePickerControllerSourceTypeCamera])
```

```
            [self doPhotoAlbumBtn:nil];                    <-- Calling action method
    startedUp = YES;
}
```

Now that you've created your masterpiece of decorated art, how can the world share in your artistic expression? If only there were a way to electronically distribute your creation directly from your device!

3.6 Providing email capabilities

There are two ways to send email from an app using the SDK. One way is to launch a `mailto:` URL, which opens the Email app. You can specify the subject, recipient(s), and so on. This is an okay method for sending an email, but there's no reason to kick your user out of your app. The other method uses the email composer controller to use the same email UI but continue your app's execution.

Whenever you're interacting with the internet, there are special considerations. In the case of images, you might want to scale or compress the image to increase performance. Also, manipulating the image, emailing, uploading, or other processing may take an undetermined amount of time. In these cases, some form of feedback to the user is a good idea.

Programmatic methods of scaling, compressing, and feedback are all useful ways to help the functionality of your app. Apple also helps by providing some standard frameworks for emailing with attachments. Let's have PicDecor email the decorated images.

TECHNIQUE 11 Adding in-app email

Often there's reason to initiate sending email for the user. They may want to provide feedback on the given app, share a prepopulated link to the app in iTunes with their friends, or send other text and/or attachments. The `MessageUI` framework provides not only the built-in UI, but also the functionality to do most of this for you.

PROBLEM

You want the user to be able to email their creation to others as an email attachment within the app.

SOLUTION

You'll use the built-in `MessageUI` framework to add email functionality to the app.

DISCUSSION

For sending email, `VCImageEditing` needs to implement the `MFMailComposeViewControllerDelegate` protocol (see the following code snippet). There's only one method in the delegate's protocol. It's called whenever the controller is done for whatever reason. The signature is `mailComposeController:didFinishWithResult:error:`. The code can check the result and error and proceed accordingly:

```
@interface VCImageEditing : UIViewController
    <MFMailComposeViewControllerDelegate> {
```

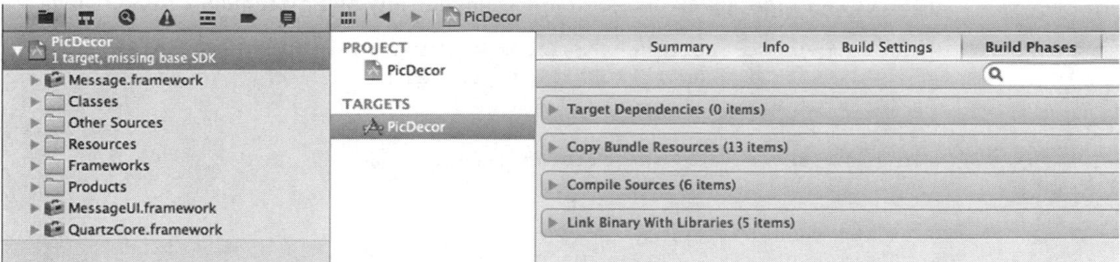

Figure 3.32 Adding a framework to a project

A couple of other items are required for sending email within the app. You'll need to add two more frameworks. Click on the PicDecor project item on the top left of Xcode. From there, select the PicDecor target and the Build Phases tab at the top. Expand the Link Binary with Libraries area (see figure 3.32).

Click (+) and select Message.framework from the list (you can filter the list by typing at the top) to add it to your project (see figure 3.33). Similarly, add the QuartzCore framework, which is used in view transformations and animations, to your project. Also, import `QuartzCore/`QuartzCore.h and `MessageUI/`MessageUI.h into your header file.

After the required items are in place, you need to do two things—create an image from the editing image view and attach it to an email (see the following listing).

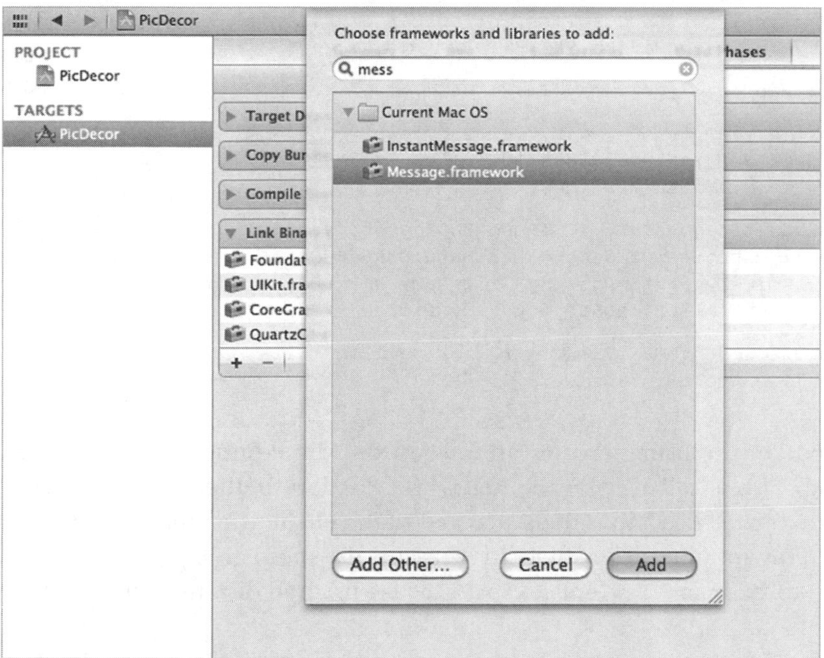

Figure 3.33 Adding the `MessageUI` framework to the Xcode project

`VCImageEditing` creating an image from the image view and attaching it to an email

```
- (void)mailComposeController:(MFMailComposeViewController*)controller
        didFinishWithResult:(MFMailComposeResult)result
        error:(NSError*)error
{
    [self dismissModalViewControllerAnimated:YES];           Normally check for error
 }

-(UIImage *)saveImage:(UIView *)view {
    CGRect mainRect = [[UIScreen mainScreen] bounds];

    UIGraphicsBeginImageContext(mainRect.size);
    CGContextRef context = UIGraphicsGetCurrentContext();
    [[UIColor blackColor] set];

    CGContextFillRect(context, mainRect);
    [view.layer renderInContext:context];
    UIImage *newImage = UIGraphicsGetImageFromCurrentImageContext();   Create the image

    UIGraphicsEndImageContext();

    return newImage;
}

-(IBAction)doEmailBtn:(id)sender;
{
    MFMailComposeViewController *mailController
        = [[MFMailComposeViewController alloc] init];
    mailController.mailComposeDelegate = self;

    for (UIView *v in [self.view subviews])                  Hide toolbar
         if ([v isKindOfClass:[UIToolbar class]])
             [v setHidden:YES];

    UIImage *i = [self saveImage:self.view];                 Call to get image

    for (UIView *v in [self.view subviews])
        if ([v isKindOfClass:[UIToolbar class]])
            [v setHidden:NO];

    NSData *imageAsData = UIImagePNGRepresentation(i);
    [mailController addAttachmentData:imageAsData            Add image to email
         mimeType:@"image/png" fileName:@"PicDecor.png"];
    [mailController setSubject:@"My PicDecor Image"];

    [self presentModalViewController:mailController animated:YES];
    [mailController release];
}
```

The code in the listing creates an image from the editing image in the `saveImage` method. This is called from the `doEmailBtn` action method. The resulting image is converted to `NSData` and is then attached to the email using the `MFMailComposeViewController` instance. The subject is set, and the message UI controller is displayed. The `MFMailComposeViewControllerDelegate` method dismisses the controller.

Note that there's code before and after the `saveImage` method call to hide the toolbar. This is so that the toolbar isn't in the image being emailed. Another way to do this would be to declare an `IBOutlet UIToolbar *tbButtons` in the header, wire it up to the toolbar in IB, and set its hidden property in the method.

TECHNIQUE 12 Scaling an image for email

Whether it's for the UI, email, or a variety of other uses, scaling images can be useful. Sometimes you may only use an image for an icon in the app (for example, letting the user set a profile picture). In these cases, there's no need to keep the full image copied on the device taking up space and possibly bandwidth (if transmitting/uploading).

PROBLEM

In many cases, the image might be large, and you should always consider not only the performance of the network activity of the device, but also the battery life. For this, you might want to scale the image to a smaller size.

SOLUTION

You'll scale and compress the user's created image to allow for faster emailing.

DISCUSSION

Scaling an image to a new size only takes a few lines of code (see the following listing). This is helpful in many cases and is necessary in some.

Scaling an image to another width and height

```
+ (UIImage*)imageWithImage:(UIImage*)image
              scaledToSize:(CGSize)newSize;
{
    UIGraphicsBeginImageContext( newSize );
    [image drawInRect:CGRectMake(0,0,newSize.width,newSize.height)];
    UIImage* newImage = UIGraphicsGetImageFromCurrentImageContext();
    UIGraphicsEndImageContext();

    return newImage;
}
```

In fact, the resolution from the camera doesn't fit your image view. Where would you put the call to scale the image?

Another option is to compress the image as a JPEG:

```
[UIImageJPEGRepresentation(imageObj, 0.4f)
       writeToFile:self.myFilePath atomically:YES];
```

TECHNIQUE 13 Using the activity indicator

It's never fun to wait on an app to process something, but it's even worse if you have no indication that something productive is happening while you wait. If the user has to wonder what's happening or if the app is hung, that can be a bad user experience leading to an eventual loss in users. It's always good to give visual feedback to the user if they do have to wait.

PROBLEM

During processing, you want to display something to the user so that they know something is going on. This not only provides feedback to the user, but also helps prevent them from initiating other actions or quitting the app.

SOLUTION

You'll see how to provide visual feedback of activity.

DISCUSSION

Two generic ways to show activity are an activity indicator and a network activity indicator (on the carrier bar).

For a standard activity indicator, you can add one to your view in the UI and have an `IBOutlet` reference to it declared in your code. When desired, you can turn its animation on and/or its hidden status off. When done, change the settings back.

To set the network activity indicator, get the shared `UIApplication` instance and set the network activity indicator to `YES`:

```
[[UIApplication sharedApplication]
        setNetworkActivityIndicatorVisible:YES];
```

When your app is doing some processing on the main thread that prevents the user from interacting with it, you should display an activity indicator to give clear feedback to the user. An example of this is loading a web page or refreshing a list from a database.

The network activity indicator (see figure 3.34) is useful to let the user know that the radios in the device are being used to communicate online. This is especially useful when your app is processing on another thread. The user may not be aware that there's other processing going on if they're still able to use the interface.

Figure 3.34 Network activity indicator displayed on the status bar by network signal meter

3.7 Summary

Now that you understand the basic view controller, you'll be able to build on that using others such as the table view and navigation controllers. You've seen how you need to think differently about your UI design—not only function, not only form, but both and more. Using IB, you confirmed your UI design and laid the basis for your app. In the code, you prepared to relate the code to the interface and then used IB to relate them.

PicDecor is a fairly basic app, but it touches on many concepts and fundamentals of iOS development. Going forward with this knowledge allows you to capitalize on this. You'll be able to advance through more complex projects quickly.

Through your defined outlets and actions, you developed the UI to behave in the way you intended. And then, through the code, you fleshed out your implementation. You took a couple of extra steps like bypassing the selection for the user if they don't have a camera (such as an older iPod Touch). This type of thinking will pay off down the line in designing intuitive apps.

Using delegation, you were able to handle some cases and functionality that might have otherwise required more checks, data members, outlets/actions, and so on. Being informed of when something will happen or has happened can be powerful—and we have only touched on the basics.

Using email within an app can be useful and can take your app outside of itself and into people's lives. For example, allowing the user to email a report or other data can bring your app into their accounting world. This is not only powerful to the user, but also adds a lot of value to your app and the likelihood of it being used.

Of course, attachments aren't the only things you can email. Using the `setMessageBody` method on the `MFMailComposeViewController` class lets you set the email body as plain text or html. This is great for tables and other formatted content.

Going forward, you'll learn about other controllers, including the navigation controller. You'll see the table view controller, which is powerful and commonly used. You'll also use input widgets other than simple buttons and see what implications come along with them.

We've covered many of the concepts that you'll encounter throughout iOS development. With these tools in your belt, you'll be able to see how more intricate aspects of the SDK work and how to utilize them in your projects.

Accessing the address book/contacts in Dial4

4

This chapter covers

- Master-detail applications
- Table views
- Working with the address book

In this chapter, you'll create an app called Dial4, which will tap into the iPhone's address book. Although apps aren't allowed access into all areas of the device (such as a user's phone number), there are areas in the address book that you can access and even modify. This allows an app to display contact data and even update it based upon a user's actions. This can be useful for a variety of apps, including those that select a location based upon a contact address or those that dial a contact's phone number.

As you'll soon see in this chapter, the iOS SDK provides developers with a direct UI into the address book to display entries and allow users to select those entries. Although this is handy, there are some limitations in how the data is displayed. For this reason, when creating your Dial4 app, you'll allow the user to access the contacts directly, allowing them to navigate into the list. To do this, you'll display the applicable contact data in a table view for the user. In this way, you avoid displaying nonapplicable data like their mailing address. Another advantage of displaying your Dial4 data in a table view is that it gives you an easy route for filtering the data as the user types into the app.

Another thing to notice in dealing with the address book framework is the handling of pointers. You'll notice that when using the address book records from the array, `objc_unretainedPointer` is called to the object pointer without transferring any ownership of the memory. In other cases, `__bridge_transfer` is used to typecast pointers to comparable Objective-C objects.

You'll now create an application called Dial4. When I had "olde tyme" cell phones, I liked being able to dial the last four digits of a phone number to have that number dialed automatically for me. By memorizing a handful of four-digit numbers, I could quickly and easily call my friends and family. Dial4 will mimic this same functionality by displaying the user's contacts and allowing them to filter the list as they type numbers. Whether it's the last four digits, the area code, or something else, you can filter the list and display only matching records. This is a great technique that you can use with other apps as well.

4.1 Creating a master-detail application with a table view

View controllers are great for presenting a view to the user and can even present other views for user interaction. But a navigation into a hierarchy is better handled by a *navigation controller*. In Dial4 you'll select rows from a table. If you've used an iPhone at all, you've seen a row selection sliding into a new view. You'll use that same dynamic.

Table views are a natural fit for hierarchy navigation. With each selection you navigate down the hierarchy and slide in the applicable data. Table views provide a great means of viewing data and interacting with it. Viewing the list doesn't need to be controlled by another mechanism—you interact directly with the list.

You'll start by creating a new project. You can specify it as a *master-detail application* so that you'll have some applicable items configured for you. From there, you'll look at the aspects of populating the table as well as how to handle user taps on a table cell.

TECHNIQUE 14 Creating a master-detail application

You want the project to display the contacts from the address book in a table view. Tapping on a row will slide a new controller (and its view) in from the right, thus navigating to the new controller. This type of hierarchy-based navigation is created with a navigation controller.

PROBLEM

Because you know your app will display data in a table view and navigate down into the data, you need to lay the foundation for your app by selecting the Master-Detail Application option in Xcode.

UINAVIGATIONCONTROLLER (FROM APPLE CLASS REFERENCE DOCS) You use navigation controllers to manage the presentation of hierarchical data in your app. A navigation controller manages a self-contained view hierarchy (known as a *navigation interface*) whose contents are composed partly of views managed directly by the navigation controller and partly of views managed by custom view controllers you provide. Your custom view controllers provide screens' worth of data while the navigation controller manages the navigation between those screens.

SOLUTION

You'll create a new project in Xcode and use a navigation controller as the base view controller.

DISCUSSION

Start a new project in Xcode and select Master-Detail Application. Click Next, specify the product name as Dial4, specify the other settings, click Next, and set the location. Open the project's Dial4MasterViewController.xib file under Resources and note the table view that appears (see figure 4.1).

A master-detail application defaults the first view controller to a table view controller. How convenient for you! Also, it reinforces the concept that table views lend themselves to navigation controllers and vice versa because often tapping on a row navigates to another controller. You could use other controllers instead of the navigation controller, but this one should be best for Dial4.

ALTERNATE SOLUTIONS

UIVIEWCONTROLLER (FROM APPLE CLASS REFERENCE DOCS) In the Model-View-Controller (MVC) design pattern, a controller object provides the custom logic needed to bridge the app's data to the views and other visual entities used to present that data to the user. In iOS apps, a view controller is a specific type of controller object that you use to present and manage the views of your app. View controller objects are descendants of the `UIViewController` class, which is defined in the UIKit framework.

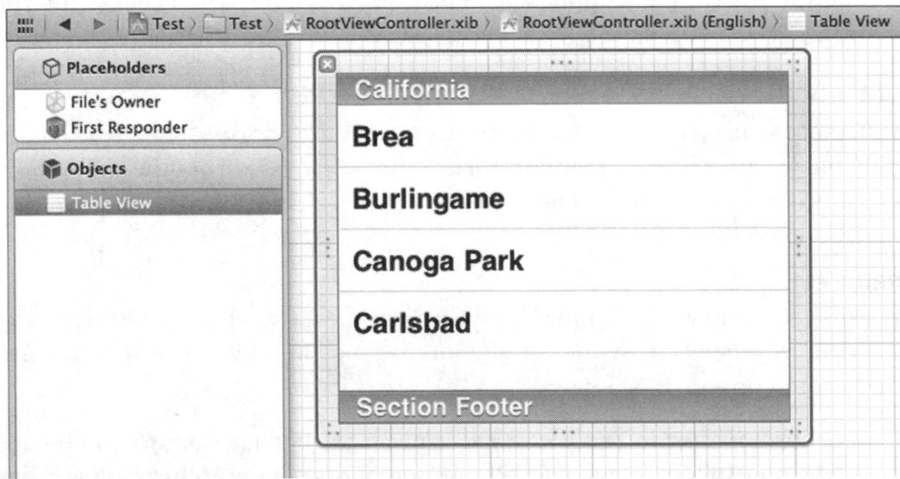

Figure 4.1 Master-Detail Application defaults to using a table view

For PicDecor in chapter 3, you used a view controller and presented the other screens sliding up from the bottom. That was fine for that project because you were making selections more than navigating. For Dial4, you'll allow the user to drill down into the data by selecting an item in the table view. A navigation controller is best for that concept.

> **UITABBARCONTROLLER (FROM APPLE CLASS REFERENCE DOCS)** You use tab bar controllers to organize your app into one or more distinct modes of operation. A tab bar controller manages a self-contained view hierarchy (known as a *tab bar interface*) whose contents are composed partly of views managed by the tab bar controller and partly of views managed by custom view controllers you provide.

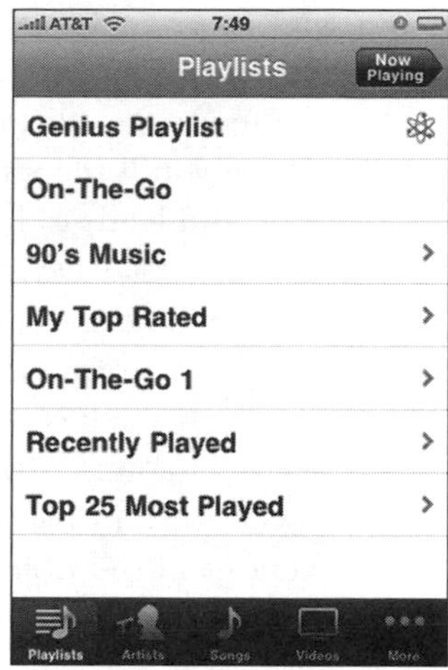

Figure 4.2 Apple uses a tab bar controller in the iPod interface

Another option is the *tab bar application*. This option gives you a tab bar at the bottom of the window. It can contain a variable number of buttons, each corresponding to a controller and therefore a view. You may have seen this utilized in the iPod app (see figure 4.2).

You don't have multiple facets of the data set or other reasons to use a tab bar controller. In your case, you want to display a list of items that are tappable and that lead to a more detailed view of the data. A navigation controller with a table view controller as the top controller is the best choice.

Without the navigation controller, you could display the table view just the same, but how would you proceed down into the data details? Sliding a view up from the bottom would be one option, but that doesn't imply the same focusing and drilling-down aspect you're looking for. A tab bar controller allows for separate controllers, but not with much relationship between them so, again, the navigation aspect is missing.

The navigation and tab bar controllers are the only controllers that are meant to house and manage multiple controllers. They allow the user to visit and view other controllers' views via the mechanism of a drilling-down hierarchy or a sibling-based hierarchy.

There're plenty of uses for the view controller and tab bar controller. Again, the primary reason for this is the implications of using a table view: tapping on a row to slide in the next controller.

4.2 Presenting data using a table view

A table view isn't much by itself. If you compile and run your project you'll see an empty table. It needs not only to get data to display from somewhere, but also another class to handle any actions the user initiates. The table view uses a *data source* to provide its data and a *delegate* to handle the interactions.

Table views are vertical displays of data using rows or *cells*. Each cell displays text and/or images to allow the user to make their selection by tapping on the cell. In some cases, selection may not be allowed because the data may be for display only. Often you'll see a disclosure indicator similar to (>) to indicate that the cell is selectable and leads to further details.

The table view class `UITableView` handles most of the visual functionality of scrolling, highlighting, selecting, and so on. What your project needs to do indicates the parts that are specific to your app. Primarily that is what data is displayed and what to do when a cell is selected.

In chapter 2, you used delegates for your buttons, so you may remember that a delegate for an object houses the functionality to be performed based on the needs or actions of the object (such as tapping a button). What follows will be similar to what you've already done, but let's look at how the table view gets and displays the data.

TECHNIQUE 15 Displaying data in a table view

A table view needs another object to provide it with the data to be displayed. This other object is called a *datasource*. It also needs a delegate to handle when the user taps on a row. The datasource and delegate can be the same object or different objects depending on your specific case. The vast majority of the time, I use the given view controller as the datasource and delegate. If you use IB to create a table view controller, IB automatically sets up a table view and the datasource and delegate relationships back to the table view controller.

> **DATASOURCE** A datasource is almost identical to a delegate. The difference is in the relationship with the delegating object. Instead of being delegated control of the UI, a datasource is delegated control of data. The delegating object, typically a view object such as a table view, holds a reference to its datasource and occasionally asks it for the data it should display. A datasource, like a delegate, must adopt a protocol and implement, at minimum, the required methods of that protocol. Datasources are responsible for managing the memory of the model objects they give to the delegating view.

PROBLEM

You need to make sure that your default table view is set up to use the appropriate class as the datasource and delegate: `Dial4MasterViewController` or `RootViewController`, depending on your setup.

SOLUTION

Using Xcode, you'll inspect the settings in your default XIB file to verify the correct settings.

DISCUSSION

Viewing the table view's connections with IB shows you that the necessary connections have already been made (see figure 4.3). The table view's delegate and

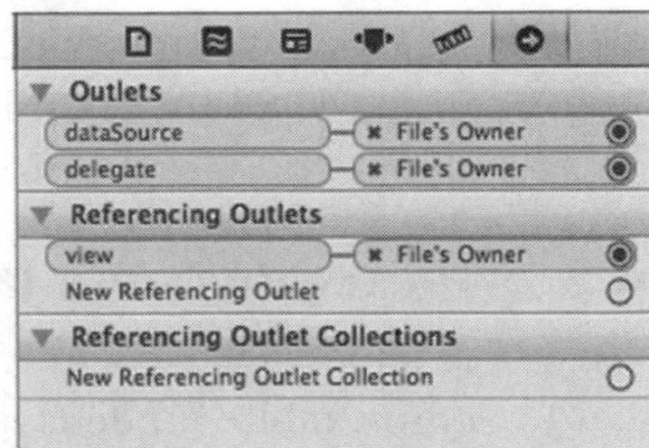

Figure 4.3 IB defaults the table view connections to File's Owner.

datasource are set to File's Owner. In the Identity Inspector for File's Owner, you see that it's an instance of `RootViewController`.

Open the RootViewController.m file in Xcode, and you'll see that when you created the project, Xcode created default methods for some of the datasource interface (see the following listing).

Default table view method implementations

```
- (NSInteger)numberOfSectionsInTableView:(UITableView *)tableView {
    return 1;                                                     Number of
}                                                                 sections

// Customize the number of rows in the table view.
- (NSInteger)tableView:(UITableView *)tableView
    numberOfRowsInSection:(NSInteger)section {
    return 0;                                                  Number of cells
}                                                              in sections

// Customize the appearance of table view cells.
- (UITableViewCell *)tableView:(UITableView *)tableView
    cellForRowAtIndexPath:(NSIndexPath *)indexPath
{                                                                 Unique string
    static NSString *CellIdentifier = @"Cell";                    for table

    UITableViewCell *cell =
        [tableView dequeueReusableCellWithIdentifier:CellIdentifier];
    if (cell == nil) {
        cell = [[UITableViewCell alloc]
            initWithStyle:UITableViewCellStyleDefault
            reuseIdentifier:CellIdentifier];
    }

    // Configure the cell.

    return cell;
}
```

The `numberOfSectionsInTableView:` method needs to return the number of sections your table will be split into. If you wanted to list car models you might have a section for each make (such as Acura, BMW, and so on). Then, in each section, you'd have cells for the various models.

The `numberOfRowsInSection:` method needs to return the number of rows for the passed-in section index. Using the previous example, this is the number of models for a given make.

The `cellForRowAtIndexPath:` returns the cell used at the given `indexPath`, which is the section and row. Based on your data, you can create and configure a table cell view and return it for display.

You'll build an array to hold the address book data you're interested in. Declare it as an `NSArray` pointer in the header and name it `myContacts`. Now, in the `numberOfRowsInSection` method, you can return the count of `myContacts`.

In your array, you'll have the references to all of the contacts in the device. Make sure the table view is pointing to the `RootViewController` (File's Owner) for its datasource and delegate so that the data is fetched from the correct class. There may be plenty of data there, so you need to decide what to display and how.

4.2.1 Apple cell styles

Four different default Apple table view cell styles are available (see table 4.1). The default cell style displays one line of text. The Value1 and Value2 cells display a title on the left and details on the right. The subtitle displays two lines of text. The top line is bolded and is typically used as a title. All of the cell styles have a built-in image view on the left and an accessory view on the right for disclosure indicator, check mark, disclosure button, or a custom view.

Table 4.1 Default Apple table view cell styles (from Apple class reference docs)

`UITableViewCellStyleDefault`	A simple style for a cell with a text label (black and left-aligned) and an optional image view. Note that this is the default style for cells prior to iOS 3.0.
`UITableViewCellStyleValue1`	A style for a cell with a label on the left side of the cell with left-aligned and black text; on the right side is a label that has smaller blue text and is right-aligned. The Settings app uses cells in this style.
`UITableViewCellStyleValue2`	A style for a cell with a label on the left side of the cell with text that is right-aligned and blue; on the right side of the cell is another label with smaller text that is left-aligned and black. The Phone/Contacts app uses cells in this style.
`UITableViewCellStyleSubtitle`	A style for a cell with a left-aligned label across the top and a left-aligned label below it in smaller gray text. The iPod app uses cells in this style.

As with the Contacts app, you're mostly interested in displaying the user name even though you'll filter on the phone number. For that reason, you retain the default table view cell style.

If you wanted to list several parts of the address book entry data in the cell, one of the default cell styles might not work. In that case, you'd need to create a custom cell class.

4.2.2 Cell customization

Creating a custom cell is facilitated by creating a new view class. When you select to create a new class, select Objective-C Class and click Next. Set the Subclass Of to `UITableViewCell` (see figure 4.4).

This creates a new class in Xcode with the basic implementation of a table view cell. In the resulting initialization method, you can create whatever other items for the cell you need. You're also free to add methods to set anything else in the cell.

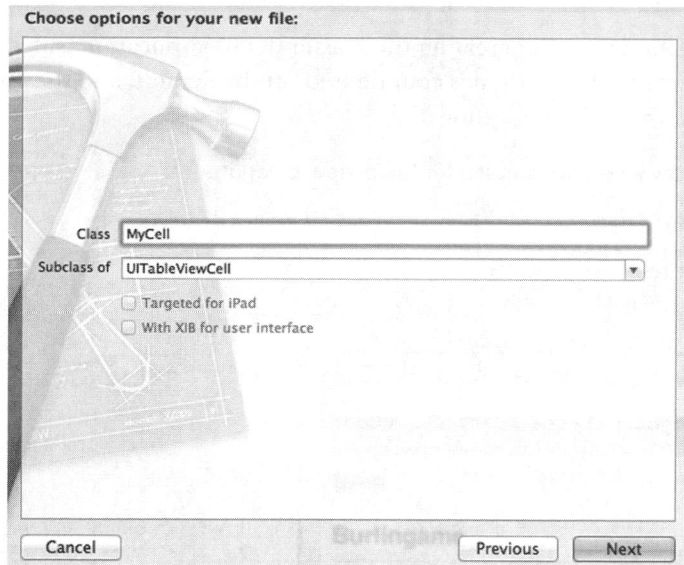

Figure 4.4 Creating a new class descending from UITableViewCell

The bottom line is that `UITableViewCell` descends from `UIView` and you can manipulate it as you would any other view. You can add text fields, buttons, images, and just about anything else.

`UITableViewCell` has a `setSelected` method that's overridden in a custom class when created. This is your chance to handle the appearance of a cell when a user selects it. But this isn't where you handle the functionality for a cell selection. That's done in the delegate which, in your case, is `RootViewController`. Let's look at that now.

> **NOTE** If you use Storyboard to design your UI, a tableview can contain a prototype cell returned when dequeuing a cell. This prototype cell can be customized via Interface Builder.

TECHNIQUE 16 Handling table view cell selection

Some tables are only for displaying data, but most allow the user to select the cell for some action. It might be to play a song, display a picture, visit a website, or any number of other actions.

The delegate of the table view has a callback to handle the selection and is passed to the `indexPath` (section and index) of the selected cell. The default implementation of this method doesn't do anything, but the comments suggest that navigating to another view is common.

PROBLEM

Based on a user's tap, you need to know when a row in the table view has been selected and handle it accordingly.

SOLUTION

Using the `UITableViewDelegate` callback methods, your class is notified when a row is selected. In that callback, you'll call the method to handle the selection appropriately.

Discussion

Another default method to use in creating the master-detail application is the method for a row being selected. The method is commented out by default, and the content is only comments (see the following listing).

Default contents of row selection method for table view delegate

```
// Override to support row selection in the table view.
- (void)tableView:(UITableView *)tableView
    didSelectRowAtIndexPath:(NSIndexPath *)indexPath
{

    // Navigation logic may go here.
    //             Create and push another view controller.
    /*
     <#DetailViewController#> *detailViewController =
        [[<#DetailViewController#> alloc]
            initWithNibName:@"<#Nib name#>" bundle:nil];
     // ...
     // Pass the selected object to the new view controller.
     [self.navigationController pushViewController:detailViewController
        animated:YES];
     */
}
```

You only need to do two things in your selection method—deselect the selected row (for appearance) and pass off the selected row index to a handler method (see the following listing).

Deselect selected row and call method to handle functionality

```
-(void)handleRowSelection:(int)rowIndex
{
}

- (void)tableView:(UITableView *)tableView
    didSelectRowAtIndexPath:(NSIndexPath *)indexPath
{
    [[tableView cellForRowAtIndexPath:indexPath]
                                    setSelected:NO animated:YES];
    [self handleRowSelection:indexPath.row];
}
```

Note that the `handleRowSelection` method is empty. You'll flesh this out later in technique 20. For now, you're concerned with the table handling. To populate the cells with data, you need to access the address book, which you'll do next.

4.3 Accessing the address book

The address book isn't like anything else you've worked with so far. Most of the related data from the address book descends from `CFTypeRef`, and the data's accessed in a way different from other classes you've seen.

TECHNIQUE 17 Retrieving the address book entries

The address book framework provides the means to access the data, but some legwork is involved to determine whether you have the right data. Some items have a single value like *first name*. But in some cases, for example, phone numbers, there may be several values. In those cases, the access is slightly different and it's important to get it right.

You'll see both routes mentioned above in accessing single-value items for names and multiple-value items for the phone numbers. You'll start slow by accessing the entries in the address book as an array.

PROBLEM

You need to access the entries in the user's address book using the provided framework.

SOLUTION

Through classes and methods in the address book framework, you'll create an address book object and copy the contacts from it.

DISCUSSION

It's easy to get an array of the address book entries. This is just the thing you need to access the data for your app. You can get the array and store it in your `myContacts` object (see the following listing). Let's do this in the `numberOfSectionsInTableView` method of your delegate. That way your address book isn't loaded until the table is loaded and, in your case, only if your array is `nil`.

Loading the array of contacts from the address book

```
- (NSInteger)numberOfSectionsInTableView:(UITableView *)tableView {
      if (nil == myContacts)
      {
        addressBook = ABAddressBookCreate();
        if ([self checkAddressBookAuthorizationStatus:tableView])
            myContacts = [NSArray arrayWithArray:(__bridge_transfer NSArray*)
            ABAddressBookCopyArrayOfAllPeople(addressBook)];
      }
    return 1;
}
```

You first need to create the address book reference with `ABAddressBookCreate()`. Then you check for user authorization to the address book. If it's allowed, you copy the people from the address book into your array.

Let's look at the method where we check for the user's address book authorization called `checkAddressBookAuthorizationStatus:`

```
-(bool)checkAddressBookAuthorizationStatus:(UITableView*)tableView;
{
    ABAuthorizationStatus authStatus =
        ABAddressBookGetAuthorizationStatus();

    if (authStatus != kABAuthorizationStatusAuthorized)
    {
```

```
        ABAddressBookRequestAccessWithCompletion
            (addressBook, ^(bool granted, CFErrorRef error)
        {
            dispatch_async(dispatch_get_main_queue(), ^{
                if (error)
                    NSLog(@"Error: %@", (__bridge NSError *)error);
                else if (!granted) {
                    UIAlertView *av = [[UIAlertView alloc]
                        initWithTitle:@"Authorization Denied"
                        message:@"Set permissions in Settings>General>Privacy."
                        delegate:nil
                        cancelButtonTitle:nil
                        otherButtonTitles:@"OK", nil];
                    [av show];
                }
                else
                {
                    ABAddressBookRevert(addressBook);
                    myContacts = [NSArray arrayWithArray:
                          (__bridge_transfer NSArray*)
                          ABAddressBookCopyArrayOfAllPeople(addressBook)];
                    [tableView reloadData];
                }
            });
        });
    }

    return authStatus == kABAuthorizationStatusAuthorized;
}
```

First you get the current authorization. If it's `kABAuthorizationStatusAuthorized`, then the if statement is skipped and the final return line will return true. Otherwise, the framework will prompt the user for authorization and the completion block will check for an error and if the authorization was granted.

If the user denied access, the app displays a message that they need to grant permissions in the Settings app. If access was granted, the address book is reverted to the current state, the people are copied to the array, and the table is reloaded to display the address book contents copied.

> **NOTE** Address book authorization, similar to photo album, calendars, and reminders authorization, was added in iOS 6, so be wary of backward and forward compatibility here.

If you try to compile now, you'll get some errors. You need to include the AddressBook framework and import the AddressBook/AddressBook.h file from the `RootViewController` header.

Now that you can compile and run, check it out. Still blank, right? Well, you didn't populate the cells yet. Now it's time to get the properties from the address book records and display them.

TECHNIQUE 18 Obtaining address book image property

The Contacts/Address Book app, like many iOS apps, allows for images to be used. In this case, images can be used for profile pictures for the different entries. Fortunately, this is another property you can access from an app through the framework.

I'm a fan of using images and icons whenever possible. Maybe this isn't best all the time, but it's a good idea to do when possible and when they add to the interface. The address book allows for setting an icon image for a contact's entry. Dial4 can certainly show that same image in your list. It improves the app's feel and makes finding a given person easier.

PROBLEM

You want to display the image associated with an address book contact entry in the table view.

SOLUTION

In the callback method for creating the cell for the table view, you'll access the image data and set it in the cell's image view.

DISCUSSION

The three things you need to set in your table view cells are the name, the image, and the accessory type. If the name doesn't exist, you'll display a phone number. If the image isn't set, you'll ignore that. The accessory type doesn't rely on anything.

Now that you have the address book contents, let's go back to your cell method and set your values. You'll set the cell accessory type to `UITableViewCellAccessory-None`, which is blank. Four accessory types are defined by Apple (see table 4.2).

Next, let's set the name in the cell. You'll want to check the name before setting it in case it's empty. Let's create a method to do it. You'll call the method `personDis-playText` and define it to receive and access only one person record from the address book (see the following listing). The `personDisplayText` method will be further implemented in the next technique.

Table 4.2 Apple-defined table view cell accessory types (from Apple class reference docs)

'	The cell doesn't have any accessory view. This is the default value.
`UITableViewCellAccessory-DisclosureIndicator`	The cell has an accessory control shaped like a regular chevron. It's intended as a disclosure indicator. The control doesn't track touches.
`UITableViewCellAccessoryDetail-DisclosureButton`	The cell has an accessory control that's a blue button with a chevron image as content. It's intended for configuration purposes. The control tracks touches.
`UITableViewCellAccessory-Checkmark`	The cell has a check mark on its right side. This control doesn't track touches. The delegate of the table view can manage check marks in a section of rows (possibly limiting the check mark to one row of the section) in its `tableView:didSelectRowAtIndexPath:` method.

Configuring the table view cell for the address book name

```
- (UITableViewCell *)tableView:(UITableView *)tableView
    cellForRowAtIndexPath:(NSIndexPath *)indexPath {
    static NSString *CellIdentifier = @"Cell";
    UITableViewCell *cell =
        [tableView dequeueReusableCellWithIdentifier:CellIdentifier];
    if (cell == nil) {
        cell = [[UITableViewCell alloc]
            initWithStyle:UITableViewCellStyleDefault        <-- One-line style
             reuseIdentifier:CellIdentifier];
        [cell setAccessoryType:UITableViewCellAccessoryNone];
    }
    // Configure the cell.
    [[cell textLabel]                                     <-- Set cell title text
         setText:[self personDisplayText:
            [myContact objectAtIndex:indexPath.row]]];
    return cell;
}
```

Now you'll set the image. After the code where you set the name, you'll get the image data, convert it to an image, and set it in the cell's default image view (see the following listing).

Getting the address book record's image data and setting it in the cell

```
NSData *d =
        (NSData*)ABPersonCopyImageData(
                        [myContacts objectAtIndex:indexPath.row]);
    if (nil != d)
    {
        UIImage *i = [UIImage imageWithData:d];
        [[cell imageView] setImage:i];
    }
    else
        [[cell imageView] setImage:nil];
```

Getting the person's name is fairly easy, but you want to consider a couple of things: what if there's no name set; what order does the user prefer for the names; and what if there are no phone numbers? Getting phone numbers is different because they're grouped.

TECHNIQUE 19 Obtaining grouped properties from the address book

Some values in the address book are grouped together, such as phone numbers and email addresses. A person may have none or several of each of these, and iOS stores them in a multivalue item.

To access these values, you must first retrieve them as a group. After you have the group for the multivalue item, you can access a specific value in an index-based fashion.

PROBLEM

You want to be able to access meaningful information for a contact in order to have an identifiable value.

SOLUTION

You'll access the first and last name for a given contact and format them given the selected preferences on the device. If there's no first or last name, you'll access the phone number as the identifiable value.

DISCUSSION

To access these items, you must first copy the property into an `ABMultiValueRef` (see 3rd annotation in the following listing). With the multivalue reference, you can copy out by index number. Using the `ABMultiValueGetCount` method, you can determine how many values (such as phone numbers) there are.

Method to determine what text to display for an address book record

```
-(NSString*)personDisplayText:(ABRecordRef)person
{
    NSString *firstName = (__bridge_transfer NSString *)
        ABRecordCopyValue(person, kABPersonFirstNameProperty);
    NSString *lastName = (__bridge_transfer NSString *)
        ABRecordCopyValue(person, kABPersonLastNameProperty);

    NSString *fullName = nil;
    if (firstName || lastName)
    {
        if (ABPersonGetCompositeNameFormat() ==
            kABPersonCompositeNameFormatFirstNameFirst)        <- Consider name order preference
             fullName = [NSString stringWithFormat:@"%@ %@",
                firstName, lastName];                          <- Assumes both names are set
         else
            fullName = [NSString stringWithFormat:@"%@, %@",
                lastName, firstName];
    }
    else
    {
        ABMultiValueRef phoneNumbers = ABRecordCopyValue(person,   <- Get first phone number if no name
                                     kABPersonPhoneProperty);
        if (phoneNumbers &&
            ABMultiValueGetCount(phoneNumbers) > 0)
        {
            fullName = (__bridge_transfer NSString*)
                ABMultiValueCopyValueAtIndex(phoneNumbers, 0);
            CFRelease(phoneNumbers);
        }
    }

    return fullName;

}
```

Other common properties that have multiple values are `kABPersonEmailProperty` and `kABPersonAddressProperty`. All of these values also have associated labels such as

Home, Work, and Other. If you want a specific one, you call the ABMultiValueCopyLabelAtIndex with the ABMultiValueRef and an index. This returns the label, which you can compare against kABWorkLabel,kABHomeLabel, and kABOtherLabel (see the following listing). This is an example of how to find a value within a multivalue ref, but you don't use this method in this app.

Cycle through the email addresses with preference to the work email

```
NSString *retVal = nil;
    ABRecordRef person = [myContacts objectAtIndex:rowIndex];
    ABMultiValueRef vals =
        ABRecordCopyValue(person, kABPersonEmailProperty);
    if (ABMultiValueGetCount(vals) > 0)
    {
        CFIndex i;
        for (i=0; i < ABMultiValueGetCount(vals); i++)
        {
            CFStringRef label = ABMultiValueCopyLabelAtIndex(vals, i);

            if (retVal == nil ||
                CFStringCompare(label, kABWorkLabel, 0)
                  == kCFCompareEqualTo)
             {
                CFStringRef val = ABMultiValueCopyValueAtIndex(vals, i);
                retVal = (NSString *)val;
                CFRelease(val);
             }
            CFRelease(label);
        }
    }
    CFRelease(vals);
    return retVal;
```

Consider name order preference

Now that you have the image and name or phone number, you can run the app with some meaningful results (see figure 4.5).

Because your handleRowSelection method is still empty, nothing happens when you select the row. The purpose of this app is to make a call when you tap the row, so let's see how that's done.

TECHNIQUE 20 Making a call

Dial4 is primarily for the iPhone, which makes calls. Many apps have a case for allowing the user to make a call. Maybe it's to contact support or place an order. In your case, it's to call someone from their address book.

Programmatically, making a call with the iPhone is quite easy. Several URLs are automatically supported by the SDK—tel: for calls, mailto: for email, sms: for sms, http: for a website, and maps: for a map.

Carrier 3:39 PM
Bear Cahill
(214) 555-1313

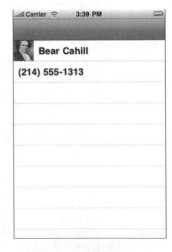

Figure 4.5 Executing Dial4 app with address book data listed

PROBLEM

You want to allow the user to select a row and initiate a call to the selected contact displayed in that table view row.

SOLUTION

In the table view cell selection method above, you called a then-empty method: `handleRowSelection`. You'll now implement this method to determine the related phone number and call it or present the user with a list of numbers to select from and call.

DISCUSSION

To make a call, you need to construct the URL with the phone number and launch it via the app. The easiest way to do that would be to get the phone number like you did before and make the URL for the call:

```
NSString *url = [NSString stringWithFormat:@"tel:%@", phoneNum];
     [[UIApplication sharedApplication] openURL:[NSURL URLWithString:url]];
```

This would work, but what if the user has multiple phone numbers? You need to prompt the user for a phone number preference. You should cycle through the phone numbers, store them in an array, and prompt the user using an alert view. When they tap on a number, you use that number to make the call.

This means you need to check the number of phone numbers available. If it's just one, you can get it, build the URL, and make the call. But if it's more than one, you need to create the alert view, add the various phone numbers as buttons, and display the alert view. You'll use delegation to receive the index of which button the user tapped (see the following listing).

Fetch the single phone number and make a call or prompt for the user's choice

```
-(void)callThisNumber:(NSString*)phoneNum
{
    NSString *url = [NSString stringWithFormat:@"tel:%@", phoneNum];
    [[UIApplication sharedApplication]
                                 openURL:[NSURL URLWithString:url]];
}

-(void)handleRowSelection:(int)rowIndex
{
    ABRecordRef person = objc_unretainedPointer([myContacts
                                        objectAtIndex:rowIndex]);
    ABMultiValueRef phoneNumbers = ABRecordCopyValue(person,
                                              kABPersonPhoneProperty);

    if (ABMultiValueGetCount(phoneNumbers) == 1)
        [self callThisNumber:(__bridge_transfer
              NSString*)ABMultiValueCopyValueAtIndex(phoneNumbers, 0)];
    else if (ABMultiValueGetCount(phoneNumbers) > 1)
    {
        UIAlertView *av = [[UIAlertView alloc]
                                  initWithTitle:@"Pick A Number"
                         message:@"Which number would you like to call?"
                               delegate:self
                                   cancelButtonTitle:@"Cancel"
```

Set self as delegate

```
                                      otherButtonTitles:nil];        Set button
                                                                     titles to nil
        for (int i=0; i < ABMultiValueGetCount(phoneNumbers); i++)
            [av addButtonWithTitle:(__bridge_transfer NSString*)
                ABMultiValueCopyValueAtIndex(phoneNumbers, i)];      Add phone
                                                                     numbers as
    if (phoneNumbers)                                                buttons
        CFRelease(phoneNumbers);
}

- (void)alertView:(UIAlertView *)alertView
    clickedButtonAtIndex:(NSInteger)buttonIndex
{
    if (buttonIndex > 0)                                   0 = Cancel
         [self callThisNumber:
            [alertView buttonTitleAtIndex:buttonIndex]];   Use button title
 }
```

Now if you select a row with multiple phone numbers, you'll be prompted to select the number to dial (see figure 4.6).

As is often the case, the final action isn't really that complicated. It's getting to that action—wading through the address book, figuring out the display test, prompting the user for which number to use, and the rest of the interface—that's hard.

TECHNIQUE 21 Displaying address book record details

Suppose you want to also view the address book record details. The obvious thought is to display the details when the user taps the row. That's what the user would expect. But the priority of this app is to make calls quickly, and you don't want to add an extra step into the process, so how should you handle this in the UI?

PROBLEM

You want to display a contact's details from the table view but not as the default table view row selection.

SOLUTION

You'll add a toggle button on the top of the display to put the list into a display-type mode. When toggled, tapping a row in the table will display the contact details. Tapping again will toggle the mode back to the calling mode.

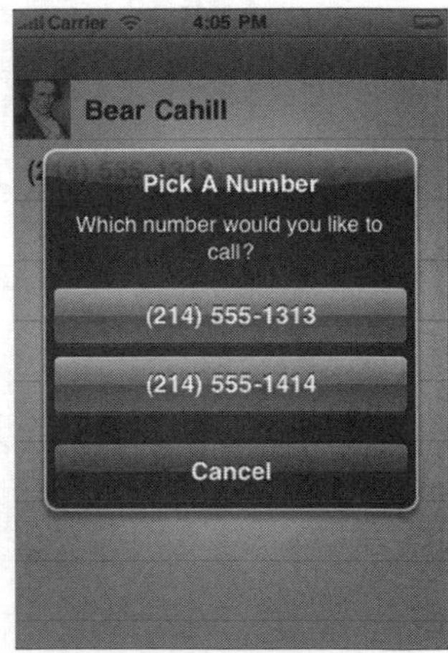

Figure 4.6 Prompted in the simulator for phone number preference

DISCUSSION

Let's put a button on the top left of the navigation item that, when pressed, allows the user to tap a row for display. You need the button, a method it calls, and a view controller to display when you have the selected address book record.

Instantiating and setting the button on the navigation item is fairly straightforward. The method it calls will simply toggle the button's title between Display and Call (see the following listing). Remove the comment delimiters above (/*) and below (*/) the viewDidLoad method and add a call to the doCallDisplayBtn method, passing in nil, which causes the button text to read Display.

Button bar item to toggle between Call and Display

```
-(void)doCallDisplayBtn:(id)sender
{
    NSString *bbiTitle = @"Display";

    if (nil != sender && [[sender title] compare:@"Display"]
                                                   == NSOrderedSame)
        bbiTitle = @"Call";

    UIBarButtonItem *bbi = [[UIBarButtonItem alloc]
        initWithTitle:bbiTitle style:UIBarButtonItemStyleBordered
        target:self action:@selector(doCallDisplayBtn:)];
    self.navigationItem.leftBarButtonItem = bbi;
}

- (void)viewDidLoad {
    [super viewDidLoad];
    [self setTitle:@"Dial4"];

    self.navigationItem.rightBarButtonItem = self.editButtonItem;

    [self doCallDisplayBtn:nil];
}
```

While you're in viewDidLoad, uncomment the line for setting the right button item. This will allow for row-level table edits later. Call setTitle on self to put the app name in the navigation bar.

Run the app and verify that the Call/Display button toggles between the two titles. Also, feel free to tap the Edit button to check that out.

Now you need a controller on which to display the details. Right-click on the Classes group in Xcode and select Add > New File. From the display window, select the template of Objective-c Class and then specify the Subclass of UITableViewController on the next step (see figure 4.7). Set the name to TVCDetails and create the file.

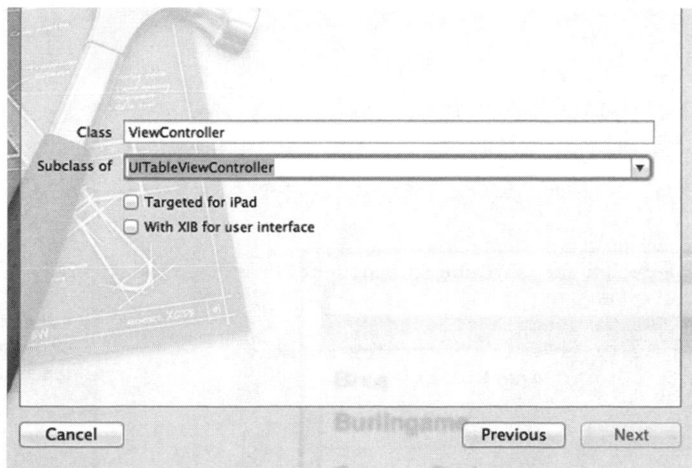

Figure 4.7 Creating a new table view controller in Xcode

In the new class, declare the person member in the header (see the following listing). Also, don't forget to synthesize and `CFRelease` call in the .m file.

Table view controller's declaration of the person member

```
#import <AddressBook/AddressBook.h>

@interface TVCDetails : UITableViewController {

    ABRecordRef person;

}

@property (nonatomic, assign) ABRecordRef person;

@end
```

This class will obtain the address book data (first name, last name, and phone numbers) the same way as before. The number of rows will be based on the number of phone numbers in the record. Also, the table view cell values will use these values. Finally, tapping on a row with a phone number will call that number (see the following listing).

Details table view controller data display and call initiation

```
-(void)callThisNumber:(NSString*)phoneNum
{
    NSString *url = [NSString stringWithFormat:@"tel:%@", phoneNum];
    [[UIApplication sharedApplication]
                                    openURL:[NSURL URLWithString:url]];
}

- (NSInteger)tableView:(UITableView *)tableView
    numberOfRowsInSection:(NSInteger)section
{
    ABMultiValueRef phoneNumbers = ABRecordCopyValue(person,
                kABPersonPhoneProperty);

    int retNum = ABMultiValueGetCount(phoneNumbers)+2;        <-- Plus 2 for names
     CFRelease(phoneNumbers);
    return retNum;
}

- (UITableViewCell *)tableView:(UITableView *)tableView
    cellForRowAtIndexPath:(NSIndexPath *)indexPath
{
    static NSString *CellIdentifier = @"DetailsCell";

    UITableViewCell *cell =
        [tableView dequeueReusableCellWithIdentifier:CellIdentifier];
    if (cell == nil) {
        cell = [[UITableViewCell alloc]
        initWithStyle:UITableViewCellStyleValue2
        reuseIdentifier:CellIdentifier];                    <-- Value2 looks better for these types of values
     }
```

```
    if (indexPath.row < 2)
        [cell setSelectionStyle:UITableViewCellSelectionStyleNone];)
     else
        [cell setSelectionStyle:UITableViewCellSelectionStyleBlue];

    NSString *title;
    NSString *text;
    switch (indexPath.row)
    {
        case 0:
            title = @"First Name";
            text =
                (__bridge_transfer NSString *)ABRecordCopyValue(person,
                kABPersonFirstNameProperty);
            break;
        case 1:
            title = @"Last Name";
            text =
                (__bridge_transfer NSString *)ABRecordCopyValue(person,
                kABPersonLastNameProperty);
            break;
        default:
            title = @"Phone";
            ABMultiValueRef phoneNumbers = ABRecordCopyValue(person,
                    kABPersonPhoneProperty);
            if (phoneNumbers &&
                             ABMultiValueGetCount(phoneNumbers) > 0)
            {
                text =
              (__bridge_transfer NSString*)ABMultiValueCopyValueAtIndex
                    (phoneNumbers, indexPath.row-2);
                 CFRelease(phoneNumbers);
            }

            break;
    }
    [[cell textLabel] setText:title];
    [[cell detailTextLabel] setText:text];

    return cell;
}

- (void)tableView:(UITableView *)tableView
    didSelectRowAtIndexPath:(NSIndexPath *)indexPath {
    if (indexPath.row > 1)
         [self callThisNumber:[[[tableView
            cellForRowAtIndexPath:indexPath] detailTextLabel] text]];
}
```

Don't allow names to be selected

Account for names rows

Only process phone number rows

Setting the title in the `viewDidLoad` method in the same way as for the `RootViewController` finishes off the appearance of this view. You now only need to use the control from the `RootViewController`. The `RootViewController` needs to import the TVCDetails.h file in its header. Then a simple check of the Navigation Item button text tells you what you need to do (see the following listing).

Processing the row selection in `RootViewController` based on the Navigation Bar button

```
- (void)tableView:(UITableView *)tableView
    didSelectRowAtIndexPath:(NSIndexPath *)indexPath {
    [[tableView cellForRowAtIndexPath:indexPath]
        setSelected:NO animated:YES];

    if ([self.navigationItem.leftBarButtonItem.title compare:@"Call"]!=
        NSOrderedSame)
        [self handleRowSelection:indexPath.row];
    else
    {
        TVCDetails *tvc = [[TVCDetails alloc]
            initWithStyle:UITableViewStyleGrouped];
        [tvc setPerson:objc_unretainedPointer(
                          [myContacts objectAtIndex:indexPath.row])];
       [self.navigationController
                                pushViewController:tvc animated:YES];
    }
}
```

Note that you should initialize the `TVCDetails` instance with `UITableViewStyleGrouped`. This will prevent any extra blank lines from displaying when you don't have rows. Run the app, tap the Display button, and then a row will display the details (see figure 4.8).

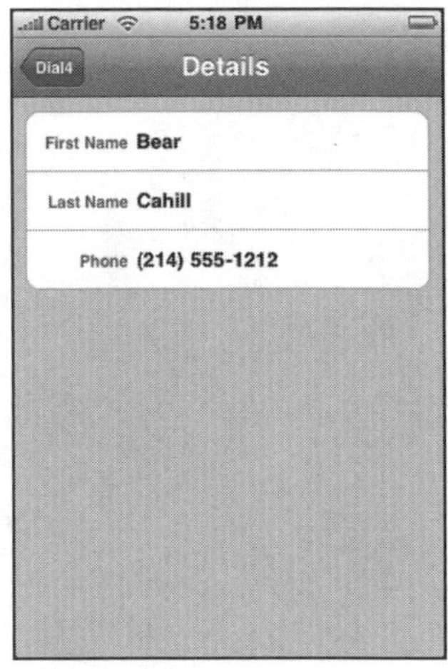

Figure 4.8 Displaying address book details in a table view

You might be wondering when you use this class with the UI editor. You don't. Creating it as a `UITableView-Controller` creates it with an implicit table view. This table view automatically has your class as its datasource and delegate. Because your `RootViewController` instantiates it, you don't need any IB connections to it. Similarly, because you don't have any buttons or other widgets to handle, there's no need for IB (not that you can't do buttons and such programmatically).

Displaying data in a table can be a great way to show address book data to a user. Also, as you've seen, it lets you drill down into the data for further details or related data. Table views can also facilitate managing data, so let's look at that now.

4.4 Managing table data

Table views can provide means for users to manage data in a table view. Users can insert, rearrange, and delete rows. Deleting is the most common editing style, and you may have noticed the default style given your Edit button's results.

As mentioned before, the touch screen allows the data to be directly manipulated. The user drags the table to scroll it instead of a separate mechanism. Similarly, the table view provides the means to manage the data with user interaction.

TECHNIQUE 22 Deleting and rearranging table view rows

The `VCDetails` class has a default method to handle edits when they're performed on a row. Search (Command-f) for `commitEditingStyle` and uncomment that method. The default implementation handling the delete style, `UITableViewCellEditing-StyleDelete`, just deletes the specified row at the `indexPath`.

Run the app in the simulator, tap the Edit button, and try to delete a row. Crash. That's expected. Looking in the Debugger Console (Command-Shift-r) shows the message that the number of rows after the delete isn't correct. That's because you didn't actually delete anything.

Deleting an item from the table view is only the visual part of the delete. You need to also delete the item from the data you're viewing. In many cases, the data being viewed is stored in an array. In that case, you'd need to delete the array item (which is most likely at index `indexPath.row`, assuming a one-section table displayed in the array's given order).

PROBLEM

You need a way to delete data from a table view and allow users to delete contacts right from your app.

SOLUTION

By using the callback method for handling table view edits, the class can be notified when the user chooses to delete a row.

DISCUSSION

To delete the data from the table's datasource, you need to delete it from your array: `myContacts`. More important, you need to delete the item from the address book. The table view row delete will then take care of calling the necessary methods for updating the table (see the following listing). You'll set the array, `myContacts`, to `nil` so that the call for number of sections in the table during the update will repopulate the array.

Committing the editing delete to the address book and table view

```
- (void)tableView:(UITableView *)tableView
    commitEditingStyle:(UITableViewCellEditingStyle)editingStyle
    forRowAtIndexPath:(NSIndexPath *)indexPath
{
    if (editingStyle == UITableViewCellEditingStyleDelete) {
        ABRecordRef person = objc_unretainedPointer([myContacts
             objectAtIndex:indexPath.row]);
        CFErrorRef *error;
        ABAddressBookRemoveRecord(addressBook, person, error);
        ABAddressBookSave(addressBook, error);          <- Save changes
        myContacts = nil;                               <- Set array to nil so it's refreshed
        [tableView deleteRowsAtIndexPaths:[NSArray
            arrayWithObject:indexPath]
            withRowAnimation:UITableViewRowAnimationFade];
    }
}
```

Table 4.3 Table view cell-editing styles provided by iOS SDK

`UITableViewCellEditingStyleNone`	The cell has no editing control. This is the default value.
`UITableViewCellEditingStyleDelete`	The cell has the delete editing control; this control is a red circle enclosing a minus sign.
`UITableViewCellEditingStyleInsert`	The cell has the insert editing control; this control is a green circle enclosing a plus sign.

Other cell-editing styles are handled according to what the style dictates. There are three editing styles (see table 4.3).

Rearranging cells is handled by another method. To allow for rearranging, you need to implement the datasource interface methods, checking whether reordering is allowed and implementing the reordering (see the following listing).

Default implementations of the reorder methods on the table view datasource

```
- (void)tableView:(UITableView *)tableView
    moveRowAtIndexPath:(NSIndexPath *)fromIndexPath
    toIndexPath:(NSIndexPath *)toIndexPath {
}

- (BOOL)tableView:(UITableView *)tableView
    canMoveRowAtIndexPath:(NSIndexPath *)indexPath
{
    return YES;
}
```

If you run the app now and tap Edit, you'll see the reorder control and even be able to reorder the rows (see figure 4.9). But because you don't do anything meaningful in the reorder method (see the listing above), when you exit the app, all changes are lost.

Setting the return value to No in the `tableView:canMoveRowAtIndexPath:` method will prevent the reorder control from displaying and thus removing this experiment. Reordering is a nice addition to an app that lets the user find what they're looking for faster. Another helpful way to do that is by searching or filtering.

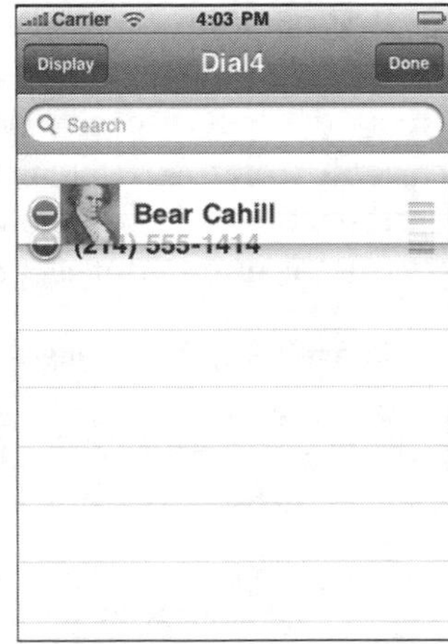

Figure 4.9 Reordering accessory (right) allows you to move table view items

TECHNIQUE 23 Filtering displayed table view data

The original motivation for this app was to allow the user to find a phone number by typing in the last four digits of the phone number. You can do this by adding an input area and wiring it to the code.

Also, you're trying to make this app something that makes finding numbers easier. You'll want to filter as the user types. Not only will this mean that the user can type four digits and probably see one or only a few numbers, but they could also type in an area code or prefix to see a subset of the numbers.

PROBLEM

You need to allow the user to type in the app and filter the displayed values based on what they type.

SOLUTION

You'll add a text field to the project and, based on the user's typing in that field, filter out contacts from the table that don't match the input.

DISCUSSION

In the UI editor, drop a Search Bar and Search Display Controller onto the top of your table view and note in the connections how the delegate is automatically set to File's Owner (see figure 4.10).

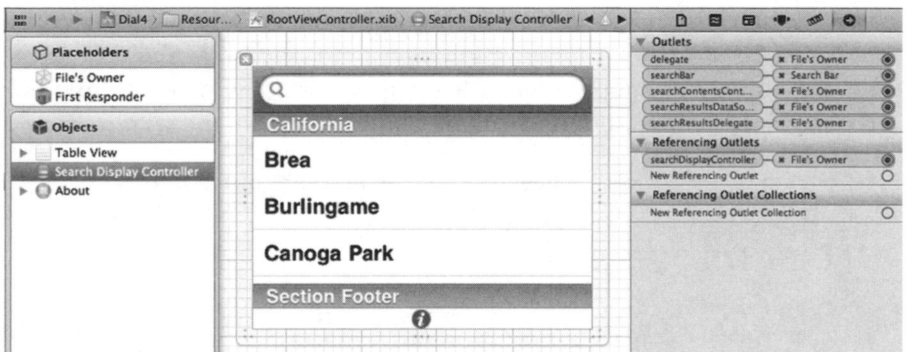

Figure 4.10 Search Bar and Search Display Controller automatically set connections when dropped

Because you're interested in filtering by the phone number, set the keyboard type to Number Pad (see figure 4.11).

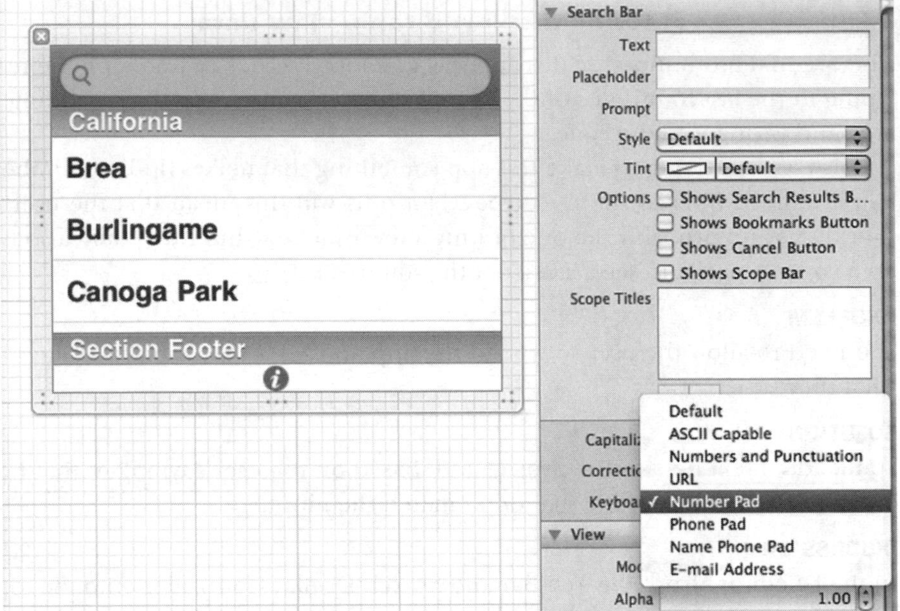

Figure 4.11 Setting the keyboard type to be Number Pad for the search bar

With it already wired up, you need to implement a couple of methods in your `RootViewController`. The first method will filter down the list as the user types (see the following listing). It simply creates a filter array and only adds the address book records where the corresponding phone numbers contain the search text.

Filter out any address book records based on the `searchText` passed in

```
- (void)searchBar:(UISearchBar *)theSearchBar
    textDidChange:(NSString *)searchText
{
    if ([searchText length] < prevSearchTextLen &&
        prevSearchTextLen != 0)
     {
        myContacts =
                   [NSArray arrayWithArray:(__bridge_transfer NSArray*)
                       ABAddressBookCopyArrayOfAllPeople(addressBook)];
        return;
    }
    prevSearchTextLen = [searchText length];

    NSMutableArray *filteredContacts =
                                 [NSMutableArray arrayWithCapacity:10];

    for (int i=0; i < [myContacts count]; i++)
    {
        ABMultiValueRef phoneNumbers = ABRecordCopyValue(
            objc_unretainedPointer([myContacts objectAtIndex:i]),
```

Reset value to use full list

Declare in header

```
                                    kABPersonPhoneProperty);
        if (phoneNumbers &&
                              ABMultiValueGetCount(phoneNumbers) > 0)
        {
            for (int j=0;
                 j < ABMultiValueGetCount(phoneNumbers);
                 j++)
            {
                NSString *phNum = (__bridge_transfer NSString*)
                ABMultiValueCopyValueAtIndex(phoneNumbers, j);
                if ([phNum rangeOfString:searchText].location
                                                        != NSNotFound)
                {
                    [filteredContacts addObject:[myContacts
                                              objectAtIndex:i]];
                     j = ABMultiValueGetCount(phoneNumbers);
                 }
            }
            CFRelease(phoneNumbers);
        }
    }
    myContacts = [NSArray arrayWithArray:filteredC
     ontacts];
}
```

Found one so set j to count to end loop

You copy the filtered array into `myContacts` so that the search's table reload will use your filtered list (see figure 4.12).

Figure 4.12 Dynamically filter the list when typing.

Now the app does what you want. You can list the contacts, filter by the number, and make a call. Also, you can see the details if you toggle the top-left button. This is a good use of the navigation controller.

There's a lot that goes into the design of this app, and there are a decent number of moving parts. But it works together well and fits together tightly. On top of that, there's not a large amount of code. The heavy lifting is done by the table view, search controller, address book, and other underlying frameworks.

4.5 Summary

You've probably seen plenty of apps that use the navigation controller and table view to display data. Now you know how it's done. The big parts are mostly the datasource and delegate of the table view. And if you create the file as a subclass `UITableViewController`, you get the skeleton of the code done for you.

Using the address book, you could list the entries in your contacts and do a variety of things like list their street address as the detail area of the cell. Using the subtitle style of cell would be good for this. Then you could display a map of their address, for example.

Navigation controllers are a natural choice for navigating down into information or other progressions of choices. Each presented controller can push the next controller, and the Back button is handled for you. Just be careful what you put in `viewWillAppear` or `viewDidAppear`. Those methods are called whenever the controller's view is displayed regardless of whether you're drilling down into a hierarchy or returning.

You'll probably use navigation controllers and table views in the majority of your apps, so it's important to master these early. Also, be sure to brainstorm about how you can use them in unorthodox ways. For example, make the cells the height of the display area and display images in the cells. Then turn on paging on the table view's scroll view attributes. That way you can create a nice vertical photo gallery that releases the cells and images from memory when they're no longer needed.

Navigation controllers and table views will be a staple of your iOS development, so get comfortable with them now and you'll be able to use these tools easily and in a variety of ways. Going forward, these aspects of your development can free up your creativity and problem solving for the real challenges of a project.

With the foundation of the main views and view controllers in place, you can move forward in the following chapters to look at more specific views and their uses. In chapter 5, you'll see how maps work in the MapKit and how to obtain the user's location through CoreData. The basic tools are provided by the SDK, which gives you the ability to use them in the custom ways you need for whatever app is being developed.

5 *MapKit and the camera in WhereIsMyCar*

This chapter covers

- The MapKit framework
- Working with maps and the current user location
- Storing and retrieving camera images

As you've seen many times over, iOS devices are a great combination of many other devices, including a computer, a phone, a camera, and more. iOS frameworks allow for using these capabilities of the devices, including mobile-related functionality like mapping. Combining these aspects of the devices together can make a simple app multidimensional. Fortunately, the iOS frameworks provide ways to display these features in views using provided view controllers.

Many types of views can be displayed on a controller, and so far you've seen buttons, images, and table views. We'll now focus on the map view, including centering, zooming, and pinning locations on the map. We'll also examine the image picker, which allows users to select an image from the camera or a photo album on the phone.

I'm sure you've had that feeling of coming out of a store and looking in the parking lot trying to remember where you parked your car. Wouldn't it be great to have an app on your iPhone to show you on a map and with a photo where your car is parked? Various apps in the App Store do this for you, but in this chapter you'll create your own app called WhereAmIParked.

To build the WhereAmIParked app, you'll add a map to the project and use that map to view the user's location. CoreLocation will also enable you to find the user's location without a map by using the CoreLocation framework (shown later in technique 26). Additionally, in this app you'll find a nearby street address to the user's location and you'll store notes from the user. Finally, I'll show how the app can display images taken with the iPhone camera.

Collecting data from the user and displaying that data requires various user interface elements in your app. Let's look at how that UI appears in the app (see figure 5.1).

Your map view, of course, shows the map, but the pin is also a view, as is the pop-up from the pin. Entering text uses a view and so does picking an image and displaying it. Also, there's a text view for taking notes and a Done button related to that view.

> **WHEREAMIPARKED APP** Like the apps in the previous chapters, WhereAmIParked is a real app in the App Store that was developed during the writing of this chapter. You can download it at http://itunes.com/apps/WhereAmIParked.

Putting views together in a meaningful and useful way is central to all apps. Let's get started building yours with a map view.

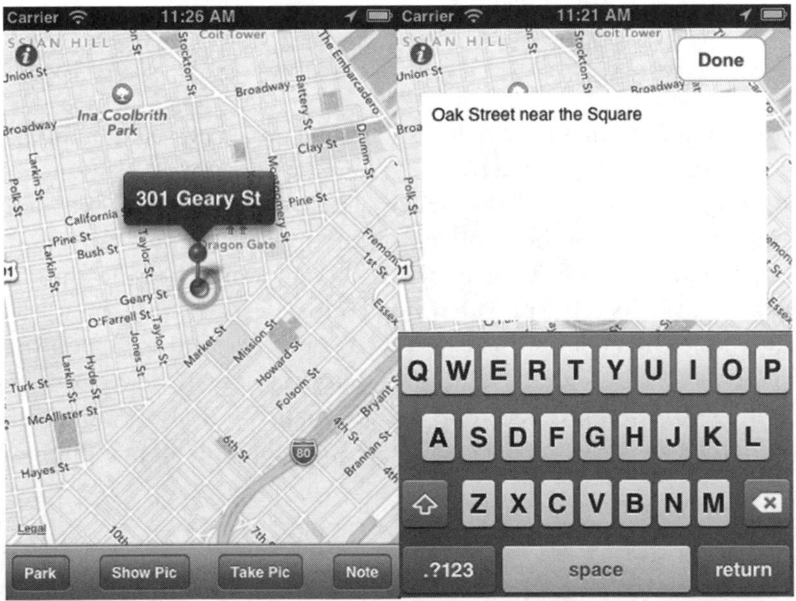

Figure 5.1 WhereAmIParked main views

5.1 Using maps with the user's location

A map view can be added to a view or set as a controller's view. By default, the map view will display a map of the world. Through various settings you can zoom in, center the map on certain coordinates, get the user's location, and display other items of interest.

The easiest and quickest way to display a map is by dropping a map view into your project via the UI editor in Xcode. You'll do that first. But displaying the user's location on the map and zooming in on that location—which you'll do in technique 25—makes it more useful for an app like yours.

TECHNIQUE 24 Adding a MapView to a project

The MapKit framework has the mapping functionality and UI. Like other controls, you'll need to add a MapView to the project in Xcode 4 and have a reference to it in the code. Also, you'll need to add the framework to your project.

Adding a framework related to a control is a common practice when adding certain controls to a project, especially if they aren't in the default frameworks included in your project. Once you've added the MapView and wired it up to the code, you'll be ready to add the real functionality.

PROBLEM

You need to add a MapView to the iPhone app. You can worry about manipulating the map later. For now, you should focus on starting the project and adding a map.

SOLUTION

Adding a basic map to a project is straightforward. You'll add a MapView to your project in Xcode 4; then you need to add the MapKit framework and run the project.

DISCUSSION

To start your project, create a new Xcode project and select a place and name for it—let's use WhereAmIParked. Click on the WhereAmIParkedViewController.xib file in your project's Resources group to open it. There you'll see the initial view is blank.

As you learned with the PicDecor project in chapter 3, you can drop any type of view (such as button, toolbar, or table view) on a `UIView`. Click on the Data Views in the IB library and drag a `MapView` to the blank view for your project. In the Attributes window, check the box to display the user's position (see figure 5.2). Save the UI in IB and go back to Xcode.

Building and running the app in the simulator now will generate an error because you haven't included the MapKit framework in your project. To do that, click on the project in the Project Navigator (far left), and select the target and the Build Phases tab. Expand the Link Binary with Libraries section and click the (+) button. From the list, filter by Map and select MapKit.framework (see figure 5.3). Click the Add button, and it's added to your project.

Now you can run the app in the simulator (Command-r) and see the map. In a couple of seconds, you should see the location displayed on the map. Because you're

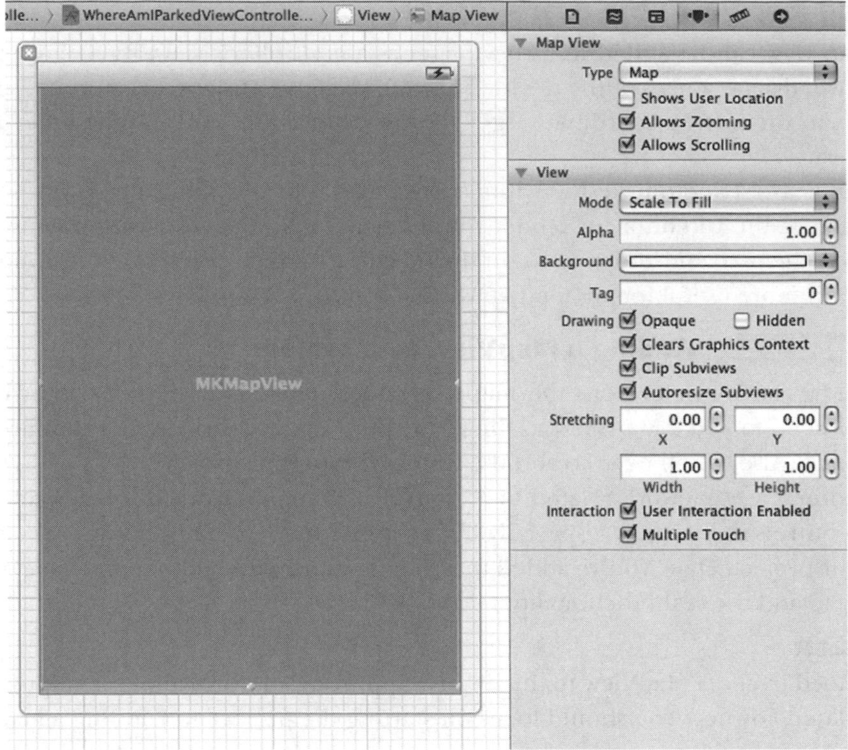

Figure 5.2 Settings for a MapView that shows user location

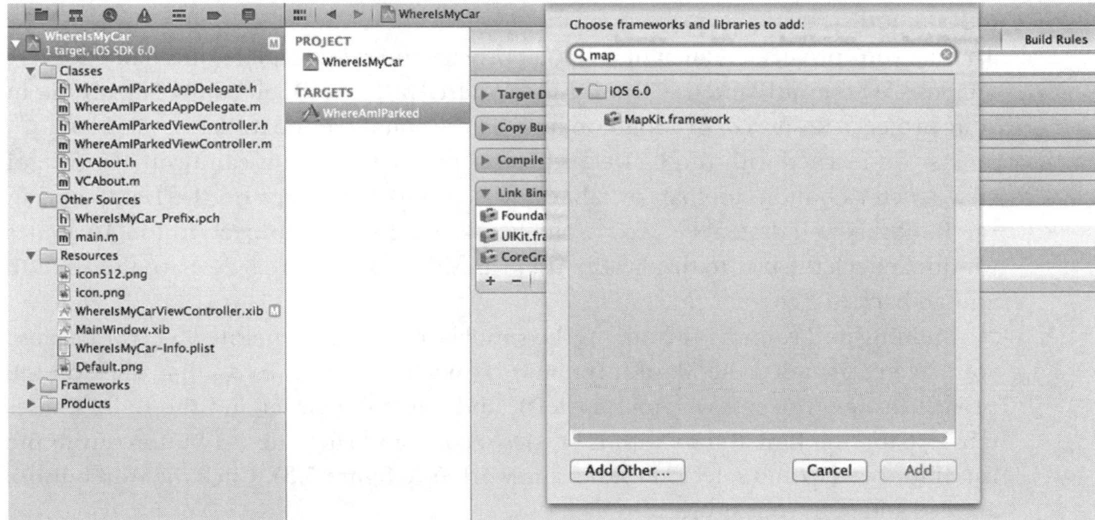

Figure 5.3 Adding the MapKit framework to a project in Xcode

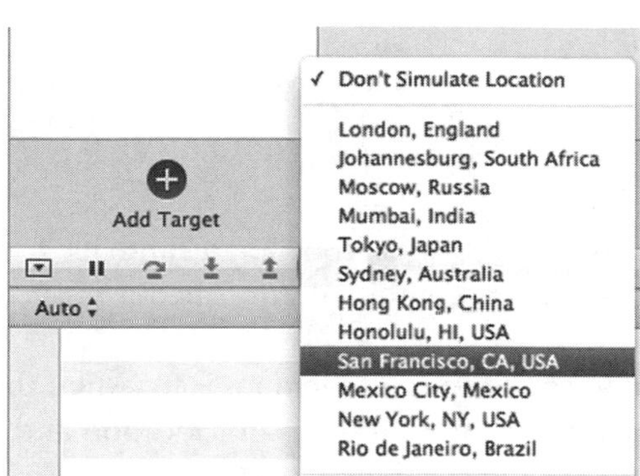

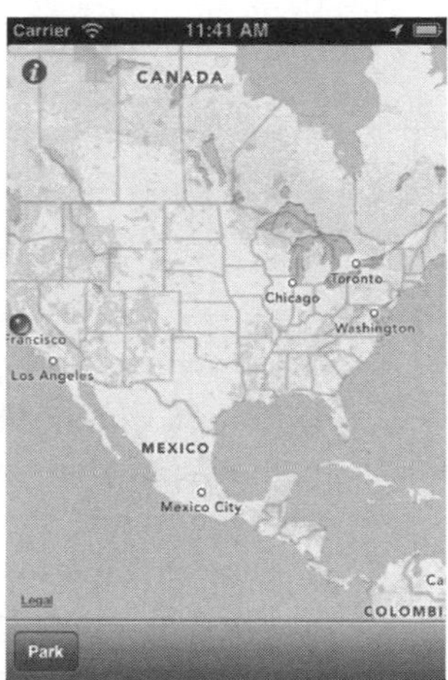

Figure 5.4 Basic Map app running in the simulator displaying user location

running in the simulator, you need to simulate your location from the bottom tool bar location button (see figure 5.4).

This app isn't all that interesting and you can't really see where you are on the map. With a few additions you can zoom into the location and get a better sense of where the user is. Let's do that now.

TECHNIQUE 25 Centering and zooming a MapView

Adding a map is fine, but being able to manipulate the map to display a specific area is what makes it meaningful to the user.

As you may have seen with other apps, there's a good bit of functionality you can add to a map such as changing the location, zooming, adding pins and display overlays, and more. The most fundamental of these is displaying a map of the area you're interested in.

PROBLEM

You need to be able to set the area that the map displays, which includes setting the center coordinate and the zoom level.

SOLUTION

To center the map on the user's location, you'll make your controller the `MapView`'s delegate and implement the `mapViewDidFinishLoadingMap:` method. In that method, you need to get the user's location from the `MapView` and center the map, but you need to make sure the `MapView` has had time to determine the user's location. Also, you'll set the span of the map, which is the amount of area to display (effectively this is the zoom), to a reasonably small area suitable for a parking app.

DISCUSSION

As you've seen before with other classes like `UITableView`, the map view has a delegate member. In WhereAmIParkedViewController.h, you'll declare that your class is an `MKMapViewDelegate` (see the following listing) and set your class to be the map view's delegate with IB.

WhereAmIParkedViewController imports MapKit.h and is an MKMapViewDelegate

```
#import <UIKit/UIKit.h>
#import <MapKit/MapKit.h>>

@interface WhereAmIParkedViewController : UIViewController
                                           <MKMapViewDelegate> {

}

@end
```

Different setters for setting the map view's center coordinate and its zoom level (called span) are available. These two aspects combined are called a *region*, which is what you'll set.

The first method for the delegation you want to implement is for when the map is finished loading. At this point, you want to center on the user's location and zoom in to a reasonable level to see where they are (where they're parked).

The delegation method you want to implement for this is `mapViewDidFinishLoadingMap:` and it passes in the map view (see the following listing). You'll use the user's location as the new center and some fairly close span for the new region to display. The span is measured in latitude and longitude degrees. Latitude degrees are always the same distance apart—approximately 69 miles. But though longitude degrees are about 69 degrees around the equator, they become increasingly closer together as they approach the poles. A setting of 0.02 is approximately 1.38 miles.

MapView delegation method called when map finishes loading to set region

```
- (void)mapViewDidFinishLoadingMap:(MKMapView *)mapView
{
    MKCoordinateRegion region;
    region.center = [mapView userLocation].location.coordinate;    <- Center on user
    region.span.latitudeDelta = 0.02;                               <- Small area
    region.span.longitudeDelta = 0.02;
    [mapView setRegion:region animated:YES];                        <- Animate change
}
```

In the UI editor, select the Map View and view its connections. Set the delegate for the object to File's Owner, which is your `WhereAmIParkedViewController` instance.

Running the app in the simulator from Xcode won't do what you hope just yet. Because the map (most likely) loads before the user's location is determined, the region setting will zoom in using a latitude and longitude of 0.000000 and 0.00000.

Let's check for the user location in your delegation method and tell the run loop to call it again in a second. If you still don't have the location, then, again, come back in one second (see the following listing).

MapView delegation method checking for user location repeatedly

```
- (void)mapViewDidFinishLoadingMap:(MKMapView *)mapView
{
    if (0.00001 > [mapView userLocation].location.coordinate.latitude)
    {
        [self performSelector:@selector(mapViewDidFinishLoadingMap:)
```

```
            withObject:mapView afterDelay:1.0];
        return;
    }

    MKCoordinateRegion region = [mapView region];
    region.center = [mapView userLocation].location.coordinate;
    region.span.latitudeDelta = 0.02;
    region.span.longitudeDelta = 0.02;
    [mapView setRegion:region animated:YES];
}
```

Call this method in one second (annotation for `withObject:mapView afterDelay:1.0];`)

Now you'll see something meaningful in the simulator. Run the app and note that after a couple of seconds, you zoom in to the default location on Infinite Loop in Cupertino (see figure 5.5).

Now you have an app that will show the user's location (that is, where the user is parking their car). As you see, finding a user's location is easy when you have a map set to display the user's location. But sometimes your app won't require a map, and you'll need to find the user's location some other way. Let's look at how to find the user's location not by using the MapView, but by using the `CoreLocation` framework.

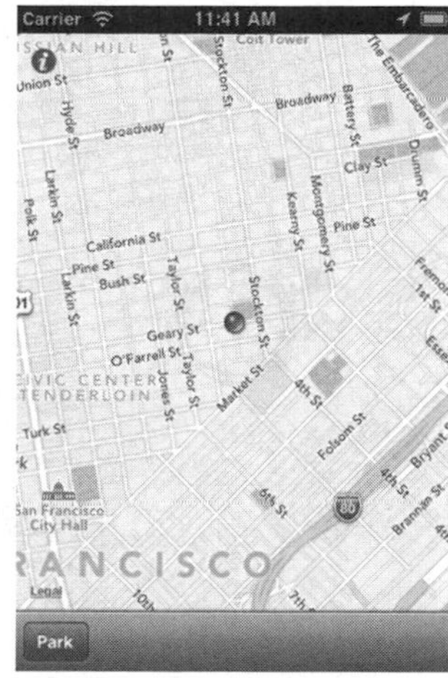

Figure 5.5 Map view centered and zoomed in on user's location

TECHNIQUE 26 Finding the user's location via CoreLocation

The CoreLocation framework is provided by Apple as part of the SDK for finding the current location of the device (and therefore the user).

The CoreLocation process for determining the user's location is an asynchronous process. After telling the framework to begin locating the user, the specified callback is called with location updates for the user. The app can specify how accurate location updates should be and also stop the process when the needed data is received. Preventing further updates is good for preserving battery life.

PROBLEM

You need to find the user's location in latitude and longitude without a MapView.

SOLUTION

You'll find the user's coordinates by creating a `CLLocationManager` instance, configuring it and starting location updates.

DISCUSSION

If you aren't using a map, but still need to find the user's location, CoreLocation provides the means to do just that. You create a `CLLocationManager` instance, set the delegate, and call `startUpdatingLocation`. The class you set as the delegate needs to implement the `CLLocationManagerDelegate` protocol (see the following listing).

Starting and handling CoreLocation updates

```
- (void)startUpdates
{
    if (nil == locationManager)
        locationManager = [[CLLocationManager alloc] init];

    locationManager.delegate = self;

    locationManager.desiredAccuracy
        = kCLLocationAccuracyKilometer;                      // Desired precision

    locationManager.distanceFilter = 10;                     // Update threshold
    [locationManager startUpdatingLocation];                 // Start updates
}

- (void)locationManager:(CLLocationManager *)manager        // Delegate method
    didUpdateToLocation:(CLLocation *)newLocation
        fromLocation:(CLLocation *)oldLocation
{
    NSDate* eventDate = newLocation.timestamp;
    NSTimeInterval howRecent = [eventDate timeIntervalSinceNow];

    if (abs(howRecent) < 120.0)                              // Only recent updates
    {
        [manager stopUpdatingLocation];                      // Stop updates and use location

        theLocation = newLocation;
        [theLocation retain];
    }
}
```

Based on your accuracy and filter settings, you may get more or fewer updates. Also, based on your needs, you may or may not stop the location updates via `stopUpdatingLocation`.

The CoreLocation runs on a separate thread once `startUpdatingLocation` is called so you're free to continue other processing with the app. You can then perform various operations based on the updates.

Using `CLLocationManager` gives you control over setting the accuracy and filter, and other things. Using MapKit gives you other advantages. The biggest advantage to maps is visual feedback to the user. Let's look at how locations on a map can be displayed to the user.

5.2 Displaying details on MapView locations and storing user's notes

Most maps show locations with pins or other images. Those items are called *map annotations*. Optionally, an app can be informed when a user taps on a given annotation to take action. Particularly, and commonly, this action is to display a pop-up view called a *callout*.

In the following techniques, you'll look at displaying pin annotations on the map for a given location. You'll also store the user's location (where they parked) to be retrieved and displayed later. To make the app more helpful, you'll reverse geocode the user's location to find a nearby address and display that in the pin callout. Also, you'll allow the user to make a note as a reminder about where they parked (such as *Section B7* or *By the bakery*).

TECHNIQUE 27 Displaying MapView pins

A basic map showing the user's location is useful, but not very meaningful in the context of an app. A map that only shows you where you are isn't very helpful or unique. But a map showing relevant locations with pins on the map is extremely powerful.

Location-based aspects to an app are unique to mobile apps—location isn't meaningful to a desktop computer because it never moves. But for functional or informational reasons, location can be very meaningful in an iPhone app. In many cases, the locations are drawn from a server or some other datasource showing you where points of interest are. In your case, your location data is determined by the user and stored in the device.

PROBLEM

You need to add a pin to the map showing the user's location.

SOLUTION

You need a button (and its associated action) for the user to tap when they park. You also need to create a class that implements the `MKAnnotation` protocol to define the location on the map. Then the action method can create the annotation and add it to the map. Finally, you'll implement the `MapView` delegate callback method to display the pin.

DISCUSSION

You first need a way to tell the app that you're parking. The most obvious way to do that is through a button on the user interface. This button needs to call a method in your `WhereAmIParkedViewController` implementation, so add an `IBAction` to the header file (see the following listing) for `doParkBtn:`. You also need an outlet for the map view so you can add the spot to the map.

`WhereAmIParkedViewController` with park button `IBAction`

```
@interface WhereAmIParkedViewController : UIViewController
                                           <MKMapViewDelegate> {

    IBOutlet MKMapView *mapParking;                    <-- Outlet for MapView

}

-(IBAction)doParkBtn:(id)sender;                       <-- Action for button

@end
```

Alternatively, you could wait until you created the object, in this case the map view, and then Control-drag it into the header file using the Assistant editor.

You've declared an outlet for the map view and an action for the button to call; now you need to create a button and wire the outlet and action. In the UI editor, resize the map view to have some room at the bottom and drop a toolbar there from the Windows & Bars group in the Library (see figure 5.6).

Figure 5.6 Add a toolbar below the map view in Interface Builder.

In the File's Owner connections, connect the `mapParking` outlet to the map view in your project. Double-click on the default Item button on the toolbar and type the new name: `Park`. In the Connection window, set the Park button's selector to be the `IBAction` (name it `doParkBtn`) you just defined in the `WhereAmIParkedViewController`, which is File's Owner in Interface Builder.

In the implementation of `doParkBtn` you'll set the user's location to be the parking spot for the user. Let's see how that's done for the map view.

Locations for a map are called *annotations*. The iOS SDK provides a protocol for `MKAnnotation`, but not a default implementation. You must create your own annotation class, which is pretty simple. There are only three members, and it's so basic that you can include it in your `WhereAmIParkedViewController` files (see the following two listings).

Parking spot implementation of `MKAnnotation` header file

```
@interface SpotAnnotation : NSObject <MKAnnotation>
{
    CLLocationCoordinate2D coordinate;
    NSString *title;
    NSString *subtitle;
}
```

```
@property (nonatomic, assign) CLLocationCoordinate2D coordinate;
@property (nonatomic, retain) NSString *title;
@property (nonatomic, retain) NSString *subtitle;

@end
```

The majority of the work is done in the declaration of the variables and properties. The only thing left is to synthesize them in the implementation file (see the following listing).

Parking spot implementation of `MKAnnotation` implementation

```
@implementation SpotAnnotation

@synthesize title, subtitle, coordinate;

@end
```

In the `doParkBtn` implementation, you need to add an instance of your `SpotAnnotation` to the map for the user's location. That's simply creating the instance, setting the coordinate to the user's location coordinate, and adding it to the map view outlet you already have (see the following listing).

Adding a `SpotAnnotation` to the map view when the user taps the Park button

```
-(IBAction)doParkBtn:(id)sender;
{
    SpotAnnotation *ann = [[SpotAnnotation alloc] init];
    [ann setCoordinate:[mapParking userLocation].location.coordinate];
    [mapParking addAnnotation:ann];
}
```

After the map view gets the annotation, it will ask its delegate what it should display as the view for this annotation. You can use one of the default pin annotation views. This is done through the delegation method, which is similar to the `UITableView` method for retrieving a given cell (see the following listing).

Specifying the annotation view to display on the map view

```
- (MKAnnotationView *)mapView:(MKMapView *)mapView
    viewForAnnotation:(id <MKAnnotation>)annotation
{
    if (![annotation isKindOfClass:[SpotAnnotation class]])
        return nil;                                              // Don't replace user location view

    NSString *dqref = @"ParkingAnnon";                           // Reuse views
     id av = [mapView
                dequeueReusableAnnotationViewWithIdentifier:dqref];
    if (nil == av)
    {
        av = [[MKPinAnnotationView alloc] initWithAnnotation:annotation
            reuseIdentifier:dqref];
        [av setPinColor:MKPinAnnotationColorRed];
        [av setAnimatesDrop:YES];                                // Animate pin drop
     }

    return av;
}
```

The app is starting to come together, and running it in the simulator is pretty exciting. You can see the map load up and zoom in, and tapping the Park button drops an annotation pin (see figure 5.7).

You may notice that each time you tap the Park button, it drops another pin in the same location. It's much more practical to replace the previous pin with the new pin assuming it's a new location. You don't want to remove the user location annotation, so you can check to see if there's more than one annotation on the map before dropping the pin. If there's more than one, you can remove the second user location pin (see the following listing).

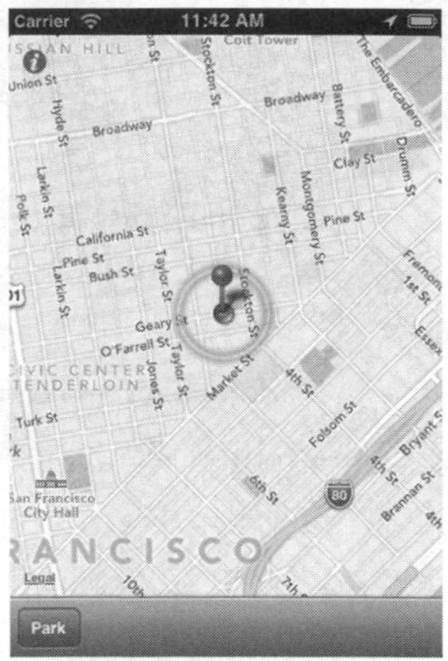

Figure 5.7 Simulator execution with user location pin drop

Remove all but the first annotation from the map before dropping new pin

```
-(IBAction)doParkBtn:(id)sender;
{
    if ([[mapParking annotations] count] > 1)
         [mapParking removeAnnotation:[[mapParking annotations]
            objectAtIndex:1]];
    SpotAnnotation *ann =
        [[SpotAnnotation alloc] init];
    [ann setCoordinate:[mapParking userLocation].location.coordinate];
    [mapParking addAnnotation:ann];
}
```

Leave zero annotations

Now you can see that when you tap the Park button it removes an existing pin, if there is one, before dropping the new pin.

Now you can display the user's location as they are parking the car. But this information is really only useful later when they're trying to find their car. For that you need to store the location and retrieve it for display later. Let's look at doing those two things now.

TECHNIQUE 28 Storing and retrieving the user's location

Having someone drop a pin on a map where they parked doesn't do you much good unless you display it when they need to find their car. To do this, you can store the spot's latitude and longitude.

The iOS SDK gives you `NSUserDefaults` which allows for storing values in the device. `NSUserDefaults` can easily store key-value pairs for floats, doubles, integers, Booleans, and some objects including `NSData`, `NSString`, `NSNumber`, `NSDate`, `NSArray`, and `NSDictionary`. You can use this to store the user's location coordinate for access in subsequent executions of the app. The same object has similar accessor methods for retrieving the stored data.

PROBLEM

You need to store and load a location value and display the location on the map.

SOLUTION

If you separate out the functionality to drop a pin on the map, you can reuse it both when the user taps the button and when the app loads with a previous location. You'll use `NSUserDefaults` to store the latitude and longitude when the user parks. When the app loads, it will check to see if a previous location was stored and, if so, drop a pin there.

DISCUSSION

The next time the app launches, it can check for the coordinate and, if one is stored, create a pin (see the following listing). The pin drop is split out into a separate method named `dropPinAtCoord` which takes a `CLLocationCoordinate2D`. The new method is called by the existing `doParkBtn` and also the `mapViewDidFinishLoadingMap` if an existing coordinate is found in memory.

Dropping a pin in the user's location, storing it, and displaying a stored location

```
- (void) dropPinAtCoord: (CLLocationCoordinate2D) coord  {
  if ([[mapParking annotations] count] > 1)
        [mapParking removeAnnotation:[[mapParking annotations]
                                                objectAtIndex:1]];
    SpotAnnotation *ann = [[SpotAnnotation alloc] init];
    [ann setCoordinate:coord];
    [mapParking addAnnotation:ann];

    [self doRevGeocodeUsingLat:coord.latitude andLng:coord.longitude];

    [[NSUserDefaults standardUserDefaults]                    <-- Store spot's coordinate
         setFloat:coord.latitude forKey:@"WIMCLat"];
    [[NSUserDefaults standardUserDefaults]
        setFloat:coord.longitude forKey:@"WIMCLng"];
}

-(IBAction)doParkBtn:(id)sender;
{
    CLLocationCoordinate2D coord =
                         [mapParking userLocation].location.coordinate;

    [self dropPinAtCoord: coord];                              <-- Call new method
 }

- (void)mapViewDidFinishLoadingMap:(MKMapView *)mapView
{
    if (0.00001 >
                 [mapView userLocation].location.coordinate.latitude)
{
        [self performSelector:@selector(mapViewDidFinishLoadingMap:)
                                withObject:mapView afterDelay:1.0];
        return;
    }

    MKCoordinateRegion region = [mapView region];
    region.center = [mapView userLocation].location.coordinate;
```

```
    region.span.latitudeDelta = 0.02;
    region.span.longitudeDelta = 0.02;
    [mapView setRegion:region animated:YES];

    if ([[NSUserDefaults standardUserDefaults]
        floatForKey:@"WIMCLat"] != 0.000)                    <- Drop pin for existing spot
     {
        CLLocationCoordinate2D coord;
        coord.latitude = [[NSUserDefaults standardUserDefaults]
                          floatForKey:@"WIMCLat"];
        coord.longitude = [[NSUserDefaults standardUserDefaults]
                          floatForKey:@"WIMCLng"];
        [self dropPinAtCoord:coord];
    }
}
```

Values can also be stored in a SQLite database or on a server. It depends on the needs of the app as to how best to store the data.

Knowing the user's location can allow you to customize the display, give location-specific information, determine the user's distance from a given item, and more. This knowledge is another dimension the mobile device has beyond a given desktop or even laptop computer. Furthermore, you can reverse geocode their location to find a nearby address. You'll see how to do that next.

TECHNIQUE 29 Reverse geocoding

Sometimes it's useful or necessary to find a nearby street address for a given coordinate. In your app, it could be helpful to see an address near where you parked.

Geocoding is the process by which you use a street address or similar to find the corresponding geographical coordinate (latitude and longitude). Built into MapKit is the ability to do the reverse process called *reverse geocoding*.

Using reverse geocoding, you can take the user's location and find a nearby street address to display to the user. In your app, this may be meaningful and helpful in finding their way back to their parking spot.

PROBLEM

You need to find a street address near the user's location.

SOLUTION

You'll need to include the CoreLocation framework in your target (Target > Build Phases > Link Libraries with Binary) and import the CoreLocation/CoreLocation.h file in the WhereAmIParkedViewController.h file. Based on this you'll be able to create the `CLGeocoder` instance and reverse geocode the coordinates.

DISCUSSION

The `CLGeocoder` is instantiated with a `CLLocation` of the coordinates and a `completionHandler` for when the reverse geocoding is complete. For now, we'll just print out the street address found to the console (see the following listing).

Reverse geocoding to find an address near to a latitude/longitude

```
-(void)doRevGeocodeUsingLat:(float)lat andLng:(float)lng;
{
    CLLocation *c = [[CLLocation alloc] initWithLatitude:lat
        longitude:lng];                                          <- Create location

    CLGeocoder *revGeo = [[CLGeocoder alloc] init];
    [revGeo reverseGeocodeLocation:c                             <- Reverses geocode
                completionHandler:^(NSArray *placemarks,
                                     NSError *error) {

        if (!error && [placemarks count] > 0)
        {
            NSDictionary *dict =
                [[placemarks objectAtIndex:0] addressDictionary];
            NSLog(@"street address: %@",                        <- Log address
                              [dict objectForKey:@"Street"]);
        }
        else
        {
            NSLog(@"ERROR: %@", error);
        }
    }];
}
```

As you see from the listing, the found address is logged out to the console:

```
2012-09-18 12:44:06.773 WhereIsMyCar[18871:13d03] street address: 243-299
    Geary St
```

In some cases, you may have multiple placemarks returned. In this case, we're only concerned with looking at one of them.

For your app, a good use of this address would be to display it on the pin callout (what's displayed when you tap on a pin). With only a few additions, you can make this happen.

TECHNIQUE 30 Adding pin callouts

Pins on a map might be meaningful to a user, but usually more specific details for each pin are necessary. If you're mapping parks, shops, restaurants, or other businesses and locations, the name, street address, distance from the user, or other information is great to display right in the map.

When you tap on a pin, an app can optionally display an annotation (or callout), which is the little pop-up that displays just above the pin. You can display a few things on that callout, such as text, called the *title*, or a *subtitle*, which is a second line of text. Like a table view cell, you can display an image on the left side and an accessory (such as a disclosure button) on the right side.

Annotations by default don't display callouts, but by just setting this value to YES, annotations will display a callout. The UI action of the user tapping the pin and displaying the callout is handled by the OS. But there are several things the app can specify to display including the title, subtitle, image, and disclosure button. Displaying the reverse geocoded address would be most helpful in your case.

PROBLEM

You need to display a title in a map pin annotation callout.

SOLUTION

Displaying a nearby street address in the callout when the pin is tapped is a three-step process. First, you'll set the callout to display when the pin is tapped; then, you need to reverse geocode the location to get the address, and then set the address as the title.

DISCUSSION

First, you need to tell the annotations they can display callouts. Then, using your reverse geocoder code, you can set the title (and possibly subtitle) of the annotation (see the following listing).

Set annotation to show a callout when tapped

```
- (MKAnnotationView *)mapView:(MKMapView *)mapView
    viewForAnnotation:(id <MKAnnotation>)annotation
{
    if (![annotation isKindOfClass:[SpotAnnotation class]])
        return nil;

    NSString *dqref = @"ParkingAnnon";
    id av = [mapView
                dequeueReusableAnnotationViewWithIdentifier:dqref];
    if (nil == av)
    {
        av = [[MKPinAnnotationView alloc]
                                   initWithAnnotation:annotation
            reuseIdentifier:dqref];
        [av setPinColor:MKPinAnnotationColorRed];
        [av setAnimatesDrop:YES];
        [av setCanShowCallout:YES];                  <- Standard callout when tapped
     }

    return av;
}
```

Having set the annotation to display its callout, you now need to set its title to the reverse geocoded address. Your `doParkBtn:` method is where you create the annotation, so in there you can now call your `doRevGeocodeUsingLat:andLng:` method (see the following listing).

Get the reverse geocoding started when the user parks

```
-(IBAction)doParkBtn:(id)sender;
{
    if ([[mapParking annotations] count] > 1)
        [mapParking removeAnnotation:[[mapParking annotations]
                                             objectAtIndex:1]];
    SpotAnnotation *ann = [[SpotAnnotation alloc] init];
    [ann setCoordinate:[mapParking userLocation].location.coordinate];
    [mapParking addAnnotation:ann];
```

```
    CLLocationCoordinate2D coord =
        [mapParking userLocation].location.coordinate;
    [self doRevGeocodeUsingLat:coord.latitude
        andLng:coord.longitude];                          Start the reverse geocode
}
```

Next, you need to set the street address in your annotation when the reverse geocoding is done. When you receive the placemark, you can cycle through the annotations from the map and look for the one that's your `SpotAnnotation` kind of class (see the following listing).

Cycle through the annotations to set the street address as the title

```
-(void)doRevGeocodeUsingLat:(float)lat andLng:(float)lng;
{
    CLLocation *c = [[CLLocation alloc] initWithLatitude:lat
        longitude:lng];

    CLGeocoder *revGeo = [[CLGeocoder alloc] init];
    [revGeo reverseGeocodeLocation:c
             completionHandler:^(NSArray *placemarks,
                                 NSError *error) {

        if (!error && [placemarks count] > 0)
        {
            NSDictionary *dict =
                [[placemarks objectAtIndex:0] addressDictionary];
            NSLog(@"street address: %@",
                [dict objectForKey:@"Street"]);

            for (SpotAnnotation *ann in [mapParking annotations])
            {
                if ([ann isKindOfClass:[SpotAnnotation class]])      Only SpotAnnotation
                    [ann setTitle:
                                [dict objectForKey:@"Street"]];      Set title

            }
        }
        else
        {
            NSLog(@"ERROR/No Results: %@", error);                   Handle error
        }
    }];
}
```

The `reverseGeocodeLocation: completionHandler` is updated to cycle through the annotations and search for the single `SpotAnnotation` instance. When that's found, the annotation title is to the street address returned from the reverse geocoding.

Now, when running the app, if the user taps on the pin, the callout is displayed. Also, the title is the street address, which in the simulator is Apple HQ's address of 1 Infinite Loop (see figure 5.8).

Based just on this, you have a decent and useful app. It's not too impressive as far as apps go, but the technology behind it is. Let's look at a few more areas where you can improve this app.

You've seen how to find the user's location and display it on the map with useful information including a nearby street address. These same steps and techniques can be used to make much more complex apps. You can show multiple locations on the map and use various annotations and more detailed callouts. You now have the basis for making significant location-based apps!

Specific to your app, let's extend the abilities to aid the user in finding where they parked. Let's look at a couple more ways to do that.

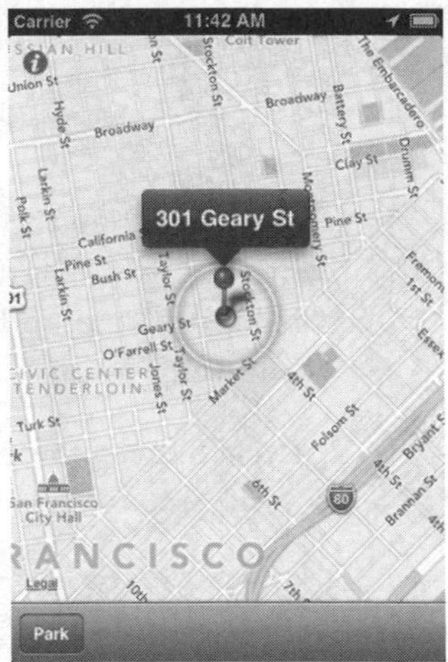

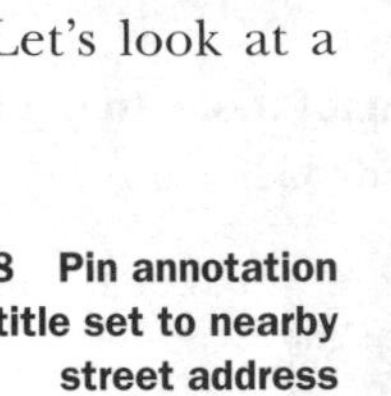

Figure 5.8 Pin annotation callout with title set to nearby street address

TECHNIQUE 31 Typing and storing user's note

You've seen how you can store values in the system using `NSUserDefaults`. This includes storing and later accessing `NSString` objects. Using `NSString` objects, you can store a text note from the user. But you still need to implement the interface for them to enter the note.

You also need to tie together the UI and the functionality to display the note when the user wants to enter a note or display it.

PROBLEM

In order for the user to remember specifics about where they parked, you can allow the user to type in some comments or a note, store it, and display it again.

SOLUTION

You'll provide UI elements for the user to take a note as well as functionality to store the note for later access.

DISCUSSION

Letting the user make a note consists of two parts: typing in a note and storing that note. This means you need to add UI elements to allow the user to take a note. This same area will display the text later for viewing and editing.

First, you need to create the actions and outlets in the code. Then, you'll use IB to create the UI and connect to the actions and outlets in the code. Finally, you'll store the text the user types in and retrieve it later to display.

First, let's prep your `WhereAmIParkedViewController` class for the items you'll add in the UI editor. You need to add outlets for the note text view and a Done button, and two actions for the new Note and Done buttons (see the following listing).

Creating the outlets and actions in your view controller header for the Note and Done buttons

```
@interface WhereAmIParkedViewController : UIViewController
    <MKMapViewDelegate, MKReverseGeocoderDelegate> {

    IBOutlet MKMapView *mapParking;

    IBOutlet UITextView *tvNote;        // Text view for note
     IBOutlet UIButton *btnDone;        // Done button for note

}

-(IBAction)doParkBtn:(id)sender;
-(IBAction)doNoteBtn:(id)sender;        // Action for Note
 -(IBAction)doDoneBtn:(id)sender;       // Action for Done

@end
```

Back in the UI, add a bar button item to the toolbar. Also, put a flexible space item between the two buttons to spread them out. You'll wire this button to the defined action after a few more changes in IB.

Drop a text view toward the top of the map—this is where the user will enter the text (see figure 5.9). Also, add a button above the text view and set its title to Done.

Next, with IB, wire the Note button to the `doNoteBtn:` action you just defined in the controller class. Wire the Done button to the `doDoneBtn:` action. Another way to wire buttons like this is to hold down the Control key on the keyboard, select the button in the UI with your mouse, and drag to the class (File's Owner, in this case) (see figure 5.10). From there, select the action in the pop-up menu.

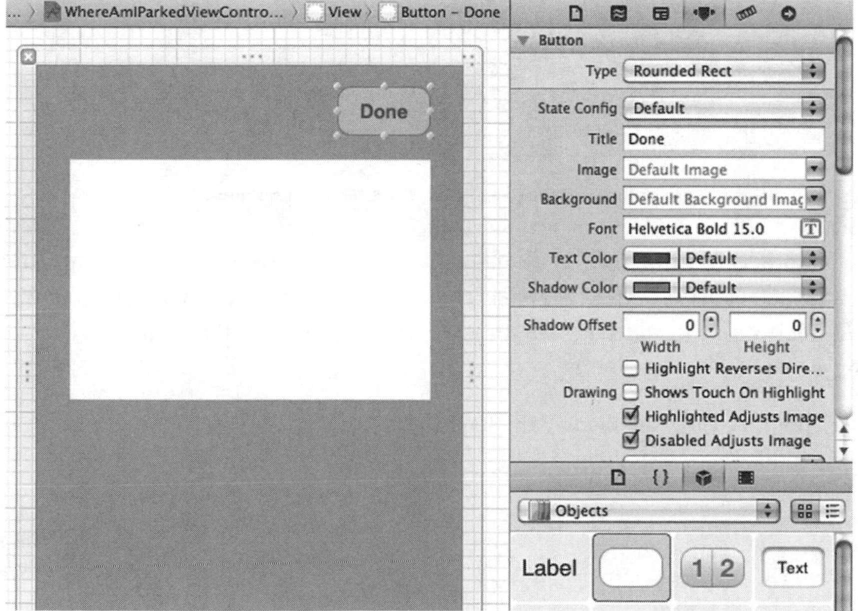

Figure 5.9 Adding the text view and Done button to allow users to make notes

Figure 5.10 Wire the Done button to its action in the code

Also, wire the text view to the `tvNote` in your controller. Finally, write the `btnDone` outlet in your controller class (File's Owner) to the Done button you dropped.

You don't want the text view or Done button visible when the app starts, so you'll set them as hidden with IB using the View settings (see figure 5.11). Be sure to set both as hidden.

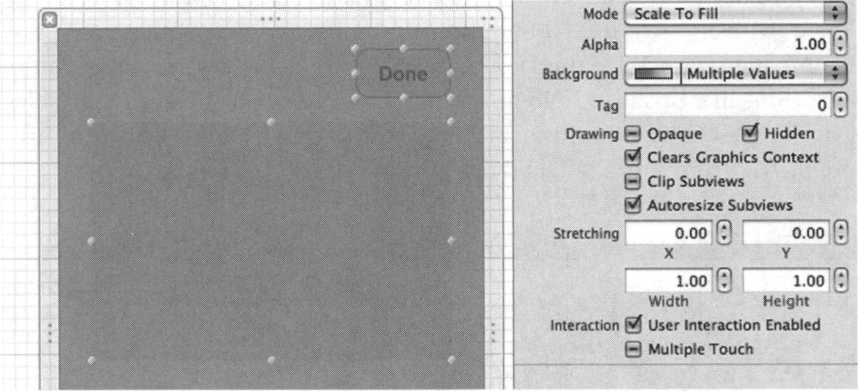

Figure 5.11 Set the text view as hidden so it's not visible until needed.

Now you need to implement `doNoteBtn:` in the code. When the user taps the button, you want to display the text view for them to type in a note. Also, you need to display the Done button. Last, make the text view the first responder to have the keyboard display (see the following listing).

Display the text view and display the keyboard

```
-(IBAction)doNoteBtn:(id)sender;
{
    [btnDone setHidden:NO];
    [tvNote setHidden:NO];
    [tvNote becomeFirstResponder];      <- Display keyboard
 }
```

That's fine, but how do you make the text view and keyboard go away? And how do you store the note? The implementation of the Done button action `doDoneBtn:` is where you'll handle that. It's basically the reverse of the `doNoteBtn:` implementation (see the following listing). You'll store the note as an object in the standard `NSUserDefaults`.

Remove the text view and Done button and save the note

```
-(IBAction)doDoneBtn:(id)sender;
{
    [btnDone setHidden:YES];                          <— Hide items
     [tvNote setHidden:YES];
    [tvNote resignFirstResponder];

    [[NSUserDefaults standardUserDefaults]            <— Save note
         setObject:[tvNote text] forKey:@"WIMCAppNote"];
}
```

Of course, a note is only good if the app can display it later. If you run the app in the simulator, you can add a note (see figure 5.12). Also, if you tap Done, it disappears correctly. Tap Note again and the note is displayed.

But if you quit the app, relaunch it, and tap the Note button, the note is gone! But is it? Not really. You're just not displaying it. To fix that, you can add a line to the `doNoteBtn:` implementation. Similar to storing the note, you can access it to display in the text view (see the following listing).

Retrieving the note text and displaying it in the text view

```
-(IBAction)doNoteBtn:(id)sender;
{
    [btnDone setHidden:NO];
    [tvNote setHidden:NO];
    [tvNote becomeFirstResponder];

    [tvNote setText:[[NSUserDefaults standardUserDefaults]
        objectForKey:@"WIMCAppNote"]];             <— Fetch with same string
}
```

Figure 5.12 Displaying the text view and Done button while editing a user note

The app often will *not* store the items in `NSUserDefaults` if you don't exit the app with the simulator Home button. If you stop the app via Xcode, don't be surprised if the note isn't saved for your next launch.

Now you have a pretty nice app. The user can pin their parking spot and add a note to help them. What else could you add?

5.3 Storing, retrieving, and displaying camera images

It would really be useful if the user could take a picture of where they parked or something nearby to give them a clear visual reference to where they parked.

Retrieving an image in your app isn't difficult. The SDK takes care of the majority of the work. Similar to the core location and reverse geocoding actions, you'll start the image picker for the camera and implement delegate methods.

Any app that wants access to the camera or photo album needs an image picker controller. You'll first look specifically at how to add an image picker controller to a project. Then you'll set the app up to receive an image taken by the camera and store that picture in the device. Finally, see how to retrieve that picture later and display it to the user.

TECHNIQUE 32 Adding a camera control

The camera UI is built in to the SDK and you can take advantage of it to add value to your app. The image picker gives the user access to their images in their device or allows them to take a picture with the built-in camera.

Like other controls you've seen (such as `WebView`), you can add the image picker via the UI editor. Wiring it up in the code allows you to manipulate the controller, and, in this case, receive the image selected/taken.

PROBLEM

To lay the groundwork for presenting an image selection to the user, you need to add an image picker controller to your project.

SOLUTION

You'll add a `UIImagePickerController` outlet to your class. Also, you need to add related actions to the declaration. In the UI, you'll add the image picker and buttons and connect them all to your class.

DISCUSSION

To take a picture, you need a `UIImagePickerController`. This can be set to use the camera or photo album. You're using the camera, of course. You'll need new buttons for taking a pic, displaying a pic, and removing the displayed pic. Also, you'll need a view controller with an image view to display the picture and hold the button to dismiss it.

Of course, you'll need actions for all of these buttons. You'll add all of this to the WhereAmIParkedViewController.h file (see the following listing).

Adding `UIImagePickerController` and actions to WhereAmIParkedViewController.h

```
IBOutlet UIImagePickerController *picController;
    IBOutlet UIViewController *vcDisplayPic;
    IBOutlet UIImageView *ivPic;

}

-(IBAction)doPicBtn:(id)sender;
-(IBAction)doShowPicBtn:(id)sender;
-(IBAction)doDonePicBtn:(id)sender;
```

Figure 5.13 View controller and subviews for displaying images

Let's create the view controller in the UI. The view controller needs a view on it, and on that view you need an image view and a button titled Done (see figure 5.13).

You also need to add the buttons to take and show the images (see figure 5.14).

Figure 5.14 Show Pic and Take Pic buttons on the toolbar

The last new thing you need in the UI is an image picker. Just add it to the list of items in your XIB file (see figure 5.15). Set its delegate to be the `WhereAmIParkedViewController` (File's Owner). Be sure to declare that `WhereAmIParkedViewController` implements `UIImagePickerControllerDelegate` in the header.

Now you need to wire these items up to the outlets and actions you added to your `WhereAmIParkedViewController` header. Click on the File's Owner item in the XIB and view the connections. You'll see the new Image Picker Controller, View Controller, Image View, and the new actions for the picture. Wire them to the applicable items with IB (see figure 5.16).

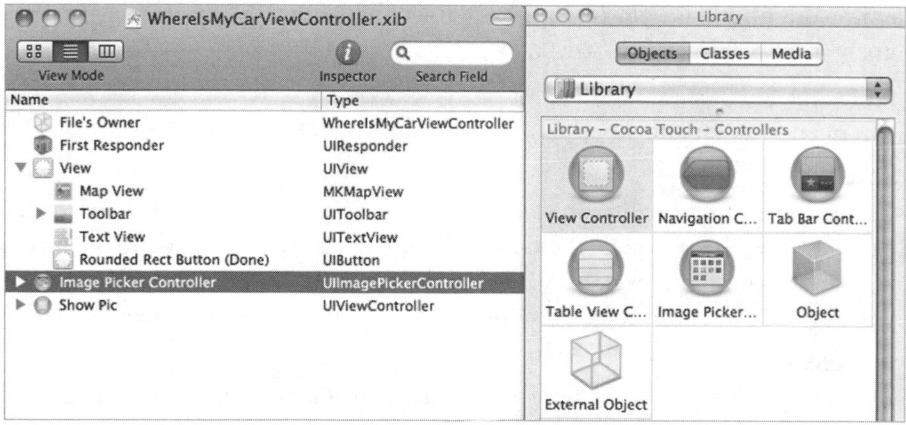

Figure 5.15 Adding an image picker to your project UI

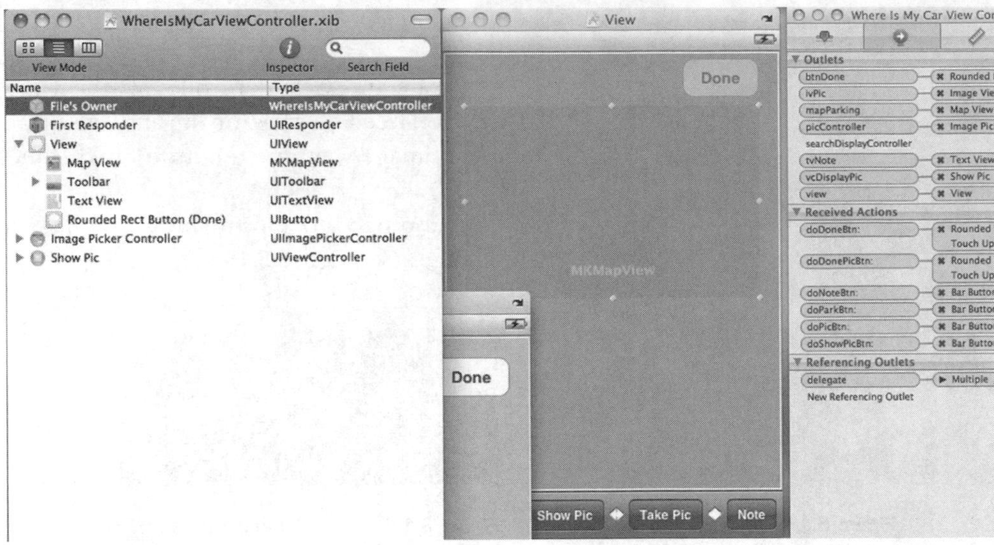

Figure 5.16 Wire up the image-related outlets/actions with Interface Builder.

You've added the camera UI to your project. That's the groundwork, which means you can display the camera to take a picture, but nothing happens with it. Next, you'll handle the image, both storing it on the device and displaying it later.

TECHNIQUE 33 Receiving and storing the picture

Displaying the camera to the user to take a picture is fine, but not worth much if you don't then allow access to the image to process in some way. The image picker controller calls two methods on its delegate. One method is for when the user taps Cancel, and one is for when they select/take a picture.

From the standpoint of the delegate, it doesn't matter if the image is from the camera or the photo album. In your case, it will be from the camera, and you'll store the image in the device to display later.

PROBLEM

You need to fetch and store an image from the camera controller.

SOLUTION

The picture functionality involves several aspects and steps. You need to display the camera when the user taps the button. Your class is the camera controller's delegate so you need to implement methods for when the user takes a picture or cancels. Then, if a picture is taken, you need to store it in the device to display it later.

DISCUSSION

The `WhereAmIParkedViewController` has an instance of the image picker controller named `picController`. The `doPicBtn` method just needs to present that, which implements the camera control (see the following listing).

Presenting the camera in the pic button action method

```
-(IBAction)doPicBtn:(id)sender;
{
    if ([[[UIDevice currentDevice] model]
         rangeOfString:@"Sim"].location == NSNotFound)       <-- Use album for simulator
         [picController setSourceType:
            UIImagePickerControllerSourceTypeCamera];
    [self presentModalViewController:picController animated:YES];
}
```

When the camera control is displayed, the user can take a picture (see figure 5.17).

The picker controller uses its delegate, `WhereAmIParkedViewController` in this case, for handling user actions. Because the `WhereAmIParkedViewController` implements `UIImagePickerControllerDelegate`, there are two methods you're concerned with: `imagePickerControllerDidCancel:` and `imagePickerController:didFinishPickingMediaWithInfo:` (see the next listing).

The cancel method is telling you that the user tapped Cancel and you can remove the image view picker controller from the screen. But the other method returns the image data you need to store. To store the image you'll want to develop the extra steps of scaling the image down and determining the path for storing the file.

Figure 5.17 A picture taken with the image picker controller camera

Receiving, scaling, and storing an image from the camera

```
+ (UIImage*)imageWithImage:(UIImage*)image
              scaledToSize:(CGSize)newSize;
{
    UIGraphicsBeginImageContext( newSize );                  <-- Scale image
     [image drawInRect:CGRectMake(0,0,newSize.width,newSize.height)];
    UIImage* newImage = UIGraphicsGetImageFromCurrentImageContext();
    UIGraphicsEndImageContext();

    return newImage;
}

-(NSString*)imagePath
{
    NSArray *paths =
              NSSearchPathForDirectoriesInDomains(NSDocumentDirectory,
                        NSUserDomainMask, YES);
    NSString *documentsDirectoryPath =
                        [paths objectAtIndex:0];

    NSString *imgPath = [NSString stringWithFormat:@"%@/WIMCApp/",
               documentsDirectoryPath];                       <-- Get documents path
```

```
    NSError *err;
    [[NSFileManager defaultManager]
     createDirectoryAtPath:imgPath withIntermediateDirectories:YES
     attributes:nil error:&err];                                    <-- Create dir

    return [NSString stringWithFormat:
        @"%@WIMCpic.png", imgPath];                                 <-- Image filename
}

- (void)imagePickerController:(UIImagePickerController *)picker
didFinishPickingMediaWithInfo:(NSDictionary *)info
{
    UIImage *pic = [info
                    objectForKey:UIImagePickerControllerOriginalImage];

    pic = [WhereAmIParkedViewController imageWithImage:pic
                               scaledToSize:CGSizeMake(320.0, 460.0)];

    [UIImagePNGRepresentation(pic)
        writeToFile:[self imagePath] atomically:YES];          <-- Append filename

    [self dismissModalViewControllerAnimated:YES];             <-- Remove camera
}

- (void)imagePickerControllerDidCancel:(UIImagePickerController
                                                          *)picker
{
    [self dismissModalViewControllerAnimated:YES];             <-- Remove camera
}
```

You can hardcode the one filename because the next time they park, they'll no longer need the previous image and can overwrite it. But if they don't take a picture the next time, the image will still be from a previous parking spot.

Now that you've taken and stored the picture, let's implement the functionality for displaying the image.

TECHNIQUE 34 Displaying a picture

Displaying the picture the user took makes it easy for them to remember where they parked. The picture might be of their car in reference to the surrounding area or some other landmark to help them find where they parked.

In technique 33, you stored the image taken by the user. To display it, you need to access the image data from the stored file and create something presentable in the OS. You can use the `ImageView` and button functionality you've already added to the project.

PROBLEM

You need to display the stored picture to the user.

SOLUTION

Displaying an existing image is quite simple after you have the UI in place for the image view, the buttons, and their applicable outlets and actions. You need to load the image from the device and then set the image in your image view and display it. Also, you need a method to remove the image when the user is done.

DISCUSSION

`WhereAmIParkedViewController` already has an outlet defined and wired for the view controller used to display the picture. Its name is `vcDisplayPic`. The `doShowPicBtn` just needs to load the picture and present the controller (see the following listing).

Loading a stored image and displaying it to the user

```
-(IBAction)doShowPicBtn:(id)sender;
{
    UIImage *pic = [UIImage imageWithContentsOfFile:[self imagePath]];

    if (nil == pic)                                    <-- Return if no pic
        return;

    [ivPic setImage:pic];                              <-- Set and show pic
     [self presentModalViewController:vcDisplayPic animated:YES];
}
```

When the user taps on the button, the stored image is displayed (see figure 5.18).

Removing the picture from display is even easier. You need to dismiss the controller the same way you presented it—by calling `dismissModalViewControllerAnimated:` on your class: `[self dismissModalViewController-Animated:YES];`.

That's it. Your app is done! It's a fully functional and quite useful app. If you haven't done so already, check it out at http://itunes.com/apps/WhereAmIParked.

Figure 5.18 Stored image displayed in the app

5.4 Summary

Creating a useful app spans a lot of aspects of the SDK including mapping, location, taking pictures, storing the image, storing notes, and all of the UI and related functionality. Plenty of apps use this same type of functionality in a variety of ways. In a short amount of time, you can probably think of even more ways.

Because the iPhone is a mobile device, many apps can benefit from the addition of maps. Much of the functionality is provided to you in the MapKit. Wrapping some additional features around that can really make for interesting apps.

While Maps is a great app built into the iPhone, there are many, many other things that can be done to make for a great map-based app. Similarly, an app that is built into the OS is the clock. It includes a timer, countdown, alarm, and more. In the next chapter, we'll look at how you can make an app similar in concept but more specific in some ways.

6 Settings, audio, and shake detection in TimeDown

This chapter covers

- Custom settings
- Working with audio
- Detecting motion

Different iOS apps interact with users in different ways. The most common way is visually—I don't know of an app that doesn't have a visible UI. Whether it's through making selections in the app, the position of the device, pushing buttons, or tapping or swiping on the screen, the app can allow for a variety of interactions.

Many times this interaction affects some functionality of the app. Some setting may change the look of the app—pushing a button may change the volume level or shaking the device may mix up pieces of a game. Similarly, the app can give feedback to the user. Like the interaction from the user, feedback can come in various forms. Visual feedback is probably the most common with audio being second.

In this chapter, we'll look at these concepts and explore how the user can access these ways of interacting and how to use them in an app. You'll build a simple app that uses the Settings app for setting values. You'll also use the audio framework to play a sound file for audio feedback. And you'll use the accelerometer to detect shaking of the device and use that in your UI.

You may not be familiar with the Settings app on the iPhone. I believe this is because using this for app settings isn't easy and it's not a good experience for the user to have to switch to the Settings app to change something. Moreover, they'd probably need to relaunch the app to have the changes apply. Most apps have settings within their app for these reasons. But it's an important topic, and because it's not easy, it will take up a good bit of space in this chapter.

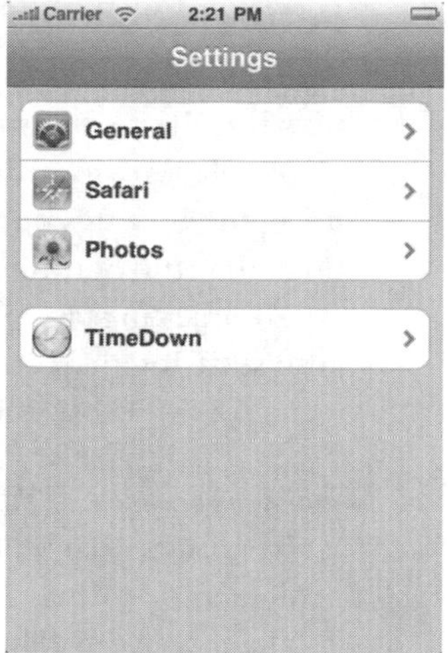

Figure 6.1 TimeDown in the built-in Settings app

Playing audio files, on the other hand, is common and quite easy to implement. This is an important and common attribute in many apps but is relatively easy to develop.

Finally, I include a special item in this chapter for rounding corners of views. It's a great technique to polish your UI and creates a look that's consistent with many other aspects of the iOS UI, especially input fields, which tend to have rounded corners.

Let's call this app TimeDown. It's a countdown timer app where the number of minutes for the timer is set in Settings (see figure 6.1).

Many apps have a settings area within the app. The "official" way to do this is by using a Settings bundle within your app. Options are meant to be set within the app.

SETTINGS/OPTIONS FROM THE APPLE "HUMAN INTERFACE GUIDELINES" Settings should represent information, such as an account name, that users set once and rarely (if ever) change. Users view app-specific settings in the built-in Settings app. Configuration options are values that users might want to change frequently, such as category types displayed in a list; configuration options should be available within the app itself.

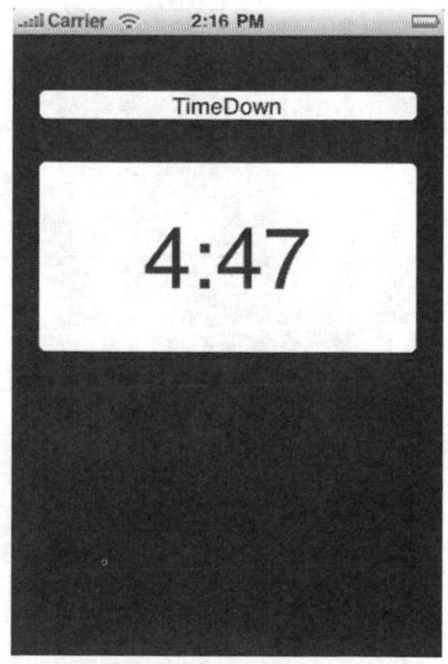

Figure 6.2 TimeDown countdown timer application UI

The UI for your TimeDown app is simple (see figure 6.2). Let's add a few extra features to your app to make it more useful. You'll use the audio framework to play a short sound file when the timer runs out and vibrate (if it's capable). Also, you'll use the accelerometer to detect a shake to allow the user to start/reset the timer.

Let's first look at how to add and use settings in a project.

6.1 Settings bundle in iOS projects

Settings are added to a project via a plist file in the Settings bundle. The Settings app uses this file to allow users to set the associated values.

Apple provides this mechanism to create the various settings for an app. When using the Settings bundle, you're limited to a set selection of entries to define your settings that the Settings app can understand and present to the user.

Your settings will include the default time limit (in minutes) for your timer and an auto-start toggle. You'll have a number, using numeric keyboard entry, and a toggle, using an on/off switch.

TECHNIQUE 35 Adding settings to an Xcode project

We've discussed a bit about what your project app will do; now let's look at starting the project and adding a Settings bundle to it.

To start your TimeDown project, open Xcode and create a new project (select View-Based Application). After the project is created and open in Xcode, you can add settings.

PROBLEM

You need to create a Settings bundle for your project and specify the user settings. The Settings bundle includes the plist file, which Xcode allows you to edit as fields and values. Your settings must include a text field for the minutes and a toggle switch for the auto-start.

SOLUTION

Right-click on your project name in the Groups & Files area in your project and select Add > New File. In the Resource section, select Settings Bundle and click OK (see figure 6.3).

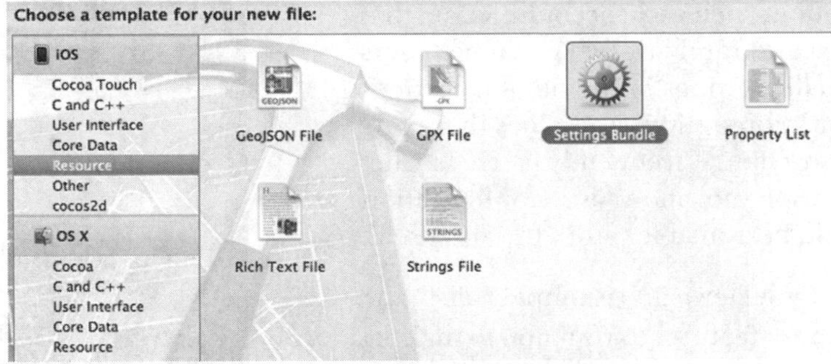

Figure 6.3 Adding a Settings bundle to an Xcode project

DISCUSSION

Name your Settings bundle whatever you like—I left the name the default, `Settings`. Run the app in the simulator and quit it. Now if you go to the Settings app you'll see the TimeDown area with the default settings (see figure 6.4).

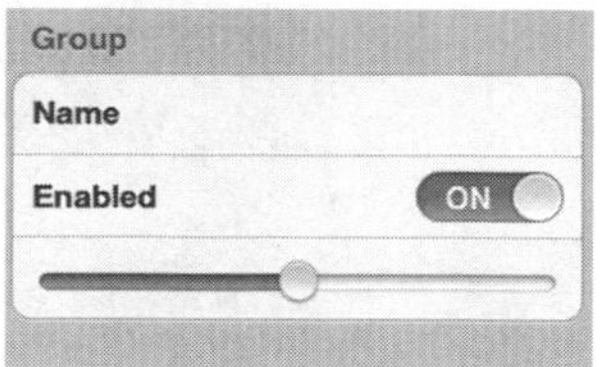

Figure 6.4 TimeDown default Settings bundle settings

Let's set the values to something meaningful to your app. Expand your `Settings.bundle` item and select the `Root.plist`. Now expand the Preference Items.

Under the Preference Items array, there are four items (see figure 6.5). The first defines the group. The next three define the settings values. You'll only use two (see figure 6.6), so you can delete the third one.

Key	Type	Value
▼Preference Items	Array	(4 items)
▼Item 0 (Group - Group)	Diction...	(2 items)
Title	String	Group
Type	String	Group
▼Item 1 (Text Field - Name)	Diction...	(8 items)
Autocapitalization Style	String	None
Autocorrection Style	String	No Autocorrection
Default Value	String	
Text Field Is Secure	Boolean	NO
Identifier	String	name_preference
Keyboard Type	String	Alphabet
Title	String	Name
Type	String	Text Field
▼Item 2 (Toggle Switch - Enabled)	Diction...	(4 items)
Default Value	Boolean	YES
Identifier	String	enabled_preference
Title	String	Enabled
Type	String	Toggle Switch
▼Item 3 (Slider)	Diction...	(7 items)
Default Value	Number	0.5
Identifier	String	slider_preference
Maximum Value	Number	1
Max Value Image Filename	String	
Minimum Value	Number	0
Min Value Image Filename	String	
Type	String	Slider
Strings Filename	String	Root

Figure 6.5 Default Settings bundle values

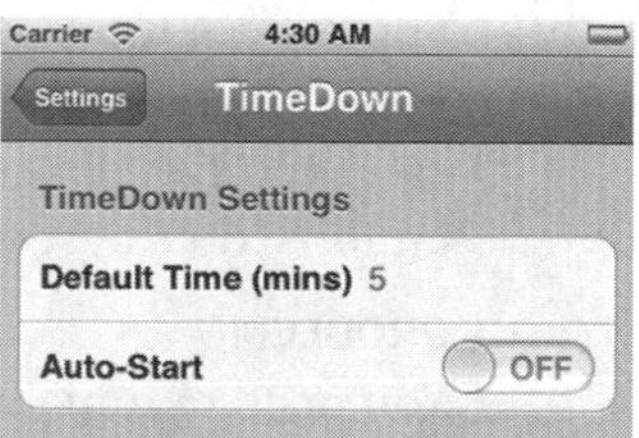

Figure 6.6 TimeDown actual settings in the Settings app

You need to make a few changes to the remaining values to make the settings applicable to your TimeDown app. You'll set the Group Title value to TimeDown settings. The first setting item will have a new title, identifier, default value, and keyboard type. The last setting will also have a new title and identifier. Match the settings to the figure (see figure 6.7).

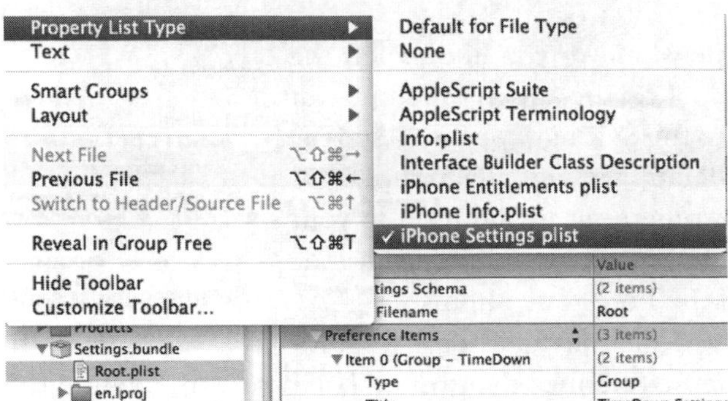

Figure 6.7 TimeDown settings `Root.plist` values

Now you can run the app, quit it, and open the Settings app to see the new items to set. If you don't run the Settings app, the values aren't actually set for use in your app. In other words, if the Settings app doesn't access your Settings bundle, no values are set for your settings. If your app tries to access the default timer value, it won't be `5` because the Settings app never set it.

In the case that the user hasn't run the Settings app, which is likely, you'll need to check for missing settings. If they're missing, you can default to the right value in the app or initialize the settings in the app as if the Settings app had done it. Let's look at how to initialize the settings in case the user doesn't run Settings for your app.

TECHNIQUE 36 Initializing iOS settings

If you opened the Settings app area for TimeDown, you technically set the values (even if you didn't change them). But if you (or your app's user) didn't run the Settings app, the values aren't actually set.

Generally, when a user downloads an app, they run the app before they run the Settings app to see what's configurable. They may never run the Settings app for your app. The settings you created in your Settings bundle may be vital and necessary for your app to run correctly. If the user doesn't set them, you still need values. In that case, you can set them in the app. Not only can you use default values within the execution, you can set the values as if the Settings app did it.

PROBLEM

You need to initialize your app's settings values for when the app needs the values, but the user hasn't gone into Settings.

SOLUTION

You can check the settings in your app and set any necessary values if they aren't set.

DISCUSSION

The Settings values are accessed via the shared `NSUserDefaults` instance from the system. `NSUserDefaults`, like an `NSDictionary`, allows values to be stored for given keys.

If you try to retrieve one of your settings from the `NSUserDefaults` instance and it returns `nil`, you know your settings haven't been stored either from the Settings app or from within your app.

To set your desired default values, you can create an NSDictionary (or NSMutable-Dictionary for multiple values) and register the defaults you set. You can add the code to your applicationDidFinishLaunching: method in TimeDownAppDelegate.m class, as shown in the following listing.

Initializing app settings in TimeDownAppDelegate

```
NSUserDefaults *settings = [NSUserDefaults standardUserDefaults];
    NSObject *timeSettings = [settings objectForKey:@"timeSettings"];

    if (nil == timeSettings)
    {
        NSDictionary *appDefaults =
            [NSDictionary dictionaryWithObject:@"5"
            forKey:@"timeSettings"];                    <-- Default setting
         [settings registerDefaults:appDefaults];
        [settings synchronize];                          <-- Store values
     }
```

If you don't set the autoStart setting, it will return as No when accessed, which is fine for the default setting.

In your case, it's easy to test to see if your timer setting is nil and set it if this is the case. In other cases, you might need to be more creative or use an NSMutable-Dictionary for more values. Either way, after the values are set, you can access them in your app. Let's see how to do that next.

TECHNIQUE 37 Accessing settings values in an app

The values stored in the NSUserDefaults instance are periodically written to disk and persisted from one execution to subsequent executions. This means that the values you set are accessible later and can affect the execution.

Beyond the Settings bundle, you may wish to store any number of values in the NSUserDefaults like last execution time, last GPS position, and various values for auto-completion. Your app stores two basic types of data, but NSUserDefaults can store a variety of data.

> **NSUSERDEFAULTS (FROM APPLE CLASS REFERENCE DOCS)** The NSUserDefaults class provides convenience methods for accessing common types such as floats, doubles, integers, Booleans, and URLs. A default object must be a property list, that is, an instance of (or for collections, a combination of instances of) NSData, NSString, NSNumber, NSDate, NSArray, and/or NSDictionary. If you want to store any other type of object, you should typically archive it to create an instance of NSData.

Similar to checking the previous values, accessing the values for use is straightforward. You need to get the standard NSUserDefaults and access the values like dictionary key value pairs.

PROBLEM

You need to access your Settings values for use in the TimeDown app.

```
All Output
GNU gdb 6.3.50-20050815 (Apple version gdb-1518) (Sat Feb 12 02:52:12 UTC 2011)
Copyright 2004 Free Software Foundation, Inc.
GDB is free software, covered by the GNU General Public License, and you are
welcome to change it and/or distribute copies of it under certain conditions.
Type "show copying" to see the conditions.
There is absolutely no warranty for GDB.  Type "show warranty" for details.
This GDB was configured as "x86_64-apple-darwin".Attaching to process 46429.
2011-03-25 05:15:59.860 TimeDown[46429:207] timeSettings: 5 autoStart: 0
```

Figure 6.8 Console output of settings for your app

SOLUTION

Retrieving the standard instance of `NSUserDefaults` gives you access to the `NSDictionary` with the key value pairs you need.

DISCUSSION

When you have the dictionary from the `NSUserDefaults` instance, you can access the values using the identifier values you set in your `Root.plist`.

For your timer length (in minutes) setting, you used the identifier value `timeSettings`. For your auto-start toggle, you used the identifier `autoStart`. You can access both of these settings and output them to the console via `NSLog` in your `viewWillAppear` method, as shown in the following listing.

Accessing and printing out your Settings values to the console

```
-(void)viewWillAppear:(BOOL)animated
{
    NSUserDefaults *settings = [NSUserDefaults standardUserDefaults];
    timeSettings =
        [[settings objectForKey:@"timeSettings"] intValue];        <— Stored asString
     autoStart = [[settings objectForKey:@"autoStart"] boolValue];

    NSLog(@"timeSettings: %d autoStart: %d", timeSettings, autoStart);
}
```

If you now run the app, you'll see the values printed to the console. Running the Settings app, changing the values, and running the app again will show the new values in the console (see figure 6.8).

Identifying which item in the Settings to choose for TimeDown is easy in the simulator because there are so few. But let's look at how to add an icon to the row to make it more visible in a real-world situation.

TECHNIQUE 38 Setting the app settings icon

Apple documentation explains the various icons that are required and other icons that may be created and used. Go to http://developer.apple.com/library/ios/navigation/ and search for Creating Custom Icons to find the "Custom Icon and Image Creation Guidelines" section of the "Human Interface Guidelines" document.

All apps have an icon on the device. Whether it's a 57 × 57 iPhone/iPod Touch icon or a 72 × 72 iPad icon, they all have them. But there are several other types of icons you can include in your app for use within the OS. Each type of icon has guidelines and requirements to be used in a given case. Following the documented size, resolution, and naming conventions allows the OS to find the right icon file to use.

PROBLEM

Not adding a specific icon to the settings means that the Settings app will only display your app's name in the table. This not only looks unprofessional, but it also makes it harder for the user to find your app in a long list. You want to add an icon to your app's area in the Settings app.

SOLUTION

You'll add an icon of the right dimensions to your project, and the Settings app will use it for your app's row in the list.

DISCUSSION

The Settings app uses png icons found in the app that have the size of 29 × 29 (and 58 × 58 for higher resolution devices). You need to create an image, add it to your project, and set the `CFBundleIconFiles` settings. Create this image and name it `Icon-Small.png`.

Drag the `Icon-Small.png` image you create into your Resources area in your project. Open the TimeDown-Info.plist file to view the icon setting. Right-click on one of the keys and select Show Raw Keys/Values to see the key names. For any case where you have a higher resolution image for higher resolution devices, add `@2x` to the image name so the OS knows to use that version (see figure 6.9).

Key	Type	Value
Localization native development region	String	English
Bundle display name	String	${PRODUCT_NAME}
Executable file	String	${EXECUTABLE_NAME}
▼Icon files	Array	(4 items)
Item 0	String	Icon.png
Item 1	String	Icon-Small.png
Item 2	String	Icon@2x.png
Item 3	String	Icon-Small@2x.png
Bundle identifier	String	com.brainwashinc.${PRODUCT_NAME:rfc1034identifier}
InfoDictionary version	String	6.0
Bundle name	String	${PRODUCT_NAME}
Bundle OS Type code	String	APPL
Bundle creator OS Type code	String	????
Bundle version	String	1.0
Application requires iPhone environme	Boolean	YES
Main nib file base name	String	MainWindow

Figure 6.9 TimeDown-Info.plist items displaying raw keys/values

OLDHAM COUNTY PUBLIC LIBRARY

If the key `CFBundleIconFiles` doesn't exist, create it and right-click it to set its type to `Array`. Add entries for your app icon (such as `Icon.png`) and the settings icon (such as `Icon-Small.png`). Feel free to create a 57 × 57 png icon for your app named `icon.png` and add it to the project.

The icons section of the Apple documentation mentioned above goes into the various file types, sizes, names, resolutions, and more of the types of icons required and supported on the various devices.

You've created a Settings bundle for your app and even initialized the values to the defaults within the code. By using an array entry in the app plist file, you specified the various icon images to use on the device. But none of this really results in anything viewable within your app—only outside of your app. Let's look at the UI of the app itself.

6.2 Runtime and time-based UI changes

Sometimes settings in the UI are best handled with Interface Builder (IB) in Xcode, and other times it's best done in the code. There are also cases where you might want to update the UI programmatically, not based on a user's actions, but time-based.

IB gives you access to many of the visual settings of the UI, but not all of them. If you want to manipulate some lower-level settings, you need to do that in the code. Rounded corners are a pretty common look in iOS apps (see any grouped table view like in the Contact app). If you want that in your app, you could use images, but there's an easier way to do it in the code.

Other values in the UI are easy to set with IB, but may depend on the state of the app. TimeDown is a timer app, and everyone expects to see the time decrement visually. You'll see how to update your remaining time value in the label every second based on a timer.

TECHNIQUE 39 Rounding corners of a view

As stated above, many apps have views that use rounded corners. Look at the icons on the device to see an example. The Settings app uses a grouped table view with rounded corners. As you can see in the image of TimeDown (see figure 6.2), you're using rounded corners with your views.

IB doesn't give you access to the `CALayer` of the `UIView` class, which is where the corner radius is set. But you can access it in the code. Let's look at how you rounded the corners of views in your app.

PROBLEM

You want to round the corners of your app's views without using images or other complex techniques.

SOLUTION

You can round the corners of your views by accessing the underlying `CALayer` aspect of the views and setting the `cornerRadius`, which you don't have access to via the UI editor.

OLDHAM COUNTY PUBLIC LIBRARY

DISCUSSION

First, let's actually create a UI for your app. Open the default xib file: TimeDownViewController.xib file. Add a view with a black background and add two labels with center justification. Size the labels and fonts to match the image approximately (see figure 6.10).

Add the QuartzCore framework to your project and import it into your `TimeDownViewController` header file. Also in the header file, declare the `UILabel` outlets and wire them up with IB, as shown in the following listing.

Import QuartzCore.h and declare the `UILabel` outlets

```
#import <UIKit/UIKit.h>
#import <QuartzCore/QuartzCore.h>

@interface TimeDownViewController : UIViewController {
    IBOutlet UILabel *lblTimer, *lblTitle;

}

@end
```

Because you're not actually doing anything with the label's text values, the app appears quite plain and the corners aren't rounded. In fact, it should look like the design in figure 6.10.

To round the corners, you use the `setCornerRadius` method from the QuartzCore framework on the layer member of your `UILabels`. You can add this code to some

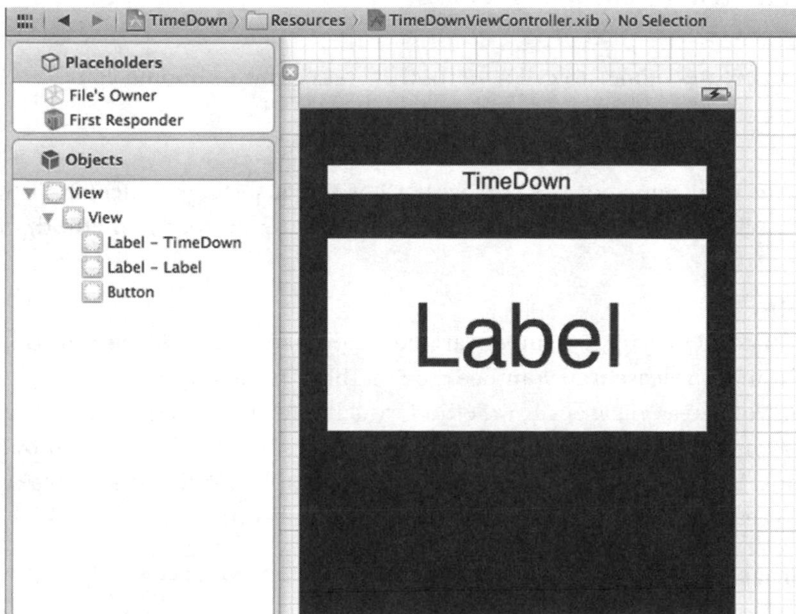

Figure 6.10 TimeDown UI design

method called before the controller's view is displayed, like `viewWillAppear:`, as shown in the following listing.

Rounding the corners of your `UILabel` layer members via QuartzCore

```
-(void)viewWillAppear:(BOOL)animated
{
    [super viewWillAppear:animated];
    [lblTimer.layer setCornerRadius:5.0];
    [lblTitle.layer setCornerRadius:5.0];
}
```

Now if you run the app again, you'll notice the corners are rounded (see figure 6.11).

You can experiment with the different values for the corner radius to see what you think looks best. In the case of the corner radius change, you only want to do that once. But some changes you want to happen at various times and/or multiple times. Let's look at how to change something based on a timer.

Figure 6.11 TimeDown in the simulator without UI updates

TECHNIQUE 40 Updating the UI with a repeating timer

A timer app is a great example of an app that needs to update the UI at certain time intervals. You can use the `NSTimer` class to help you know when to update the UI.

Timers can fire once after a specified time period or repeatedly based on a set time period, which is what your app will do.

PROBLEM

You want to create a timer to call a method every second to update your `UILabel` with the current remaining time.

SOLUTION

You'll create an instance of `NSTimer` with a few select settings to accomplish your UI update. You'll set it to repeat every second and call its `oneSecond:` method, which will update the UI.

DISCUSSION

First, you need to declare a member variable reference of the `NSTimer` in your header. Also, you want to release it in your `dealloc` method in the implementation.

Back in your `viewWillAppear:` method, you already have your `timeSettings` set to the value from the Settings app. This is set in minutes, so you'll multiply it by 60 to get the seconds. You'll set the timer display label to Blank, and if the `autoStart` value is on, you'll create the timer, as shown in the following listing.

Set the time, clear the label, and create the timer if `autoStart` is on

```
timeSettings *= 60;
    [lblTimer setText:@""];
    if (autoStart)
```

```
setTimer = [NSTimer
    scheduledTimerWithTimeInterval:1.0      <-- One second
     target:self
    selector:@selector(oneSecond:)          <-- Call oneSecond:
     userInfo:nil
    repeats:YES];                           <-- Set to Repeat
```

Your timer will fire every second and call the oneSecond: method on itself. In your oneSecond: method, you want to decrement the remaining time by one (second) and update the label with the remaining time. Also, you'll need to check to see if the time has run out and stop the timer, as shown in the following listing.

Decrement the remaining time, update the label, stop the timer when done

```
-(void)oneSecond:(NSTimer*)timer;
{
    timeSettings--;
    if (timeSettings > -1)
        [lblTimer setText:
            [NSString stringWithFormat:@"%d:%02d",
            timeSettings/60, timeSettings%60]];
    else
    {
        [secTimer invalidate];                  <-- Releases reference
         secTimer = nil;
    }
}
```

While the time is 0 or more, update the label. After that, invalidate the timer (which also releases it) and set the member to nil.

Open the Settings app, set the time to 1, the autostart to On, and run the app. You should see it start the timer when the app launches. The countdown should display in the lower label (see figure 6.12).

Figure 6.12 TimeDown running with `autoStart` starting the timer

Now you've seen how to create the UI and update it in the app both as a one-time event and a timer-based event. The app even handles the case when the time runs out, but it doesn't do much to notify the user that the timer is done. In the next section, we'll look at a couple of ways to notify the user that time is up, including playing an audio file.

6.3 Playing audio and vibrating the device

Most of Apple's success in the last several years started from the iPod and playing audio. The iOS also gives the developer a lot of ways to play audio including access to the iPod functionality. Here we'll look at a couple of basic ways to access some of this functionality.

TECHNIQUE 41 Playing an MP3 file

Including audio files in your app is as easy as an image or any other type of file—drag it into the project's Groups & Files area. Playing the file isn't much more complicated.

The AVFoundation framework provides the AVAudioPlayer which, as you can see by its name, plays audio. The framework takes care of most of the work. You need to tell it what audio file you want it to play and then tell it to begin playing it. Other functions to the audio player class exist, but they are equally straightforward.

PROBLEM

You need to play an audio file when the TimeDown timer runs out of time. This signifies to the user that time has expired in the timer.

SOLUTION

You'll use the `AVAudioPlayer` class in the AVFoundation framework to create an instance with an MP3 file from your project and play it through the device.

DISCUSSION

Because you'll use the `AVAudioPlayer` from the AVFoundation framework, you first need to add the AVFoundation framework to your project. Also, you need to import the AVFoundation.h file into your `TimeDownViewController` header file and declare an `AVAudioPlayer` member (such as `aAudioPlayer`). Don't forget to release it in the `dealloc` method also.

Next, add an MP3 file to your project. I created an MP3 called "beeps.mp3" and dropped it in my project Resources group.

Let's write a separate method that expects the filename (no extension), creates the `AVAudioPlayer` instance with your file, and plays it, as shown in the following listing.

Method to take a filename and play an MP3

```
-(void)playSound:(NSString*)soundFileName
{
    NSString *aFilePath = [[NSBundle mainBundle]
        pathForResource:soundFileName ofType:@"mp3"];
    if (nil != aAudioPlayer)
    {
        [aAudioPlayer stop];                              // Stop before release
         [aAudioPlayer release];
    }
    aAudioPlayer =[[AVAudioPlayer alloc]                  // Create with MP3
         initWithContentsOfURL:[NSURL fileURLWithPath:aFilePath]
                        error:NULL];
    [aAudioPlayer play];
}
```

If you already have an instance of the player, stop the playing and then release it. The initialization method of the AVAudioPlayer takes an `NSURL` to your file that you got from the `NSBundle`'s `mainBundle`. After it's set up, you call play on the player.

To play my beeps.mp3 file, I call `playSound:` with the name where the timer runs out back in your `oneSecond:` method, as shown in the following listing.

Call the `playSound:` method where the timer runs out

```
-(void)oneSecond:(NSTimer*)timer;
{
    timeSettings--;
    if (timeSettings > -1)
        [lblTimer setText:
            [NSString stringWithFormat:@"%d:%02d",
            timeSettings/60, timeSettings%60]];
    else
    {
        [secTimer invalidate];
        secTimer = nil;
        [self playSound:@"beeps"];
    }
}
```

This is a great way to notify a user of an event, especially a timer or alarm event. Another way to notify a user is through vibrating the device. Let's look at how to do that.

TECHNIQUE 42 Vibrating the iPhone

Vibration is a great dimension added to most phones these days. It's great for silent mode ringing and alarms and also great feedback for games and other apps. You'll use it like an alarm and have the device vibrate when the timer runs out.

Not all iOS devices vibrate, but the iPhone does. If you try to vibrate the device on an iPod or iPad, the vibration command is simply ignored.

PROBLEM

You want to vibrate your iPhone when the TimeDown timer runs out.

SOLUTION

You'll use the AudioToolbox framework to play the vibration system sound.

DISCUSSION

Similar to playing an MP3 file in technique 41, you'll create a separate method for vibrating the device. You'll simply call the method *vibrate* and call it when you want the iPhone to vibrate.

First add the AudioToolbox framework to your project and import the AudioToolbox header file in the `TimeDownViewController` header file. Then create a vibrate method that calls `AudioServicesPlaySystemSound`, specifying the system sound `kSystemSoundID_Vibrate`, as shown in the following listing. That's it!

Vibrate the device with a play system sound call

```
-(void)vibrate;
{
    AudioServicesPlaySystemSound (kSystemSoundID_Vibrate);
}
```

Now call your new vibration method the `playSound:` method. This way your app will play the MP3 and vibrate (if possible) when the time is done.

Now you've seen how easy it is to play an audio file and make the device move by vibrating. But what if the user makes the device move? Let's look at how you can use the accelerometer to detect the device being shaken and use that in your app.

6.4 Detecting and handling device motion

Your app has very little in the way of a UI. The settings are handled via the Settings bundle in the Settings app, and your output is mainly one `UILabel` (with nicely rounded corners).

Let's continue with this bare UI by using the accelerometer to detect shaking and handle that as part of your interface instead of buttons.

TECHNIQUE 43 Detecting shaking with the accelerometer

iOS devices have the ability to detect motion and pass that information on to the given apps through the Accelerometer in the UIKit framework.

Detecting motion with the accelerometer is useful in various ways for different apps. In many apps, shaking is used to allow the user to undo a previous action. Let's look at how to detect a shake versus a given motion.

PROBLEM

You want to detect shaking the device from within your app.

SOLUTION

You first need to detect motion of the device from within the app and then compare it to another motion to see if it's a shake or simply being moved.

DISCUSSION

In the `TimeDownViewController` header file, specify that your class implements the `UIAccelerometerDelegate` interface:

```
@interface TimeDownViewController : UIViewController
    <UIAccelerometerDelegate>
```

Then, in the `viewWillAppear:` method, set the shared accelerometer's delegate to be your `TimeDownViewController`:

```
if ([UIAccelerometer sharedAccelerometer].delegate == nil)
        [UIAccelerometer sharedAccelerometer].delegate = self;
```

If you put this in `viewWillAppear:`, it may be called (in some apps) every time the view appears. This can be redundant. In this case, it will only be called once.

Declare `prevAcceleration` in the header to be a reference of `UIAcceleration`. Declare the property of it, synthesize it in the implementation file, and release it in the `dealloc`.

Next, write a method that takes two `UIAccelerations`, the `prevAcceleration` and the current one, and a threshold (of movement) to determine if the device is shaking, as shown in the following listing.

Take two `UIAccelerations` and a threshold and check the motion threshold

```
-(BOOL)shakingEnoughFromPrev:(UIAcceleration*) prevShake
                toThisShake:(UIAcceleration*) thisShake
          withThisThreshold:(double) shakeThreshold;
{
    double dX = fabs(prevShake.x - thisShake.x);              <-- Calculate deltas
     double dY = fabs(prevShake.y - thisShake.y);
    double dZ = fabs(prevShake.z - thisShake.z);

    return (dX > shakeThreshold && dY > shakeThreshold) ||
           (dX > shakeThreshold && dZ > shakeThreshold) ||
           (dY > shakeThreshold && dZ > shakeThreshold);     <-- True if threshold exceeded
 }
```

In your accelerometer callback method, you'll check the current `UIAcceleration` against the previous and set the flag to YES if it's shaking. If there's no previous acceleration, you'll skip the comparison method call and set the `prevAcceleration`, as shown in the following listing.

Check for shaking against previous acceleration or set if none

```
- (void) accelerometer:(UIAccelerometer *)accelerometer
                      didAccelerate:(UIAcceleration *)acceleration {

    if (self.prevAcceleration)
    {
      if (!isShaking &&
        shakingEnough(self.prevAcceleration, acceleration, 0.5))
          isShaking = YES;                                     <-- YES if shaking
     }
    self.prevAcceleration = acceleration;
}
```

You only want to detect shaking when your shaking flag is NO. If it has already detected shaking, there's no need to check again.

Now you know how, based on a threshold, to determine if the device is shaking. Your threshold of 0.5 may be too small or too large depending on the particular app and use. Also based on the particular app, you may do different things when the app is shaking. Let's see how you can handle shaking in the UI for your TimeDown app.

TECHNIQUE 44 Handling shaking with an action sheet

Quickly presenting the user with a list of options for selection or confirmation of an action is a common practice. Using the action sheet is a common technique for accomplishing that. It presents the user with the various allowed options to choose from and calls a callback with the index of the button selected.

Your app has little in the way of a UI, so let's use the device shaking to reset the timer for your app. You'll verify with the user that they want to reset using an action sheet.

PROBLEM

You want to prompt the user to start/reset the timer when they shake the device.

SOLUTION

When you detect the device shaking, you'll prompt the user to start the timer via a `UIActionSheet` with applicable options.

DISCUSSION

You already know when the device is shaking, and now you need to add an action sheet to give the user options and handle their selection.

For handling the action sheet, you need to declare that `TimeDownViewController` implements the `UIActionSheetDelegate`interface. In the code where you set the shaking flag to YES, you can create and display an action sheet to prompt the user to start the timer, as shown in the following listing.

Prompt the user to start the time with an action sheet

```
UIActionSheet *as = [[UIActionSheet alloc]
                initWithTitle:@"Start Timer"
                delegate:self                          Delegate is self
                 cancelButtonTitle:@"Cancel"
                destructiveButtonTitle:nil
                otherButtonTitles:@"Start", nil];      One option plus Cancel
             [as showInView:self.view];
```

Because the delegate is set to self, you can implement the callback for when the user makes a selection on the action sheet, as shown in the following listing. You'll know which button they press based on the button index. In this case, your Start button has index 0. When you detect that, you'll start (or restart) the timer.

Start/Restart the timer based on the user's action sheet selection

```
- (void)actionSheet:(UIActionSheet *)actionSheet
    clickedButtonAtIndex:(NSInteger)buttonIndex
{
    if (0 == buttonIndex)
    {
        [lblTimer setText:@""];
        NSUserDefaults *settings =
                                 [NSUserDefaults standardUserDefaults];

        timeSettings =
                    [[settings objectForKey:@"timeSettings"] intValue];
        timeSettings *= 60;                                   Reset time

        if (!secTimer)
            secTimer = [NSTimer scheduledTimerWithTimeInterval:1.0
               target:self
               selector:@selector(oneSecond:)             Create timer if none
               userInfo:nil
               repeats:YES];
    }
    isShaking = NO;                                       Reset shaking flag
 }
```

You essentially reset the label and time value to the original length. This effectively starts the timer over. If you don't have a timer, you need to create a new one the same way you did in `viewWillAppear:` earlier. You also want to reset the shaking flag so you can detect shaking later.

You'll have to run the app on your device to test whether it detects the shaking. When you're running it, you can shake the device and see the action sheet appear. Select Start and see that the action sheet is removed and the timer starts over (see figure 6.13).

Now, even though you have no real interactive UI in your app, it's fully functional as a timer using the Settings bundle and accelerometer to detect shaking.

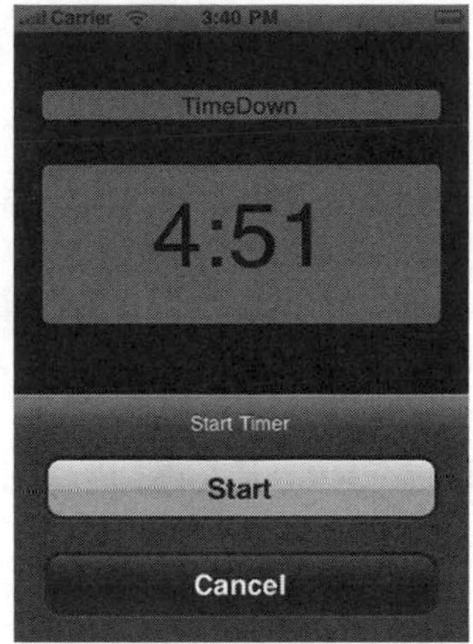

Figure 6.13 Action sheet prompting the user to start the timer

6.5 Summary

From developing the TimeDown app, you've seen how to use the Settings bundle for the Settings application for your app's values. You've seen how to initialize, set, and access the Settings values and even set the icon for the Settings app.

You've also seen how to update the UI in the app including rounding corners and updating based on a repeating timer. When the timer completes, you've seen how to notify the user by playing a file and vibrating the device (when applicable). Finally, you saw how to detect motion as shaking and how you can use that detection as your user interface.

While your use of some of these aspects was quite simplified, you can see the basics of how they work and how they can be employed for any number of uses. Other aspects need more advanced development for more complex uses. Playing a single MP3 file in the app is easy, but accessing the iPod to play user's audio tracks is a bit more complex. We'll see in the next chapter how to do that.

7 CoreData, iPod access, and playing music—PlayMyLists

This chapter covers

- The CoreData framework
- Accessing databases
- Creating and working with music playlists

The iPhone, iPod, and iPad are great music playing devices and allow you to create playlists. You may want to write an app that includes the ability to create a playlist used within the app. With access to the music in the iPod on a device and a database for the app, apps can allow the user to select tracks and create their own playlists within an app.

Creating playlists is useful, but being able to play them is what's important. Using the iPod access to select tracks, CoreData to store the selections, and the music player to play the music makes for a usable app.

You'll build this app as a learning exercise, so it's not a replacement for the iPod app. But with the techniques you learn in this chapter, you can make a functional app and have the ability to create more complex apps in the future.

As with many data-driven apps, you need a way to store data, and CoreData is a great tool for that. You'll design a database within Xcode and have the related code generated for you. You'll use CoreData to store and retrieve the data related to your playlists. Because this is the basis of your app, and because you've covered UI-based topics in previous chapters, we'll now focus attention on CoreData concepts.

With the database designed and the code generated, we'll then look at accessing the music for the app user to make their selections. This UI part of the app will largely be provided by the framework used, but receiving user selections and storing them in the database is crucial to the concept and functionality of the app.

Finally, we'll look at playing the music selected and stored by the user in a given playlist. This includes handling notification callbacks when one track ends to know when to play the next track in the playlist.

Let's first look at setting up the project to support your table view navigation.

7.1 Creating a table view project

All apps deal with some form of data and many need to store that data in a meaningful way. Often the solution is a database including tables, rows, and relationships between them.

A common way to display data to the user in a meaningful way is with rows in a table.

TECHNIQUE 45 Create a project with table navigation

Data-driven apps typically need an interface to allow the user to select items and/or details for a given item. While the data's stored in a database with CoreData handling the storing and retrieving, what the user sees in the UI is often a table view representing the data. And often when the user of table views taps on a given row, they expect to see details slide in from the right, which is the functionality of a navigation controller.

PROBLEM

You need to create a project, a table view, and a navigation controller.

SOLUTION

You'll create a Master-Detail Application project in Xcode using Storyboard and CoreData. Then you'll set up the UI to have a table view embedded in a navigation controller.

DISCUSSION

Open Xcode as normal and select Create a New Project. From the pop-up window, select Master-Detail Application, and click Next (see figure 7.1).

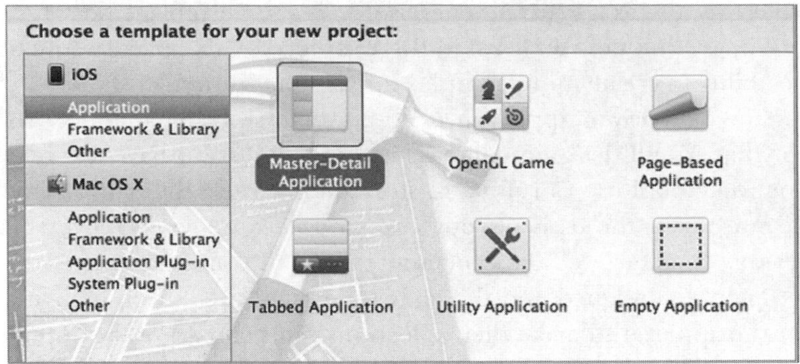

Figure 7.1 Create a new Master-Detail Application Xcode project

The next step of the project creation is to set the product name (such as `PlayMyLists`) and company identifier (see figure 7.2). Notice that you'll use Storyboard and CoreData for this project. One thing to note is that Storyboard requires iOS version 5, so if you want to support past versions of iOS, you shouldn't use Storyboard.

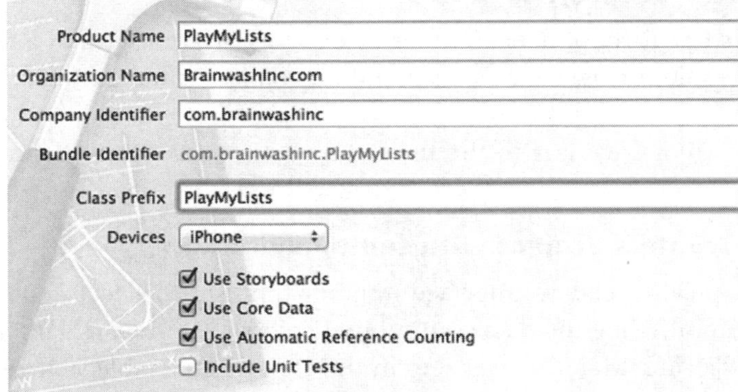

Figure 7.2 Project options including Storyboard and CoreData

Continue with the project creation by selecting the location and click Create to create the project and view the summary (see figure 7.3).

Figure 7.3 Newly created project summary data

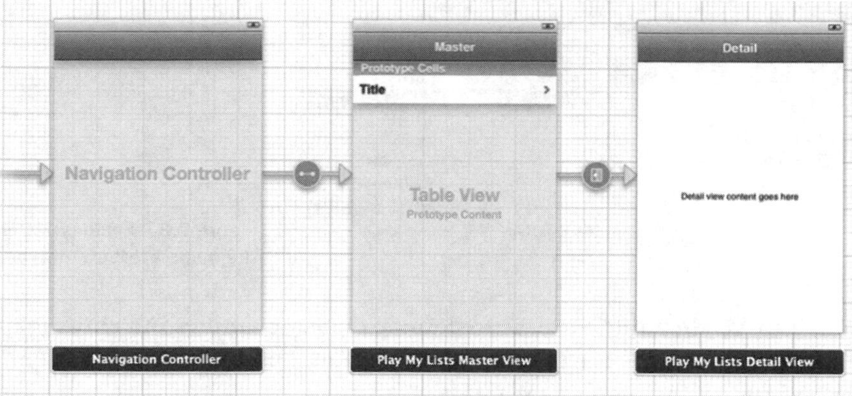

Figure 7.4 Storyboard of Master-Detail Application UI

Open the Storyboard file using the navigator. As you can see, the base view controller is created as a navigation controller with a root controller of a table view controller that leads to a view controller for displaying data details (see figure 7.4). This confirms that this hierarchy-style data display and drill-down into details is a commonly used design.

Figure 7.5 Executing the template code in the simulator

At this point, Xcode has handled most of the heavy (and light) lifting for you. It included the CoreData framework in your project and it created your app delegate, master view controller, and detail view controller classes, as well as the Storyboard to use them. On top of that, your master view controller is a table view controller. Finally, both the app delegate and your master view controller have a lot of code relating to a common table view controller that CoreData generated for you.

If you run this app in the simulator, you can create new database data using the (+) button, delete it using the Edit button, and view details for the items by tapping on the listed rows (see figure 7.5).

Now you're set up on the UI side, but what about the data side? You need to configure your project to be ready to store and access data using CoreData.

TECHNIQUE 46 Defining entities in CoreData

Your entities will be simple, but more complex entities are possible. You'll have two entities for your playlists: the playlist and its member tracks.

The playlists will contain tracks, so you'll need to set up the relationship between the playlists and tracks later. In this technique, you'll focus on the entities of creating and adding attributes.

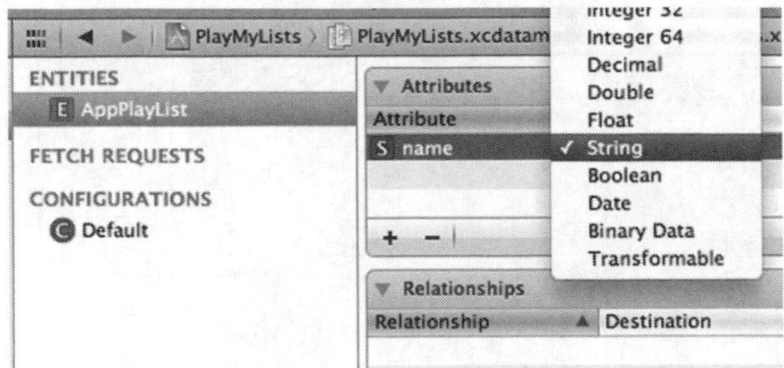

Figure 7.6 AppPlayList entity with the name attribute of type String

Built into Xcode is the interface to develop database entities. An entity maps to a table and the attributes are the fields in the table. You'll use this interface to enter all of the data you'll need for your database.

PROBLEM

You need to create two CoreData entities for your app, `AppPlayList` and `PlayList-Track`, to map to your database tables. The playlist needs to have a name and the track needs a persistent ID that you'll later relate to the persistent ID in the iPod.

SOLUTION

Using the data model editor, you'll define your entities and their attributes.

DISCUSSION

Select the `PlayMyLists.xcdatamodel` item in the Groups & Files area on the left in Xcode. Notice the template entity of Event is listed in the Entities area. Select and delete this item so you can start fresh.

Now that your list is empty, click the Add Entity button at the bottom of Xcode. A new entity is now created and needs to be named (let's use `AppPlayList`).

> **ENTITY NAMING WARNING** Be careful of your choices when naming your entities. If they duplicate existing class names within iOS frameworks, you may wind up with confusing errors at compile time.

Next, add an attribute to the entity. Click the (+) button at the bottom left of the Attributes area, type `name`, and then set its Type to `String` (see figure 7.6).

Now create another new entity with the button at the bottom of the frame. Set its name to `PlayListTrack`. Add a new attribute, name it `persistentID`, and set its type to `String` (see figure 7.7).

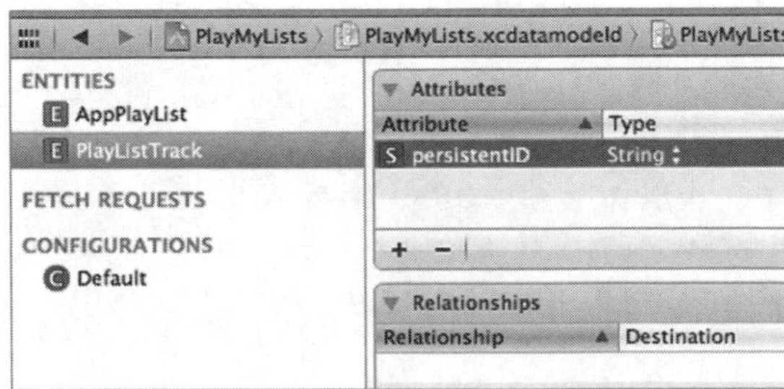

Figure 7.7 `PlayListTrack` entity with attribute `persistentID` of type String

You now have your two entities. But they aren't related. How does the app know which tracks go with which playlists? You need to define the relationship between these two entities. Let's do that now.

TECHNIQUE 47 Creating relationships in CoreData

As is usually the case, your database needs relationships. Playlists need to have access to multiple tracks and tracks should know which playlists they belong to. The relationship from the playlists to the tracks is a *to-many* relationship: one playlist can point to many tracks.

The model editor lets you build the relationships, including to-many relationships. A relationship can also be set to handle object deletion in different ways, such as whether to delete the object only or also the objects that it's related to in the database.

PROBLEM

You need to define a to-many relationship between the playlists and tracks.

SOLUTION

Using the CoreModel editor, you can define relationships between the two entities. Also, you can specify that the relationship from the `AppPlayList` entity to the `PlayListTrack` is a to-many relationship. You'll also define the relationship from the `PlayListTrack` as the inverse of the `AppPlayList`'s relationship.

DISCUSSION

Select the same `xcdatamodel` as before from the left pane. Select the `AppPlayList entity` in the definition. Click and hold the Add Attribute button for the drop-down menu to display and select Add Relationship.

A new relationship will be defined for the `AppPlayList` entity. Name the new relationship `tracks`. To the right of it, set the Destination to `PlayListTrack`. Don't specify an inverse.

Bring up the Utilities view on the right for the new relationship and make sure the Data Model Inspector is selected (at the top of Utilities). Check the To-Many Relationship in the Plural area (see figure 7.8). Set the Delete Rule to Cascade. This means that if the playlist is deleted, the track data is also deleted. You don't want tracks orphaned in the database.

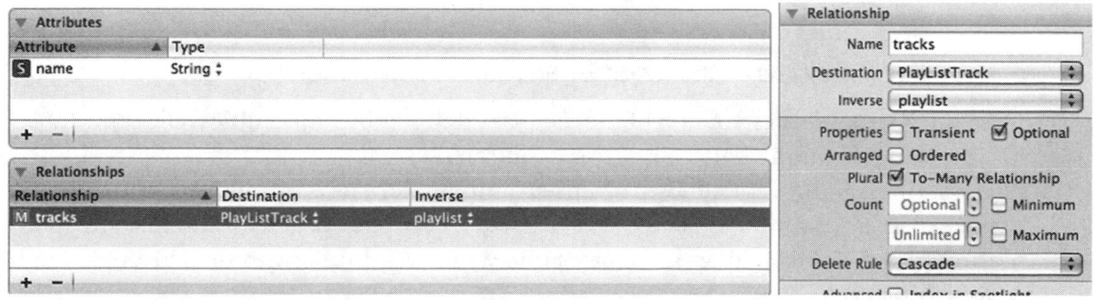

Figure 7.8 Creating a to-many relationship between `AppPlayList` and `PlayListTrack`

Now select the `PlayListTrack` entity and create a new relationship from the drop-down menu as you did before. Name it `playlist` because it points to the given track's playlist. Set its destination to `AppPlayList`. Set its inverse to `tracks`, which is the relationship you defined for `AppPlayList` (see figure 7.9). This means that it's the other end of that same relationship.

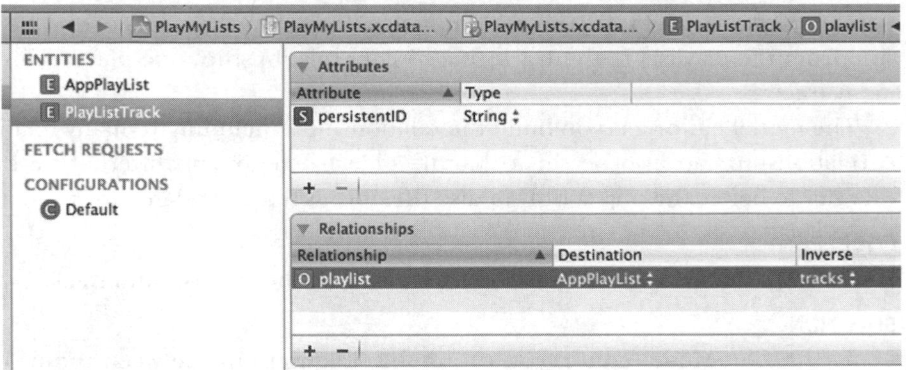

Figure 7.9 Creating the inverse relationship from `PlayListTrack` to `AppPlayList`

If you didn't set this to be the inverse (or even create it at all), the playlist would have a relationship to the tracks. But the track wouldn't know what playlist it belongs to. Depending on your app, this aspect may be useful.

Now you've created your entities and the relationship between the two. To get a high-level view of the entities, select them both on the right (see figure 7.10).

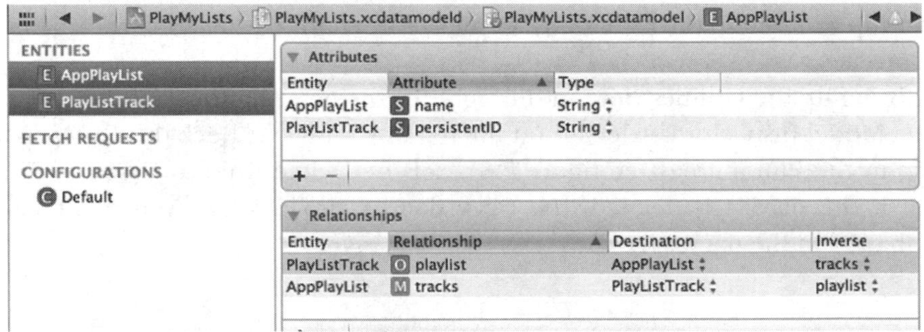

Figure 7.10 Viewing all entities defined and their attributes and relationships

To see a visual representation of the database defined by your entities, click the Table/Graph toggle on the bottom right (see figure 7.11).

At this point, your entities are defined and usable. The iOS framework provides the means to access your objects as `NSManageableObject` instances and the attributes through key-value coding. Let's look at how you can do this with the existing code in your project.

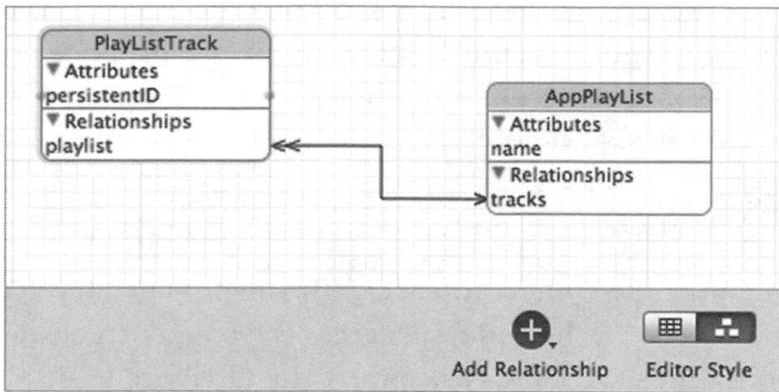

Figure 7.11 Graph representation of the database entities and relationship

TECHNIQUE 48 Inserting and deleting CoreData objects

You've changed your database definition so the app is no longer valid—it still uses the previous defined entity and attribute. But with only a few changes, you can see how CoreData allows you to access the data.

Because the default project already handled some of the CoreData functions, including creating new objects, listing them in the table view, and deleting them, you can reuse some of that code. But you need to update the code to reflect the changes you made to the `Event` entity.

PROBLEM

You need to access your database `AppPlayList` entity from the code and display its attribute.

SOLUTION

You'll change the references in the code to use your definition changes.

DISCUSSION

Because the default CoreData code in your project uses key-value coding, you don't need to change any of the class names. Also, because the default entity and your `AppPlayList` entity only have one attribute, you only need to change that one attribute's references.

The app needs to know what entity it's dealing with (such as creating, accessing, or deleting). In the method that creates and/or returns the object to fetch data, you need to tell it to use the new entity name.

Find the method named, `fetchedResultsController`. It has one line that specifies what entity it's dealing with. Find that line and change `Event` to `AppPlayList`:

```
NSEntityDescription *entity = [NSEntityDescription
        entityForName:@"AppPlayList"
        inManagedObjectContext:self.managedObjectContext];
```

That's the only place the entity name is used. Now your `NSFetchedResultsController` instance will access that entity. But you need to tell it the name of the attribute as well.

The fetchedResultsController instance needs to know how to sort the fetched objects from the database. This is done via the NSSortDescriptor instance created for the fetchedResultsController. In the same method, fetchedResultsController, set the value from timeStamp to name where the sort descriptor is created:

```
NSSortDescriptor *sortDescriptor = [[NSSortDescriptor alloc]
                            initWithKey:@"name" ascending:NO];
```

The previous entity had an attribute named timeStamp. If you change all references in the code to your new attribute, name, the code will access the data correctly.

In the method that configures the table cell, specify the attribute to display in the table. Change that from timeStamp to name, as shown in the following listing.

Specify the name attribute to be displayed in the table cell

```
- (void)configureCell:(UITableViewCell *)cell
    atIndexPath:(NSIndexPath *)indexPath {

    NSManagedObject *managedObject =
        [self.fetchedResultsController
            objectAtIndexPath:indexPath];
    cell.textLabel.text = [[managedObject
                            valueForKey:@"name"] description];
}
```

Now you're accessing the right attribute, but the app also needs to set the right attribute. Make the same change from timeStamp to name in the insertNewObject method. Default the value of the name to New List, which is more meaningful in your app:

```
[newManagedObject setValue:@"New List" forKey:@"name"];
```

Now you can run the app and create database items of your entity—AppPlayList. Of course, you can delete them as well. But right now these playlists are only entries in the database—all with the same name value and no tracks (see figure 7.12). Be sure to delete the old version of the app first to avoid issues with the existing database.

To add tracks to the playlist, you can use the same key-value coding mechanism or you can generate code for your entities and access it all via member items. Let's look at how to generate Objective-C code from your CoreData entities.

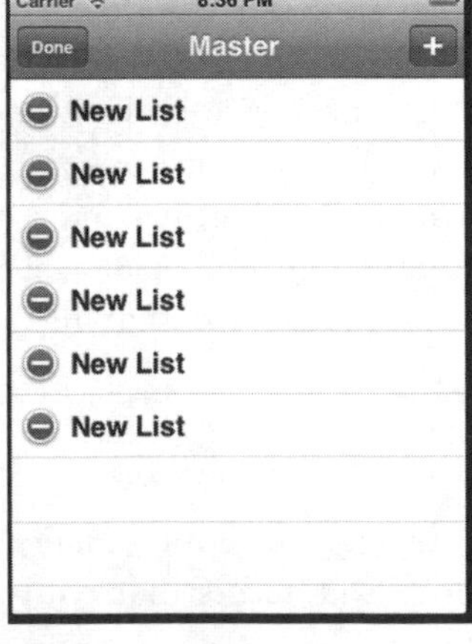

Figure 7.12 PlayMyLists listing newly created AppPlayList entities

TECHNIQUE 49 Creating classes for CoreData entities

Creating classes based on CoreData entities can be useful in accessing the data. But you probably don't want to edit that code after you create it. If you need to change your entity definition later and regenerate the code, it will blow away your changes. To avoid this, you can create helper classes or child classes instead.

Helper classes can be classes that inherit from your generated CoreData classes or are completely separate. These are classes that can possibly filter your objects, sort them, convert them for transmission, or any other functionality you might need.

PROBLEM

You need to generate code based on your CoreData entity definitions.

SOLUTION

You'll use the Xcode new file mechanism to generate the code into your project.

DISCUSSION

Open the data model again and select the entities (or just one). You can right-click on the entity name and get helpful documentation relating to CoreData operations here.

To create the subclass, select the entity(ies) for which you'd like to create a source code. From the Editor menu, select the Create NSManagedObject Subclass option (see figure 7.13).

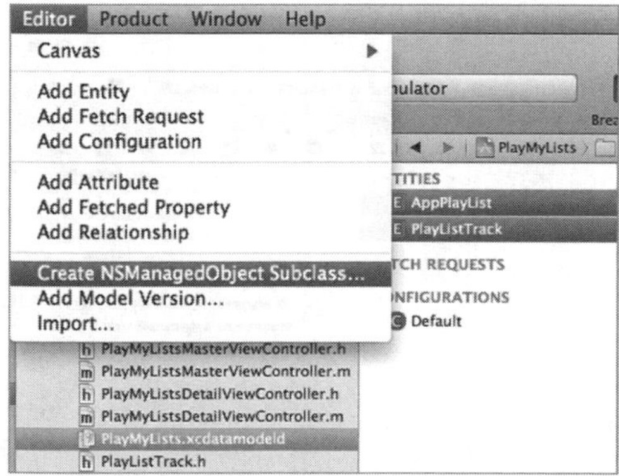

Figure 7.13 Selecting entities for generating Objective-C code

On the next form, select the location and target (see figure 7.14).

There should be from two to four new classes generated based on the entities selected—a header and implementation file for each. The files will have the same names as the entities you created. Again, this can cause problems if you named your entities something that may already exist somewhere else.

By looking at the implementation files, you'll see there's not much to the classes. The header files are more interesting because they tell you the methods you have access to (see the following two listings). Notice how the attributes and relationships both translate into items.

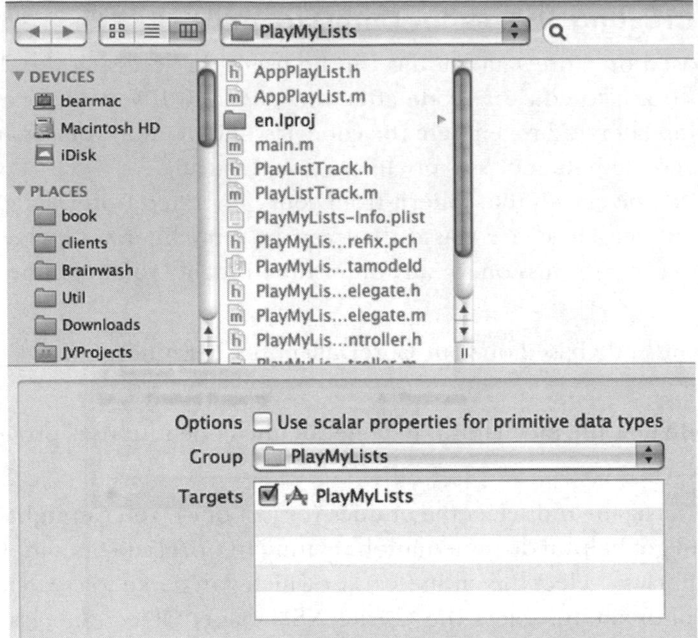

Figure 7.14 Specify the directory, group, and target for the new `NSManagedClass` files

Header file for `AppPlayList` with name and tracks

```
#import <CoreData/CoreData.h>

@interface AppPlayList :  NSManagedObject
{
}

@property (nonatomic, retain) NSString * name;
@property (nonatomic, retain) NSSet* tracks;

@end

@interface AppPlayList (CoreDataGeneratedAccessors)
- (void)addTracksObject:(NSManagedObject *)value;
 - (void)removeTracksObject:(NSManagedObject *)value;
- (void)addTracks:(NSSet *)value;
- (void)removeTracks:(NSSet *)value;

@end
```

NSSet for multiples

Relationship accessors

CoreData objects use `NSSet` instances for the *to-many* relationships. `NSSet` is similar to `NSArray` but isn't ordered. In your case accessing tracks returns the set of tracks for the given playlist as one or more `PlayListTrack` instances. There are also generated methods to add and remove single and multiple tracks.

Header file for `PlayListTrack` with `persistentID` and `playList`

```
#import <CoreData/CoreData.h>
@class AppPlayList;

@interface PlayListTrack :  NSManagedObject
{
}

@property (nonatomic, retain) NSString * persistentID;
@property (nonatomic, retain) AppPlayList * playList;        <- Relationship is member

@end
```

Because the playlist has a to-many relationship with the tracks, the accessors need to support that. It uses `NSSet` to return the tracks and has methods to add additional tracks as well.

That's how to generate the code for CoreData entities. You can use these classes for data in the database and access the attributes as data. Let's look at how to do that.

You've now seen how to create a project using CoreData. You've also looked at how to define entities, their attributes, and relationships, and even how to insert and delete instances of the data and the source code. Now you should look at how to display this data to the user in a meaningful way.

7.2 Displaying CoreData for data-driven apps

In the previous section, you saw all about how to create a data-driven project using CoreData as well as how to manage that data in creation of the database and source code.

What you ultimately want is to allow the user to create and manipulate the data via the UI. You need to be able to display the data to the user, allow the user to navigate around the data, and add/delete items in the database (and therefore the UI). Let's see how that's done.

TECHNIQUE 50 Display selected item details

The default project code has a nice table view controller to display the default—and now, your—entity data from the database. This default table view displays a list of your playlists. Because your playlists contain a set, or list, of tracks, let's continue the design and use another table view to display the contents of a given playlist.

You can largely use the same code with changes for the different entity name and attributes. This allows you to create and also access the playlist tracks in the same way as your playlists.

PROBLEM

You need to create a table view controller to display the list of tracks in a selected playlist.

SOLUTION

You can create a new table view controller class based on the default one created for you in the project. Then you'll specify the new table view to display the tracks for the playlist passed into the class.

DISCUSSION

Right-click in the Classes area and select New File. Pick the NSObject as the base class, but this doesn't really matter because you'll replace the contents. Name your new class VCPlayListItems.

Copy and paste the contents of the PlayMyListsMasterViewController.h file into the header of your new class. Do the same from PlayMyListsMasterViewController.m to the VCPlayListItems.m file. Be sure to keep the appropriate class name and import statements.

Like you did when you changed the Event entity to AppPlayList in your code, so you'll do for this class using PlayListTrack where you have AppPlayList. And you'll change the places you have name to be persistentID in your new class.

In the insertNewObject method, you'll need to set the value of your entity to be the right attribute:

```
[newManagedObject setValue:@"New Track" forKey:@"persistentID"];
```

In fetchResultsController, change the entity named to be PlayListTrack:

```
NSEntityDescription *entity =
        [NSEntityDescription entityForName:@"PlayListTrack"
        inManagedObjectContext:self.managedObjectContext];
```

This implementation of the configureCell method doesn't need to access the name attribute because it doesn't exist for the PlayListTrack. You can change it to use the persistentID:

```
- (void)configureCell:(UITableViewCell *)cell
    atIndexPath:(NSIndexPath *)indexPath {

    NSManagedObject *managedObject = [[[playList tracks] allObjects]
        objectAtIndex:indexPath.row];
        // [self.fetchedResultsController
        objectAtIndexPath:indexPath];
    cell.textLabel.text =
        [[managedObject valueForKey:@"persistentID"] description];
}
```

The configureCell method is called from your tableView:cellForRowAtIndexPath: method.

There are several differences to displaying tracks for a given playlist that you'll want to consider. To start, you'll need the selected playlist.

The Master-Detail Application template created the master view controller such that it passes in the selectedObject to the detail view controller in the prepareForSegue method. You can piggyback on this functionality to get the selected playlist to your new table view controller.

TECHNIQUE 51 Passing a Playlist to the Detail View controller

The master view controller already passes in the selectedObject to the detail view controller via the synthesized detailItem member. You can add that same code to your new VCPlayListItems table view controller.

From there, you can access the data in the playlist to display to the user.

PROBLEM

You need the `VCPlayListItems` table view controller to have access to the selected playlist from the master view controller. When you have the reference, you can list the tracks in the table view.

SOLUTION

You can copy the `detailItem`-related code from the detail view controller to your `VCPlayListItems` class and use the reference accordingly.

DISCUSSION

You need to add two lines of code to your `VCPlayListItems` class: one to the header and one to the implementation.

The header file needs the member declaration:

```
@property (strong, nonatomic) id detailItem
```

The implementation needs to synthesize the member:

```
@synthesize detailItem = _detailItem
```

> **NOTE** Optionally, you can change the `detailItem` member to `playList` if you like and change the member type, references, and `setDetailItem` call from the master.

Now, after the playlist is passed in, you can access the tracks to list them in the table view.

Your playlist track listing will have only one section, so you can set that in the `numberOfRowsInSection` method. This is also a good place to make some initializations, so let's call it the `fetchedResultsController` accessor. Because you ignore the returned value, it's going to set up the instance to be used later:

```
- (NSInteger)numberOfSectionsInTableView:(UITableView *)tableView {
    [self fetchedResultsController];
     return 1;
}
```

For the number of rows in that section, you'll return the number of tracks in the play list. Note that the following code will produce an error because the `_detailItem` is declared as ID as opposed to an `AppPlayList` instance. You can fix this by importing the AppPlayList.h file and typecasting the `_detailItem` in each case to `AppPlayList`:

```
- (NSInteger)tableView:(UITableView *)tableView
    numberOfRowsInSection:(NSInteger)section {
    return [[_detailItem tracks] count];
}
```

Now that you have the new `VCPlayListItems` table view displaying the playlist tracks, you can replace the old detail view controller with your new one.

TECHNIQUE 52 Replacing the detail view controller

The default detail view controller was a simple view controller that used a label to display basic data about whatever selected item was passed in. For your app, you have more knowledge about the object and want to display something more appropriate.

Beyond that, you also want the user to be able to add and remove tracks from the selected playlist.

PROBLEM

You need to replace the default detail view controller in the project Storyboard file with your `VCPlayListItems` table view controller.

SOLUTION

In the Storyboard file, you'll remove the detail view controller, drop a new table view controller object in the file, and specify its class to be your `VCPlayListItems` class.

DISCUSSION

Open the Storyboard file, select the Detail View Controller, and delete it. Drop a new table view controller where the old detail view controller was and specify its class to be `VCPlayListItems` in Utilities.

Click on the new `tableview`'s prototype cell and set it's identifier to `TrackCell` in the Attributes Inspector. This will be used as the reuse identifier, `CellIdentifier`, in the code. Set that in the `cellForRowAtIndexPath`: method now.

Control-drag from the table cell of the master view controller's table view to the new `VCPlayListItems` object and specify its segue value to be Push (see figure 7.15). Select the newly created segue and make sure its identifier is set to `showDetail` in the Attributes Inspector of Utilities (see figure 7.16).

Now the existing functionality of the segue will be invoked when the user taps a playlist in the table view. The master view controller will pass in the selected object and the `VCPlayListItems` instance will slide in from the right.

Figure 7.15 Connecting the new detail view controller via master view controller segue

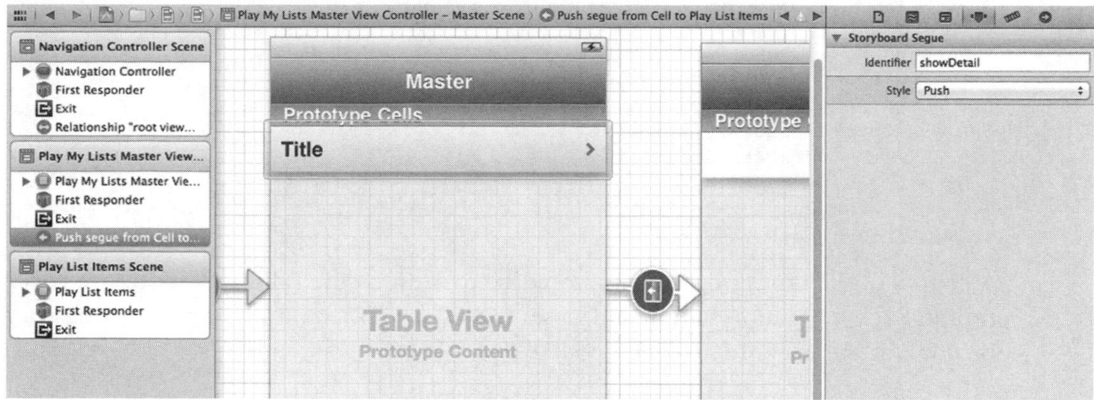

Figure 7.16 Newly created detail view controller and segue from master view controller

You already set up a `VCPlayListItems` class to list the tracks for the playlist, but you haven't created a way for users to add tracks to a playlist. Let's do that now.

TECHNIQUE 53 Managing tracks in the selected playlist

You've mostly prepped the new detail view controller, `VCPlayListItems`, but now you need to implement adding tracks to a playlist.

PROBLEM

The table view isn't updated when the user adds a new track to the playlist. This means the user won't know that the track was added. Also, the table view doesn't update for removing tracks from the playlist.

SOLUTION

Whenever a track is added to the database, the app needs to also add it to the selected playlist. The delegate callbacks will then cause the table view to update with the new data. Similarly, for the table view callback method for deleting a track, you can update the database, which leads to updating the table view.

DISCUSSION

You want to update your table view when a new track is added to the playlist via the (+) button. You know when one is created (in the `insertNewObject` method), so you can update the table there. Because your table is based on the tracks in the playlist and not the database, you need to add the new track to the list and the related `NSFetchedResultsControllerDelegate` callback methods will update the table:

```
[_detailItem addTracksObject:newManagedObject];
```

Like you added the track to the playlist when it was created, you want to remove it when it's deleted. In the `tableView:commitEditingStyle:forRowAtIndexPath:` method, you want to remove the track and delete it. Be sure to remove it from the playlist before you delete it, as shown in the following listing, because removing a deleted track can cause errors.

Remove the track from the playlist, delete it, and reload

```
NSManagedObjectContext *context =
  [self.fetchedResultsController managedObjectContext];
[playList removeTracksObject:
  [self.fetchedResultsController
    objectAtIndexPath:indexPath]];
[context deleteObject:
  [self.fetchedResultsController
    objectAtIndexPath:indexPath]];
```

A couple of nice finishing touches would be to set it so the Edit button doesn't cover up the Back navigation button and to set the title to Tracks. Both of those things can be done in the viewDidLoad method like this:

```
self.navigationItem.leftItemsSupplementBackButton = YES;
    self.title = @"Tracks";
```

Another option would be to set the title to the playlist name passed in, but I'll leave that up to you to decide and implement.

Now that you have the structure for the playlists and tracks, let's look at accessing the user's music to build an actual playlist.

7.3 Accessing iPod music

Every iOS has the Music app in it for playing music. For playing music in general, the Music app is great. But when you want to do something specific to your app with music (such as allowing the user to select a song to play during a game), the app has to handle that itself.

The SDK provides the means to access the music directly and also a UI to allow the user to select audio items. Your app needs to allow the user to select tracks to add to their playlists. Then you'll use the direct API into the music to get the selected items' titles.

TECHNIQUE 54 Using the media picker to access music

As with the address book and image picker, the iOS frameworks give you access to the music in the device. You're provided not only with the data for the audio, but also with a nice, consistent UI for selecting it.

Also, similar to the address book and image picker scenarios, you have callback methods for the media picker classes to notify your app when the user has selected items from the music library.

In creating playlists, you need to use this UI to allow the user to select tracks and notify the app of their choices.

PROBLEM

You need to allow the user to choose audio tracks from their device to add to their playlists.

SOLUTION

You'll use the `MPMediaPlayerController` from the MediaPlayer framework to display a UI that allows the user to select audio tracks. The app will then extract the `persistent ID` from the track data, create a new entry in the database, and relate it to the given playlist being edited.

DISCUSSION

There are four steps in a process like using the media picker controller to select items—you need to lay the groundwork, create and display the controller, handle the callback with the user's selections by extracting out the applicable data, and process the data. In your case, processing the data means storing it in the database as `PlayListTrack` data.

To use the media picker, add the `MediaPlayer.framework` to your project. Also, import the `MediaPlayer/`MediaPlayer.h file into your `VCPlayListItems` header file. The final piece of groundwork here is to change the `addButton` target action to be a new method named `showMediaPicker`, which you'll implement next, as shown in the following listing.

Specify the `addButton` to call `showMediaPicker`

```
UIBarButtonItem *addButton = [[UIBarButtonItem alloc]
                  initWithBarButtonSystemItem:UIBarButtonSystemItemAdd
                  target:self
                  action:@selector(showMediaPicker)];
```

The second part of creating and displaying the controller is handled in `showMediaPicker`. For the most part, you instantiate the media picker, set a few values, and present it, as shown in the following listing.

Creating and displaying the media picker

```
-(void)showMediaPicker
{
    MPMediaPickerController *picker =
                                   [[MPMediaPickerController alloc] init];
    [picker setDelegate: self];                          // For callbacks

    [picker setAllowsPickingMultipleItems: YES];         // Allow multiselect

    picker.prompt = @"Pick Tracks";                      // Title bar text

    [self presentModalViewController: picker animated: YES];
}
```

For the iPhone and iPod, this is fine. But for the simulator, which doesn't have the iPod, this will bog down the app and make it look like there are significant problems. To prevent this, all you have to do is put in a check at the top of the app:

```
if (NSNotFound != [[[UIDevice currentDevice] model]
                        rangeOfString:@"Simulator"].location)
      return;
```

At this point, you can run the app, select a playlist, and tap the Add button to see the media picker (see figure 7.17).

But you're not handling the callbacks, so not only does selecting tracks do no good, but you can't even remove the media picker from the display. Let's take care of that.

The first, and easiest, callback you'll handle is the Cancel callback. When the user taps Cancel, this is what's called and you'll simply dismiss the media picker:

```
- (void)mediaPickerDidCancel:
      (MPMediaPickerController *)mediaPicker
{
    [self dismissModalViewControllerAnimated:YES];
}
```

Figure 7.17 Displaying the media picker

The other callback you're concerned about is when the user taps Done. In that case, you'll check to see if they've made any music selections, create the new database entries, and dismiss the picker, as shown in the following listing.

Pass the media items into `insertNewObject`, reload the table, and dismiss the picker

```
- (void)mediaPicker: (MPMediaPickerController *)mediaPicker
    didPickMediaItems:(MPMediaItemCollection *)mediaItemCollection
{
    for (MPMediaItem *mi in [mediaItemCollection items])
        [self insertNewObject:mi];

    [self.tableView reloadData];                    <-- Remove other call

    [self dismissModalViewControllerAnimated:YES];
}
```

Notice that you're reloading the table here after all the new items have been added. You can remove the same call to the `insertNewObject` method so that it's only called once. Also, you'll see the `insertNewObject` method is being passed to the `MPMediaItem`. Let's update that method to use it.

Previously you entered `New Track` as the persistent ID. That doesn't do you any good now. You need to get the real ID from the media item and store it in the database. Media item properties are accessed through the `valueForProperty:` method similar to what you did with `NSManagedObject` instances, as shown in the following listing.

Fetch the persistent ID and store it in the entity object

```
- (void)insertNewObject:(MPMediaItem*)mediaItem {

    NSString *pID = [NSString stringWithFormat:@"%@",
        [mediaItem valueForProperty:MPMediaItemPropertyPersistentID]];
    if ([[[detailItem tracks] allObjects] containsObject:pID])
        return;                                       <-- Don't duplicate
      ...
    [newManagedObject setValue:pID forKey:@"persistentID"];
```

You check to see if the track is already in the list and return if it is. Also, you can remove the call to `reloadData` here if you haven't done so already (because you're calling it in the media picker callback now).

Now when you run the app on your device and pick media, not only are you able to cancel, but you can also select media and add it to your list (see figure 7.18).

It uses the persistent ID for the display, which is only exciting if you're a developer! Let's look at how to display the title of the track instead.

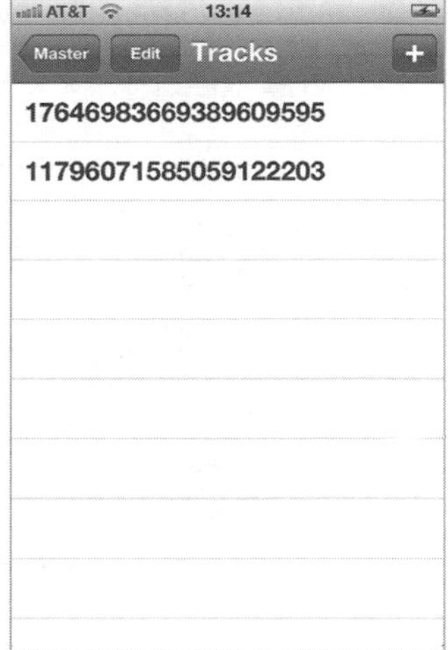

Figure 7.18 Selected media persistent IDs listed for a playlist

TECHNIQUE 55 Finding media info from the iPod

All tracks in the iPod are given a persistent ID that's unique to that track on that device. It won't change on that device, but it won't be the same in another person's iPod database.

Because you stored the persistent ID, you'll be able to find the selected media via the `MPMediaQuery` class. When you have the media item back, you can look up other information including the title. The title would certainly be a more useful piece of information to display in your app.

PROBLEM

You need to find the selected media using the stored persistent ID, retrieve its title, and display that in the table.

SOLUTION

Using the `MPMediaQuery` class, you can retrieve media items matching your selected criteria including your persistent ID. The media query class uses the `MPMediaPropertyPredicate` class to specify the query criteria. You'll specify your `persistentID` and query for your media items.

DISCUSSION

From the `configureCell` method, you already know the index of the item selected from the `indexPath.row` value. With this information, you can get the `managedObject` and retrieve the `persistentID`. By creating an `MPMediaPropertyPredicate` with that, you can filter the items in a `MPMediaQuery` to find your item, as shown in the following listing.

Retrieve your media item via the persistent ID and set the cell text to the title

```
- (void)configureCell:(UITableViewCell *)cell
                                  atIndexPath:(NSIndexPath *)indexPath {

    NSManagedObject *managedObject = [[[detailItem tracks] allObjects]
        objectAtIndex:indexPath.row];
    NSString *pID = [managedObject valueForKey:@"persistentID"];
    NSNumber *longID =
                 [NSNumber numberWithLongLong:[pID longLongValue]];
    MPMediaPropertyPredicate *pred = [MPMediaPropertyPredicate
            predicateWithValue:longID
                      forProperty:MPMediaItemPropertyPersistentID];
    MPMediaQuery *mpQ = [MPMediaQuery songsQuery];
    [mpQ addFilterPredicate:pred];

    NSArray *items = [mpQ items];

    if ([items count] > 0)
        cell.textLabel.text = [[items objectAtIndex:0]
            valueForProperty:MPMediaItemPropertyTitle];
    else
        cell.textLabel.text = @"Unknown Title";          <— If not found
}
```

There are a lot more capabilities in filtering media items via the property predicate that I encourage you to read about. But you get the basic concept: filtering the media items based on the criteria specified.

Now if you run the app (on your device), you'll see the track list with the titles displayed in the table (see figure 7.19).

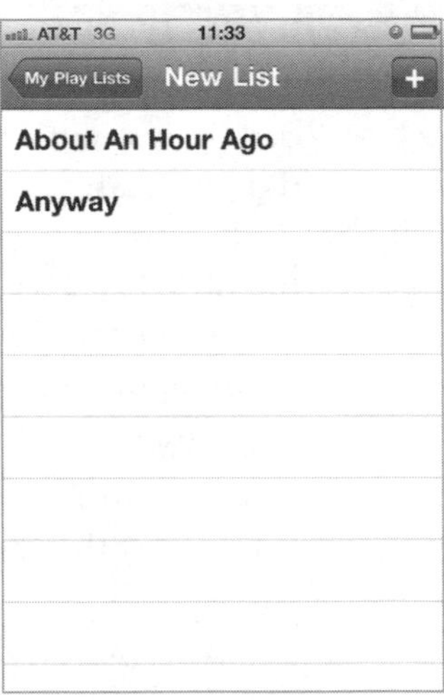

Figure 7.19 Playlist tracks listed with the track titles in the table

In most cases, it would be wiser to store the track title in the database along with the `persistentID` and any other data you'd want to access frequently. But depending on the case, it might be better to always use the latest information (for example, if the data in question changes often, which isn't the case for track titles).

Whether you store a lot of data or very little, you definitely need the `persistentID` to reliably retrieve the track later to play the music. Let's look at how to play the tracks.

7.4 Playing music with iOS

The mobile Apple device family was largely launched by the iPod, which is still a great device, and the iOS devices benefit from that technology. It's still a core use and a core ability of the iPhone, iPod, and iPad, and playing music from within your app isn't complicated.

You've stored the persistent IDs for the selected tracks. That allows you to access the music on the device. From there, you'll need to play the tracks. Because you're dealing with playlists, you'll need to handle when a track ends and when to start playing the next track. You know the order to play them in, so you need to handle the update from the system when the track ends.

TECHNIQUE 56 Playing the playlist

You have the playlist and you know how to access the tracks and find them with `MPMediaQuery`. Now you need to know how to play them.

The SDK provides a controller for playing music. Unlike many of the other framework controllers you've seen, this controller doesn't have a UI. But it does have a delegate that you'll implement to receive updates.

PROBLEM

You need to access the playlist tracks and play the music.

SOLUTION

You'll create an `MPMusicPlayerController`, retrieve all the `MPMediaItems`, and play them in the music player.

DISCUSSION

To keep the UI intuitive and simple, let's start playing the songs when the user taps on a given track. That means you'll launch the playing in the `didSelectRowAtIndexPath:` method. The first thing it should do is return if it detects it's running in the simulator.

You already have the MediaPlayer framework in the project, so you can declare a `MPMusicPlayerController` member named `musicPlayer` in the header. In the `didSelectRowAtIndexPath:` method, you'll create it if it's `nil` (for example, subsequent taps on rows won't create new instances), as shown in the following listing.

Create the music player if necessary or stop playing if you have one

```
if (nil == musicPlayer)
    {
        musicPlayer = [MPMusicPlayerController applicationMusicPlayer];
        [musicPlayer setRepeatMode:MPMusicRepeatModeAll];
    }
    else
        [musicPlayer stop];
```

Next, you can create a list of media items to play in the music player. As you did before, you can use the `MPMediaQuery` class to fetch each track in your playlist. If you add them to a mutable array, you can create an `MPMediaItemCollection` and set that to play, as shown in the following listing.

Creating an `MPMediaItemCollection` to play tracks from a `playList` instance

```
NSMutableArray *tracksToPlay = [NSMutableArray arrayWithCapacity:
        [[[playList tracks] allObjects] count]];
```

```
    for (NSManagedObject *managedObject in [detailItem tracks])
    {
        NSString *pID = [managedObject valueForKey:@"persistentID"];
        NSNumber *longID =
                [NSNumber numberWithLongLong:[pID longLongValue]];
        MPMediaPropertyPredicate *pred = [MPMediaPropertyPredicate
            predicateWithValue:longID
            forProperty:MPMediaItemPropertyPersistentID];
        MPMediaQuery *mpQ = [MPMediaQuery songsQuery];
        [mpQ addFilterPredicate:pred];                          <-- Find the media

        NSArray *items = [mpQ items];

        if ([items count] > 0)
            [tracksToPlay addObjectsFromArray:items];
    }

    MPMediaItemCollection *collection = [MPMediaItemCollection
        collectionWithItems:tracksToPlay];                     <-- Create collection
     [musicPlayer setQueueWithItemCollection:collection];      <-- Add and play
     [musicPlayer play];
}
```

If you run the app, you might notice the tracks have no set order. If you try to play the tracks, there's no logical order they play in. While the preceding code will play the playlist, selecting any row starts the music—not exactly what the user expects!

To correct the order, you can add an `Order` attribute to the `Track` entity in the data model and recreate the code. When each track is added to the playlist, you can set its order to be the number of tracks in the playlist at that time. Now when the playlist tracks are iterated over to be added to the `tracksToPlay` array, they should be sorted first by calling `[[detailItem tracks] sortedArrayUsingDescriptors:[NSArray arrayWithObject:[NSSortDescriptor sortDescriptorWithKey:@"order" ascending:YES]]]`.

TECHNIQUE 57 Handling music player updates

The music player will play continuously because you specified the repeat mode to repeat all (see "Create the music player if necessary or stop playing if you have one"). But you can be notified when the track changes or there are other changes in the music player. Like many music players, it might be nice to display the track name when it starts playing. Let's do that with your player.

The music player can be set to send notifications. The notifications are sent when the state (such as play, pause, or stop) changes or when the item being played changes (for example, goes to the next track). This is how the app will know when to display the track title.

PROBLEM

You'd like to display the track name when it begins playing with the music player.

SOLUTION

You'll specify that the music player should send notifications when changes occur. Also, you'll set your class to be an observer for those notifications and display the track title when a new track begins playing.

DISCUSSION

Back where you created your music player and set the repeat mode, you can also tell it to send notifications and set your class as the observer:

```
[musicPlayer beginGeneratingPlaybackNotifications];
        [[NSNotificationCenter defaultCenter]
            addObserver:self
                selector:@selector(handleNowPlayingChange:)
```

You need to implement the `handleNowPlayingChange:` method to display the track title. The music player can return the currently playing track to your method. You already know how to get the title property. All you have to do is create a label, set the text, and display it, as shown in the following listing.

Begin monitoring music player notifications

```
-(void)handleNowPlayingChange:(NSNotification*)notification
{
    MPMediaItem *nowPlaying = [musicPlayer nowPlayingItem];
    NSString *title =
                [nowPlaying valueForProperty:MPMediaItemPropertyTitle];
    if (nil == lblTitle)
    {
        CGRect r = self.view.frame;
        r.size.height = 44;
        lblTitle = [[UILabel alloc] initWithFrame:r];
        [lblTitle setTextAlignment:UITextAlignmentCenter];
        [lblTitle setTextColor:[UIColor blueColor]];
        [lblTitle setFont:[UIFont boldSystemFontOfSize:22]];
        [lblTitle setBackgroundColor:[UIColor blackColor]];
        [lblTitle setAlpha:0.8];                                   Partially transparent
         [self.view addSubview:lblTitle];
    }
    [lblTitle setText:title];
    [lblTitle setHidden:NO];
    [lblTitle performSelector:@selector(setHidden:)                  Hide after 2 seconds
         withObject:[NSNumber numberWithBool:YES] afterDelay:2.0];
}
```

As you can see, you separate the track display in a few ways including text color, background color, and bold font. Also, after 2 seconds, you have the `setHidden:` method called to remove the label. Run the app on the device and select a track to play to see the label display (see figure 7.20). The label will display over your content, but only for the 2-second delay.

Other notifications from the music player include volume changes and state changes (such as when a track is paused). Depending on your app, you may wish to handle these notifications.

There are also various notifications from the background that allow an app to respond to the lock screen audio controls and even change the lock screen image. See http://wp.me/puRFY-hX.

You can see that it's not too difficult to play music and even have the user select the tracks to play. This can be a great add-on to an app—user-selected soundtrack. Whether it's a game, an exercise app, or something else, adding music can be a great option for the user experience.

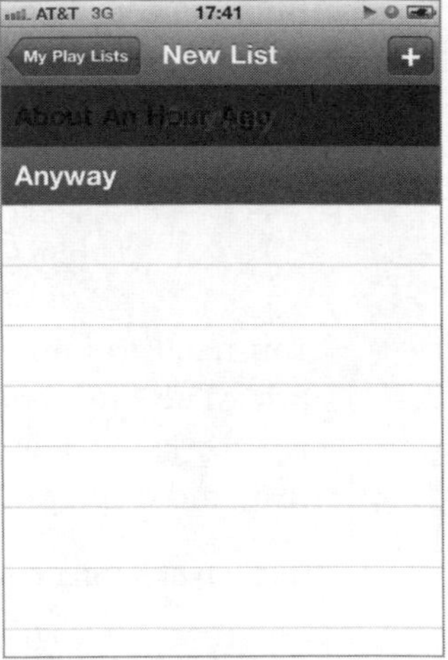

Figure 7.20 Displaying the track title when music player track change notification fires

7.5 Summary

Playing music may only apply to a subset of the apps you develop, but CoreData and databases will probably apply to many more. There are many ways to store data—user defaults, settings, flat files, and so on. But databases get you fast, reliable access and storage while also providing ways to easily associate data via relationships.

While some concepts and implementation of more complex CoreData aspects might be intimidating, I encourage you to practice, experiment, and explore other examples and tutorials. Soon you'll be comfortable with it, and when CoreData is second nature, it's a great and powerful tool to use in your development.

If your app has a server-side component with an online database, CoreData can be even more helpful if you design the databases the same. In the next chapter, you'll design an app that communicates with other users' devices over the internet. Through that, you'll see that having data in the device and on the server can be benefited by the database design in both places.

You've seen how to design CoreData entities with attributes and relationships and manage the data via the code. Using the media picker UI and callbacks, you allowed the user to define playlists. And using the music player without a UI, you played music and responded to notifications of changes to display the track title.

This shows you several more ways that the iOS SDK and frameworks support accessing features and functionality within the device. This functionality and the UI let you leverage some great functionality of the device. In the next chapter, see some ways that Apple allows you to leverage functionality on their servers including Push Notification and In-App Purchase.

8 Push notification and in-app purchase—Rock, Paper, Scissors

This chapter covers

- Push notifications with UrbanAirship
- Setting up in-app purchases
- Building a simple game

Push notification is a way to have a server send a message to a device. The message can include text, a badge number for the specified app's icon, and an audio file included in the app to play.

If the app isn't currently running, the user will see the notification and can open the app. If the app is running, a certain method is called with the notification details, which the app is designed to handle.

In-app purchases are facilitated by the app, but supported by the server, which handles the payment processing. The items available for sale within the app are stored on the server. The information stored is little more than an ID, description, and price. The app can query for salable items from the server, present them to the user, and then initiate the sale.

Apple servers handle the sales transaction, which prompts the user for their iTunes account password. The sale is handled like buying an app, and the user is emailed a receipt. The app is informed of the outcome of the sale (such as success or failure) and can then provide the user with whatever they bought.

Push notifications are initiated on the server, but in-app purchases are initiated by the user in the app. Users purchase something from within the app (such as a new level for a game or additional features). The Apple server then prompts the user to log in using their iTunes account, and the app is notified of the result to handle errors, enable new features, or enable whatever the user purchased.

In this chapter, we'll take a look at how both of these technologies work in an app. You'll learn about and configure both push notifications and in-app purchases and then you'll design the Rock, Paper, Scissors app.

After you set up push notifications and in-app purchases, you'll add them to your project. For your Rock, Paper, Scissors game, you'll allow the user to purchase options to overturn a game they lose. And when they do overturn a loss, the app will send out a notification to let others know what they did.

It's often best to see new concepts in some form of project, so adding these features to your app will be a good learning experience. You'll also use this same project in the next chapter to design GameCenter features.

8.1 Using Apple Push Notification

Push notification is a big way for an app to live outside of itself. While many apps have a server-side portion, it's often in support of the app's use by the user. The server side can be for queries of a database, storing data, or downloading content.

Push notifications allow the app (as the server side) to work even when it's not running. Reminders, updates, and messages are examples of how the app can be effective even when it's not running.

There are various ways to develop the functionality necessary to create push notifications that are pushed to devices through Apple servers. UrbanAirship has an easy-to-use process to facilitate push notifications, and you'll use it in this technique.

Through this technique, you'll see how to provision the app for push notifications on the Apple site as well as the UrbanAirship site, and look at how the two are related. From there, you have the necessary configuration pieces in place, and you can code the app to send and handle push notifications. The code for push notifications in the app is relatively insignificant work compared to the configuration.

TECHNIQUE 58 Provisioning for push notification

There are a few cases where the provisioning in the Provisioning Portal actually needs to be different from the default setting. Push notification and in-app purchase are two of these cases. GameCenter is a third and will be covered in the next chapter.

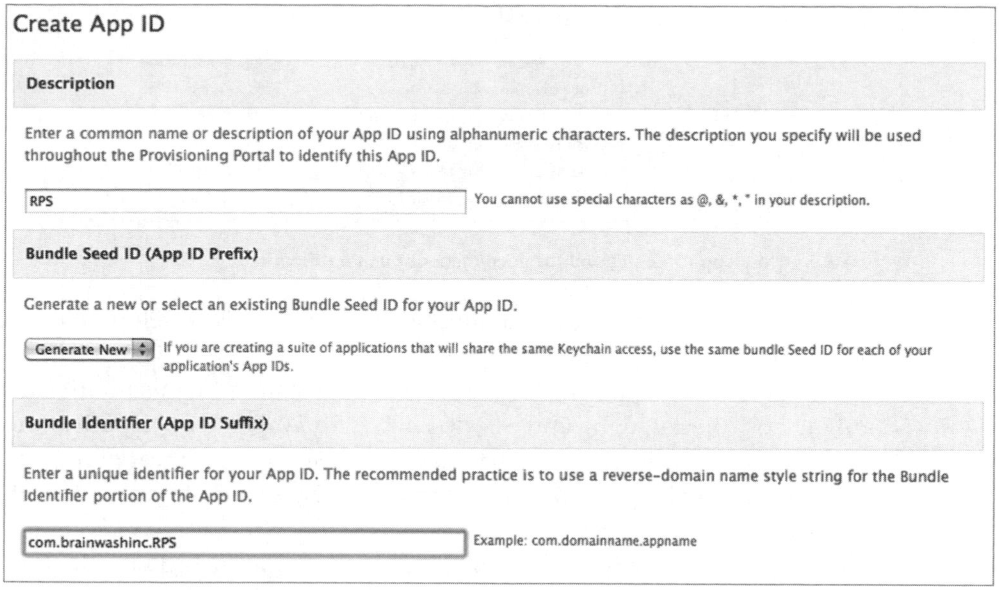

Figure 8.1 Creating a new app ID for Rock, Paper, Scissors in the Provisioning Portal

For provisioning, most of the process is the same as any other case. But you need to export the created certificate to the server for push notifications.

PROBLEM

You need to create a new app ID in the Provisioning Portal with push notification enabled and configured.

SOLUTION

Using the Provisioning Portal, you can create a new app ID. You'll use `com.brainwashinc.RPS`.

DISCUSSION

Because you've set up your certificates in the past, you need to go to the Provisioning Portal, log in (if necessary), and click App IDs. From there, you click New App ID and fill in the necessary info (see figure 8.1).

Click Submit to create the new app ID; notice the new app ID in the listing (see figure 8.2). Also notice that GameCenter and in-app purchase are enabled, but

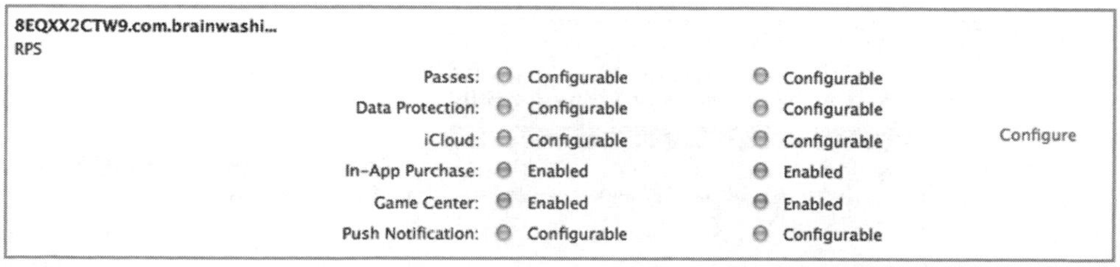

Figure 8.2 New app ID created with GameCenter, in-app purchase, and push notification settings

8EQXX2CTW9.com.brainwashi...
RPS

	Development	Production	
Passes:	Configurable	Configurable	
Data Protection:	Configurable	Configurable	
iCloud:	Configurable	Configurable	Configure
In-App Purchase:	Enabled	Enabled	
Game Center:	Enabled	Enabled	
Push Notification:	Enabled	Enabled	

Figure 8.3 New app ID configured for development push notification

that push notification is set to Configurable. Left column is Development and right is Production.

Now that the new app ID is created, you need to configure push notification. Click Configure on the far right and check Enable for Apple Push Notification Service. Click Configure on the line for Development Push SSL Certificate and submit your Certificate Signing Request like you do for a regular certificate in the Portal. See the How-To tab for details.

When the certificate is ready, click the Download button and save the file. Double-click the saved file in Finder to install it. Now your new app ID is configured for Apple Push Notification (APN) (see figure 8.3).

You'll need to create new provisioning profiles in the Provisioning tab using this app ID. Be sure to name your profiles appropriately, and select the new app ID—RPS. Once created, download these profiles and double-click on them in Finder to install them.

You'll also need the new push notification certificate for whatever server you use for the notifications. Open Keychain, locate the new certificate, and export it by right-clicking and selecting export (see figure 8.4).

When prompted, name the file whatever you like and click Save. You can then choose to enter a password or leave it empty. You won't go through the various options for server-side development of push notifications. Instead, you'll use UrbanAirship for your app. In this case, it's easiest to not use a password for your export, as suggested by their site.

That's the groundwork for using APN. You've created a new app ID for your app and have configured it with the push notification certificate and new provisioning profiles to use in Xcode. Now to configure the server side.

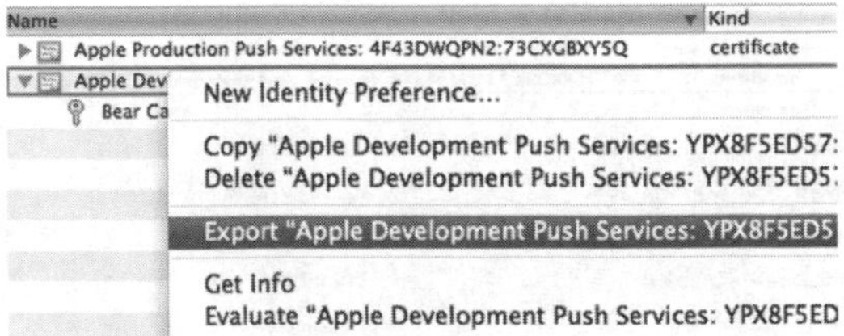

Figure 8.4 Exporting the APN certificate in Keychain

TECHNIQUE 59 Configuring UrbanAirship for APN

As I mentioned in the last technique, there are a variety of ways to develop push notifications from the server side. Depending on your level of server-side development, you might choose one over another.

UrbanAirship provides a solution that's not only already developed and has a good API, but is free (depending on what traffic you generate or package you choose). You'll concentrate on the iOS development and leave the server-side coding to another book. Let's use UrbanAirship!

Fortunately, UrbanAirship has done a great job both with their service and their interface on the web. Their process online is helpful and quick, even the first time you use it.

PROBLEM

You have an app ID that's configured for push notification, but you need to configure the server side. You've decided to use UrbanAirship, so you'll step through their process to configure the app on their server.

SOLUTION

First, you'll create an account with UrbanAirship and then you'll create an app within that account. You'll then try their test app, with the app details generated from the app you create in your account.

DISCUSSION

Create an UrbanAirship account at http://urbanairship.com like you've done on many other websites. After it's created and verified, create a new app in the account (see figure 8.5).

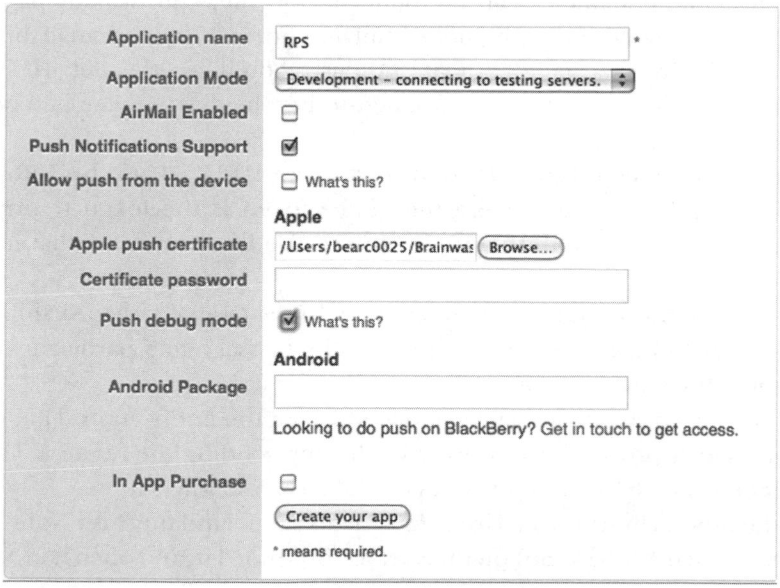

Figure 8.5 Creating a new app in UrbanAirship account

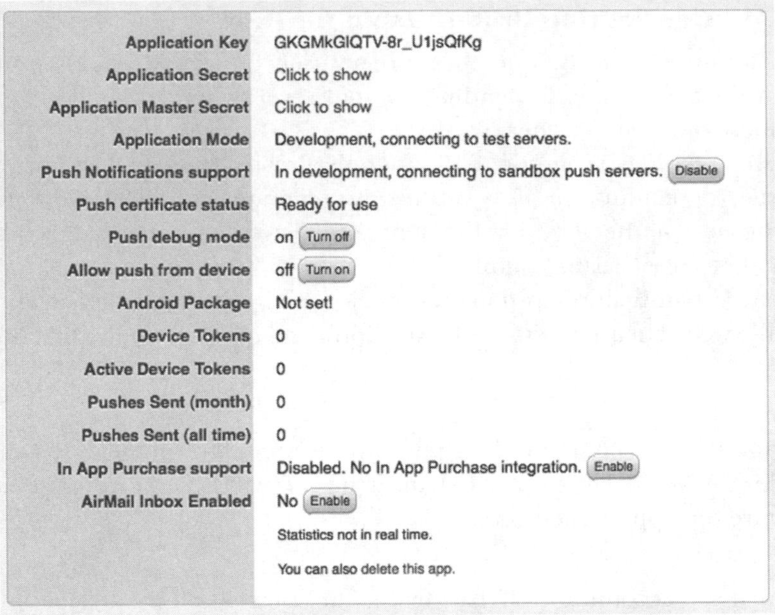

Application Key	GKGMkGIQTV-8r_U1jsQfKg
Application Secret	Click to show
Application Master Secret	Click to show
Application Mode	Development, connecting to test servers.
Push Notifications support	In development, connecting to sandbox push servers. Disable
Push certificate status	Ready for use
Push debug mode	on Turn off
Allow push from device	off Turn on
Android Package	Not set!
Device Tokens	0
Active Device Tokens	0
Pushes Sent (month)	0
Pushes Sent (all time)	0
In App Purchase support	Disabled. No In App Purchase integration. Enable
AirMail Inbox Enabled	No Enable
	Statistics not in real time.
	You can also delete this app.

Figure 8.6 App details in UrbanAirship including app key and secrets

After your app is created, you'll see the app details, including the app key, app secret, and app master secret (see figure 8.6).

Make note of the key and secrets; you'll need those in the app code for use with the UrbanAirship API.

The UrbanAirship documents can be found on the site, and two key pages are http://urbanairship.com/docs/push_index.html and https://docs.urbanairship.com/display/DOCS/Getting+Started%3A+iOS%3A+Push. You'll see the details there—two areas that are particularly interesting are registering the device token and posting a push request.

Registering your device token is done by sending an HTTP PUT to this URL:/api/device_tokens/<device_token>, where the device token is the token returned to your device when it registers with the Apple servers. You'll see more on that in technique 60.

As I said, push notifications are initiated online. In the case of UrbanAirship, their server sends a request to the APN servers to send the message to a particular device. The device is identified by the token.

But something needs to tell UrbanAirship to send out the notification. That can be from a website, server process or, in your case, the app sending the request. The format of the request can be found in the docs on the UrbanAirship site.

Let's test the process by using the UrbanAirship text app. Find the Push Notification Test Client (also called APNS Demo) on their server, download it, and open it in Xcode.

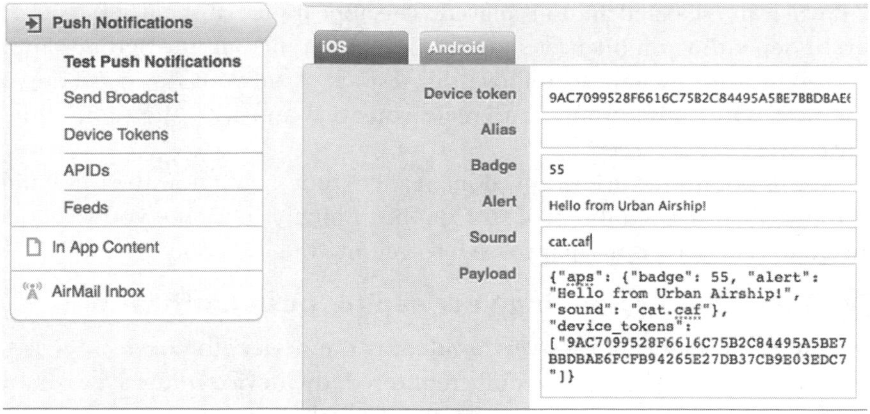

Figure 8.7 Testing push notification to a device via http://urbanairship.com

Use your development profile you created for the new app and set the bundle identifier to match the settings in the Provisioning Profile. Make it appear as though this is your new app configured with Apple and UrbanAirship. Use the key and secrets from UrbanAirship in APNSAppDelegate.m.

Run the app on your device and open the console to view the log. When the device token is printed, copy it. At http://urbanairship.com, go to the Push Notifications tab and select Test Push Notifications. Paste the device token and use whatever other settings you'd like (see figure 8.7).

Send the push notification both with the app running (see figure 8.8) and not running (see figure 8.9) and notice the difference. Notice when the badge number is set

Figure 8.8 UrbanAirship push notification test with demo app running

Figure 8.9 UrbanAirship push notification test with demo app not running

and when the selected audio is played. The appearance of the notification may be different depending on the user's notification preferences in the Settings app.

You'll probably want to remove this test app from your device when you're done testing it. Otherwise, when you create your real app with the same bundle ID, the device will get confused.

At this point, you've basically done it all, except seeing how the iOS handles its side of things. You've used the process from beginning to end, but you've actually written the code. The servers are happy, so let's get into the iOS code.

TECHNIQUE 60 Registering your app for push notifications

For the push notification servers to identify the device, the device needs to be registered with them. When successfully registered, the device returns a token used by the servers. UrbanAirship needs to know this token to know what device to tell the Apple servers to notify.

Apple can take care of the majority of the work here, but you do need to first ask Apple to do it and to handle the response. Let's also look at how you handle the notification when the app is running.

PROBLEM

You need to register the device with the APN servers and handle the returned token. You also need to handle the case when the app is sent a notification while it's running. In your case, you want to display the notification payload.

SOLUTION

First, you'll create a new project and use the settings you decided on when you created the app ID. Next, you'll register the app with the push servers and handle the responses. Similarly, you'll handle the notification itself by implementing the appropriate callback method.

DISCUSSION

Create a Single View project in Xcode like you've done before, and use the app ID settings you set in the portal (see figure 8.10).

In the app delegate class, you add code to register with the APN servers, as shown in the following listing.

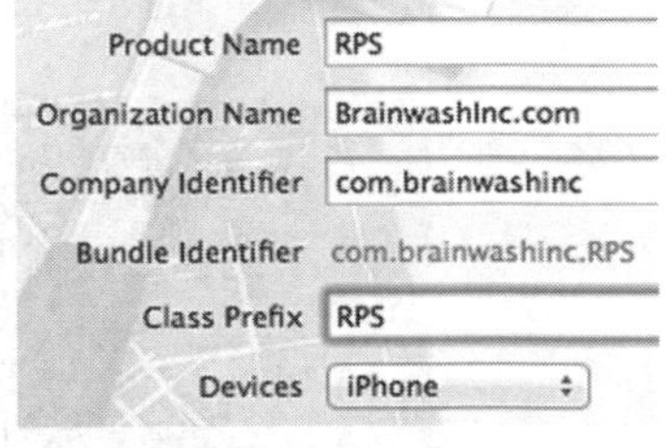

Figure 8.10 Create a new Xcode project based on the new app ID created

Register the device with the APN servers

```
[[UIApplication sharedApplication]
    registerForRemoteNotificationTypes:
                                        (UIRemoteNotificationTypeBadge |
                                         UIRemoteNotificationTypeSound |
                                        UIRemoteNotificationTypeAlert)];
```

There are two callback methods you need to implement. One is for the case where you get a token returned successfully, and one is for when the registration fails, as shown in the following listing.

Push notification server registration callback methods

```
- (void)application:(UIApplication *)app
    didRegisterForRemoteNotificationsWithDeviceToken:(NSData
                                                     *)deviceToken
{
    NSLog(@"deviceToken: %@",deviceToken);
}

- (void)application:(UIApplication *)app
    didFailToRegisterForRemoteNotificationsWithError:(NSError *)err
{
     NSLog(@"APN Registration Error: %@", err);
}
```

In both preceding listings, you log out the applicable information. In the first method, you typically will want to send that token to your server (or UrbanAirship, in your case). You can check to see if the token is different from the last time and not update the server if it hasn't changed.

A similar method is used in the case of receiving a notification during execution. Again, in your case, you'll log on and display the information (see the following listing). Depending on the app, you may need to take more useful action.

Log and display the notification payload when received during app execution

```
- (void)application:(UIApplication *)application
    didReceiveRemoteNotification:(NSDictionary *)userInfo
{
    NSLog(@"APN: %@", [userInfo description]);

    UIAlertView *alert = [[UIAlertView alloc]
               initWithTitle:@"APN"
                  message:[userInfo description]
                 delegate:nil
        cancelButtonTitle:@"OK"
        otherButtonTitles:nil];
    [alert show];                                          <- Display APN
 }
```

This is the core of the app prepping to receive push notifications with Apple. Apple is satisfied at this point, and it's up to you and your server solution to decide what you need and to do it. In your case, you'll send out a notification when the user overturns a loss. Let's look at your server solution setup for that.

TECHNIQUE 61 Registering your app with UrbanAirship

At this point, you have your apps created and configured on the Apple and UrbanAirship servers. You've also registered your device with the APN server. Apple knows how to send you notifications, but UrbanAirship doesn't know how to tell Apple to do it.

In technique 60, you registered the device with the APN server, but didn't do anything with the token returned to the app. You'll register that token with UrbanAirship, so it knows how to tell Apple where to send a notification.

PROBLEM

Your UrbanAirship app configuration is ready to receive commands to send notifications to the APN server, but it doesn't have any device tokens. After the app has registered with the APN server and received a token, you need to register that token with the UrbanAirship server.

SOLUTION

From the UrbanAirship API, you know that you need to send your device token to `/api/device_tokens/<device_token>`. You also need to send the query as a `PUT` and complete authorization using your app key and app secret from your UrbanAirship app configuration.

DISCUSSION

There are three key things that make the HTTP query work in registering the token—the format of the token, the HTTP method, and the authorization.

The token needs to have no spaces in it and have the (<) and (>) symbols removed. It's then appended to the end of the URL from the API (see the following listing). This changes the method that receives the token so it reformats the token and prints it to the console.

Reformat the APN token and log it to the console

```
- (void)application:(UIApplication *)app
    didRegisterForRemoteNotificationsWithDeviceToken:(NSData
                                                         *)deviceToken
{
    NSString *stringToken = [[[[deviceToken description]
             stringByReplacingOccurrencesOfString: @"<"
                                          withString: @""]
             stringByReplacingOccurrencesOfString: @">"
                                          withString: @""]
             stringByReplacingOccurrencesOfString: @" "
                                          withString: @""];

    NSLog(@"stringToken: %@",stringToken);
```

The HTTP method is `PUT`, which is a method call on the URL request. Let's create the URL from the API using the token and set the method to `PUT`, as shown in the following listing.

Create the URL request for the UrbanAirship API and set method to `PUT`

```
NSString *UAServer =
                   @"https://go.urbanairship.com/api/device_tokens/";
    NSString *urlString = [NSString stringWithFormat:@"%@%@/",
                          UAServer, stringToken];
    NSURL *url = [NSURL URLWithString:urlString];

    NSMutableURLRequest *urlRequest = [[NSMutableURLRequest alloc]
                   initWithURL:url];
    [urlRequest setHTTPMethod:@"PUT"];
```

The authorization is more complex, but nothing too crazy. You add a header field to the request for authorization using the app key and secret (see the following listing). Create a string using the app key and secret, separated by (:), and convert that to base 64 (see the UrbanAirship demo app for an example of a method to convert to base 64). Then add that as a value on the URL request for the header field authorization, and send the request.

Create the authorization header field on the request and send

```
NSString *keySecret = [NSString stringWithFormat:@"%@:%@",
                             appKey,
                             appSecret];
    NSString *base64KeySecret = [RPSAppDelegate base64forData:
                   [keySecret dataUsingEncoding:NSUTF8StringEncoding]];
    [urlRequest addValue:[NSString stringWithFormat:@"Basic %@",
                                                   base64KeySecret]
      forHTTPHeaderField:@"Authorization"];

    [[NSURLConnection connectionWithRequest:urlRequest
                       delegate:self]
                        start];
```

Delegate is self

Because the NSURLConnection delegate is self, you need to handle the callback methods for the response or failure (see the following listing). You log out the responses—there's nothing really to do in your case.

Handling the NSURLConnection callback for the server request's response

```
- (void)connection:(NSURLConnection *)theConnection
    didReceiveResponse:(NSURLResponse *)response
{
    NSLog(@"Server Response: %@\nStatus Code: %d",
          [(NSHTTPURLResponse *)response allHeaderFields],
          [(NSHTTPURLResponse *)response statusCode]);
}
- (void)connection:(NSURLConnection *)connection
    didFailWithError:(NSError *)error
{
    NSLog(@"Error Server Response: %@",
          [error userInfo]);
}
```

Now you're fully prepped for UrbanAirship to receive commands to send notifications. The Apple server was already ready to send them when told to, and now UrbanAirship knows how to tell it how and where to send the notifications. Let's look at how to finally send a notification.

TECHNIQUE 62 Sending a batch push notification

There are a variety of notifications you can send and a variety of ways you can send them. Using the UrbanAirship API docs, you can see how to do the various types of sends.

A common option is to send a notification to a single user. Another option is to send a broadcast message, which means everyone with the app will receive the notification (unless they have notifications for the app turned off in the Settings app).

PROBLEM

You need to send a broadcast message to everyone with your app. You'll need to format your payload and send it to the UrbanAirship server using the proper URL.

SOLUTION

From the UrbanAirship API, you know the format of the payload needs to be in JavaScript Object Notation (JSON). You also know the URL is `/api/push/broadcast/`.

By setting the app key and master secret, the request is authorized by the server and sent out to the registered tokens/devices. Typically, the master secret shouldn't be stored in the app, but for your purposes you'll store the master secret in the app.

DISCUSSION

You'll create a new class called `APNSender` to manage your push notification functionality. `APNSender` is based on `NSObject`, and houses a fairly generic `HTTPPost` method to handle the various push notification queries to UrbanAirship.

For the broadcast notification, you really need to specify the URL and the notification payload (see the following listing). You'll include a text message but no badge number or audio file to play.

Method to prepare the notification-specific data to send to UrbanAirship

```
+(void)sendAPNWithMsg:(NSString*)msg;
{
    NSString *url = @"https://go.urbanairship.com/api/push/broadcast/";
    NSString *payload = [NSString
                    stringWithFormat:@"{\"aps\":{\"alert\":\"%@\"}}",
                       msg];

    NSString *resp = [APNSender HTTPPost:url body:payload];
    NSLog(@"Response: %@", resp);
}
```

Notice that the method is static because you don't really need an instance to hold any information. You may decide you'd like to keep something around and do a different route.

Similar methods could be written to send other types of notifications. Either way, you can use the same code to perform the HTTP request, as shown in the following listing.

Method to send HTTP `POST` for a push notification using key and master secret

```
+(NSString*)HTTPPost:(NSString *)urlString body:(NSString*)body;
{
    NSData *postData = [body dataUsingEncoding:NSASCIIStringEncoding
                       allowLossyConversion:YES];
    NSURL *url = [NSURL URLWithString:urlString];

    NSMutableURLRequest *urlRequest = [NSMutableURLRequest
                requestWithURL:url
```

```
                cachePolicy:NSURLRequestReturnCacheDataElseLoad
                timeoutInterval:10.0];

    [urlRequest setHTTPMethod:@"POST"];
    [urlRequest setValue:@"application/json; charset=utf-8"
      forHTTPHeaderField:@"Content-Type"];                    <-- JSON content
     [urlRequest setHTTPBody:postData];

    NSString *keySecret = [NSString stringWithFormat:@"%@:%@",
                           appKey,
                           masterSecret];
    NSString *base64KeySecret = [RPSAppDelegate base64forData:
               [keySecret dataUsingEncoding:NSUTF8StringEncoding]];
    [urlRequest addValue:[NSString stringWithFormat:@"Basic %@",
      base64KeySecret] forHTTPHeaderField:@"Authorization"];

    NSData *urlData;
    NSURLResponse *response;                                   <-- Wait for response
     NSError *error;

    urlData = [NSURLConnection sendSynchronousRequest:urlRequest
                               returningResponse:&response
                                           error:&error];

    if (!urlData)
        return @"";

    NSString *dataString = [[NSString alloc]
                  initWithData:urlData                         <-- Convert to string
                   encoding:NSASCIIStringEncoding];
    return dataString;
}
```

As with registering the token with the UrbanAirship server, this request sets the method, but to `POST` this time. The request also includes the app key and master secret, using base 64 encoding for the authorization header field.

This time, however, you don't use a delegate to receive the response. Instead, you wait for it using a synchronous request call. The response is then converted to a string and returned to the caller to process.

Let's test this functionality by adding a button to the UI to call a `doBtnPush` method that calls your `APNSender` method (see figure 8.11).

Have the `doBtnPush:` method call `APNSender`'s `sendAPNWithMsg:` and send in a test string like `@"Test"` as the message. Don't forget to import the `APNSender` class in the view controller. Run the app on the device and tap your new button to test it (see figure 8.12). Be sure to remove the UrbanAirship demo app before trying to install and run this app.

From the UrbanAirship API docs, you can see the other options and parameters that you can send in the notification. Try using other messages and sending the notification when the app isn't running to see how it goes.

Now you've learned the basics of APN. From this point on, it's mostly variations on a theme—sending to other devices, sending other types of messages, and handling the messages differently. You can see that, depending on the text sent, your app could actually perform other actions.

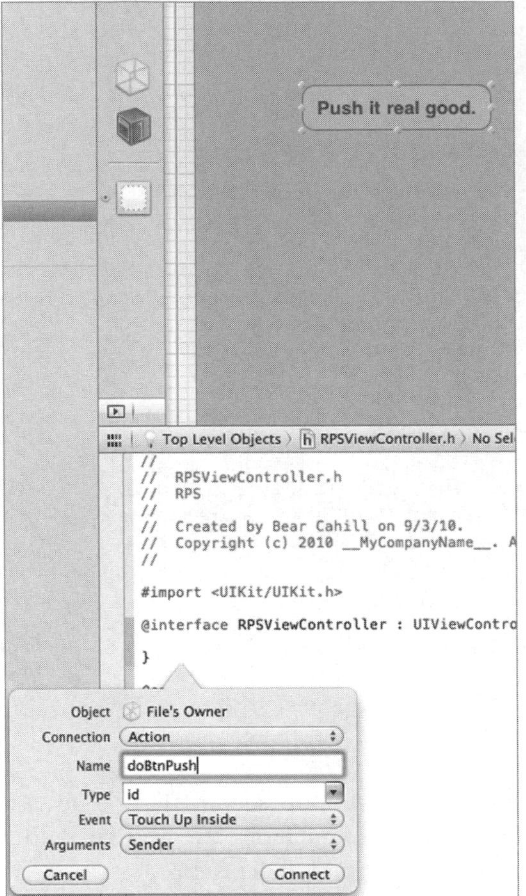

Figure 8.11 Adding a button for `doBtnPush:` action for testing push notification

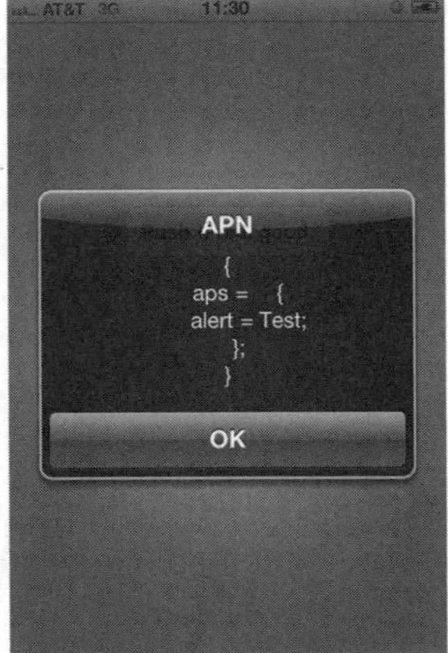

Figure 8.12 Push notification displayed while the app is running

Having a server side to the app allows offline notifications to be sent. Your app could allow for usernames to be set and various users to send messages to other users. Reminders, updates, and state changes—like when a mover takes a turn in a game—are all examples of how push notifications can be used.

Fortunately, Apple handles a lot of the work for the foundation of push notification. You're left to dream up other uses, and to implement the functionality to make those uses work. The use in your game is to announce that the user overturned a loss. But first they have to purchase the ability the overturn a loss. Let's take a look at how you can add that to an app.

8.2 In-app purchase

It's great to have a free game and a paid version, but what if the user has to abandon their data, progress, and images from the free version to upgrade to the paid version?

What about when you add levels to a game and want to release a new version, but all of the current users would then get the added levels for free?

Adding in-app purchase to your app requires a few steps, including configuring iTunesConnect, creating a test account for testing, and adding it to your code. Let's look at these steps in detail.

TECHNIQUE 63 Setting up iTunesConnect for in-app purchase

As with push notification, Apple needs to know that the given app intends to accept in-app purchases. When you created the new app ID back in technique 58, in-app purchase was enabled. That takes care of the Provisioning Portal. You still need to configure iTunesConnect to know about the purchase details.

iTunesConnect stores all of the items the user can purchase. They're specified by a product ID that the app will use to identify what the user wants to buy. These product IDs can also be queried from the server at runtime. That way, you can add new items for sale without updating the app.

PROBLEM

You need to create a new item for in-app purchase in iTunesConnect. You could create many items to sell in iTunesConnect, but you'll look at one item as an example and go from there.

SOLUTION

First you'll create a new app in iTunesConnect, and then you'll add an in-app purchase item to it for the user to purchase.

DISCUSSION

Log on to http://iTunesConnect.apple.com and click Manage Your Applications. Click Add New Application and set the app name, SKU, and bundle ID (see figure 8.13).

Click Continue and set the data, price, description, and other settings including the icon and at least one screenshot. These values can be changed later, so feel free to use placeholder type values for now. Click Save and you should see your new app created (see figure 8.14). I used a white image as my placeholder, so there's not much to look at. Click Done to return to the apps area and click Go Back to return to iTunesConnect front page.

Next, you'll add an in-app purchase item to your app. Click Manage Your In-App Purchases, click Create New, and click on the app you just created.

There are many potential problems that are solved by using in-app purchases, including subscription-based payments. There are three different types of items that a

App Name Rock, Paper, Scissors Network
SKU Number RPS
Bundle ID RPS - com.brainwashinc.RPS
You can register a new Bundle ID here.

Figure 8.13 Creating a new app in iTunesConnect

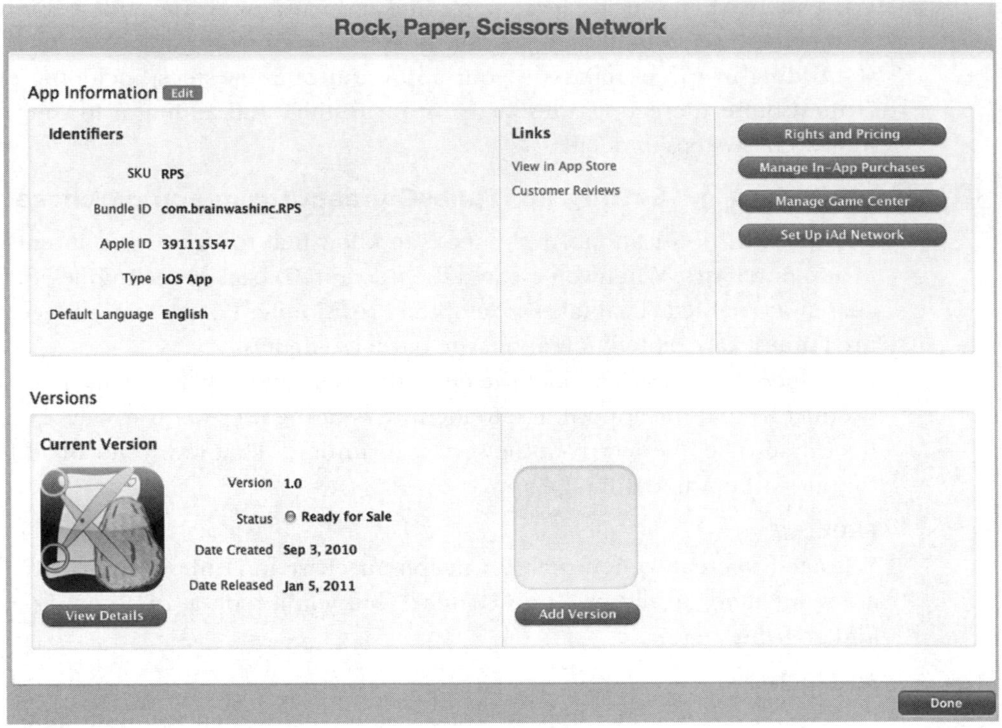

Figure 8.14 New app created in iTunes

user can buy through in-app purchase: consumable, nonconsumable, and subscription-based items.

A nonconsumable item is something that the user buys one time and has from then on. Examples include new game levels, media content, and advanced features of an app.

A consumable item is something the user buys and then uses, so at some point it's gone. This might include fuel for a vehicle in your game, a temporary ability for a character, or access to a one-time event.

Subscriptions are a combination of the other two types. Users may make subscription purchases repeatedly, but the content provided doesn't go away. Examples of this are monthly access to reports or media content like magazines.

You'll sell an *overturn* consumable item. This is an item that allows users to overturn a loss when playing the game. It's only used one time, so it's a consumable, and users can buy as many as they like.

Set a reference name, product ID, type, and price (see figure 8.15). None of these values except the price will be seen by the user. The product ID will be sent from the code and can be descriptive or not. As an example, I used a number to show that there's no defined format. Reverse DNS is a good, real-world value for this, because you may have several items to purchase for several apps.

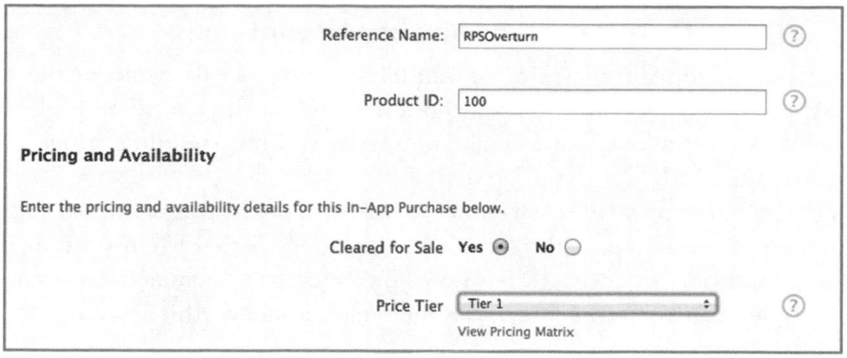

Reference Name: RPSOverturn

Product ID: 100

Pricing and Availability

Enter the pricing and availability details for this In-App Purchase below.

Cleared for Sale Yes No

Price Tier Tier 1

View Pricing Matrix

Figure 8.15 Settings for adding an in-app purchase

You have to add at least one language to the item (see figure 8.16). I added English and set the display name to be something meaningful. The display name and description should be worded in such a way as to explain to the user what they're purchasing.

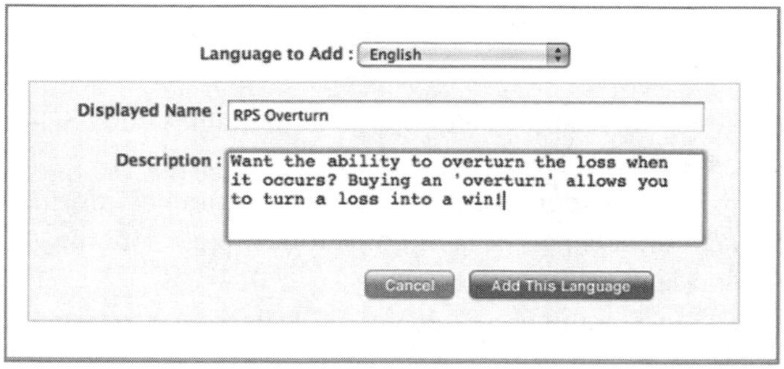

Language to Add : English

Displayed Name : RPS Overturn

Description : Want the ability to overturn the loss when it occurs? Buying an 'overturn' allows you to turn a loss into a win!

Cancel Add This Language

Figure 8.16 Adding a language and details to an in-app purchase item

When you're done here, be sure to click Save and you'll see your new item listed (see figure 8.17).

Notice the status is set to Pending Developer Approval. Click on the item in the list, add a screenshot to the item, and click Approve.

Notice the note that appears with the text: "To have this in-app purchase reviewed along with your app version, go to the app's Version Details page and select this in-app purchase." If you don't do this, your in-app purchase item will need to be reviewed separately—this is also true in the case of adding in-app purchase items later without updating your app.

At this point, your in-app purchase is ready to be tested. It's available for sale in the sandbox testing area. But you may not have an account in the sandbox area. Let's create an account now so you can test your purchase.

1 result

Reference Name	Product ID	Cleared for Sale	Status
RPSOverturn	100		Pending Developer Approval

Figure 8.17 New in-app purchase item listed in iTunesConnect

TECHNIQUE 64 Creating an in-app test account

Testing your in-app purchase in the sandbox allows you to perform the purchase using Apple servers and processes without actually having the item available in the real world. Also, it allows you to make purchases without spending money. Unfortunately, this is the only place you can do that!

All of the steps you've done so far are in line with the testing sandbox. The production version of these steps is the same. The difference is that when your app's in production, real users can access it. For now, you'll need a special account to access and test purchases. iTunesConnect provides the means to create this account.

PROBLEM

You need a way to test your in-app purchase. Apple allows the item to be available in the sandbox so that you can test it on their servers. But you need an account there for testing.

SOLUTION

In iTunesConnect, you'll create a test in-app purchase account that allows you to perform in-app purchases.

DISCUSSION

Log on to http://iTunesConnect.apple.com and click Manage Users. Select In App Purchase Test User and click Add New User.

Fill out the account information using real and memorable information. You shouldn't receive any validation emails or communications, but it's always good to use details you can remember later (see figure 8.18).

After you click Save, your account is created and is available for testing in the sandbox for in-app purchases.

You've created the in-app purchase item to sell and an account to buy it. Let's get into the code and add the functionality to test the purchase.

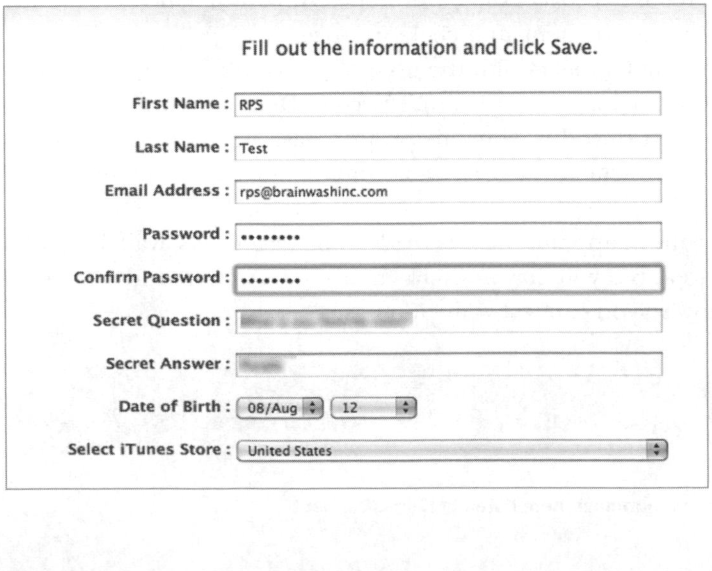

Figure 8.18 Creating an in-app test user account in iTunesConnect

TECHNIQUE 65 Adding in-app purchases to the project

Two of the three pieces for in-app purchases are in place now. You've created the item to sell and the account to buy it; now you need to add the code.

The Apple process handles most of the heavy lifting and even helps with the lighter stuff. The user uses their iTunes account to make the purchase and Apple handles the login process for you. Basically, you need to initiate the purchase when the user asks you to and handle the result.

Using StoreKit classes, you'll create a payment and add it to the queue for processing by the Apple servers. By setting your class to be the *observer*, you'll receive the result of the transaction to handle accordingly.

PROBLEM

You need to add in-app purchase to your project by interfacing with the process both in starting the purchase and handling the result.

SOLUTION

You'll use the StoreKit framework to initiate a payment for an in-app purchase item. You'll set the class as the observer so that the callback methods are called based on the results of the purchase. You need to handle the purchase as succeeding, failing, or being a duplicate purchase.

DISCUSSION

You need to add the StoreKit framework to your project and import it into your `RPSViewController` header file. You also need to add a Buy button to the project that calls a new action called `doBtnBuy:`.

The `doBtnBuy:` method needs to initiate the purchase, but it also needs to check to see if this account is set up to make purchases. Some accounts aren't configured to make payments. For example, parents can disable payment for their children.

If the account is able to make payments, you'll create an instance of `SKPayment`, add it to the default payment queue, and set Self as the observer (see the following listing). `RPSOverturn` needs to be defined as your in-app purchase item ID. In your case, this is `100`.

Initiating a purchase if the account is authorized to make payments

```
- (IBAction)doBtnBuy:(id)sender;
{
   if ([SKPaymentQueue canMakePayments])
    {
       SKPayment *payment = [SKPayment
                         paymentWithProductIdentifier:RPSOverturn];     <- Your item ID
        [[SKPaymentQueue defaultQueue]
           addPayment:payment];                        <- Add to queue
        [[SKPaymentQueue defaultQueue]
           addTransactionObserver:self];               <- To receive results
    }
    else
    {
       UIAlertView *alert = [[UIAlertView alloc]
```

```
                                      initWithTitle:@"Not Authorized"
                                      message:@"Not authorized to purchase."
                                      delegate:self
                                      cancelButtonTitle:@"OK"
                                      otherButtonTitles: nil];
        [alert show];
    }
}
```

You need to implement the method to handle the transaction updates. The transactions come back as an array, because several purchases may have been made. Depending on the state, you'll call the applicable method (see the following listing). Because you're only selling one thing, even if the user started several purchases before you received a response, you can handle them all the same.

Based on the transaction state, call the appropriate method

```
- (void)paymentQueue:(SKPaymentQueue *)queue
          updatedTransactions:(NSArray *)transactions
{
    for (SKPaymentTransaction *transaction in transactions)
    {
        switch (transaction.transactionState)
        {
            case SKPaymentTransactionStatePurchased:
                [self completeTransaction:transaction];
                break;
            case SKPaymentTransactionStateFailed:
                [self failedTransaction:transaction];
                break;
            case SKPaymentTransactionStateRestored:
                [self restoreTransaction:transaction];
            default:
                break;
        }
    }
}
```

Next, you need to implement these three new methods for the various states. In each case, you'll finish the transaction by calling the `finishTransaction:` method on the default payment queue.

In the case of a failure, you can show some possibly helpful information to the user. The transaction's error number may contain information as to why it failed and a possible suggestion, as shown in the following listing.

Displaying information about the failed transaction to the user

```
- (void) failedTransaction: (SKPaymentTransaction *)transaction
{
    if (transaction.error.code != SKErrorPaymentCancelled)
    {
        NSString *messageToBeShown = [NSString
            stringWithFormat:@"Reason: %@, You can try: %@",
```

```
            [transaction.error localizedFailureReason],
            [transaction.error localizedRecoverySuggestion]];
        UIAlertView *alert = [[UIAlertView alloc]
            initWithTitle:@"Unable to complete your purchase"
            message:messageToBeShown
            delegate:self
            cancelButtonTitle:@"OK"
            otherButtonTitles: nil];
        [alert show];
    }
    [[SKPaymentQueue defaultQueue] finishTransaction: transaction];
}
```

A restore state means the user has purchased this item before and that it can be restored. This is for nonconsumable items, where the user already bought the new game level, for example. This may happen if the user somehow loses some data, including what they purchased. They aren't charged for the item, but the app is told to restore what was previously purchased. In your case, this won't happen because you are only selling consumable items, but you'll handle it anyway and finish the transaction, as shown in the following listing.

Finish the transaction in the case of restore state

```
- (void) restoreTransaction: (SKPaymentTransaction *)transaction
{
    [[SKPaymentQueue defaultQueue] finishTransaction: transaction];
}
```

Finally, in the case of a successful purchase, you'll increment the number of overturns purchased and save the purchase to the device. You'll also log this out, so you can see that it happened, as shown in the following listing.

Increment the overturns count for successful purchase and store it

```
- (void) completeTransaction: (SKPaymentTransaction *)transaction
{
    int overturns = [[NSUserDefaults standardUserDefaults]
                      integerForKey:RPSOverturnCount];
    overturns++;
    NSLog(@"number of overturns: %d", overturns);
    [[NSUserDefaults standardUserDefaults]
        setInteger:overturns
        forKey:RPSOverturnCount];

    [[SKPaymentQueue defaultQueue] finishTransaction: transaction];
}
```

You're now ready to test the purchase. Before you run the app, open iTunes on your device, go to the Featured tab and scroll to the bottom. Click on your account name and log out. If you skip this step, when you try the purchase, it will try to use your current iTunes account.

Run the app on the device and tap the Buy button (see figure 8.19). You'll be prompted to log in—be sure to use the in-app purchase test account.

Feel free to put additional log statements in the code and watch the log console as you go through the process. You should see the overturns count increment with each purchase and a "Thank You—Your purchase was successful" message displayed.

You're only selling one item, but you may sell several or many. In that case, you may not want to add all of the IDs to your code. You may not even know what all of the items will be over time. The framework has other methods to support greater functionality with purchases, such as querying for details on given product identifiers.

Figure 8.19 Logging in with the in-app purchase test account in making a purchase

Congrats! You've accomplished a lot. The concepts we've covered so far in this chapter are fairly stout. These are low-level functions that are great for supporting the functionality and usefulness of an app, but they don't really make an app on their own.

You now have these items to support your app so let's go write it!

8.3 The Rock, Paper, Scissors game

You've put a lot of foundational work in place with configuring the app online and writing support methods for push notification and in-app purchases. But you need a game to hang these pieces on.

You'll use the basic but timeless game of Rock, Paper, Scissors. The user can make their selection, and then a random number will determine the computer opponent's selection and determine the win or loss.

You'll also handle the case when the user wants to overturn a loss. If they've purchased overturns, a loss will turn into a win. Otherwise, you'll let them know they need to purchase overturns.

TECHNIQUE 66 Designing the game

You need to write code that adds some form of interface for the game, as well as handles the game play itself. The game is fairly simple, but has limitless replay value for most people.

The UI is basically three buttons for the three selections and a button to overturn. Your UI will handle these actions like most other buttons. But you'll need to process the user selections in light of the game logic.

PROBLEM

You need to design the UI for your Rock, Paper, Scissors game using three options and the Overturn and Buy buttons.

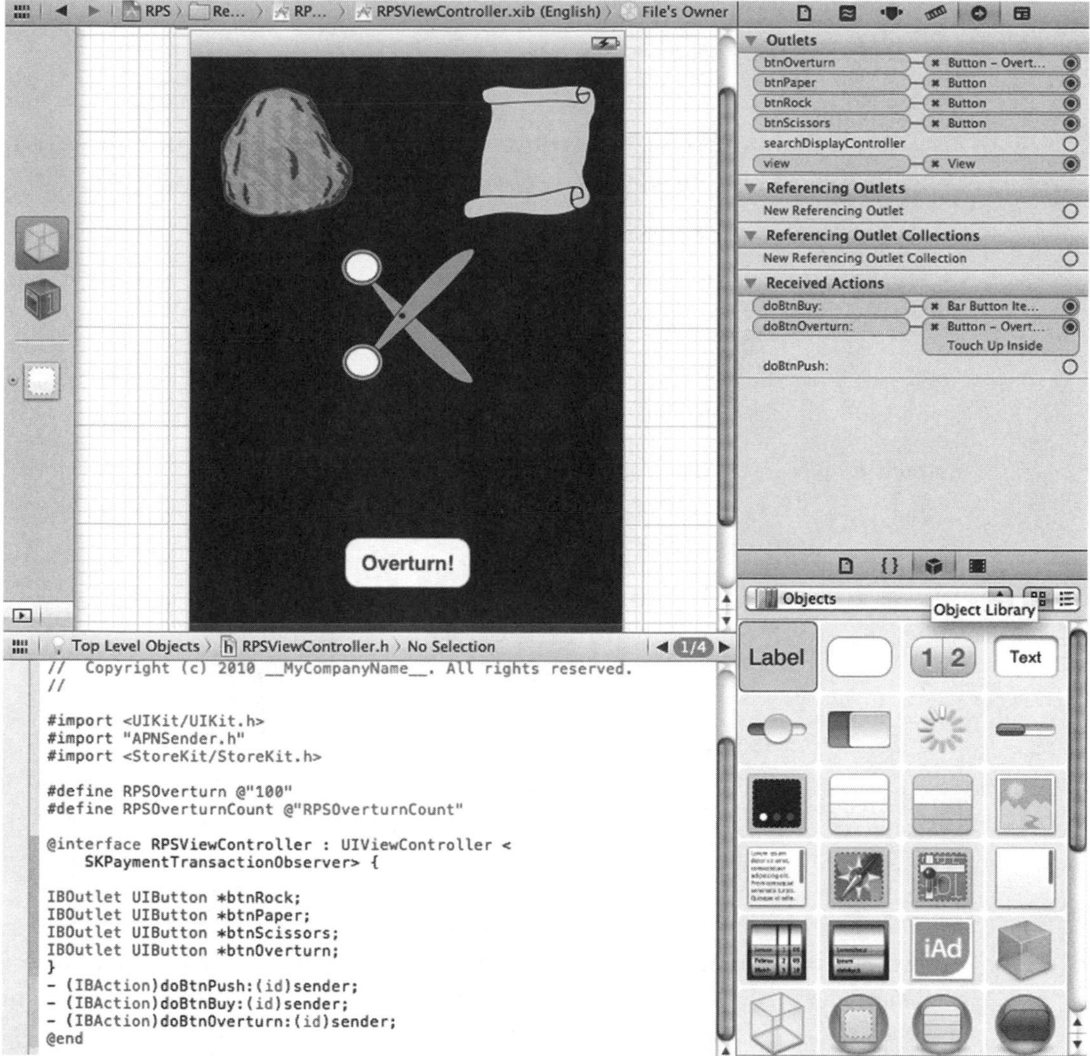

Figure 8.20 Designing the UI for Rock, Paper, Scissors

SOLUTION

You'll use IB and the UI editor in Xcode to create the interface, outlets, and actions.

DISCUSSION

Open the RPSViewController.xib file and create the UI layout for the buttons, actions, and outlets (see figure 8.20).

A toolbar at the bottom is best for a Buy button because it's more a function of the app than a part of the game.

In the header file, you need to define some values used for player selections, as shown in the following listing.

Player selection choices defined in the header

```
#define ROCK 0
#define PAPER 1
#define SCISSORS 2
```

You also need to store some values during the game, like what the user chose, if this game is a win, and the total points for this session, as shown in the following listing.

Data members for storing aspects of the game during play

```
int myChoice;
    bool isWin;
    int gamePoints;
```

Next, you'll handle the button actions when the users make their selections, as shown in the following listing.

Methods for processing the user's selection during play

```
- (IBAction)doBtnRock:(id)sender;
{
    myChoice = ROCK;
    [self waitForOtherPlayer];
}

- (IBAction)doBtnPaper:(id)sender;
{
    myChoice = PAPER;
    [self waitForOtherPlayer];
}

- (IBAction)doBtnScissors:(id)sender;
{
    myChoice = SCISSORS;
    [self waitForOtherPlayer];
}
```

In this case, the computer will be the other player and generate a random number for the *other* player (see the following listing). After the computer has selected, you'll process the results of the game.

Computer player selection and call to process the results

```
-(void)waitForOtherPlayer;
{
    int otherPlayerChoice = rand()%3;
    [self processOtherPlayersChoice:otherPlayerChoice];
}
```

Processing the results consists of comparing the two selections, setting the win flag, and increasing the points for the user, as shown in the following listing.

Process the results to determine a win and points

```
-(void)processOtherPlayersChoice:(int)otherPlayerChoice;
{
    isWin = NO;
```

```
    NSLog(@"My Choice: %d Other Player's Choice: %d",
                    myChoice, otherPlayerChoice);
    if (otherPlayerChoice != myChoice)
    {
        int diff = myChoice - otherPlayerChoice;
        if (diff == 1 || diff == -2)
        {
            gamePoints++;
            isWin = YES;
        }
    }
    NSLog(@"Win: %@ Points: %d", isWin ? @"Yes" : @"No", gamePoints);
}
```

Because the selections are essentially numeric, you can do a fairly basic comparison to see if they're equal or not. If they're not equal, you can do a difference to see if it's a win: 1 beats 0, 2 beats 1, and 0 beats 2. If the difference is 1 or 2, the user wins.

You're printing out to the log the choices, points, and win info. But it would be nice to display to the user the total points. You can add a label to the UI as an outlet in the class and update it in the processing method, as shown in the following listing.

Update the label with the total points to display to the user

```
[lblPoints setText:[NSString stringWithFormat:@"Points: %d",
                                                    gamePoints]];
```

Now you have the log and label to display score data (see figure 8.21).

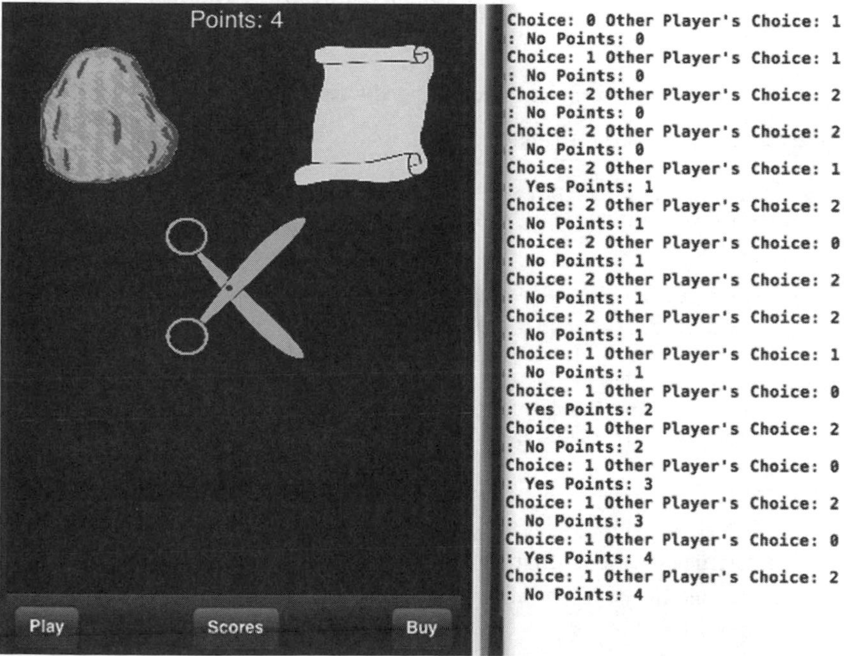

Figure 8.21 Xcode console and simulator running the app with score data

Playing the game will randomly result in some wins and some losses. Losing stinks, so let's give the user a way to overturn a loss and pay you some money at the same time—it's a win-win!

TECHNIQUE 67 Overturning a loss

Overturning a loss is easy … at least in this game. You need to implement your action for the Overturn button. The `doBtnOverturn:` action needs to check the number of available overturns and use one if available.

If the user doesn't have any overturns, you can let them know and suggest they buy some more. It's not a good idea to automatically start the purchase process without the user selecting it specifically. That could be a real turnoff and frustrate the user. They may not even realize they're making a purchase until they get a receipt. Both are bad possibilities.

PROBLEM

You need to give the user the option to overturn a loss. The app needs to check the overturn count and handle it appropriately.

SOLUTION

If the user has purchased overturn credits, they'll be stored in the device. If they haven't purchased any, this value will be zero, which works perfectly. You'll check that value and overturn the loss.

DISCUSSION

You can access the overturn count on the device and notify the user if they don't have any, as shown in the following listing.

Checking the number of overturns and prompting the user if zero

```
-(IBAction)doBtnOverturn:(id)sender;
{
    int overturns = [[NSUserDefaults standardUserDefaults]
        integerForKey:RPSOverturnCount];
    if (overturns == 0)
    {
        UIAlertView *av = [[UIAlertView alloc]
            initWithTitle:@"No Overturns"
            message:@"You do not currently have any overturns.\n\nTap
'Buy' below to buy overturn credits."
            delegate:nil cancelButtonTitle:@"OK"
            otherButtonTitles:nil];
        [av show];
        return;
    }
```

If there are overturns and the current game is a win, you can tell the user they don't need to overturn, as shown in the following listing.

Notifying the winning user they don't need an overturn

```
if (isWin)
        {
            UIAlertView *av = [[UIAlertView alloc]
                initWithTitle:@"No Overturns"
                message:@"Ummm, but you won."
                delegate:nil cancelButtonTitle:@"Oops"
                otherButtonTitles:nil];
            [av show];
            return;
        }
```

Finally, if you're past those steps, you have at least one overturn, and the current round is a loss. You'll decrease the number of overturns, store that, reset the win flag, and increment the points, as shown in the following listing.

Handling an overturn by setting the new overturn value, flag, and points

```
overturns--;
[[NSUserDefaults standardUserDefaults]
    setInteger:overturns
    forKey:RPSOverturnCount];
isWin = YES;
gamePoints++;
[lblPoints setText:[NSString
    stringWithFormat:@"Points: %d", gamePoints]];
[APNSender sendAPNWithMsg:@"Loss overturned!"];        <- Tell the world
```

Notice that you also set the points in the label and send out a push notification (to everyone) that a loss was overturned. In the real world, this probably isn't a good idea, but for now it's fun … and you're the only person that will see this!

8.4 Summary

We've covered a lot of concepts and have been between the Provisioning Portal, iTunesConnect, and UrbanAirship, and all over Xcode. These are great concepts to be familiar with and to add to your apps when and where they're applicable.

Using iTunesConnect, you're able to provision the app to use push notification and in-app purchase. You can then export the certificate from KeyChain to use on the server for notifications. In iTunesConnect, you can also create and manage the items your app can sell and create a test account to purchase within the sandbox.

These concepts are pretty hefty, though your game isn't. In the next chapter, you'll continue with your game to see how you can make it better. One great addition would be to allow the user to play other users over the network. Then it gets interesting, and overturns actually mean something!

9 GameCenter leaderboards and achievements— Rock, Paper, Scissors

This chapter covers

- Working with GameCenter
- Creating leaderboards for your games
- Playing and chatting with others

GameCenter is a great way to open your app up to a more social aspect of gaming. It includes leaderboards, achievements, and even chatting within the app. In this chapter you'll take the Rock, Paper, Scissors game from chapter 8 and add GameCenter functionality to it.

Using GameCenter, a player can view their past game scores and achievements, as well as the scores and achievements of friends. They can invite friends to play games through GameCenter, which matches the devices up to play together.

In this chapter, you'll look at techniques for authenticating players in GameCenter and using leaderboards and achievements. Leaderboards allow your app to store a user's score and display the leaderboard as a view. Achievements are similar to leaderboards, but are stored as a percentage (for example, 100% means the player achieved the goal).

The last few techniques will explore matching players up for games, and even voice chatting within the app using GameCenter.

9.1 Game Center authentication and leaderboards

GameCenter requires the user to create a username and password in order to store and display score and achievement data. A lot of the work and user interface (UI) is provided in GameKit, but there's still work to do in the app and in iTunesConnect.

In this section, you'll look at setting up the Rock, Paper, Scissors app to authenticate the user in GameCenter, configuring the app for leaderboards in iTunesConnect, and saving and displaying users' scores.

TECHNIQUE 68 Authenticating the player

PROBLEM

Users can't interact with GameCenter to store and view scores without authenticating their account. GameKit helps out a lot, but the app has to tell GameKit to authenticate.

SOLUTION

The Rock, Paper, Scissors app needs to use GameKit to get the `GKLocalPlayer` instance and kick off the authentication process. The UI will be displayed if necessary or the authentication will happen automatically (in subsequent launches).

DISCUSSION

The GameKit framework handles the majority of the heavy lifting for GameCenter. With the Rock, Paper, Scissors project open, add the GameKit framework to the project. Create a new class based on `NSObject` and name it `UtilGameCenter`. You'll isolate your GameCenter-related code here for reuse in other projects later.

In your new header file, UtilGameCenter.h, import `GameKit/`GameKit.h and declare a bool flag named `gameCenterFeaturesEnabled` (see the following listing). The flag will be set to `Yes` when the user has been authenticated so the app knows it can communicate with GameCenter.

UtilGameCenter header file with imported GameKit and flag

```
#import <Foundation/Foundation.h>
#import <GameKit/GameKit.h>

@interface UtilGameCenter : NSObject  {

    bool gameCenterFeaturesEnabled;
}
@property (nonatomic, assign) bool gameCenterFeaturesEnabled;

@end
```

Be sure to synthesize `gameCenterFeaturesEnabled` in the implementation file.

Declare an authenticate method in the header file and implement it in the .m file to get the local player and to authenticate the player with GameCenter, as shown in the following listing.

Get the `GKLocalPlayer` and authenticate with GameCenter

```
-(void)authenticate;
{
    GKLocalPlayer *locPlayer = [GKLocalPlayer localPlayer];
    [locPlayer authenticateWithCompletionHandler:^(NSError *error)
    {
        if (!error)
            self.gameCenterFeaturesEnabled = YES;
        else
            self.gameCenterFeaturesEnabled = NO;
    }];
}
```

Set enabled flag

The authenticate method can be called at almost any time, so let's call it when the `UtilGameCenter` is initialized, as shown in the following listing.

`UtilGameCenter` init method calls authenticate for GameCenter

```
- (id)init {
    if ((self = [super init])) {
        [self authenticate];
    }

    return self;
}
```

Back in `RPSViewController`, you need to kick the whole process off for GameCenter. You can import the UtilGameCenter.h in the `RPSViewController` header and declare a GameCenter variable of `UtilGameCenter`. In the `viewDidLoad` method, you can create the `UtilGameCenter`, which does the authentication, as shown in the following listing.

`RPSViewControllerviewDidLoad` starts GameCenter authentication

```
- (void)viewDidLoad {
    [super viewDidLoad];
    gameCenter = [[UtilGameCenter alloc] init];
}
```

Now, when you run the app, GameCenter will be engaged, you can set up your account, and you're in. The next time you run the app, the authentication will be automatic (see figure 9.1).

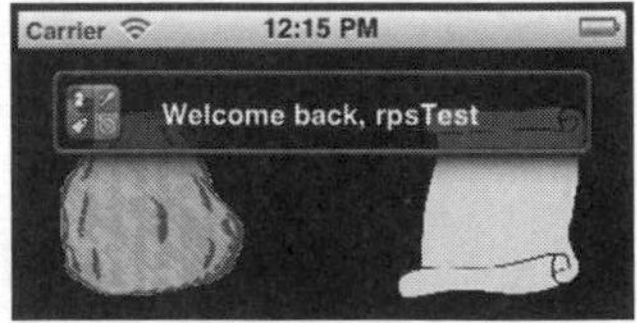

Figure 9.1 GameCenter authentication at launch welcome back

Now the app authenticates the user with GameCenter, but it doesn't do anything else. One of the main uses of GameCenter is to store user scores. Let's look at how to set up iTunesConnect for an app to use GameCenter leaderboards.

TECHNIQUE 69 Configuring leaderboards in iTunesConnect

Configuring a leaderboard in iTunesConnect is a fairly straightforward process. Mostly iTunesConnect needs to know that there is a leaderboard for the given app and some details like the format of the data and a name for the leaderboard.

PROBLEM

You need to set up a leaderboard for your Rock, Paper, Scissors app in iTunesConnect. This will allow the app to store users' scores.

SOLUTION

iTunesConnect provides an interface online to create and configure leaderboards for apps. Through fairly clear forms, someone can log into the site and create a leaderboard with little technical process.

DISCUSSION

To get to the leaderboard creation area for an app, log into iTunesConnect (http://itunesconnect.apple.com). Click Manage Your Applications, click on your app icon, and click Manage GameCenter. Click Enable and, in the leaderboard area, click Add Leaderboard and then select Choose under Single Leaderboard (see figure 9.2).

Enter values for your new leaderboard including reference name, leaderboard ID, format type, and sort order (see figures 9.3 and 9.4).

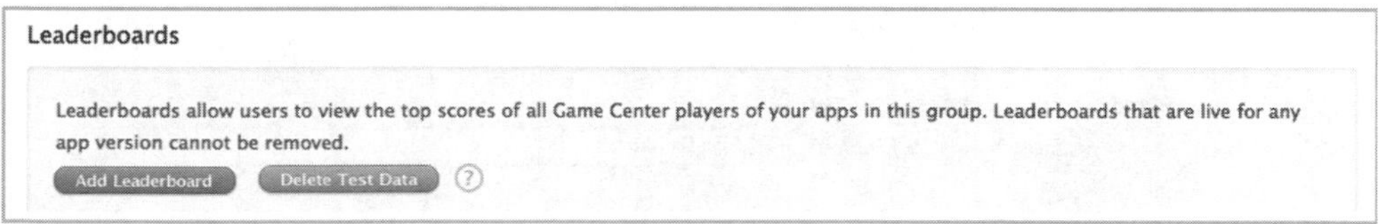

Figure 9.2 Create a leaderboard for an app in iTunesConnect.

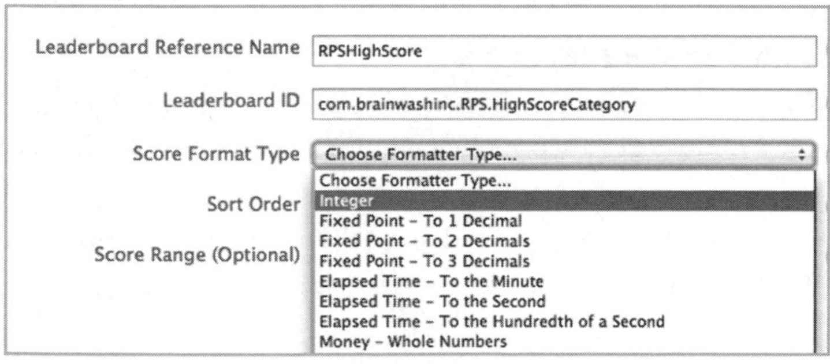

Figure 9.3 Configure the sort order and format type for a leaderboard.

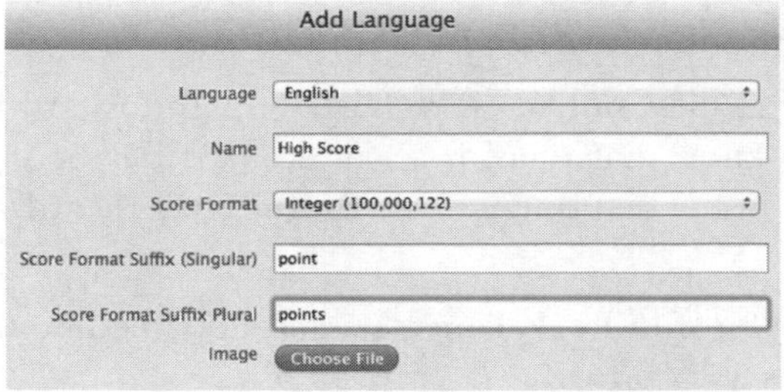

Figure 9.4 Add a language for the leaderboard.

The last step is to add at least one language. This will specify the format of the leaderboard data, the score format suffix, and the name for the given language. Click Add Language and make the applicable selections based on your type of scores (figure 9.5). The leaderboard ID will be used in technique 71 to specify which leaderboard to display in the app.

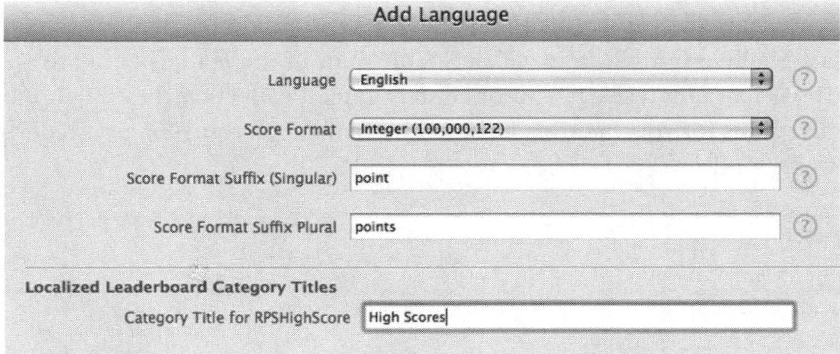

Figure 9.5 Adding a language to the leaderboard and setting display data

Now the leaderboard is online, ready for your app to start reporting scores to it. In the next technique, you'll see how the app can upload scores to the leaderboard.

TECHNIQUE 70 Saving the player's score

As with authenticating the user, reporting a score is mostly handled by GameKit. The main thing you need to do is get a score object and tell it to report to GameKit.

PROBLEM

Now that you have a leaderboard online and an authenticated user, you need a mechanism to send the score online.

SOLUTION

You'll use built-in GameKit classes and methods to send the score to the leaderboard associated with this app. If there is an error, there is a way to enable uploading a score later.

DISCUSSION

Like authenticating a user used a GKPlayer class, reporting the score uses the GKScore class. You'll need to create a method to receive the points value for the score.

In UtilGameCenter, you'll create the GKScore instance, set the score, and tell it to report the score to the leaderboard by calling the method reportScoreWithCompletionHandler, as shown in the following listing.

Create a GKScore instance, set the score value, and report

```
-(void)reportScore:(int)score;
{
    GKScore *theScore = [[GKScore alloc] init];

    theScore.value = score;
    [theScore reportScoreWithCompletionHandler:^(NSError *error)
    {
        if (error)
        {
            NSData *archivedScore = [NSKeyedArchiver
                    archivedDataWithRootObject:theScore];
            [self archiveScoreToSendLater:archivedScore];        Report later
         }
    }];
}
```

Given the reportScore method above, the score is either reported or you call archiveScoreToSendLater with the data to send later. You need to have a meaningful archiveScoreToSendLater method to store this data.

Declare an NSMutableArray called archivedScoresToSendLater in the header. In your meaningful archivedScoresToSendLater method, you can instantiate the array (if needed) and add your score to be reported later, as shown in the following listing.

Method to store a score to be reported later

```
-(void)archiveScoreToSendLater:(NSData*)score;
{
    if (nil == archivedScoresToSendLater)
        archivedScoresToSendLater = [NSMutableArray
                arrayWithCapacity:5];

    [archivedScoresToSendLater addObject:score];
}
```

With the groundwork in place, you need a way to start your reporting process. Why not use a button? In your case, it's a great solution because you can manually engage a button for testing and observation.

Add a button (such as Save) to the UI and wire it up to an action (such as doBtnSave:) in RPSViewController. This action needs to check your flag to make sure GameCenter features are enabled and then call your reportScore method with the point value, as shown in the following listing.

UI action method to check GameCenter flag and report player's score

```
-(IBAction)doBtnSave:(id)sender;
{
    if (gameCenter.gameCenterFeaturesEnabled)
        [gameCenter reportScore:gamePoints];
}
```

Launch the app, see that you get the Welcome Back authentication message, and play a while to score points. Tap Save and step through the code to see if the score is reported or if you get an error. In the case of an error, an app can present the user with a message and possible causes, such as, "No network connection."

But what do you really want to see? You want to see that score on a leaderboard and your name proudly listed beside it. That will happen when you display the leaderboard. Let's add that display function to your app now.

TECHNIQUE 71 Displaying the leaderboard

Again, GameKit does a lot of work for you here. It's a great combination of functionality from the framework of the app and server-side support.

The `GKPlayer` authenticated the player, `GKScore` reported the score, and the `GKLeaderboardViewController` will display the leaderboard within the app.

PROBLEM

You've reported scores for your game, but can't see them. You need to display the leaderboard associated with your app.

SOLUTION

GameKit comes to your aid again and provides the means and UI to display leaderboards for your app. You'll create the leaderboard view controller, set the appropriate settings to specify the leaderboard, and then display it.

DISCUSSION

You'll display the leaderboard as a modal view controller, so you need a view controller on which to call the present method. You also need to specify the category (from technique 69) to display.

> **NOTE** The leaderboard ID is the category value: `com.brainwashinc.RPS.HighScoreCategory`.

You can write another method in your `UtilGameCenter` class to take a view controller to present the leaderboard and the category for the leaderboard. From there, it can create the needed view controller, specify the category, and display the leaderboard, as shown in the following listing.

Specify the category and present the leaderboard modally

```
-(void)showLeaderboardToVC:(UIViewController*)displayWithVC
              forCategory:(NSString*)cat;
{
    GKLeaderboardViewController *vcLeaderboard =
        [[GKLeaderboardViewController alloc] init];
```

```
    vcLeaderboard.timeScope = GKLeaderboardTimeScopeAllTime;
    vcLeaderboard.leaderboardDelegate = self;
     vcLeaderboard.category = cat;
    [displayWithVC
        presentModalViewController:vcLeaderboard animated:YES];
}
```

Callback for finish

There are other timeScope settings: GKLeaderboardTimeScopeToday and GKLeaderboardTimeScopeWeek. When the leaderboard is displayed, the user can select to view those as well (see figure 9.6).

Because UtilGameCenter is set as the delegate for the leaderboard view controller, you need to implement that protocol, which is one required method: leaderboardViewControllerDidFinish: (see the following listing). You just need to dismiss the controller when finished.

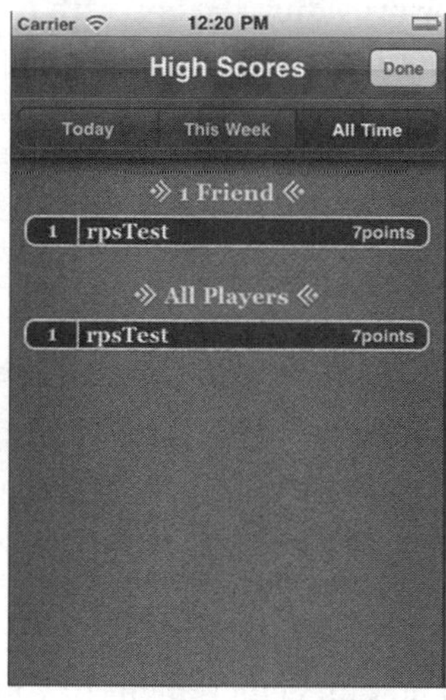

Figure 9.6 Displaying the leaderboard with scores and user options

`GKLeaderboardViewController` callback method when finished

```
- (void)leaderboardViewControllerDidFinish:
            (GKLeaderboardViewController *)viewController
{
    [viewController.parentViewController
        dismissModalViewControllerAnimated:YES];
}
```

As with saving the scores, you need an action to kick off displaying the leaderboard. How about a button? Add a button to the UI (such as Scores) and wire it to an action (such as doBtnScores:) in RPSViewController. This action can check the GameCenter features-enabled flag and call the showLeaderboardToVC method in your UtilGameCenter instance, as shown in the following listing.

`Scores` button action to check GameCenter flag and display leaderboard

```
- (IBAction)doBtnScores:(id)sender;
{
    if (gameCenter.gameCenterFeaturesEnabled)
        [gameCenter showLeaderboardToVC:self
        forCategory:@"com.brainwashinc.RPS.HighScoreCategory"];
}
```

There you go—when the button is tapped, the leaderboard is displayed (see figure 9.6) and you can see your name and your awesome score, and you can even take a screenshot of it to share with friends. Of course, if your friends are connected to you in GameCenter, they'll see it in the GameCenter app. They can also see your scores from other games and achievements. Speaking of achievements...

9.2 GameCenter achievements

Achievements are fun that continues beyond scores. They keep you playing game after game by providing the app with more long-term goals. Some can be silly or overwhelming, but it seems like they keep people coming back for more.

Adding an achievement to your game, or any app, is an easy process that can increase an app's replay value and overall appeal.

In this section, you'll look at adding an achievement in iTunesConnect, reporting a user's progress of an achievement, and displaying the achievement board related to the app.

TECHNIQUE 72 Adding an achievement in iTunesConnect

Adding an achievement in iTunesConnect is similar to and probably simpler than adding a leaderboard. The process mainly consists of setting the name, the ID, and the point value for the achievement. The point value is basically a way to have a meaningful and measurable value to report against (for example, *60% done*).

PROBLEM

You need to add an achievement to your app in iTunesConnect so that your app can store user progress against it.

SOLUTION

You'll use iTunesConnect to create the achievement and the necessary values for the app to meaningfully send achievement progress online.

DISCUSSION

Log in to iTunesConnect as you did when setting up leaderboards, go into your app, select Manage GameCenter, and click Edit in the Achievements area.

Click Add New Achievement, and you're presented with the fields to set for your achievement (see figure 9.7). For your Rock, Paper, Scissors achievement, you'll set the reference name to be *100 Points*, the ID to be `com.brainwashinc.RPS.HundredPoints` and the point value to be `100`.

Achievement

Achievement Reference Name	100 Points
Achievement ID	com.brainwashinc.RPS.Hundred- Points
Point Value	100 800 of 1000 Points Remaining
Hidden	Yes ○ No ◉
Achievable More Than Once	Yes ○ No ◉

Figure 9.7 Achievement settings in iTunesConnect for a new achievement

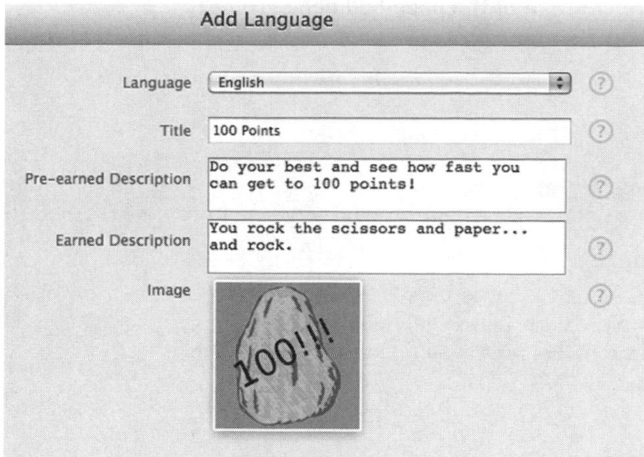

Figure 9.8 Achievement add language settings

As you did with the leaderboard configuration, you also need to add a language. Click Add Language and specify a Title, Pre-earned Description, and Earned Description to display the user's progress accordingly (see figure 9.8). This is also where you upload an image to represent the achievement.

Click Save Changes and you've created your achievement. It's now ready to have progress reports sent for users. The app will need the achievement ID you used above (`com.brainwashinc.RPS.HundredPoints`) and can now report the achievement progress for a user as a percentage. Let's set up your app to do that.

TECHNIQUE 73 Reporting achievement progress

Once again, GameKit is your friend here. Like `GKPlayer`, `GKScore`, and `GKLeaderboardViewController` handled the related UI and functionality, guess what will report progress on the achievement? If you said `GKAchievement`, then you're right.

PROBLEM

You need to set your app up to report progress for the achievement you created in iTunes. You know the achievement ID and need GameKit to do the rest for you.

SOLUTION

You can use `GKAchievement` to report the progress as a percentage of the achievement when given the achievement ID. If there's an error, you want to store the progress to be reported later like you did with the scores in technique 70.

DISCUSSION

Using the `GKAchievement` class in your `UtilGameCenter`, you'll set the same achievement ID that you set in iTunesConnect (`com.brainwashinc.RPS.HundredPoints`), as well as the progress of the given user, and tell it to report to the server. If there's an error, you'll store it and report it later, as shown in the following listing.

Method to report the given percentage of the specified achievement

```
-(void)reportPercentage:(int)percentage
                       ofAchievement:(NSString*)achievementID;
{
    GKAchievement *theAch = [[GKAchievement alloc]
                            initWithIdentifier:achievementID];
    theAch.percentComplete = percentage;
    [theAch reportAchievementWithCompletionHandler:^(NSError *error) {
        if (error)
        {
            NSData *archiveAch = [NSKeyedArchiver
                        archivedDataWithRootObject:theAch];
            [self archiveAchievementToSendLater:archiveAch];     <- Report later
         }
    }];
}
```

If there's an error, your created data object and call to `archiveAchievementToSend-Later:` handles it. Let's create that method, too (see the following listing). You need to declare the `archivedAchievementsToSendLater` as an `NSMutableArray` in the header. If it's `nil` when this method is called, then create it and store the data.

Add achievement to report later

```
-(void)archiveAchievementToSendLater:(NSData*)achievement;
{
    if (nil == archivedAchievementsToSendLater)
        archivedAchievementsToSendLater =
            [NSMutableArray arrayWithCapacity:5];

    [archivedAchievementsToSendLater addObject:achievement];
}
```

What better way to put all of this into action than with a button? You already stored the score with the Save button, so let's add the achievement progress reporting to the same action in `RPSViewController`. Change `doBtnSave:` to also call the `report-Percentage` method on your `UtilGameCenter` instance (see the following listing). Pass in the points and achievement ID to the `reportPercentage` method and let GameKit handle the rest.

Save button action storing the score and achievement progress

```
-(IBAction)doBtnSave:(id)sender;
{
    if (gameCenter.gameCenterFeaturesEnabled)
    {
        [gameCenter reportScore:gamePoints];
        if (gamePoints < 101)
            [gameCenter reportPercentage:gamePoints
                ofAchievement:@"com.brainwashinc.RPS.HundredPoints"];
    }
}
```

When you report progress on an achievement, you report the percentage complete. So if your achievement requirement is based on having 100 points and your user has 90 points, you would report 90% complete for the achievement. However, if the achievement is 1000 points, having 90 points would require reporting 9% complete. Notice in the code that the app doesn't report progress past 100 points (this is to save bandwidth for this example app). However, it also means that if you don't report progress right at 100 points, you won't receive the achievement.

Similarly, if you run the app at a later date, rack up 20 points, and tap Save, your leaderboard score will go back down to 20 and your achievement progress will decrease to 20%.

Once again, you have the app reporting something you can't see. How do you display the achievement progress?

TECHNIQUE 74 Displaying achievement boards

Like leaderboards, you want to be able to see the achievement boards in the app. And like leaderboards, the UI is handled by GameKit.

PROBLEM

You need to be able to display within the app the achievement board for your app's achievement.

SOLUTION

You'll use the GameKit-provided class to display the achievement board as a view controller.

DISCUSSION

Like you did with leaderboards in technique 71, you'll use a GameKit-provided view controller to display the achievement board. `GKAchievementViewController` only needs a delegate for calling the finish callback. Let's write a show achievements method in your `UtilGameCenter` class (see the following listing). The finish callback will then dismisses the achievement view controller.

Achievement view controller and finish callback to dismiss

```
-(void)showAchievementsToVC:(UIViewController*)displayWithVC;
{
    GKAchievementViewController *vcAchievements =
        [[GKAchievementViewController alloc] init];
    vcAchievements.achievementDelegate = self;
    [displayWithVC presentModalViewController:vcAchievements
                                                       animated:YES];
}

- (void)achievementViewControllerDidFinish:
    (GKAchievementViewController *)viewController
{
    [viewController.parentViewController
        dismissModalViewControllerAnimated:YES];
}
```

By adding a button to the UI and an action in `RPSViewController`, you can call the `showAchievementToVC:` method above with your `RPSViewController` and display the achievements.

One of the fun things about achievements is competing for them. Whether it's against yourself or others, it's competitive and fun. But playing Rock, Paper, Scissors is more fun when you play against someone else. In the next section, you'll see how GameCenter facilitates playing against other people.

9.3 Matching and playing via GameCenter

With GameCenter, Apple has provided an amazing set of common functionality to app developers and removed the barriers to network gaming. In the past, you had to develop your own server-side friends network with invitations, UI, messaging, and so forth. Not only is that now done for you, but it's a common friends network for all the games you have.

For playing games with others, GameCenter allows you to match random players, invite friends together for games, send messages back and forth, and even voice chat within your app. Your app also doesn't need to be a game. You can use GameCenter for the friends network, interaction, and voice chat for nongame uses as well.

Matching players allows your app to find other players wanting to play the same game. Using the GameKit framework classes, you can specify criteria for matching players, like how many players will be playing. Another option for playing other people is to invite a specific person to play.

Regardless of the technique used to match up players for a game, GameCenter can also be used to provide voice chat for players in the game. Let's look at techniques for matching up players and adding chat.

TECHNIQUE 75 Matching players

The basics of instigating a match between players is quite simple. GameKit again does the hard part. You need to tell it what game you want to play and who you want to play it with, have it look for a match, and then handle things when a match is found.

PROBLEM

You need to use GameKit to find a match to play a game of Rock, Paper, Scissors.

SOLUTION

Using `GKMatchRequest`, you'll specify your parameters and tell it to find a match.

DISCUSSION

Your `UtilGameCenter` class can once again handle starting the process. You'll pass in a delegate for handling the various callbacks of finding a match and such. This delegate will be your `RPSViewController`, but first let's look at your method, as shown in the following listing.

`GKMatchRequest` starts the match request search for players

```
static NSObject *matchDel;
-(void)fetchMatchWithMatchDelegate:(id)del;
{
    GKMatchRequest *req = [[GKMatchRequest alloc]
        init];
    req.minPlayers = 2;                                  Two players
     req.maxPlayers = 2;
    req.playerGroup = 1;                                 All match

    matchDel = del;                                      Store delegate

    GKMatchmaker *mmaker = [[GKMatchmaker alloc]
        init];
    [mmaker findMatchForRequest:req
        withCompletionHandler:^(GKMatch *match,
        NSError *error)
    {
        if (!error)                                      Set delegate
         {
            gameMatch = match;
            [gameMatch setDelegate:(id)matchDel];
        }
    }];
}
```

For the match request, you specify that you need a minimum and maximum of two players. Also, you set the `playerGroup` to be `1` for everyone. The `playerGroup` can be any `int` you like and can limit the players that get matched together. You may want to only match players together by skill level, location, or other criteria.

You store the delegate passed in a static `NSObject` (`matchDel`). In the header, you declare a GameMatch member variable, and if there's no error, you set it to the match that's returned. In that match, you set the delegate to the `matchDel` static object you stored. Now whatever delegate passed in will receive the match-related callbacks. Let's look at those.

In `RPSViewController`'s header, you need to create some variables for game play. You need a flag, `inAGame`, to know when a user is in a game or not. You'll use an `int` variable (`opponentChoice`) to know what the other player selected, and you'll create an outlet for a label (`lblMessage`) to display messages to the user.

Let's add some initialization settings to your new member variables in your `doBtnPlay:` method and call the fetch match method on your `UtilGameCenter` instance, as shown in the following listing.

Initialize game related member variables when Play button is tapped

```
- (IBAction)doBtnPlay:(id)sender;
{
    inAGame = NO;
    myChoice = -1;
```

```
    opponentChoice = -1;
    if (gameCenter.gameCenterFeaturesEnabled)
        [gameCenter fetchMatchWithMatchDelegate:self];
}
```

If the user is authenticated, fetch a match and pass in the self for the delegate. Now you need to be sure to handle the GKMatchDelegate methods.

The callback for when a match is found passes in the match instance, the playerID, and their connection state (which is also sent when they disconnect). You want to save the match, which is what you'll use to allow the devices to communicate (see the following listing). If they disconnected, you want to notify the user.

Handle the match callback for playerID and connection state

```
- (void)match:(GKMatch *)match
        player:(NSString *)playerID
        didChangeState:(GKPlayerConnectionState)state
{
    if (state == GKPlayerStateConnected)
    {
        inAGame = YES;                                          Save
        gameMatch = match;                                   <- GKMatch
     }
    else if (state == GKPlayerStateDisconnected)
    {
        UIAlertView *alert = [[UIAlertView alloc]
                  initWithTitle:@"Disconnected"
                  message:@"The other player disconnected."
                  delegate:self
                  cancelButtonTitle:@"OK"
                  otherButtonTitles: nil];
         [alert show];
    }
}
```

Now you have a match with another (random) player. The other callback for the match in your case is the other player's move. The callback for a message sent via the GKMatch class is sent for the match, an NSData instance, and the playerID. For your game, you already have the match, so you can ignore that. There's only one other player, so the playerID isn't important for you. But the data class contains their rock-paper-scissors selection. You'll see how that's passed when the player makes a selection later. You first need to store the player's selection, as shown in the following listing.

Processing a GameCenter player match

```
- (void)match:(GKMatch *)match
    didReceiveData:(NSData *)data
    fromPlayer:(NSString *)playerID
{
    NSString *otherPlayersChoice =
        [[NSString alloc] initWithData:data
        encoding:NSUTF8StringEncoding];                          Store
    opponentChoice = [otherPlayersChoice intValue];           <- move
     if (myChoice != -1)                                <- Check my move
```

```
        {
            [lblMessage setText:@"Player selected."];
            [self processOtherPlayersChoice:opponentChoice];
        }
        else
         [lblMessage setText:@"Other player selected. Waiting for you..."];
}
```

You store the move passed to you, and if you've made a move (`myChoice != -1`) you process the other player's move. This assumes two things—that the data sent via the match is a string of their selection and that when you make your selection, it's stored in `myChoice`. Your `doBtnPaper:`, `doBtnRock:`, and `doBtnScissors:` methods need to help out with this, as shown in the following listing.

Selection processing methods store choice and then wait or send and process

```
- (IBAction)doBtnRock:(id)sender;
{
    myChoice = ROCK;
    if (opponentChoice == -1)
        [self waitForOtherPlayer];
    else
    {
        [self sendMyChoice];
        [self processOtherPlayersChoice:opponentChoice];
    }
}
```

You store the selection, and if the `opponentChoice` isn't set (`== -1`), you wait for the other player (call `waitForOtherPlayer`). If the other player has already selected, you send your selection and process theirs.

While waiting for the other player, you can send your move. If you're not in a game, you can tell the user that, as shown in the following listing.

`waitForOtherPlayer` updated for sending selection

```
-(void)waitForOtherPlayer;
{
    if (inAGame)
    {
        [lblMessage setText:@"Waiting for other player..."];
        [self sendMyChoice];
    }
    else
    {
        UIAlertView *alert = [[UIAlertView alloc]
                  initWithTitle:@"Not Playing"
                  message:@"Please press play to start a game."
                  delegate:self
                  cancelButtonTitle:@"OK"
                  otherButtonTitles: nil];
        [alert show];
    }
}
```

Either way, you're sending your selection to the other user. Your method that receives the data stores it and only processes it if you've made your selection already, so it's safe to send it multiple times if that happens.

What does sendMyChoice do? How do you send the selection? You convert the selection to an NSString, convert that to NSData, and pass that to the GameMatch instance method, as shown in the following listing.

Convert the selection to data and send it through GameMatch

```
-(void)sendMyChoice;
{
    NSString *choice = [NSString stringWithFormat:
        @"%d", myChoice];
    NSData *data = [choice dataUsingEncoding:
        NSUTF8StringEncoding];
    NSError *error;
    [gameMatch sendDataToAllPlayers:data
        withDataMode:GKMatchSendDataReliable error:&error];
}
```

While you've mostly seen and thought of this from one user's perspective, you're handling both sides here. If you make a selection, you send it to the other user. The user's device receives and stores your selection, and if they've made theirs, it processes your selection to conclude the winner, award points, and so on.

If the other player receives your selection and they haven't made a selection yet, the game doesn't have anything to do. When they do select, the game already has your choice and can process it. At the same time, they're sending you their choice, and because you have your choice, the game can process it on your end.

Because the matching can be random or directed (playerGroup), you can see how connecting users together can be easy. From there, sending data can also be easy and can contain about anything converted to NSData. This has obvious applications for competitive games, but could be used for all sorts of apps.

Playing a random person is fine, but what if you want to play one of your friends? Let's look at inviting a specific user to connect via GameCenter.

TECHNIQUE 76 Inviting friends to play

You have a built-in friends network with GameCenter, and you want to be able to invite those friends to play games. GameCenter and GameKit do a great job of handling this in terms of the UI and functionality. You can invite friends, launch the app, and play the game in a smooth and seamless process.

PROBLEM

Inviting friends to play a game has two sides to it. You want to be able to invite friends to play your game via GameCenter. But you also need to handle the match when GameCenter provides it to the app.

SOLUTION

GameCenter handles its part automatically. It knows what apps have GameCenter enabled and can send invitations to your friends independent of anything else.

Figure 9.9 GameCenter invitation sending

Figure 9.10 GameCenter requests list

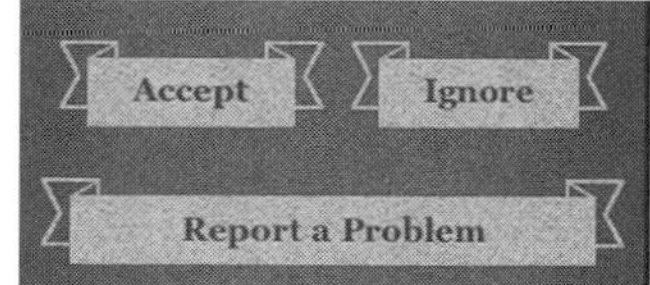

Figure 9.11 Options on a GameCenter invitation

But for your app to send friends invitations, it needs to use some more GameKit classes. There are also related delegate callback methods to handle the process in your app. Specifically, you'll need to set the match maker's `inviteHandler` code.

DISCUSSION

When you start GameCenter, you can select a game, select a friend, type out an invitation message or use the default, and send it (see figure 9.9).

When you receive an invitation from a friend, you can also view that in GameCenter (see figure 9.10).

Tapping on an invitation gives you the option to accept, ignore, or report a problem with the request (see figure 9.11).

To use the related UI in the app, you need to use a GameKit class called `GKMatchmakerViewController`. The matching setup is similar to the random matching, where you set the minimum and maximum number of players and `playerGroup` on a `GKMatchRequest`. You then pass that match request to the `GKMatchmakerViewController`, set the delegate, and display the view controller.

You can create a method in your `UtilGameCenter` to do this (with values somewhat specific to your game) by accepting a delegate for that matchmaker view controller, as shown in the following listing.

Displaying GameCenter matchmaker UI with request

```
-(void)inviteMatchWithMatchDelegate:(id)del;
{
    GKMatchRequest *req = [[GKMatchRequest alloc]
        init];
    req.minPlayers = 2;
    req.maxPlayers = 2;
    req.playerGroup = 1;
```

```
    GKMatchmakerViewController *vcMMaker =
        [[GKMatchmakerViewController alloc]
            initWithMatchRequest:req];
    [vcMMaker setMatchmakerDelegate:del];
    [del presentModalViewController:vcMMaker animated:YES];
}
```

You'll implement the delegate methods for the matchmaker view controller later in this technique. For now, let's develop how the matchmaker gets launched.

You'll make your Play button now display an alert view, giving the user the option to invite a friend or play a random person (see figure 9.12).

In the alert view callback, you'll call a new method, `inviteFriend`, if they select Invite and another new method, `autoMatch`, if they select Random. The `autoMatch` method will be the old `doBtnPlay:` method renamed, as shown in the following listing.

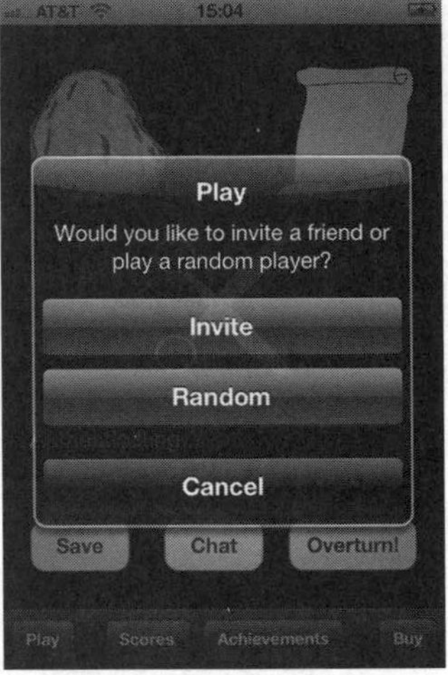

Figure 9.12 Prompt the user to invite a friend or match randomly

Ask the user how they'd like to be matched: invite or random

```
- (IBAction)doBtnPlay:(id)sender;
{
    UIAlertView *av = [[UIAlertView alloc]
        initWithTitle:@"Play"
        message:@"Would you like to invite a friend or...
        play a random player?"
        delegate:self
        cancelButtonTitle:@"Cancel"
        otherButtonTitles:@"Invite", @"Random", nil];
    [av show];
}

- (void)alertView:(UIAlertView *)alertView
    clickedButtonAtIndex:(NSInteger)buttonIndex
{
    if (buttonIndex == 1)
        [self inviteFriend];
    else if (buttonIndex == 2)
        [self autoMatch];
}
```

The new `inviteFriend` method will be similar to the `autoMatch` (the renamed `doBtnPlay:`) method. It'll init the game variables, check the GameCenter features-enabled flag, and notify the user if they aren't authenticated; it'll also call the matchmaker-related method on `UtilGameCenter`, as opposed to the random match method, as shown in the following listing.

Starting the process to create a GameCenter player match

```
-(void)inviteFriend;
{
    inAGame = NO;
    myChoice = -1;
    opponentChoice = -1;
    if (gameCenter.gameCenterFeaturesEnabled)
    {
        [lblMessage setText:@"Inviting friend..."];
        [gameCenter inviteMatchWithMatchDelegate:self];    <- Matchmaker method
     }
    else
    {
      UIAlertView *alert = [[UIAlertView alloc]
        initWithTitle:@"Authenticate"
        message:@"You have not been authenticated into GameCenter yet."
        delegate:self
        cancelButtonTitle:@"OK"
        otherButtonTitles: nil];
      [alert show];
    }
}
```

The matchmaker UI looks like the GameCenter UI with the button to Invite Friend (see figure 9.13).

You're passing `self` into the matchmaker method, so you need to implement the related callbacks. There are several callbacks; a couple of them aren't very interesting and are called when the invite is cancelled or failed and you can dismiss the matchmaker view controller (see the following listing). These are still required methods and need to be implemented, even if they are empty.

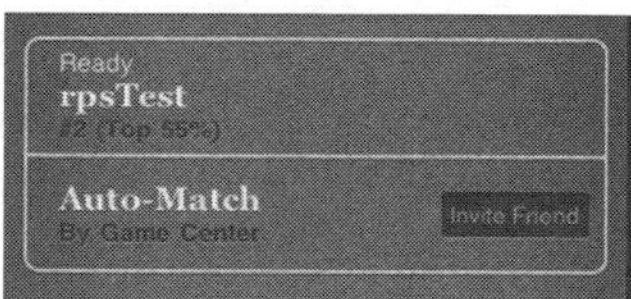

Figure 9.13 Matchmaker UI to invite friends to play

Handling GameCenter matchmaker delegate calls

```
- (void)matchmakerViewControllerWasCancelled:
    (GKMatchmakerViewController *)viewController
{
    [self dismissModalViewControllerAnimated:YES];
    [lblMessage setText:@"Nevermind."];
}

- (void)matchmakerViewController:
    (GKMatchmakerViewController *)viewController
    didFailWithError:(NSError *)error
{
    [self dismissModalViewControllerAnimated:YES];
    [lblMessage setText:@"Invite failed."];
}
```

A more interesting callback is the one called when a match is found (for example, the invitation is accepted). In your case, you'd set the inAGame flag to Yes and dismiss the matchmaker, as shown in the following listing.

Invitation accepted/match found—set flag, dismiss controller

```
- (void)matchmakerViewController:
    (GKMatchmakerViewController *)viewControllerdidFindMatch:
        (GKMatch *)match
{
    inAGame = YES;
    gameMatch = match;
    [lblMessage setText:@"Match Found. Play!"];
    [self dismissModalViewControllerAnimated:YES];
}
```

Finally, to be able to handle requests to play, you need to add the block shown in the following listing to your code.

Block used in `viewDidLoad` to handle incoming invitations

```
[GKMatchmaker sharedMatchmaker].inviteHandler =
        ^(GKInvite *invite, NSArray *playersToInvite) {
        GKMatchmakerViewController *controller =
            [[GKMatchmakerViewController alloc]
                initWithInvite:invite];
        controller.delegate = self;
        [self presentModalViewController:controller
            animated:YES];                                  Display matchmaker
```

I hope you agree that while there are more steps to inviting other users to play through GameCenter and GameKit, it's not all that complicated. If you have a game, I encourage you to open it up to GameCenter for leaderboards, achievements, friend invitations, and voice chat. Let's add voice chat to your app now.

TECHNIQUE 77 Voice chat via the GameCenter

GameCenter allows for voice chat when a game match is established. It's easy to set up with a few lines of code and only requires a GameMatch. This means you have to be connected to at least one other player, but that should be obvious—otherwise, it wouldn't be a chat.

PROBLEM

You need to add voice chatting to your app using GameCenter.

SOLUTION

When you have a match between two players, you can begin a chat session.

DISCUSSION

You can add a Chat button to the interface and wire it to a `doBtnChat:` method in your `RPSViewController`. It can check to make sure you have a GameMatch and, if so, start a chat with a specified channel name.

A single match can have more than one voice channel, and players in the match can join multiple channels simultaneously.

To start a chat, make sure you have a GameMatch instance (notify the user if not) and then create the chat with the `voiceChatWithName:` method passing in the channel name. Store the returned `GKVoiceChat` in a member variable, as shown in the following listing.

Create a chat with channel name RPS if you have a GameMatch

```
-(IBAction)doBtnChat:(id)sender;
{
    if (nil == gameMatch)
    {
        UIAlertView *alert = [[UIAlertView alloc]
          initWithTitle:@"No Game"
          message:@"You are not currently in a game."
          delegate:self
          cancelButtonTitle:@"OK"
          otherButtonTitles: nil];
        [alert show];
        inAGame = NO;
        return;
    }

    chat = [gameMatch voiceChatWithName:@"RPS"];
    [chat start];
}
```

As you can see, adding great voice chat capability to your app requires only a few lines of code and can greatly enhance your app.

9.4 Summary

GameCenter gives you a lot of features for very little cost in effort or anything else. It enabled you to provide reliable and integrated matching and gaming functionality to your Rock, Paper, Scissors app. Also, it allowed you to add score reporting and leaderboard viewing to your game. Much of this couldn't be done without Apple's integration of the members network.

With the ease and accessibility of the GameCenter functions, many types of apps (especially games) can grow into the next dimension by allowing users to engage with their friends, experience the app in a new way, or strive for more achievements and higher scores.

10 iTunes API, iPad, and iAd—MusicSearch

This chapter covers

- Connecting to iTunes
- Converting your apps for iPad
- Adding ads to your app

Integrating various systems seems to be a big area of growth for technology in general, and especially in the mobile world. A growing number of apps let you post to Twitter, the Facebook app can sync with your contacts, and ShareKit will let you integrate with a variety of online options.

Another great app for integration is iTunes. The iTunes API is easy-to-understand JSON (JavaScript Object Notation) text, which can be parsed and scavenged for interesting data.

Two other growing areas for development are with the iPad and iAds. Both were launched with a great deal of hype and continue to grow. The iPad has sold a record number of devices, and I don't think advertising is going to disappear anytime soon, either.

In this chapter we'll look at these three items—the iTunes API, the iPad/iPod, and iAds—and learn how to integrate them with an app. You'll create an app that searches music through the iTunes API, displays the results, and allows you to preview songs. You'll convert that app to universal binary for both the iPhone/iPod and the iPad. Then you'll add iAds to the app, so it will be full of Apple-related content.

10.1 Searching for music with the iTunes API

A quick online search of "iTunes api" returns plenty of results. Look for results with a real Apple URL and you'll find plenty of information on the API.

You'll create an app, MusicSearch, that allows the user to search for an artist, song, album, and so forth, and displays the results in a table that includes the song title, album title, and cover artwork of the album (see figure 10.1).

Tapping on a row will allow the user to play the track preview, load iTunes for the related media, and view the details (such as the album artwork in a slightly larger format).

TECHNIQUE 78 Querying with the iTunes API

The published iTunes search API allows for good searches with a simple URL. The results are returned in JSON and are easy to parse. You'll focus on searching for music related to the text the user enters.

PROBLEM

You need to search the iTunes online database for given search text entered by the user.

SOLUTION

Using the iTunes API, you can search for music with the related terms and obtain data that's textual, visual (images), and auditory (song previews).

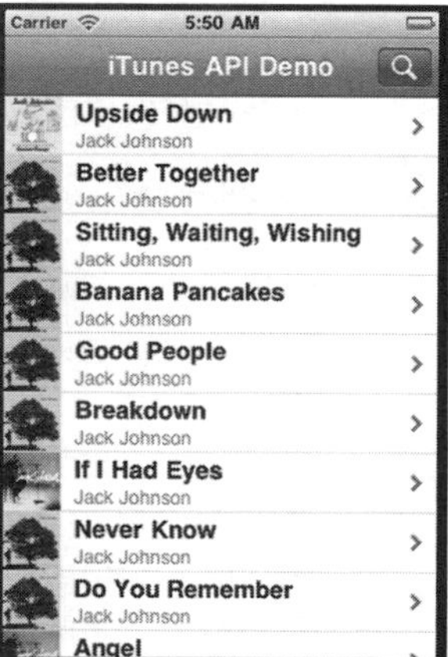

Figure 10.1 Search results listing from iTunes for Jack Johnson

DISCUSSION

The API defined online is easy to figure out. The URL is http://ax.itunes.apple.com/WebObjects/MZStoreServices.woa/wa/wsSearch. If you add the parameters `?term=<text>&entity=<entity>` where `text` is the search text and `entity` is the media type (such as `tvShow` or `movie`), you can see the details. You'll use `musicTrack` and let the user enter the search text.

First, you'll create a new view-based project and name it MusicSearch. In the UI editor, you'll replace the default view with a table view. This is where you'll display the results. You'll need to change `RootViewController` to a `UITableViewController` in the code and wire up the table view to it.

Next, you need a simple search input view controller with Interface Builder (IB) (see figure 10.2).

`RootViewController` will need an outlet for a `UIViewController` and an action for a Cancel button (such as `doBtnCancel:`). Also, make `RootViewController` a `UITextFieldDelegate`. Wire up `RootViewController` to the search view controller, making `RootViewController` the text field's delegate.

In the `RootViewController`'s `viewDidLoad` method, you can add a Search button and set the navigation title (see the following listing).

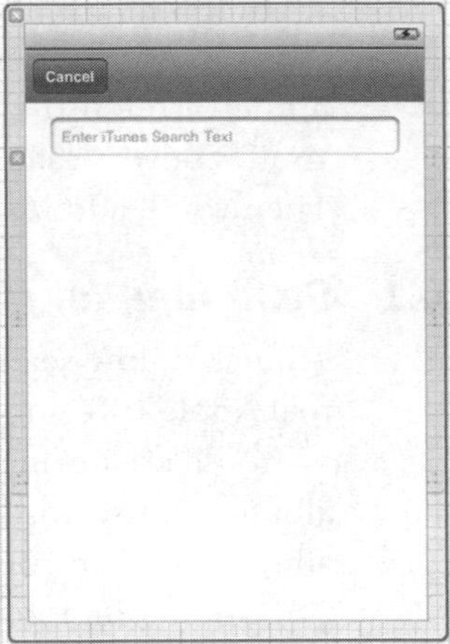

Figure 10.2 Search text input view controller

Set the title and create a search button for the navigation item

```
- (void)viewDidLoad {
    [super viewDidLoad];
    self.title = @"iTunes API Demo";

    UIBarButtonItem *bbi = [[UIBarButtonItem alloc]
                initWithBarButtonSystemItem:UIBarButtonSystemItemSearch
                target:self
                action:@selector(doBtnSearch:)];
    [self.navigationItem setRightBarButtonItem:bbi];
}
```

The `doBtnSearch:` method needs to display your search view controller (see the following listing).

Display the search view controller when Search is tapped

```
-(void)doBtnSearch:(id)sender;
{
    [self presentModalViewController:vcSearch animated:YES];
}
```

Since the `RootViewController` is the search text field's delegate, you can do the search when `textFieldShouldReturn` is called (when the user taps the Return key while editing that field). You'll need somewhere to store the results, so declare an `NSArray` named `results` in the header and use it in the callback method (see the following listing).

Use the text entered to query iTunes and retrieve the results

```
- (BOOL)textFieldShouldReturn:(UITextField *)textField
{
    [self dismissModalViewControllerAnimated:YES];          Back to table
     [textField resignFirstResponder];
    NSString *searchText = textField.text;
    searchText = [searchText stringByReplacingOccurrencesOfString:@" "
                            withString:@"+"];
    NSString *url =
 [NSString stringWithFormat:@"http://ax.itunes.apple.com/WebObjects/...
        MZStoreServices.woa/wa/wsSearch?term=%@&entity=musicTrack",
    searchText];

    NSError *error;
    NSString *search = [NSString stringWithContentsOfURL:
        [NSURL URLWithString:url]
        encoding:NSUTF8StringEncoding error:&error];

    return NO;
}
```

A sample of what the results look like is shown in the following listing.

Partial example results from iTunes API search


```
{
 "resultCount":50,
 "results": [
{"wrapperType":"track", "kind":"song", "artistId":909253,
"collectionId":120954021, "trackId":120954025,
"artistName":"Jack Johnson", "collectionName":"Sing-a-Longs and
Lullabies for the Film Curious George", "trackName":"Upside Down",
"collectionCensoredName":"Sing-a-Longs and Lullabies for the Film
Curious George", "trackCensoredName":"Upside Down", "artistViewUrl":
 "http://itunes.apple.com/us/artist/jack-johnson/id909253?uo=4",...
```


The results are in a format called JSON, which is mostly readable and easily parsed into usable formats like arrays and dictionaries. Let's see what you can do with the JSON data passed back from iTunes.

TECHNIQUE 79 Displaying JSON results

You'll need to parse the JSON data into something usable in the code. There's a great JSON framework here: https://github.com/stig/json-framework/. It's easy to add to a project and nicely parses and generates code from/to `NSArrays` and `NSDictionaries`. Then you can display it to the user.

PROBLEM

You need to parse JSON into an array of dictionaries, one for each query result, to be able to display the data to the user.

SOLUTION

You'll use the JSON framework to parse the returned data. The dictionaries will contain key/value pairs for the various items, including `artistName`, `trackName`, `previewUrl`, and `artwork` items.

DISCUSSION

After you have the framework in your project, you can manage the response data from iTunes. You can add code after you receive the response to trim out the newlines and parse the JSON into a dictionary (see the following listing).

Prepping and parsing JSON data into your results member variable array

```
search = [search stringByReplacingOccurrencesOfString:
          @"\\n" withString:@""];
    NSDictionary *dict = [search JSONValue];          <- High-level dictionary
     results = [dict objectForKey:@"results"];        <- Content items

    [self.tableView reloadData];
```

Now that you have the results in an array, you know how many items were returned from the query. With that, you can specify how many rows are in the table (see the following listing).

Return the count of the results array as the number of rows

```
- (NSInteger)tableView:(UITableView *)tableView
        numberOfRowsInSection:(NSInteger)section {
    return [results count];
}
```

Each item in the results array is to be the contents of a row. You'll display the `trackName` on top, the `artistName` on bottom, and the artwork on the left. You also want to specify a disclosure indicator as the accessory so people know they get more by tapping on a row (see the following listing).

Setting the data in the table cells based on the query results

```
- (UITableViewCell *)tableView:(UITableView *)tableView
                      cellForRowAtIndexPath:(NSIndexPath *)indexPath {

    static NSString *CellIdentifier = @"Cell";

    UITableViewCell *cell = [tableView
        dequeueReusableCellWithIdentifier:CellIdentifier];
    if (cell == nil) {
        cell = [[UITableViewCell alloc]
            initWithStyle:UITableViewCellStyleSubtitle
            reuseIdentifier:CellIdentifier];
        cell.accessoryType =
            UITableViewCellAccessoryDisclosureIndicator;       <- Disclosure indicator
     }

    NSDictionary *trackDict = [results objectAtIndex:indexPath.row];
    cell.textLabel.text =
```

```
        [trackDict objectForKey:@"trackName"];                    <— Track name

    cell.detailTextLabel.text =
        [trackDict objectForKey:@"artistName"];                   <— Artist name

    NSString *imageURL =
        [trackDict objectForKey:@"artworkUrl60"];                 <— Artwork
     cell.imageView.image = [UIImage imageWithData:
        [NSData dataWithContentsOfURL:[NSURL URLWithString:imageURL]]];

    return cell;
}
```

Run the app, search for an artist or album, and see the results displayed from iTunes (see figure 10.1). Now that you're displaying the results in the table, you want to do something meaningful and expected when you tap on a given row. Let's look at using the `previewUrl` in the results to play the iTunes song preview.

TECHNIQUE 80 Playing song preview

A few ways to play a song when using a URL are available; the easiest is to launch the URL using the shared application. Another way would be to load the URL in a web view inside the app. The cleaner way would be to download the song and play it with the built-in media player. Let's look at a couple of these techniques.

PROBLEM

Given the `previewUrl` for the results, you need to play the track preview audio file. Let's try two solutions—launching the URL, and downloading the audio file.

SOLUTION

The `UIApplication` class has a method to launch a given URL. It uses the OS to determine what app to use and how to best handle the data. This can be especially useful if you don't know what types of links an app may try to load.

You'll look at that method, but because you know you're dealing with audio, you'll also look at the solution to download the file and play it locally.

DISCUSSION

When the user taps on a row, you can get the data item dictionary based on the row number they tapped. From that, you can get the value for the `previewUrl` key. A simple call to `openURL` on the `UIApplication` instance will launch this URL and play the audio (see the following listing).

Based on the row index, launch the previewUrl for the given data dictionary

```
- (void)tableView:(UITableView *)tableView
      didSelectRowAtIndexPath:(NSIndexPath *)indexPath {
   NSDictionary *dict = [results objectAtIndex:indexPath.row];
   [[UIApplication sharedApplication]
           openURL:[NSURL URLWithString:[dict                     Open
           objectForKey:@"previewUrl"]]];                         <— previewUrl
}
```

A better way, especially because you know the data format you're working with, would be to download the data and play the file locally. First, you'll fetch the data from the server into an `NSData` object. Then, you can store the file locally and play it with a built-in audio player from the `AVFoundation` framework (be sure to add that to your project).

You'll also need a way to get a path to store the file and a separate method to play the file. First, let's focus on getting the data from the server (see the following listing).

Given the preview URL, fetch the sound file, store it locally, and play it

```
NSData *fileData = [NSData dataWithContentsOfURL:
            [NSURL URLWithString:
            [dict objectForKey:@"previewUrl"]]];
        NSString *path = [NSString
            stringWithFormat:@"%@/soundTrack.mp4",
            [self getFilePath]];                          <—— Writeable path
         [fileData writeToFile:path atomically:YES];
        [self playSound:path];                            <—— Play audio
```

The logic is clear—fetch the data, store the data, and play the data. The fetching is handled by the `NSData` call to `dataWithContentsOfURL`. What about getting the path for storing the file? You'll use the same name for all files, `soundTrack.mp4`, because you'll only store them for temporary use.

To get the path, you get the document directory—there's only one on an iOS device. You then append the `exeName` to it and create that directory if it doesn't already exist. Basically, you're creating a place for this app to store files (see the following listing).

Creating a storage dir based on the document directory and executable name

```
-(NSString*)getFilePath;
{
    NSArray *paths = NSSearchPathForDirectoriesInDomains
            (NSDocumentDirectory, NSUserDomainMask, YES);     <— Document dir
     NSString *documentsDirectoryPath = [paths objectAtIndex:0];
    NSString *exeName = [[NSBundle mainBundle]
            objectForInfoDictionaryKey:@"CFBundleName"];
    NSString *path = [documentsDirectoryPath                  <— Append exeName
             stringByAppendingPathComponent:exeName];

    NSError *error;
    [[NSFileManager defaultManager]
              createDirectoryAtPath:path
              withIntermediateDirectories:YES
              attributes:nil                                  <—— Create dir
               error:&error];
    return path;
}
```

Last, you can play the file. From AVFoundation.Framework, you can declare an `AVAudioPlayer` in the header. Then, in the `playSound` method, you can initialize it with data from your path and play the song (see the following listing).

Create an `AVAudioPlayer` with your sound file path and play it

```
-(void)playSound:(NSString*)aFilePath
{
    if (nil != aAudioPlayer)
    {
        [aAudioPlayer stop];                                    Stop playing
    }
    aAudioPlayer =[[AVAudioPlayer alloc]
        initWithContentsOfURL:
            [NSURL fileURLWithPath:aFilePath] error:NULL];
    [aAudioPlayer stop];
    [aAudioPlayer play];
}
```

Lots of other data and URLs will be in the query results. One URL is the `trackViewUrl`, which would load a view of the track data. Another option would be to replace the *http* in the url with *itms* and load it in iTunes, where the user could then buy the track (see the following listing).

Load the `trackViewUrl` into iTunes

```
NSString *url = [dict objectForKey:@"trackViewUrl"];
        url = [url stringByReplacingOccurrencesOfString:@"http"
                    withString:@"itms"];
        [[UIApplication sharedApplication]
                    openURL:[NSURL URLWithString:url]];
```

If you log out the data to the console, you can inspect the data returned from iTunes for other interesting items you might use in your app. Again, this is only a music search, but you could develop something that searches for various types of media.

Like many iPhone apps, this app can be converted to run on the iPad with a UI specifically for the iPad. By creating a universal binary, the same project can run on both size devices and display the proper UI. Let's look at creating the iPad aspects now.

10.2 Converting an app to iPad

While people still think of the iPhone first, the iPad is popular and is, in some cases, more effective for certain uses. If nothing else, it's got a bigger screen, which can allow it to do more with visual media.

It's common to take an existing app developed for the iPhone/iPod and convert it to an iPad app or a universal binary that will run on all the devices. You might also have the goal of making a universal binary, but it's best to develop the iPhone version first and then add the iPad aspects later.

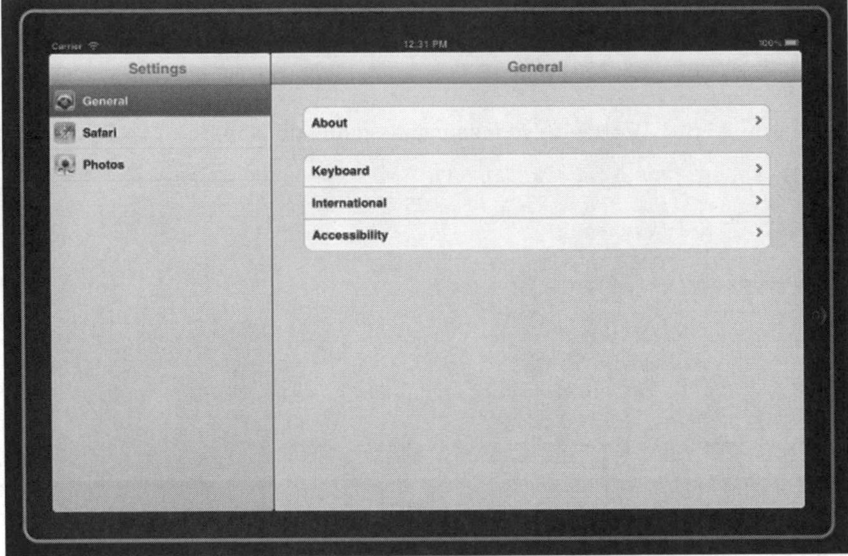

Figure 10.3 Settings app on iPad using the split view controller

In this section, you'll take your MusicSearch app and convert it to a universal binary. You'll use a combination of built-in functionality of Xcode to convert the project. Xcode also has capabilities to convert the UI to iPad. Xcode will do that for you as part of the project upgrade, but it can be done separately.

You'll use an iPad-specific control called a *split view controller*. This is the controller used in the Email and Settings apps (see figure 10.3).

Typically, the split view controller has two built-in view controllers. The left is the master and the right is the details. In the master, the user navigates and the content is displayed in the details.

Let's start by letting Xcode do what it can to get you set up as a universal binary.

TECHNIQUE 81 Converting the project in Xcode

Xcode has a feature to upgrade an existing target to be compiled for iPad. You'll start by using that upgrade, and then do specifics needed in the code and UI editor from there.

PROBLEM

You need to convert an iPhone/iPod app into a universal binary to be run on all iOS devices.

SOLUTION

You'll start by using the built-in Xcode functionality to upgrade your project and related xib file. That will technically do what you need.

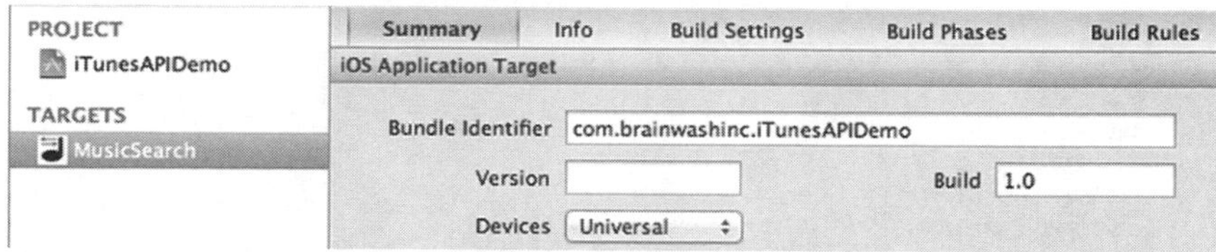

Figure 10.4 Xcode's built in feature to convert an iPhone app for iPad

DISCUSSION

Select the target you want to upgrade. Under the Summary tab, select Universal for Devices (see figure 10.4). You'll be prompted to indicate if you want to convert your UI for iPad—select Yes.

You'll now have access to iPad-specific settings for orientation, app icons, launch images, and so on (see figure 10.5).

As part of the upgrade process, Xcode creates a new resources group called Resources-iPad. In that new group is an upgraded version of the MainWindow.xib file named MainWindow-iPad .xib (see figure 10.6).

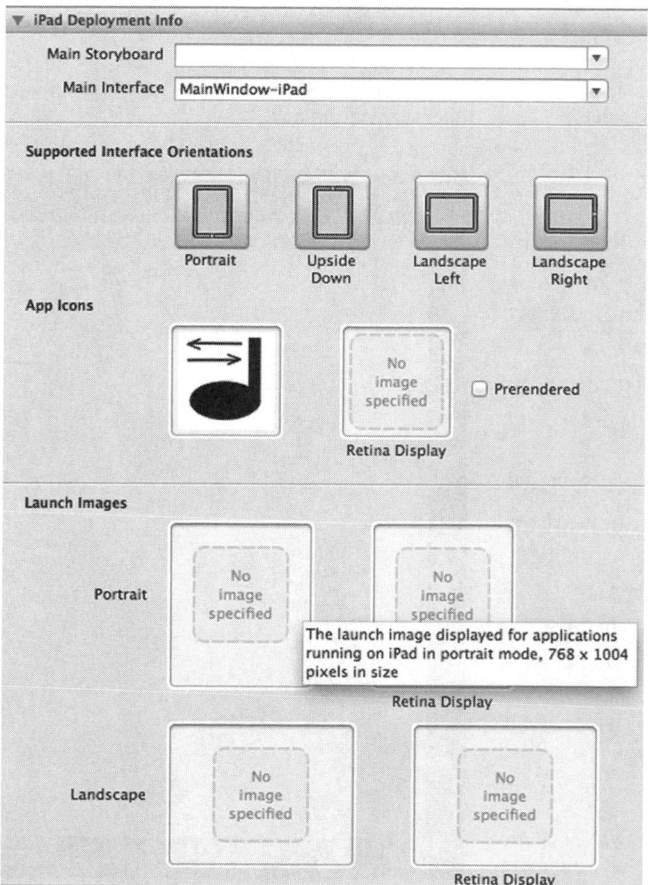

Figure 10.5 Xcode allows settings for iPad-specific images

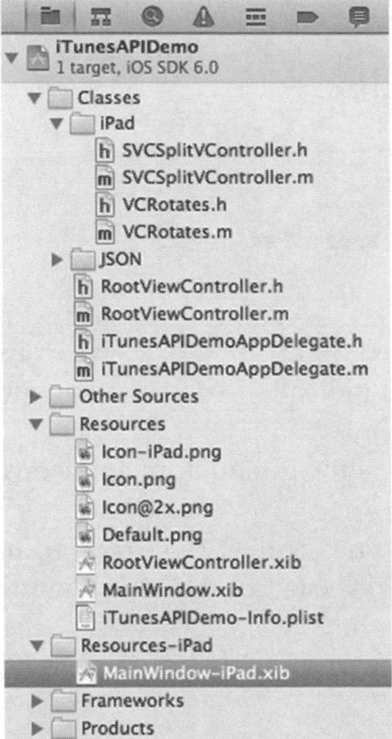

Figure 10.6 Xcode creates a new resources group with an upgraded MainWindow-iPad.xib file.

Figure 10.7 Xcode now has an iPad simulator option for running the app.

You can run the app now in the iPad simulator, but be sure to select the iPad simulator before running it (see figure 10.7).

You'll notice that running the app displays a blank list (see figure 10.8).

Rotating the simulator to landscape doesn't make much difference (see figure 10.9).

Adding a method to `RootViewController` will allow the app to rotate properly in landscape (see the following listing).

Figure 10.8 Upgraded universal binary app running in the iPad simulators

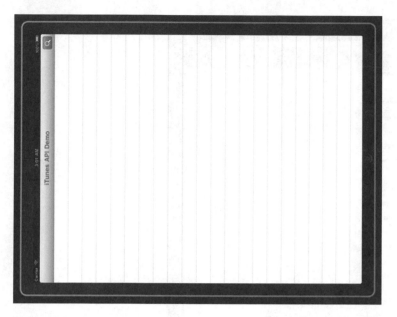

Figure 10.9 Upgraded universal binary running in the iPad simulator landscape

Callback for a view controller to determine if the view controller should rotate

```
- (BOOL)shouldAutorotateToInterfaceOrientation:
    (UIInterfaceOrientation)interfaceOrientation {
    return YES;
}
```

Yes for all cases

Going through the rest of the app, you can see the other screens have issues as well. For one, the search view's toolbar is out of whack (see figure 10.10).

But the functionality is still mostly fine. You can enter text in the search field, tap Send, and see the results back on the first table view (see figure 10.11).

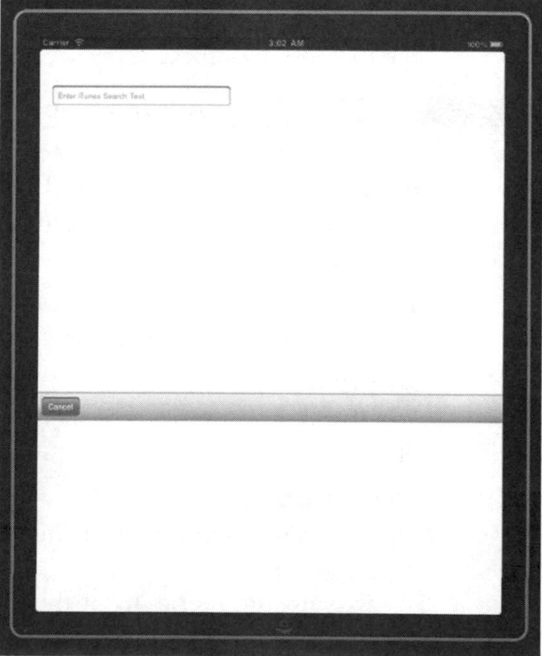

Figure 10.10 Search view layout is wrong after Xcode upgrade to iPad

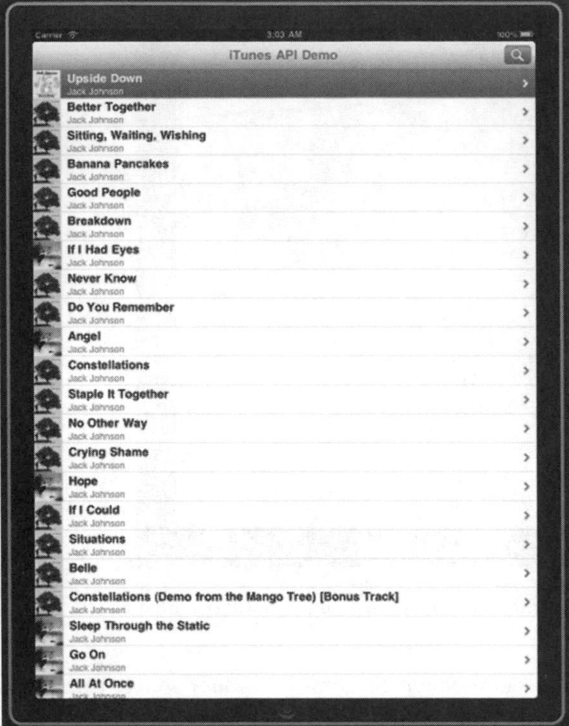

Figure 10.11 Search results displayed in the table view from iTunes

While the upgrade technically works, the layout of the UI isn't quite right. It runs like a giant iPhone/iPod, but with small text. For some apps, this might work fine, but for table views, the look is off and the navigation feels awkward. It would be better to use the `UISplitViewController`.

TECHNIQUE 82 Adding a split view to the app

A common use of the split view controller is to use the master view for navigation and drilling down into a hierarchy. The detail view on the right can then be used to show information related to the selection on the left.

PROBLEM

You want to use a split view controller to display your table view on the left and the detail view to display the related artwork image.

SOLUTION

You'll add a split view controller to your project's UI and display your data in a more elegant way.

DISCUSSION

Open the MainWindow-iPad.xib file and drag a `UISplitViewController` into the file (see figure 10.12).

Expand the hierarchy of the split view controller and notice the first child view controller is a navigation controller. Because you already have a navigation toolbar for

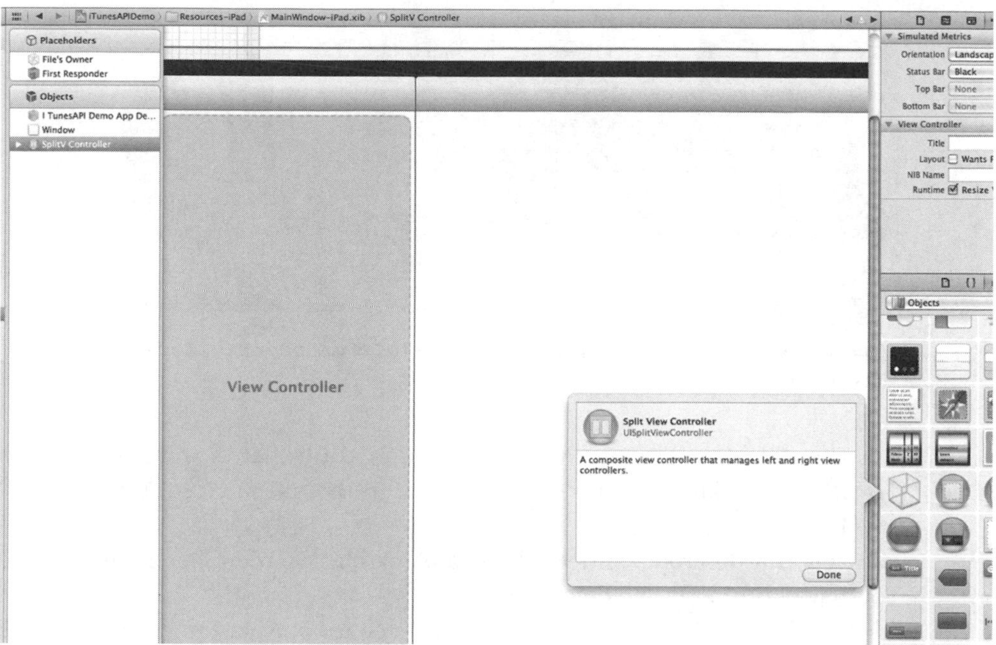

Figure 10.12 Adding a split view controller to the MainWindow-iPad.xib file

your project, drag your existing one over the one in the split view controller and replace it (see figure 10.13).

Create a new class in the project and name it `SVCSplitController`, which extends a `UISplitViewController`. In IB, change the class type of the split view controller to your new `SVCSplitController` class. Also, add the same rotate method to the implementation file of the `SVCSplitController` as you did for `RootViewController` (see the listing "Callback for a view controller to determine if the view controller should rotate").

Next, you need to make the main controller of the app dependent upon which device it's running on. To do this, you abstract out the base view controller in `MusicSearchAppDelegate`. Currently it's `UINavigationController`, but for iPad, you put your navigation controller in the master view of the split view controller.

If you leave the navigation controller as the main view, that's what will be displayed all the time. Remember the giant table view? In `MusicSearchAppDelegate`, change the type of the `navigationController` to `UIViewController`. Also, right-click on the `navigation-Controller` and select Refactor (make sure all of your Xcode run processes are stopped—click the icon that looks like a stop sign if it's active). Select Refactor and type in the new name: `main-Controller`.

Figure 10.13 Replace the navigation controller in the split view controller.

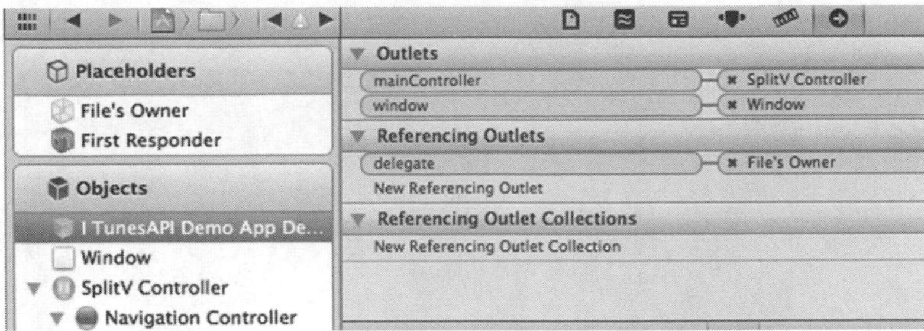

Figure 10.14 Associating the split view controller to the `mainController` in the app delegate

For the old MainWindow.xib, the navigation controller is still the `mainController`. For iPad, associate the split view controller to the `mainController` member (see figure 10.14).

Now run the app... and you'll see a blank black screen (see figure 10.15) because you have nothing in the detail view.

But if you rotate it to landscape, you'll see the navigation controller and its table view in the master view (see figure 10.16)

Figure 10.15 iPad with split view controller running in the iPad simulator

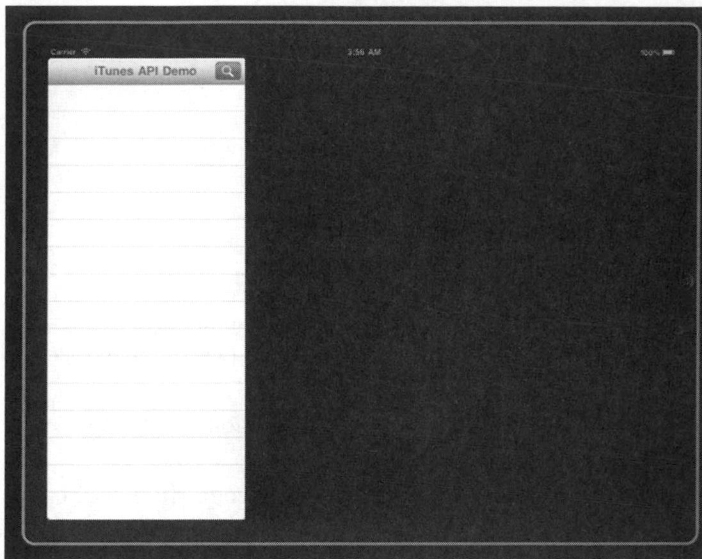

Figure 10.16 App with split view controller running in the iPad simulator landscape

Drop a plain `UIView` in the details area, then a toolbar across the top of that, and then another `UIView`, taking up the rest of the space (see figure 10.17).

Back in the `SVCSplitController`, declare a `UIToolbar` in the header and connect it to the toolbar at the top of the detail view with IB.

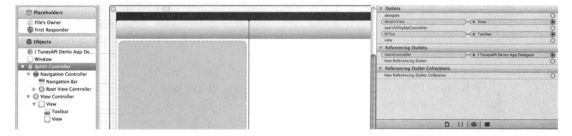

Figure 10.17 Laying out the detail view with a toolbar and views

If you run the app now, the toolbar will be missing because it doesn't know how to handle the various orientations. This is because the autosizing isn't right (see figure 10.18).

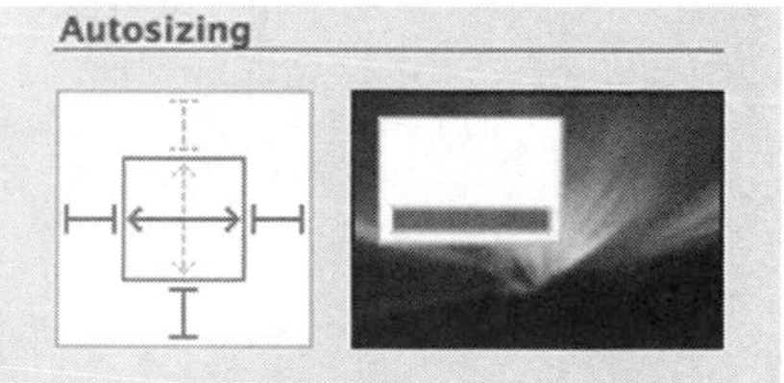

Figure 10.18 Auto-sizing of the toolbar keeps the widget offscreen

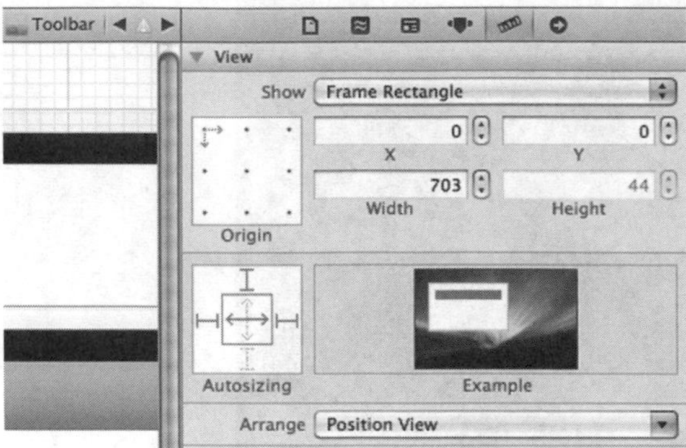

Figure 10.19 Appropriate auto-sizing settings to keep the toolbar at the top

Set the auto-sizing to match figure 10.19 to keep the toolbar at the top, regardless of the orientation.

Now the detail view has a toolbar that stays at the top regardless of the orientation. When the split view is in portrait, the master view isn't displayed, but there are callbacks called on the split view controller's delegate.

Let's handle those callbacks in the split view controller class itself, which means it's its own delegate. Declare in the header that it implements `UISplitViewControllerDelegate` and set `self` as the delegate in `viewDidLoad` (see the following listing).

Set `self` to be the delegate in `SVCSplitControllerviewDidLoad`

```
- (void)viewDidLoad {
    [super viewDidLoad];
    self.delegate = self;
}
```

When the split view controller rotates to landscape, a callback specifies that the master view controller will be hidden, and a `UIBarButtonItem` is passed in that's related to the master view. You can add this Bar button to your toolbar in the details area (see the following listing).

Callback when split view controller is going portrait and hiding master

```
- (void)splitViewController:(UISplitViewController*)svc
    willHideViewController:(UIViewController *)aViewController
        withBarButtonItem:(UIBarButtonItem*)barButtonItem
        forPopoverController:(UIPopoverController*)pc
{
    [barButtonItem setTitle:@"Menu"];
    [tbTop setItems:
            [NSArray arrayWithObject:barButtonItem]
            animated:YES];
}
```

Add Bar button (annotation)

Similarly, a callback is raised when the split view controller goes to landscape to invalidate the button and show the master view controller (see the following listing).

Invalidate the Menu button

```
- (void)splitViewController:(UISplitViewController*)svc
    willShowViewController:(UIViewController *)aViewController
    invalidatingBarButtonItem:(UIBarButtonItem *)button
{
    [tbTop setItems:nil animated:NO];
}
```

Remove Bar button

Now when the user turns the app to portrait in the iPad simulator, the Menu button appears. And if that button is tapped, the master view with the table view is displayed (see figure 10.20).

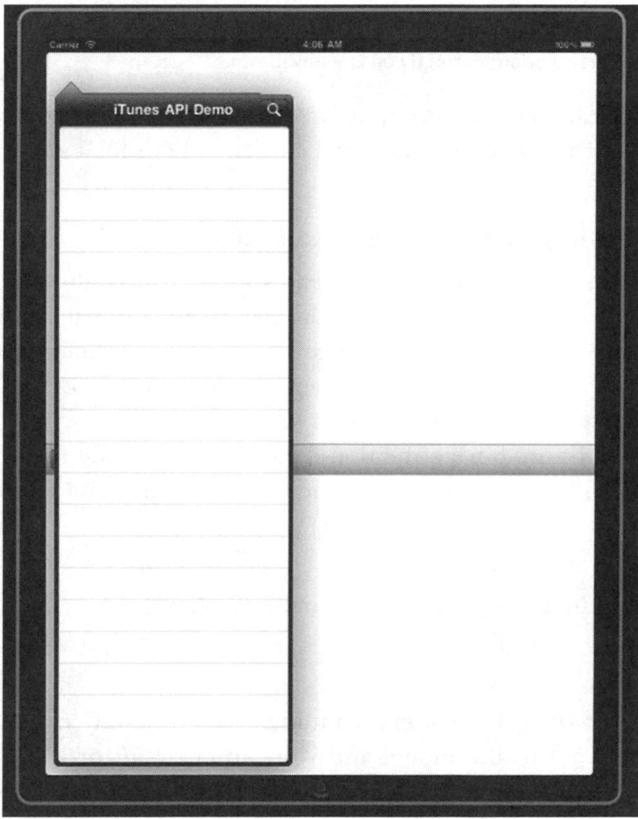

Figure 10.20 iPad app running portrait with master view displayed as pop-over

The search view toolbar needs to have its auto-sizing fixed, as does the web view controller (see figure 10.21).

Depending on the various widgets, you may want to set the auto-sizing to different settings so that it stays centered, stays to the right or left, or scales.

Getting the various controls on the views to display correctly may take more or less work, depending on the given app. Also, you'll need to test the views on different-sized devices to make sure fixing it in one place doesn't break it in another.

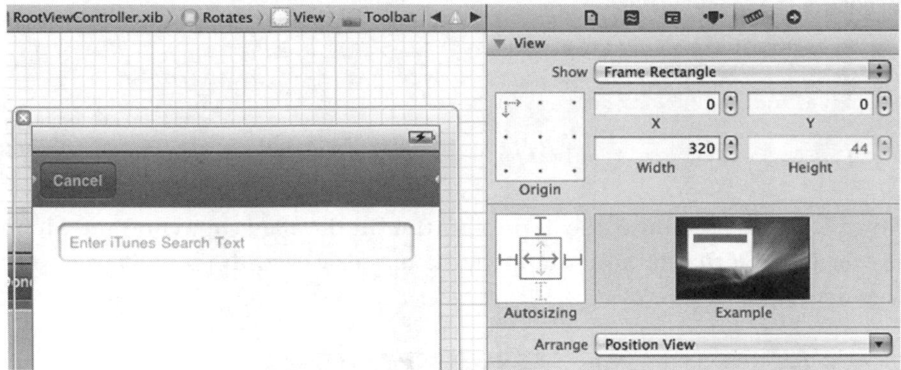

Figure 10.21 Fixing the toolbars to orient correctly on the new device

The master will often handle the navigation, but at some point you'll want to display some related data in the detail view (such as email content). Let's look at a way to do that in a universal binary.

TECHNIQUE 83 Displaying items in the detail view

As stated earlier, using the split view controller in iPad apps tends to follow the pattern that the master view handles navigation and the detail view handles detail information.

You'll follow that same pattern using MusicSearch. There's not much navigation, but the master view has the table view where the user selects the query results. You can display the artwork in the detail view when the user selects to do so.

But because this is a universal binary, the non-iPad devices running the app won't use the split view controller. How do you handle the difference in UI functionality for the given devices?

PROBLEM

You want to display the album artwork in a modally displayed view controller for iPhone, but in the detail view for iPad.

SOLUTION

You can use several ways to detect if the app is running on a given device. `[[UIDevice currentDevice] model]` returns the model and you can check it for iPad or other model designations. `UI_USER_INTERFACE_IDIOM()` returns either `UIUserInterfaceIdiomPhone` (for iPhone and iPod) or `UIUserInterfaceIdiomPad` (for iPad).

You could also set a variable in the main navigation controller (for iPhone/iPod) and similarly in the `SVCSplitController`. The `mainController` value is different based on the device type (`UINavigationController` for iPhone/iPod and `SVCSplitController` for iPad). This variation could be used to determine the device type. The variable could be similarly based on the resolution of the device, but that may not be consistent in the long term.

You'll use the `UI_USER_INTERFACE_IDIOM()` route, but also in the case of iPad, you'll post a notification using `NSNotificationCenter`, which the `SVCSplitController` will register to listen for. The view to be displayed will be included in the notification, and `SVCSplitController` will display the view in the detail view.

DISCUSSION

`SVCSplitController` needs to register for the notification of a posted view for the detail view display (see the following listing), which can be done in the `viewDidLoad` method.

`SVCSplitController` registers for `DisplayDetailsView` notifications

```
[[NSNotificationCenter defaultCenter] addObserver:self
        selector:@selector(displayInDetails:)
                                name:@"DisplayDetailsView" object:nil];
```

When a notification named `DisplayDetailsView` is posted, `SVCSplitController` will be notified and passed an `NSNotification` instance. The `NSNotification` instance will contain the view to be displayed in the detail view (see the following listing).

Notification processing to display details

```
-(void)displayInDetails:(NSNotification*)notif;
{
    UIView *view = [notif object];
    for (UIView *v in [detailsView subviews])
        [v removeFromSuperview];
     [detailsView addSubview:view];
}
```

Remove subviews

Now whenever a class wants to display something in the detail view, it can post a notification and include the view to be displayed (see the following listing).

For iPhone/iPod present the detail view modally; iPad posts notification with view

```
if (UI_USER_INTERFACE_IDIOM() == UIUserInterfaceIdiomPhone)
        [self presentModalViewController:vcWebView animated:YES];
    else
    {
        NSString *artistViewUrl =
            [dict objectForKey:@"artworkUrl100"];
         [webView loadRequest:[NSURLRequest
            requestWithURL:[NSURL URLWithString:artistViewUrl]]];
        [[NSNotificationCenter defaultCenter]
            postNotificationName:@"DisplayDetailsView"
            object:webView];
     }
```

Load artwork

Display web view

Apple has made something really great with the iPad. To me it's an obvious idea and a great execution. They've done a great job of taking a positive mobile experience and making it slightly different and maybe more immersive. Another area they've managed to make somewhat exciting is advertising. The first iAds I saw were fun to watch. Let's look at how to add those to an app.

10.3 *Adding iAds to an app*

Advertising is not a new way to make money. It's not even new to mobile apps. But Apple does it differently, because the distributor of your app is also the advertiser (sort of—they may not be advertising, but they are the warehouse serving the ads and securing the deals).

In your case, your app isn't really exceptional for selling because it does about the same thing as iTunes. And you don't have any In-App Purchases to offer the user. Let's add ads and see if you can monetize it that way.

You may not be able to sell your app for $.99, but if you can get $.10 from a user 20 times, you've done better. Let's look at adding iAds to your app.

TECHNIQUE 84 Configuring iTunes for iAds

As with some other special additions to apps (GameCenter, In-App Purchases, and APN), iAds require some online configuration in iTunesConnect, but not much.

PROBLEM

You need to configure your app in iTunesConnect to include iAds.

SOLUTION

You'll simply log into iTunesConnect and enable iAds for your app.

DISCUSSION

There's not much to it, but it's important. Without enabling iAds for your app, it won't get any ads.

In the Provisioning Portal, create a new app ID. Then log into iTunesConnect and click on your app to manage it. Click on Set Up iAd Network (see figure 10.22).

On the iAds page, select your target audience age and click Enable iAds (see figure 10.23).

You may need to check your contracts area in iTunesConnect to make sure you have all the necessary agreements in place. This is a good idea to do periodically, anyway. Sometimes clients ask me

Figure 10.22 iTunesConnect allows you to set up iAd network for your app

The iAd Network gives you an opportunity to earn advertising revenue through ads in your application. Learn more.

- Once you click Save, iAd cannot be disabled. To remove ads from an application, you will need to resubmit your application with the iAd Network functionality removed.

My primary target audience is users under 17 years of age. Yes ◉ No ○

Enable iAds

Figure 10.23 Select your target audience age and enable iAds in iTunesConnect.

why their app is no longer in the AppStore. The first thing I do is get them to log into iTunesConnect and see if there are any new or updated contracts they need to agree to.

Now that you've set up iAds in iTunesConnect, let's add it to the app.

TECHNIQUE 85 Adding iAds to an app

Adding iAds to your app is a lot like adding a regular view. In IB, there's an `ADBannerView` you can drag and drop into your project.

PROBLEM

You need to add iAds to your project and handle it accordingly.

SOLUTION

In the UI editor, you'll add an `ADBannerView` to your UI, and in the code, you'll handle the callback methods to hide the ad view when no ad is loaded.

DISCUSSION

Open the RootViewController.xib file. Because your artwork image is small, you really don't need the `UIWebView` to be so big. Let's use that for your ad space.

Drag the top of the web view down to leave some room and drop an `ADBannerView` in there (see figure 10.24).

For the code, be sure to add the `iAd.Framework` and add an outlet in RootViewController.h for the `ADBannerView` to be connected with IB.

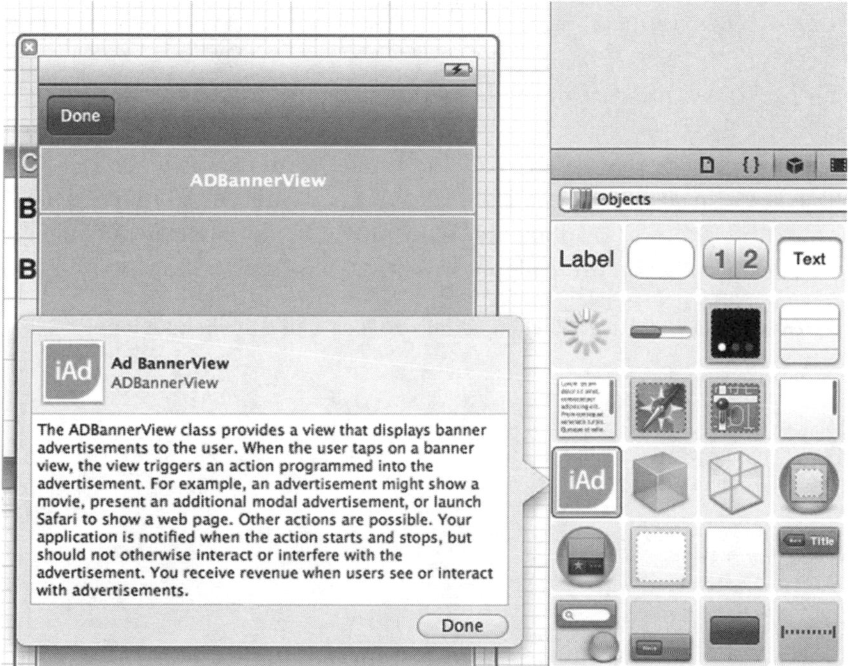

Figure 10.24 Dropping an `ADBannerView` control in your web view UI

Declare that RootViewController implements ADBannerViewDelegate in the header. Also declare a bool flag named hidingAdBanner.

When there's no ad displaying, you want to hide the ADBannerView control. A method that hides or shows the ad banner view based on what's passed in and the current state will help out here (see the following listing).

Method to hide the AdBanner by moving it offscreen with animation

```
-(void)hideAdBanner:(bool)hideIt;
{
    if ((hideIt && hidingAdBanner)
        || (!hideIt && !hidingAdBanner))
        return;                                          <— Not needed

    hidingAdBanner = hideIt;                             <— Set flag

    [UIView beginAnimations:nil context:nil];

    int adHeight = adBanner.frame.size.height;
    CGRect r = adBanner.frame;
    r.origin.y -= adHeight;                              <— Move banner
     adBanner.frame = r;

    r = webView.frame;
    r.origin.y -= adHeight;
    r.size.height += adHeight;                           <— Taller web view
     webView.frame = r;

    [UIView commitAnimations];                           <— Animate it
 }
```

You can use a few different delegate methods for the ADBannerView. With IB, set the delegate of the ADBannerView to be RootViewController. You're interested in two callback methods—when the ad loads and when the ad fails to load.

When the app starts, you can call hideAdBanner with YES so that the banner is out of view because there's no ad loaded. When an ad loads, you can call it again with NO. If an ad fails to load, you can call it again with YES (see the following listing).

Call hideAdBanner with YES when ad fails to load and NO when ad loads

```
- (void)bannerView:(ADBannerView *)banner
    didFailToReceiveAdWithError:(NSError *)error
{
    [self hideAdBanner:YES];
}

- (void)bannerViewDidLoadAd:(ADBannerView *)banner
{
    [self hideAdBanner:NO];
}
```

In the simulator, the ads will load test ads from the Apple servers. This is a good, reliable way of knowing if the code's working. They sometimes fail to load, which is helpful for testing (maybe this is intentional). When the app launches in the App Store, it will load real ads.

10.4 Summary

iTunesConnect has report features for seeing how your apps are doing as far as loading ads, displaying them, people clicking on them, and how they're paying.

There's also a lot of good information there, in the Provisioning Portal, the Apple Developer site, iOS forums, and many other places. I encourage you to get out there, see how people are solving problems and sharing solutions, and learn as much as you can.

Don't be afraid to ask questions. iOS developers tend to quite helpful, in my opinion!

11 Collection view, social, reminders, and state restoration—MeetSocial

This chapter covers

- Using collection views
- Working with the Social Framework
- Calendar items and reminders
- Saving and restoring state

iOS 6 changed and expanded many frameworks, classes, and protocols. These changes touch a lot of items both in functionality and concept. This chapter covers several of these areas in a new app called MeetSocial.

MeetSocial allows the user to search for meetings from meetup.com by specifying a location or keyword to search for events or groups. The results are displayed in a collection view. A *collection view* is similar to a table view, but the cells can have varied sizes, including width. Based on the width of the collection view cells, a variable number of cells can fit across the display.

The MeetSocial results may also be shared using the new Social Framework, which includes, but is not limited to, Twitter and Facebook. The MeetSocial project covers how to set up this sharing and display the UI to the user for sharing.

The event results have associated dates so MeetSocial allows the user to create a reminder for the event's date and time. Reminders are a new addition to the EventKit framework. State restoration is another new addition, but to the UIKit. It allows an app to store its current state to restore the UI on the next execution.

MeetSocial covers all of these areas while including familiar concepts and some functionality you've seen before. Some aspects of this project are new, but they all fit into areas we've already covered and you should feel confident in adding them to a project.

11.1 Presenting data using a collection view

Collection views use many of the same concepts as table views which you've already seen in projects like Dial4 in chapter 4. Both use a datasource and delegate and both have the concepts of sections, rows, and cells.

TECHNIQUE 86 Creating a project to use a collection view

You'll start by creating a new Master-Detail iOS project and convert it to use a collection view. Then you'll add the UI and functionality to search meetup.com for results and display them in the collection view.

PROBLEM

You need a new project containing a collection view to display your search results.

SOLUTION

Open Xcode and create a new project from the File menu. Specify it to be a Master-Detail iOS application, name it MeetSocial, and specify the other necessary settings.

DISCUSSION

You've created projects in just about every chapter so this is nothing new to you at this point. But I want to point out a couple of things. The first is that this project is using Storyboards (see figure 11.1), but not CoreData.

The second thing is that it also doesn't use Automatic Reference Counting (ARC). This is because, at the time of this writing, the JSON code I'll use isn't ARC-compliant. I'm fine with using or not using ARC at this point... as long as I remember whether I'm using it on a given project.

A few steps are necessary to convert the standard Master-Detail template to what you want for MeetSocial. First, select the MSMasterViewController.h file from the navigator and, in the editor, change its base class from `UITableViewController` to `UIViewController`. Then load the .storyboard file and delete the default master and detail view controllers.

Product Name MeetSocial
Organization Name Brainwashinc.com
Company Identifier com.brainwashinc
Bundle Identifier com.brainwashinc.MeetSocial
Class Prefix MS
Devices iPhone
☑ Use Storyboards
☐ Use Core Data
☐ Use Automatic Reference Counting
☐ Include Unit Tests

Figure 11.1 Creating a Master-Detail Storyboard project

Drop a new `UIViewController` into the UI edit area, change its class setting to `MSMasterViewController` in the Identity Inspector, and make it the new root view controller in the `UINavigationControllers` connections (see figure 11.2).

Now add a `UICollectionViewController` into IB and alter the default cell to be similar to the image (see figure 11.3). Also, be sure to set the collection view cell's identifier to `ResultsCell`. You'll use that in the code to dequeue or create a new instance of the cell.

As you develop the app, you can manipulate the cell in various dimensions to see the effects. Change the base class of `MSDetailViewController` from `UITableViewController` to `UICollectionViewController` and change the class name for your new IB `UICollectionViewController` to be `MSDetailViewController`. Remove the `configureView` method references from the details controller. This method is part of the template, but you won't use it in this case.

Now set the master view UI to be like the image (see figure 11.4) and wire it up to the related header file by Control-dragging the items to the header using the Assistant. Note the object naming, which will be referenced later in the code.

Also, Control-drag the text field to the collection view and select Push to create the segue from the search input to the results display. This is also a good time to set the text field delegate to be `MSMasterViewController` and set the attributes on the text

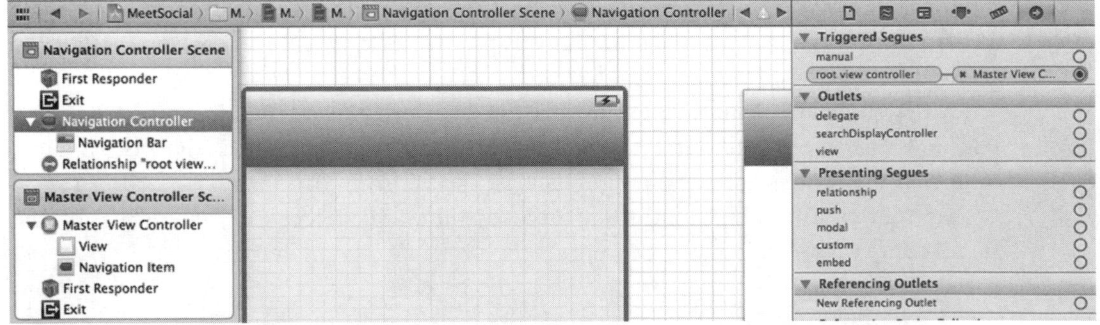

Figure 11.2 Removing table view from Master-Detail project

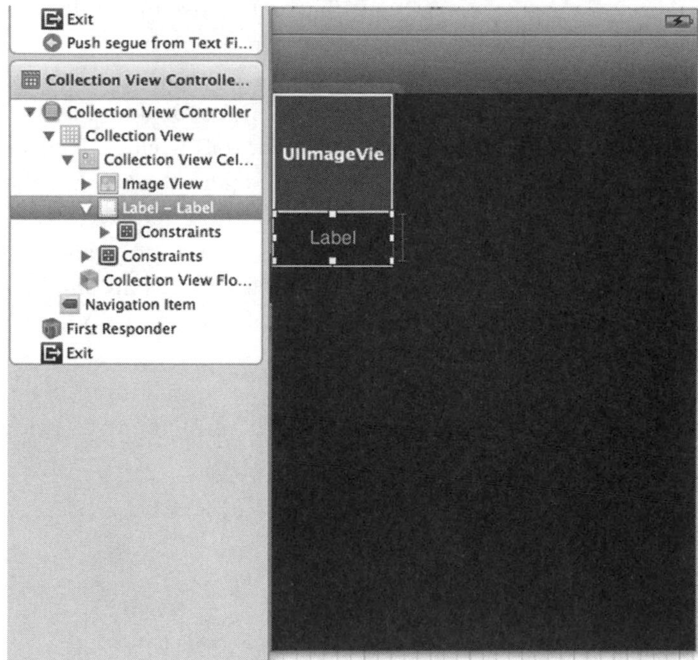

Figure 11.3 Adding a collection view controller to the UI

field in the Attributes Inspector; specifically you can set the Return key to Search. I also like to set the Clear button to appear while editing and check the Auto-enable Return Key box.

Back in the MSMasterViewController.m file, you need to remove the `_objects` data member. This is part of the template you selected, but you won't be using it. Delete the declaration of it near the top of the file: `NSMutableArray *_objects;`.

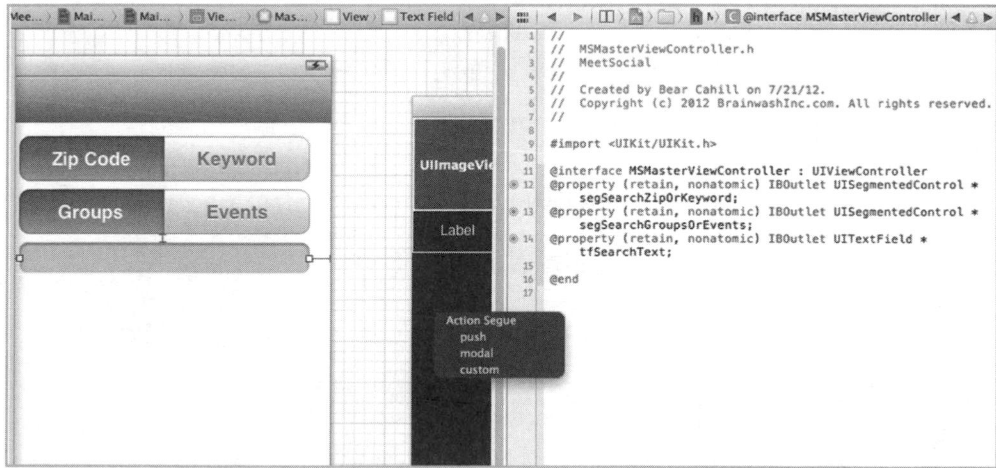

Figure 11.4 Wiring up the UI elements and segue

Now you'll have plenty of compile errors (see figure 11.5—some code removed to focus on the errors). To get rid of those, you need to address each place `_objects` was referenced. No problem. Delete the `insertNewObject:` method (the button created to call this method is in `viewDidLoad:`—delete the two lines for that `addButton`). For the implementation of `tableView:numberOfRowsInSection:` change it to return `0;`. For the `tableView:cellForRowAtIndexPath:` method, delete the two lines with *object* in them. And delete the entire body of any other method referencing `_objects`: `commitEditingStyle`, `didSelectRowAtIndexPath`, and `prepareForSegue`.

Also, specify in the interface declaration in the .h file that it implements `UITextFieldDelegate`. Feel free to compile the project now and see that it compiles without errors.

Now you have a fairly blank canvas to implement your search input, fetch results, and display them in your collection view. Next you'll implement fetching search results and displaying them.

```
- (void)insertNewObject:(id)sender
{
    if (!_objects) {
        _objects = [[NSMutableArray alloc] init];
    }
    [_objects insertObject:[NSDate date] atIndex:0];
    NSIndexPath *indexPath = [NSIndexPath indexPathForRow:0 inSection:0];
    [self.tableView insertRowsAtIndexPaths:[NSArray arrayWithObject:indexPath] withRowAnimation:
        UITableViewRowAnimationAutomatic];
}

- (NSInteger)tableView:(UITableView *)tableView numberOfRowsInSection:(NSInteger)section
{
    return _objects.count;
}

- (UITableViewCell *)tableView:(UITableView *)tableView cellForRowAtIndexPath:(NSIndexPath *)indexPath
{
    UITableViewCell *cell = [tableView dequeueReusableCellWithIdentifier:@"Cell"];

    NSDate *object = [_objects objectAtIndex:indexPath.row];
    cell.textLabel.text = [object description];
    return cell;
}

- (void)tableView:(UITableView *)tableView commitEditingStyle:(UITableViewCellEditingStyle)editingStyle
    forRowAtIndexPath:(NSIndexPath *)indexPath
{
    if (editingStyle == UITableViewCellEditingStyleDelete) {
        [_objects removeObjectAtIndex:indexPath.row];
        [tableView deleteRowsAtIndexPaths:[NSArray arrayWithObject:indexPath] withRowAnimation:
            UITableViewRowAnimationFade];
    } else if (editingStyle == UITableViewCellEditingStyleInsert) {
        // Create a new instance of the appropriate class, insert it into the array, and add a new row to the table
            view.
    }
}

- (void)tableView:(UITableView *)tableView didSelectRowAtIndexPath:(NSIndexPath *)indexPath
{
    if ([[UIDevice currentDevice] userInterfaceIdiom] == UIUserInterfaceIdiomPad) {
        NSDate *object = [_objects objectAtIndex:indexPath.row];
        self.detailViewController.detailItem = object;
    }
}

- (void)prepareForSegue:(UIStoryboardSegue *)segue sender:(id)sender
{
    if ([[segue identifier] isEqualToString:@"showDetail"]) {
        NSIndexPath *indexPath = [self.tableView indexPathForSelectedRow];
        NSDate *object = [_objects objectAtIndex:indexPath.row];
        [[segue destinationViewController] setDetailItem:object];
    }
}
```

Figure 11.5 Errors from removing `_objects` declaration

TECHNIQUE 87 Fetching search results from Meetup.com

Many apps I've developed have a server-side piece. In some cases the server side is part of the project. In other cases, the client develops the server side or it already exists. In whatever case, you need to understand the server API and develop the app functionality and user interface related to that API.

PROBLEM

Now that you've set up your UI, you need the functionality to back it up. You need the app to take the user's input from the search screen and fetch results from meetup.com.

You're only implementing a small subset of the meetup.com API—just searching events and groups and not even implementing the various search options for those. So you just have the ability to search by ZIP code (location) and keyword for either groups or events.

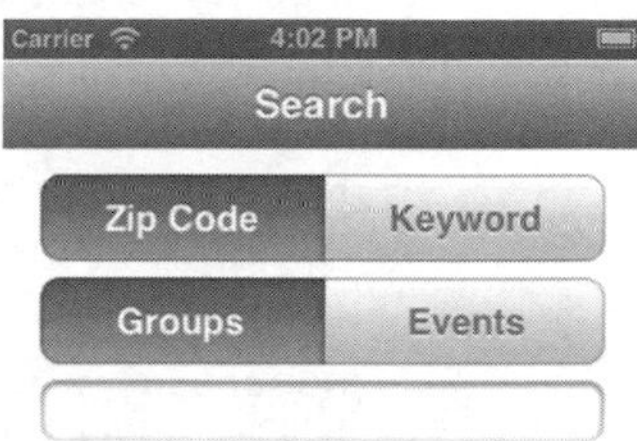

Figure 11.6 App running in the simulator

SOLUTION

MeetSocial takes the user input for search criteria including the text and constructs the appropriate query to the meetup.com server. Note: You'll need to register for a meetup.com API key at http://www.meetup.com/meetup_api/key/.

The meetup.com API is described at http://www.meetup.com/meetup_api/, where you can see the various items, documentation, libraries, and so on. For the purposes of this example, you'll only use two URLs with `GET` parameters built into them.

DISCUSSION

When your app starts, you want to do a couple things to get it started. In `viewDidLoad`, move the contents below the `super` call and add the `setTitle:` call to `self`. Similarly, create `viewWillAppear` and call `becomeFirstResponder` on the `tfSeachText` object. At this point, if you run your app, it looks ready (see figure 11.6).

You can select your search preferences and even type in search text, but nothing happens if you type in search text and tap Search. But if you add the `textFieldShouldReturn:` method to MSMasterViewController.m with the lines `[textField resignFirstResponder];` and return `NO;`, the app will display the empty collection view (see figure 11.7).

Figure 11.7 Empty collection view without search implemented

So let's implement the search based on the user's input. You'll get three pieces of information from the user: whether they want to search by ZIP code or keyword, whether they want to search for events or groups, and the search text (either a ZIP code or keyword).

Based on those pieces of information, you can construct the URL for the search and fetch the server results (see the following listing).

Fetch server results for search URL

```
-(void)doSearch;
{
    NSString *groupsOrEvents =                               <-- Search for
         segSearchGroupsOrEvents.selectedSegmentIndex == 0
                    ? @"groups" : @"2/open_events";

    NSString *zipOrKeyword =                                 <-- Search by
         segSearchZipOrKeyword.selectedSegmentIndex == 0
                    ? @"zip" : @"topic";
                                                                 Your
    NSString *apiKey = @"...";                               <-- API key
     NSString *query = [NSString stringWithFormat:
        @"https://api.meetup.com/%@?key=%@&sign=true&%@=%@",
        groupsOrEvents,
        apiKey,
        zipOrKeyword,
        tfSearchText.text];

    NSError *error = nil;
    NSURL *url = [NSURL URLWithString:query];
    NSHTTPURLResponse* retResp=nil;
    NSData *respData = [NSURLConnection sendSynchronousRequest:      Server
        [NSURLRequest requestWithURL:url]                        <-- query
         returningResponse:&retResp error:&error];

    if (error)
        NSLog(@"ERROR: %@", error);
    else
    {
        NSString *resultsJSON = [[[NSString alloc]
                    initWithData:respData
                    encoding:NSASCIIStringEncoding] autorelease];    Write
        [self writeToResultsFile:resultsJSON];                   <-- to file
     }
}
```

I want to point out two things here. One is that you'll need your own API key as I pointed out earlier. Put that in the `apiKey` variable. The other point is that you're writing the results out to a file. The collection view will use this same file to display the results instead of passing around the results in a variable. This approach has potential performance hindrances, but when you go to restore the UI in later techniques, having the data stored locally will be a big help.

To write out the code, you use a built-in method on `NSString`, as shown in the following listing. For any/all of the code, you may want other or more error handling.

Write out the search results to file

```
-(void)writeToResultsFile:(NSString*)stringToStore;
{
        NSArray *paths = NSSearchPathForDirectoriesInDomains
            (NSDocumentDirectory, NSUserDomainMask, YES);
        NSString *documentsDirectoryPath = [paths objectAtIndex:0];
        NSString *path = documentsDirectoryPath;                      Write path

        NSError *error = nil;
        [[NSFileManager defaultManager] createDirectoryAtPath:path
            withIntermediateDirectories:YES                            Create dir
             attributes:nil error:&error];
        if (error)
            NSLog(@"Dir Error: %@", error);

        path = [NSString stringWithFormat:@"%@/%@", path, @"results.json"];
        [stringToStore
             writeToFile:path atomically:YES                           Write file
            encoding:NSUTF8StringEncoding error:&error];
        if (error)
            NSLog(@"Write Error: %@", error);
}
```

NSData also has a writeOut: method that you could use to store the data and have the collection view controller convert however necessary. But I wanted to do it here for potential debugging purposes: being able to log it out, and so forth.

Add the call to doSearch, [self doSearch];, in the textFieldShouldReturn: delegate call to perform the search before the segue to the collection view controller happens. Now that you have the results, the main view controller has done its job. It's time to display the results.

TECHNIQUE 88 Displaying items in a collection view

Collection views are similar in multiple ways to table views. They both use a data source and a delegate for managing the data and user interaction. And they're both great for displaying data using cells. Collection views are more flexible in the way they display the data visually as far as shape and size.

PROBLEM

You have the search results stored in a file and need to display them meaningfully in a collection view. By *meaningfully*, I mean you'd like to display them similar to icons with a limited amount of text below for the name.

SOLUTION

MeetSocial will read the results from the file and convert the JSON text into data object instances—an array of NSDictionary instances in this case. The automatic reloading of the collection view data will drive the rest of the displaying of data.

You have your collection view controller so you have a collection view wired up to its datasource and delegate (UICollectionViewDataSource and UICollectionView-Delegate protocols, respectively). Now you need to implement the defined methods in those protocols.

For the UICollectionViewDataSource, you'll implement two methods: the first to specify how many items are in your section and the second to return the cell for the given indexPath specified in the request:

```
-(NSInteger)collectionView:(UICollectionView *)collectionView
    numberOfItemsInSection:(NSInteger)section;
-(UICollectionViewCell*)collectionView:(UICollectionView *)collectionView
    cellForItemAtIndexPath:(NSIndexPath *)indexPath;
```

The numberOfSectionsInCollectionView: method is optional and defaults to 1 if not implemented.

For the UICollectionViewDelegate, you'll implement methods for when the user selects a cell, which is covered in technique 89.

DISCUSSION

First let's cover reading the data back into the app.

Reading stored results data file

```
-(NSString*) readResultsFile
{
    NSArray *paths = NSSearchPathForDirectoriesInDomains
                    (NSDocumentDirectory, NSUserDomainMask, YES);
    NSString *documentsDirectory = [paths objectAtIndex:0];

    NSString *fileName = [NSString stringWithFormat:@"%@/results.json",
                    documentsDirectory];
    NSError *error = nil;
    NSString *content = [[[NSString alloc] initWithContentsOfFile:fileName
                    usedEncoding:nil
                     error:&error] autorelease];             Read in text
    if (error)
    {
        NSLog(@"read error: %@", error);
        return nil;
    }

    return content;
}
```

Now you can call readResultsFile when you reload the collection view. So let's call it from the numberOfItemsInSection method. I'm using a JSON framework that you can find here: http://stig.github.com/json-framework/. Be sure to include the JSON.h import in your code. Similarly, declare an NSArray object named displayItems in your interface (either in your .h or at the top of your .m) and likewise release it in your dealloc method.

Determine and return number of items in section

```
- (NSInteger)collectionView:(UICollectionView *)collectionView
                    numberOfItemsInSection:(NSInteger)section;
{
    NSString *resultsJSON = [self readResultsFile];
```

```
    NSDictionary* resultsDict =                                      Convert
                        [resultsJSON JSONValue];                  <─┘ to objects
     if (resultsDict)
    {
        [displayItems release];                                        Get
        NSString *key = @"results";                                <─┘ data
         displayItems = [[resultsDict objectForKey:key] retain];
    }
    return [displayItems count];
}
```

So you've read in the results data, converted it to data (an array of `NSDictionary` instances), and stored it. Also, you returned the number of elements in your array, which is the number of items in your collection view. Now you need to create the cells for this data when it's needed for display by the collection view.

This implementation of `collectionView:cellForItemAtIndexPath:` will use the cell you made in IB. It was simple: an image view and a label. Ideally, you'll display an image in the image view and the item name in the label. That doesn't sound too bad. It's not, but it's also not that straightforward. You have a few hurdles to clear in the process.

One hurdle is that you may be displaying events or groups, and each of those have different data returned in the results. For example, the groups have URLs for images, but the events don't. Similarly, events have dates associated with them, which is important given the context. So let's display the image for groups, but the date in that large area for events.

Since you have that default cell defined, you can dequeue your cell using a set cell identifier. If one doesn't exist that you can reuse, the framework will create one for you. Then, based on whether you have an image URL (value in dictionary for `photo_url` key), you'll fetch and display the image at that URL.

Configure the collection view cell

```
static NSString *CellIdentifier = @"ResultsCell";          <── Cell identifier

- (UICollectionViewCell *)collectionView:(UICollectionView *)collectionView
                        cellForItemAtIndexPath:(NSIndexPath *)indexPath;
{
    UICollectionViewCell *cell = [collectionView
        dequeueReusableCellWithReuseIdentifier:CellIdentifier
                        forIndexPath:indexPath];

    cell.contentView.backgroundColor = [UIColor darkGrayColor];

    NSDictionary *item = [displayItems objectAtIndex:indexPath.row];
    NSString *photoURL = [item objectForKey:@"photo_url"];

    UIImageView *iv = nil;
    UILabel *lbl = nil;                                                Find UI
                                                                       items
    for (UIView *v in cell.contentView.subviews)                   <─┘
    {
         if ([v isKindOfClass:[UIImageView class]])
            iv = (UIImageView*)v;
```

```
        else if ([v isKindOfClass:[UILabel class]])
        {
            lbl = (UILabel*)v;
        }
    }

    [iv setImage:nil];
    [lbl setText:[item objectForKey:@"name"]];

    if (photoURL)
    {
        if ([photoURL length] > 0)
            [iv setImage:[UIImage imageWithData:
                         [NSData dataWithContentsOfURL:
                         [NSURL URLWithString:photoURL]]]];
    }
    return cell;
}
```

So you get your new or reused cell and the selected item. You get the value for the `photoURL` key (there won't be one for events) and then search for your UI items of the image view and label.

You set the name of the event or group (both have a name value) in the label and if you have a `photoURL` value, you fetch that image and set it in the image view. Now if you do a search for events, you'll see meaningful results (see figure 11.8).

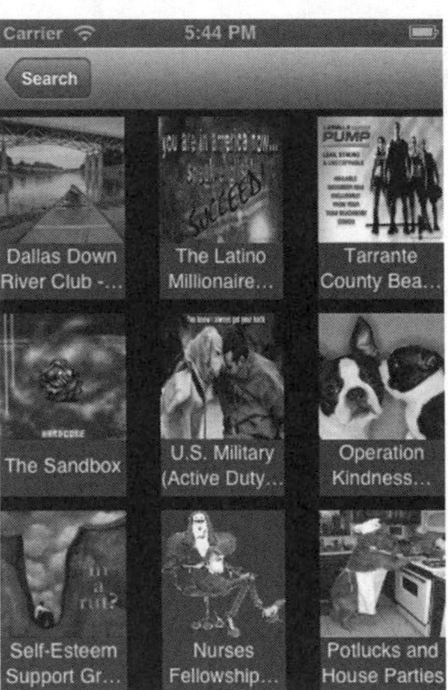

Figure 11.8 Event search results with images

So the difference for the search results for events compared to groups is that you want to display the data for the events (instead of an image). Since the date is key for a date-based event, you'll put it where the image would go and that way it's pretty large.

This will give you a chance to do two extra things: dynamically change a cell and format a date. Creating a `UILabel` for the date isn't a big deal. You can add it as a subview of the image view so that when you find it again later, you can remove it before doing something else.

So in the case where you have an event, you have the default label set to the name (as with a group). You can get the date/time value using the `time` key and use an `NSDateFormatter` to make nice readable date text. You'll also set some nice attributes on the label.

Collection view cell image and label configuration

```
- (UICollectionViewCell *)collectionView:(UICollectionView *)collectionView
                     cellForItemAtIndexPath:(NSIndexPath *)indexPath;
{
```

```
UICollectionViewCell *cell = [collectionView
    dequeueReusableCellWithReuseIdentifier:CellIdentifier
    forIndexPath:indexPath];

cell.contentView.backgroundColor = [UIColor darkGrayColor];

NSDictionary *item = [displayItems objectAtIndex:indexPath.row];
NSString *photoURL = [item objectForKey:@"photo_url"];
NSDecimalNumber *time = [item objectForKey:@"time"];        <-- Get time value

UIImageView *iv = nil;
UILabel *lbl = nil;

for (UIView *v in cell.contentView.subviews)
{
    if ([v isKindOfClass:[UIImageView class]])
    {
        iv = (UIImageView*)v;
        [iv.subviews makeObjectsPerformSelector:             <-- Remove old label
                    @selector(removeFromSuperview)];
    }
    else if ([v isKindOfClass:[UILabel class]])
        lbl = (UILabel*)v;
}

[iv setImage:nil];
[lbl setText:[item objectForKey:@"name"]];

if (photoURL)
{
if ([photoURL length] > 0)
[iv setImage:[UIImage imageWithData:
                    [NSData dataWithContentsOfURL:
                    [NSURL URLWithString:photoURL]]]];
}
else if (time)
{
    if ([time floatValue] > 0)
    {
        if (!dateFormatter)                                  <-- Create formatter
         {
            dateFormatter = [[NSDateFormatter alloc] init];
            [dateFormatter setTimeStyle:NSDateFormatterNoStyle];
            [dateFormatter setDateFormat:@"M/d/YY H:MM"];
        }

        NSDate *eventDate = [NSDate dateWithTimeIntervalSince1970:
                    [time floatValue]/1000];
        NSString *dateStr = [dateFormatter
                    stringFromDate:eventDate];

        UILabel *lblDate = [[[UILabel alloc]                 <-- Config label
                     initWithFrame:CGRectMake(0, 0, 90, 90)]
                    autorelease];
        [lblDate setNumberOfLines:2];
```

```
            [lblDate setFont:[UIFont boldSystemFontOfSize:22]];
            [lblDate setLineBreakMode:NSLineBreakByWordWrapping];
            [lblDate setTextAlignment:NSTextAlignmentCenter];
            [lblDate setTextColor:[UIColor whiteColor]];
            [lblDate setBackgroundColor:[UIColor blackColor]];
            [lblDate setText:dateStr];
            [iv addSubview:lblDate];            <- Add label
        }
    }

    return cell;
}
```

Note that you remove the date/time label from the image view when you cycle through to find the cell's image view. Also, the `dateFormatter` object is a data member declared in the interface declaration and released in the `dealloc`. You can read through the other attributes set on the `UILabel` and change those as you like to get different effects (see figure 11.9).

So that's the basic functionality. You've used user input to search for event or group results based on ZIP code or keyword. Then you stored those results and displayed them depending on the type of results using an image or the date/time. Now what should you do if the user taps on a given cell, be it a group or event?

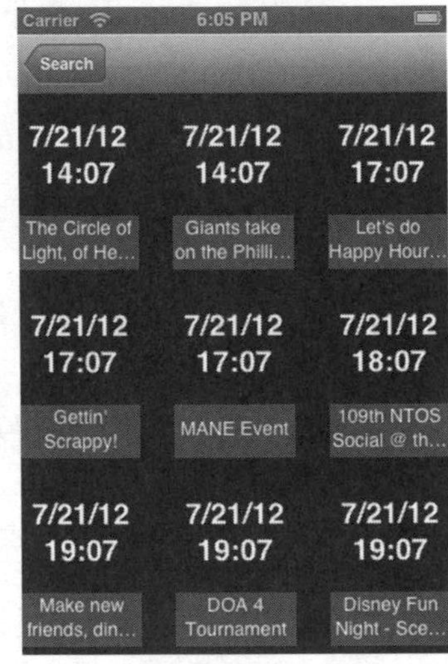

Figure 11.9 Event results displayed in collection view

11.2 Sharing via the Social Framework

Obviously it's all about socializing these days. Everyone posts updates or tweets about when they go out, what they eat, and just about everything else. MeetSocial can use the Social Framework in iOS to share items from their search.

The Social Framework provides access to the integrated social network accounts setup. If the user has configured their account (such as Twitter username and password), the app can piggyback on that. This means the app doesn't need to prompt the user to log in and manage that whole process. Before the Social Framework, this process could be complex and inconsistent for the user.

The Social Framework also provides the means and UI for the user to set this up from your app if they haven't already. Since so much of this is handled for you, MeetSocial won't directly do much with the Social Framework. You'll just specify that you want to share and use the UIKit `UIActivityViewController` to present it to the user, and the rest is handled for you.

TECHNIQUE 89 Specifying activity items

Setting what you want to share is straightforward. You'll set things like the event (or group) name, the event date, an image, and so on. From there you have what you want to share.

PROBLEM

You need to specify what to share with others based on your search results of events or groups.

SOLUTION

As with the collection view, you want access to different types of data based on the search results. In the case of a group, you have an image, but for the event, you want to share the date. You can create an array of items for the sharing activity.

The `UIActivityViewController` has an `init` method that takes an array of activity items. Yep, it's about that easy. You just implement the `collectionView:didSelectItemAtIndexPath:` method to get the selected item, get the applicable data, and create the array. We'll look at presenting the UI in the next technique.

DISCUSSION

Like in the cell method for a collection view, you can look for the "link" key value for the selected item to determine whether it's an event or group. There are other ways to do this: you could've stored some flag setting based on the user's search or even set a value in the cell method when you figured out what type of search it is. But in most cases you need the link value anyway.

Our main goal here is to share the various info via social networks, but in the real world, that's not the only thing you can do here, so let's give the user a couple of options. Specifically, let's give them the option to open a web page for the given item. Okay, you got me—the event has a URL but it's keyed differently. Busted. But that comes in the next technique.

So the `collectionView:didSelectItemAtIndexPath:` can set the selected item and, based on that, prompt the user for some actions.

Display options when item is selected

```
- (void)collectionView:(UICollectionView *)collectionView
                    didSelectItemAtIndexPath:(NSIndexPath *)indexPath;
{
    [selectedItem release];                                                  // Create member
     selectedItem = [[displayItems objectAtIndex:indexPath.row] retain];
    av = [[[UIAlertView alloc] initWithTitle:@"Details"
                message:@"Would you like to..."
                delegate:self cancelButtonTitle:@"Cancel"
                otherButtonTitles:@"See Website",
                                  @"Share", nil]
                                    autorelease];
    [av show];
}
```

In the preceding code, you get the selected item and store it in the member named `selectedItem`. Be sure to declare that in the interface in the .h file or at the top of the .m file, and add it to the `dealloc` unless you're using ARC. Also, specify in the .h that your class implements the `UIAlertViewDelegate` protocol.

You can handle it generically for now, but when you actually go to share it, you need to differentiate. You'll do that in the method to handle the tap.

Handle selection of user's `alertView` option

```
- (void)alertView:(UIAlertView *)alertView
                  clickedButtonAtIndex:(NSInteger)buttonIndex;
{
    if (buttonIndex == 0)                                          Cancel
         return;                                                   button

    if (buttonIndex == 2)
        [self share];                                              Share
     else                                                          item
    {
        NSString *url = [selectedItem objectForKey:@"link"];

        if (url)                                                   Show
             [[UIApplication sharedApplication]                    item
                    openURL:[NSURL URLWithString:url]];            site
        else
        {
            NSString *url = [selectedItem objectForKey:@"event_url"];
            [[UIApplication sharedApplication]
                    openURL:[NSURL URLWithString:url]];
        }
    }
}
```

If the user taps Cancel, you return. If they tap the Share button, you can handle that in another method (in technique 90). And if they tap the website option, you can get the applicable URL and load it. Let's look at the share part.

Using activity view controller to share

```
-(void)share;
{
    NSString *url = [selectedItem objectForKey:@"link"];
    NSString *textToShare = [selectedItem objectForKey:@"name"];

    UIImage *imageToShare = nil;
    NSArray *activityItems = nil;
    if (url)
    {
        NSString *photoURL = [selectedItem
                    objectForKey:@"photo_url"];
        imageToShare = [UIImage imageWithData:
                    [NSData dataWithContentsOfURL:
                    [NSURL URLWithString:photoURL]]];
        activityItems = @[textToShare,
                    url,                                           Share
                    imageToShare];                                 image
```

```
    }
    else
    {
        url = [selectedItem objectForKey:@"event_url"];

        NSDecimalNumber *time = [selectedItem objectForKey:@"time"];
        NSDate *eventDate = [[NSDate dateWithTimeIntervalSince1970:
                    [time floatValue]/1000] autorelease];
        NSString *dateStr = [dateFormatter stringFromDate:eventDate];

        activityItems = @[textToShare,
                          url,
                           dateStr];                              Share date
    }

                     UIActivityViewController *activityVC =
Pass in                  [[[UIActivityViewController alloc]
items                        initWithActivityItems:activityItems
                              applicationActivities:nil] autorelease];
                     [self presentViewController:activityVC
                                        animated:YES
                                      completion:nil];
}
```

Like for the `collectionView:didSelectItemAtIndexPath:` method, you key off of the link value to see whether it's a group or event. In each case, you create values for the `activityItems` array accordingly. But what do you do with these items?

TECHNIQUE 90 Presenting the activity sharing interface

In technique 89 you determined what to share. Now you need to share it. Though the Social Framework provides the infrastructure for what you want to do, UIKit provides the UI... at least the start of it.

PROBLEM

You need to present share options to the user based on what they've selected to share. Ideally, you want to allow them to share in a variety of ways without overwhelming them with steps and decisions, but instead presenting meaningful options.

SOLUTION

You'll use your array of activity items to create and preset the `UIActivityViewController`, which will present options based on your activity items. The underlying Social Framework paths will handle the rest for you.

DISCUSSION

You instantiate the `UIActivityViewController` with that array and present it (see figure 11.10). I didn't specify a completion handler but you can, and it'll be called after the controller is dismissed.

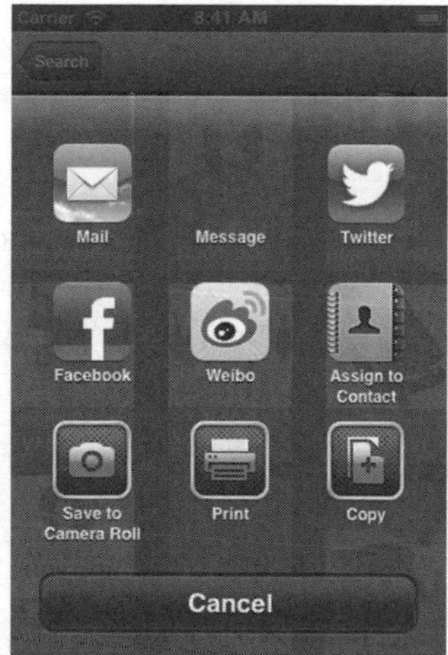

Figure 11.10 Social network share UI

Based on the items you're trying to share via the activity items, the UI will present the options. Note that since you included an image, one option is to save to the camera roll. In this case, you'll pick Facebook and will see the continued UI to go that particular route (see figure 11.11).

The user is presented with options including the image album to use, location, text, and more. The frameworks involved handle all of the heavy lifting.

Since you have a date, it'd be nice to create a calendar event or reminder. Let's look at that now.

Figure 11.11 Facebook-specific share UI

11.3 Creating calendar items in the OS

EventKit lets you easily create calendar items or even access existing ones to search, manipulate, present, and so forth. Even the UI is provided to create a smooth experience for both the developer and end user.

For MeetSocial, the events are based on dates, so let's allow the user to create meaningful date-based items from that.

TECHNIQUE 91 Creating the event store and calendar event

The EventKit framework provides much of what's needed to create and manage calendar-related events. This ties in nicely to your app so let's use it for the events, since they're date/time-based.

PROBLEM

You want to allow the user to create a calendar event based on the item selected and its related date/time.

SOLUTION

You'll add the EventKit to your app, retrieve the date and time for the event, and use the Event Store to create your particular event.

Calendar manipulation can get complex with calculating dates, repeat events, and so forth, but we'll cover the basics here and set you free to conquer the world on your own. If you're going to do a date-rich app, you'll soon get more familiar with these concepts, so we'll give you the keys here.

DISCUSSION

First, be sure to add the EventKit to your project's Build Phases (see figure 11.12). Add the EventKitUI framework also while you're here. This allows for editing of calendar events. And add the import of EventKit/EventKit.h and EventKitUI/EventKitUI.h to your class.

And you present the user with the new options.

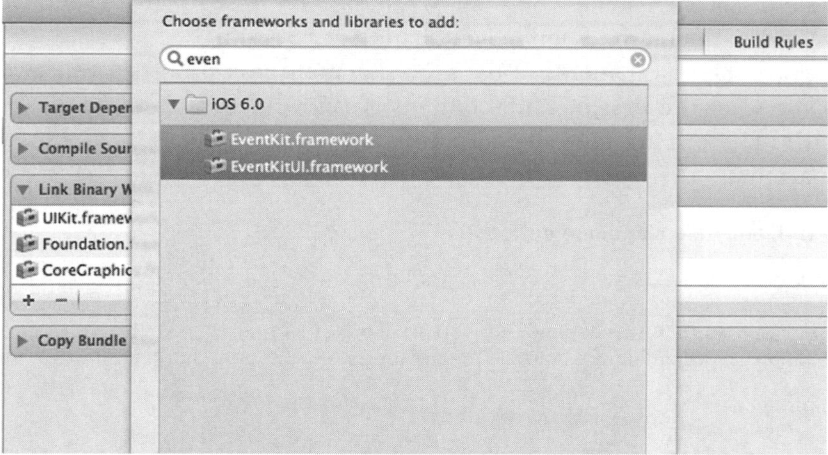

Figure 11.12 Adding EventKit frameworks

Presenting share options including calendar

```
- (void)collectionView:(UICollectionView *)collectionView
                      didSelectItemAtIndexPath:(NSIndexPath *)indexPath;
{
    [selectedItem release];
    selectedItem = [[displayItems objectAtIndex:indexPath.row]
                      retain];
    NSString *url = [selectedItem objectForKey:@"link"];

    UIAlertView *av = nil;
    if (url)
        av = [[[UIAlertView alloc] initWithTitle:@"Details"
                      message:@"Would you like to..." delegate:self
                      cancelButtonTitle:@"Cancel"
                      otherButtonTitles:@"See Group Page", @"Share",
                          nil]
                      autorelease];
    else
        av = [[[UIAlertView alloc] initWithTitle:@"Details"
                      message:@"Would you like to..." delegate:self
                      cancelButtonTitle:@"Cancel"
                      otherButtonTitles:@"See Event Page", @"Share",
                          @"Create Cal Item",                    New
                           @"Create Reminder",                   options
                          nil]
                          autorelease];

    [av show];
}
```

Now the user has two new options: one for creating a calendar event and one for creating a reminder (see next technique). You'll need to update your `alertView:clickedButtonAtIndex:` method to handle these. Currently your `else` in the method to handle the event assumes you want to see the web page for that event. Now you'll check whether the button is tapped and handle it accordingly.

Here are the new contents of the else statement that processes your event selections. Note that the previous full contents are now in the if for when the button index is 1. The rest are the calendar and reminder items. Let's look at the calendar event part first.

Handle URL and calendar share options

```
if (buttonIndex == 1)
{
    NSString *url = [selectedItem objectForKey:@"event_url"];
    [[UIApplication sharedApplication] openURL:[NSURL URLWithString:url]];
}
else
{
    NSDecimalNumber *time = [selectedItem objectForKey:@"time"];
    NSDate *eventDate = [[NSDate dateWithTimeIntervalSince1970:
                             [time floatValue]/1000] autorelease];
    EKEventStore *eStore = [[[EKEventStore alloc]                    // Create EventStore
                              initWithAccessToEntityTypes:
                             EKEntityMaskReminder | EKEntityMaskEvent]
                             autorelease];
    NSError *error = nil;
    if (buttonIndex == 3)
    {
        if ([self isAuthorizedForEntityType:EKEntityTypeEvent])
            [self createCalItem];                                    // Create if authorized
    }
}
```

Not too much about creating the event is done in this method. You're checking whether the app has been authorized to create events and, if so, call `createCalItem` to create it. Let's look at the authorization request.

Checking for calendar authorization

```
-(bool)isAuthorizedForEntityType:(EKEntityType)type;
{
    EKAuthorizationStatus authStatus =                               // Check authorization
         [EKEventStore authorizationStatusForEntityType:type];
    if (authStatus != EKAuthorizationStatusAuthorized)
    {
        [[EKEventStore alloc]
            requestAccessToEntityType:EKEntityTypeEvent
            completion:^ (BOOL granted, NSError *error)
        {
            if (granted)                                             // Create if granted
             {
                [self createCalItem];
            }
            else                                                     // Not granted message
             {
```

```
                UIAlertView *av = [[[UIAlertView alloc]
                    initWithTitle:@"Permissions"
                    message:@"If you deny the app permissions, you can not \
                        create calendar events.\n\nYou can \
                        change your permissiongs in the Settings \
                        app under Privacy."
                        delegate:nil
                    cancelButtonTitle:nil
                    otherButtonTitles:@"OK", nil] autorelease];
                [av show];
            }
        }];
        return NO;
    }
    else
        return YES;                                  Already authorized
}
```

The authorization method takes an EventKit entity type and queries for the authorization setting. The first time the status is queried, its value is the EKAuthorizationStatus enum value of EKAuthorizationStatusNotDetermined.

If the user has previously granted permission, the method drops into the else statement and returns YES. Back in the calling method, the createCalItem method is called. If the status is anything other than EKAuthorizationStatusAuthorized, you want to prompt for authorization.

If the user grants permission in the prompt, create the calendar event by calling createCalItem. Otherwise, display a meaningful message to the user. Let's look at the createCalItem method for creating the calendar event.

Create and edit a calendar item

```
-(void)createCalItem;
{
    EKEventStore *eStore = [[[EKEventStore alloc] init] autorelease];

    EKEvent *event =                                              Create event
                 [EKEvent eventWithEventStore:eStore];
    [event setCalendar:[eStore defaultCalendarForNewEvents]];
    [event setTitle:[selectedItem objectForKey:@"name"]];

    NSDecimalNumber *time = [selectedItem objectForKey:@"time"];
    NSDate *eventDate = [NSDate dateWithTimeIntervalSince1970:
                        [time floatValue]/1000];

    [event setStartDate:eventDate];
    [event setEndDate:eventDate];
    NSError *error = nil;
    [eStore saveEvent:event span:EKSpanThisEvent
        commit:YES error:&error];                                 Save event
     if (error)
        NSLog(@"Saving createCalItem: %@", error);

    EKEventEditViewController *editEvent =
        [[[EKEventEditViewController alloc] init] autorelease];
    [editEvent setEditViewDelegate:self];
```

```
    [editEvent setEvent:event];                              Display
    [self presentViewController:editEvent                    event
            animated:YES completion:nil];
}
```

In the createCalItem method, you create the event store so you can access the calendar. The event is created and you set the calendar, title, start date, and end date. Then the event is saved. Finally, you display the built-in display for the event so the user can make any changes to the event.

You don't have to present the event to the user to edit, but why not? They might want to add some details, and you get to go through the (short) process of seeing how that's done. But what about the reminder?

TECHNIQUE 92 Creating a calendar reminder

In the previous technique you saw how to present the user with new options for their date-based selected item. You also saw how to create the event store and calendar event for their item.

We presented them with the option to create a reminder, but you're not handling it yet. Let's see how the reminder is created too.

PROBLEM

You want to create a calendar reminder for a date-based event similar to creating a calendar event in the previous technique.

SOLUTION

You'll use the same event store, but will need to create a reminder and set its applicable attributes. But there's no need to present any other UI except for a confirmation the reminder was created.

DISCUSSION

That last code listing in the previous technique shows what happens if the button index is 3 for a calendar event. Let's look at an else for that if in the alertView: clickedButtonAtIndex: method to handle the reminder option.

Checking for calendar or reminder authorization

```
if (buttonIndex == 3)
{
    if ([self isAuthorizedForEntityType:EKEntityTypeEvent])
        [self createCalItem];
}
else
{
    if ([self isAuthorizedForEntityType:EKEntityTypeReminder])      New
        [self createReminderItem];                                 reminder
 }
```

Just as in the previous technique, you need to check for the user's authorization to create the reminder entity type EKEntityTypeReminder. If they have previously authorized, you call createReminderItem to create the new reminder.

Since your isAuthorizedForEntityType method takes the entity type already, you just need to update it to handle the case when the user is prompted and they authorize access.

Create item based on entity type

```
if (granted)
{
    if (type == EKEntityTypeEvent)
        [self createCalItem];
    else
        [self createReminderItem];          <-- Access granted
 }
```

In both cases your app calls the new method named createReminderItem to create the reminder if authorization is approved.

Create an iOS reminder

```
-(void)createReminderItem;
{
    EKEventStore *eStore = [[[EKEventStore alloc] init] autorelease];

    NSDecimalNumber *time = [selectedItem objectForKey:@"time"];
    NSDate *eventDate = [NSDate dateWithTimeIntervalSince1970:
        [time floatValue]/1000];

    EKReminder *reminder =                          <-- Create reminder
         [EKReminder reminderWithEventStore:eStore];

    NSCalendar *gregorian = [[[NSCalendar alloc]
        initWithCalendarIdentifier:
        NSGregorianCalendar]
        retain];
    NSDateComponents *comps = [gregorian components:
        (NSDayCalendarUnit | NSMonthCalendarUnit
        | NSYearCalendarUnit)
        fromDate:eventDate];
    [comps setDay:[comps day]];
    [comps setMonth:[comps month]];
    [comps setYear:[comps year]];

    [reminder setCalendar:                          <-- Set values
         [eStore defaultCalendarForNewReminders]];
    [reminder setTitle:[selectedItem objectForKey:@"name"]];
    [reminder setDueDateComponents:comps];

    NSError *error = nil;                           <-- Save reminder
    [eStore saveReminder:reminder
         commit:YES error:&error];
    if (error)
        NSLog(@"Saving createCalItem: %@", error);

    UIAlertView *av = [[[UIAlertView alloc]
        initWithTitle:@"Reminder"
        message:@"Reminder created!"
        delegate:nil cancelButtonTitle:nil
```

```
        otherButtonTitles:@"OK", nil]
        autorelease];
    [av show];
}
```

Similar to the calendar event, you create the event store instance, create the reminder, set the reminder values, and save the reminder in the event store. Instead of displaying a view to edit the reminder, you display a message to the user that the reminder was created.

We've been dealing a lot with various UI aspects, including the collection view and Social Framework items. You've probably been starting the app a lot and having to do your searches over and over again. What if you could start where you left off each time?

11.4 Saving and restoring the UI state

A new feature introduced in iOS 6 is the ability to save and restore the state of your app. You could always do this on your own and in your own fashion, but now it's facilitated and some parts are automated for you.

For MeetSocial, you do search for server results and store them locally. If, while viewing results, you're interrupted, run other apps, and our MeetSocial app is removed from memory at some point, you'll have to start over. You can avoid this with UI state restoration by adding new methods, protocols, and attributes to items as part of the UIKit. There are several steps and some parts are done for you.

TECHNIQUE 93 Specify that an app will save/restore

The first thing you need to do is tell the OS that your app intends to save its state when necessary and restore it when returning. This is done with a couple of short methods.

But since the app is now expected to restore, another method will be called to help fulfill that restoration and you need to implement it.

PROBLEM

You want your app to restore to the previous UI state during restoration. So you need the app delegate to declare that it intends to restore and also facilitate the restoration as necessary.

SOLUTION

In your `MESAppDelegate` class you implement the `UIStateRestoration` methods to specify your intentions to save/restore state.

You also need to implement the `application:viewControllerWithRestorationIdentifierPath:coder:` method to return restorable view controllers as requested.

DISCUSSION

There are two methods concerned with declaring saving and restoring, and they both return `YES`.

Specifying the app will save and restore

```
-(BOOL) application:(UIApplication *)application
                      shouldSaveApplicationState:(NSCoder *)coder
```

```
{
    return YES;
}

-(BOOL) application:(UIApplication *)application
                        shouldRestoreApplicationState:(NSCoder *)coder
{
    return YES;
}
```

Not much to that, but also it doesn't do much. It tells the OS to make the necessary calls and expect them to be implemented. One of those methods returns view controller instances as they're requested.

Restore view controllers based on ID

```
- (UIViewController *) application:(UIApplication *)application
    viewControllerWithRestorationIdentifierPath:
                        (NSArray *)identifierComponents
                        coder:(NSCoder *)coder {
    UIViewController* theController = nil;
    NSString* lastID = [identifierComponents lastObject];       <-- Hierarchy path

    if (!lastID) return nil;

    if ([lastID isEqualToString:@"MENavCon"])                    <-- Restoration IDs
         theController = _window.rootViewController;
    else if ([lastID isEqualToString:@"MESearchInput"])
        theController = [[(UINavigationController*)
                        _window.rootViewController
                        viewControllers] objectAtIndex:0];

    return theController;
}
```

One thing to notice is the `identifierComponents`. It's a hierarchy path of parent-children getting to the given view controller requested. So if you have a complex navigation setup to your app, just knowing the restoration ID may not be enough. It might need to know the hierarchy used to get to the view controller and instantiate it accordingly.

Also of note are the restoration ID strings used. Where did they come from? You made them up. `MSNavCon` is the main navigation controller and `MSSearchInput` is the initial user input controller. You have access to both of these objects here because they're loaded on startup. But how does the system know about these names? Let's look at setting those now.

TECHNIQUE 94 Setting restoration IDs on objects

Setting the restoration ID on an item (such as a view controller) allows the OS to specify what it's looking for during restoration so that the app can respond properly.

PROBLEM

You need to specify restoration IDs on your view controllers so they can be found during restoration.

Figure 11.13 Setting detail view controller restoration ID

SOLUTION

For your navigation controller and master view controller, you'll specify the restoration IDs in the UI editor Attributes Inspector (see figure 11.13).

DISCUSSION

Set the navigation controller's restoration ID to `MSNavCon` and the master view controller's to `MSSearchInput`. You can use the Storyboard ID if you'd like. Depending on your uses of the Storyboard, you may or may not need this set. For this case, you can do it either way, but I wanted to show you the route for using the Storyboard ID.

For the detail view controller, set the Storyboard ID to `MSResults` and check the box to use the Storyboard ID as the restoration ID. In this case, you do need them to be the same. This will facilitate using the restoration ID passed in during the restore process to fetch the instance from the Storyboard using the Storyboard ID. It's easier if they're the same.

TECHNIQUE 95 Assigning restoration classes

For view controllers that aren't loaded when the app starts up, you need to specify restoration classes. The specified class will provide the instance of the view controller to use when the app is being restored to the previous state.

The restoration class needs to implement the `UIViewControllerRestoration` protocol, which has one method expecting a view controller to be returned—the view controller to use for state restoration.

PROBLEM

You need to specify a restoration class for your detail view controller because it's not automatically instantiated during normal app execution startup. This restoration class needs to create and return a view controller instance with the same state as it was in the previous execution.

SOLUTION

You need to specify that your detail view controller implement the `UIViewControllerRestoration` protocol and assign itself to be the restoration class. Yes, that means that your detail view controller is its own restoration class (not instance, class).

In the viewDidLoad method, specify itself as the restoration class with this:

```
self.restorationClass = [self class];
```

Add UIViewControllerRestoration to the list of protocols in the .h file. Now add the protocol's method to the .m file:

```
+ (UIViewController *) viewControllerWithRestorationIdentifierPath:
                          (NSArray *)identifierComponents
                          coder:(NSCoder *)coder;
```

DISCUSSION

Note the two parameters sent in: the identifierComponents and the coder. The identifierComponents should specify the view controller to be loaded. Remember earlier you set the Storyboard ID to MSResults and checked the box for the restoration ID to be the same. This allows you to now use the restoration identifier component to fetch the instance from the Storyboard.

So all you have to do is instantiate your detail view controller and return it. But you want to load it from the Storyboard so you're consistent with normal execution. You can get the Storyboard from the coder and instantiate based on the Storyboard ID you set.

Load restoration view controller from Storyboard

```
+ (UIViewController *) viewControllerWithRestorationIdentifierPath:
                          (NSArray *)identifierComponents
                          coder:(NSCoder *)coder;
{
    UIStoryboard* sb = [coder decodeObjectForKey:
            UIStateRestorationViewControllerStoryboardKey];

    NSString* lastID =                                   <—— Storyboard ID
         [identifierComponents lastObject];
    if (sb)
        return (MSDetailViewController*)
            [sb instantiateViewControllerWithIdentifier:lastID];

    return nil;
}
```

For restoration, it's fine to return nil. In some cases you might want to, for example, if the data used previously has expired for some reason. The system won't restore to that point.

So you have all of the view controllers loading to this point, but the state itself isn't loaded. You haven't set the segment controllers, text field, or anything in the detail view controller. Let's look at that process.

TECHNIQUE 96 Encode/decode UI-related state values

So you've restored your classes, but haven't really restored the state. You want to bring the app back up as if the user were picking right back up and nothing has changed. If they were selecting search input or viewing results, you want to go right back there.

The state restoration process helps you again here by calling methods and sending in helpful information.

PROBLEM

You want to restore your UI state, not just the classes, from the previous execution. So you need to both store the state when necessary and restore it when called upon to do so.

SOLUTION

`UIViewController` has two methods called during restoration. Since you declared that your app restores, these methods are called. When saving the state, `encodeRestorableStateWithCoder:` is called with an `NSCoder` to store values. Similarly, when restoring `decodeRestorableStateWithCoder:` is called with an `NSCoder` to retrieve values.

DISCUSSION

To restore the search input values for the user's execution, let's implement these two methods.

Save restoration values into `NSCoder`

```
#define kSearchGorE @"SearchGorE"
#define kSearchZorK @"SearchZorK"
#define kSearchText @"SearchText"

- (void)encodeRestorableStateWithCoder:(NSCoder *)coder
{
    [super encodeRestorableStateWithCoder:coder];
    [coder encodeInt:segSearchGroupsOrEvents.selectedSegmentIndex
                     forKey:kSearchGorE];
    [coder encodeInt:segSearchZipOrKeyword.selectedSegmentIndex
                     forKey:kSearchZorK];
    [coder encodeObject:tfSearchText.text
                     forKey:kSearchText];
}
```

For the master view controller, the search input UI, you want to save the three user settings: two segment controllers and the text field data.

Restore values from `NSCoder`

```
- (void)decodeRestorableStateWithCoder:(NSCoder *)coder {
    [super decodeRestorableStateWithCoder:coder];
    [segSearchGroupsOrEvents setSelectedSegmentIndex:
                        [coder decodeIntegerForKey:kSearchGorE]];
    [segSearchZipOrKeyword setSelectedSegmentIndex:
                        [coder decodeIntegerForKey:kSearchZorK]];
    [tfSearchText setText:
                        [coder decodeObjectForKey:kSearchText]];
}
```

In both cases, you're calling the super version of these methods first. You can call it later in the method, but be sure to call it so that the base class has a chance to restore anything from the system.

Why don't you do something similar for the detail view controller? Well, there's no user input (granted, if the user was sharing something at the time, and so forth, there may be a case for that, but for our purposes, we won't go that far). And remember, your detail view controller loads the search results from a file. That file is still there and your class will read it in and display the results again (without going to the server).

But what about where the user was in the collection view? If they'd scrolled down and maybe selected an item, you want to be right back there. How's that done?

TECHNIQUE 97 Table/collection datasource considerations

Another way the UI state restoration setup helps is by managing some UI aspects. Scroll views automatically retain their location. But table views and collection views, though scroll views, may not display the same data at the same location.

So though you want to display the same item, its index path might be different during a later execution. The system helps with that by providing the `UIDataSourceModelAssociation` protocol to save and restore the item's `indexPath`. A given datasource for a restorable table view or collection view should implement this protocol.

PROBLEM

You want to display to the user the same item(s) they were looking at before the app quit.

SOLUTION

You implement the `UIDataSourceModelAssociation` protocol and store identifying data for the given displayed item(s) when requested.

During restoration, the system sends in that identifying data and the app returns the current `indexPath`, which may or may not be the same as the previous execution.

DISCUSSION

The `UIDataSourceModelAssociation` protocol has two declared methods. Let's look at the first one for preserving the viewed item's `indexPath`.

Specify unique ID for item at index path

```
- (NSString *) modelIdentifierForElementAtIndexPath:(NSIndexPath *)idx
                        inView:(UIView *)view;
{
    NSDictionary *item = [displayItems objectAtIndex:idx.row];
    return [NSString stringWithFormat:@"%@", [item objectForKey:@"id"]];
}
```

For the `indexPath` passed in, you can get the related item (event or group) and use the ID stored in the data from the server. That will help you identify the item during restoration when this method is called.

Return index path for restoration item

```
- (NSIndexPath *) indexPathForElementWithModelIdentifier:
                        (NSString *)identifier
                        inView:(UIView *)view;
{
```

```
    int cnt = 0;
    for (NSDictionary *item in displayItems)
    {
        if ([[item objectForKey:@"id"] isEqualToString:identifier])
            return [NSIndexPath indexPathForRow:cnt inSection:0];
        cnt++;                                                      <-- Count rows
    }
    return nil;
}
```

Since your indexPath only has one section, you know that will be zero. And the row is based on the order of the items in the array. Given that, you can cycle through the array, find the matching ID, and return the index of that item.

Now that you're returning the indexPath, the OS can position the base class scroll view properly.

If your items were simply (unique) strings, you could return that in the restoration method and return the index of that item in the array for the restoration method. Depending on your dataset, different routes will make sense. But maybe your dataset definition changes from one version to the next. How can you store that type of data?

TECHNIQUE 98 Additional app version and state data

For some overarching data that doesn't relate directly to a given view or view controller, you might want to store some values. Maybe some data relates generally to multiple parts of your app (such as version) and you want to set it during preservation and access it during restoration.

The UIApplicationDelegate can implement two methods for just this purpose.

PROBLEM

You want to store some general data during state preservation to have access to it later.

SOLUTION

Similar to the view controller, the app delegate has encode and decode methods that are called during the preservation and restoration processes. An NSCoder is passed in so values can be stored and retrieved accordingly.

DISCUSSION

The methods are defined and implemented simply enough. Let's look at some implementations.

Encode/decode general restoration values for app

```
- (void)application:(UIApplication *)application
                    willEncodeRestorableStateWithCoder:(NSCoder *)coder
{
    [coder encodeFloat:1.0 forKey:@"MSVersion"];
}

- (void)application:(UIApplication *)application
                    didDecodeRestorableStateWithCoder:(NSCoder *)coder
{
```

```
    float curVer = [[NSUserDefaults standardUserDefaults]
                        floatForKey:@"MSVersion"];
    float lastVer = [coder decodeFloatForKey:@"MSVersion"];
}
```

In the encode method, you're encoding the current version. Normally you might get this from another source—I can't imagine anyone would remember to update this number for each new version—but for our example, there it is. This method is called *before* the rest of the restoration calls on classes. So you can set general data here and/or you can do something here that might affect other restoration steps.

The decode method is called *after* the rest of the restoration steps, so you can do something to wrap up restoration and/or decode general settings. In the example, I'm retrieving the current version (presumably set during restoration) and the previous version (set during the previous execution's preservation). You could compare them and do some migration or upgrade process if necessary.

11.5 Summary

In this chapter we looked at a variety of items in a new project for searching for local meetup.com results. You displayed them in a collection view. You shared them through various outlets. You created calendar items for them and even preserved and restored the UI state for the user.

These items will translate to a variety of projects and can form the foundation for some great apps.

appendix The iOS developer program and app distribution

Unlike developing for desktop computers or websites, there are some hoops to jump through for some mobile platforms, including the iPhone. The first requirement is becoming an iOS developer by joining the iOS Developer Program. This gives you access to many resources, including the Provisioning Portal.

The Provisioning Portal is where you set up all of the necessary items to develop and distribute your app. If uploading your app to the App Store is like putting it on a plane, think of the Provisioning Portal as where you buy the ticket, check the bags, and get the boarding pass. It's a multistep process with input, output, and a purpose.

In this chapter, we'll look at enrolling in the Developer Program, each aspect of the Provisioning Portal, and the two types of distribution.

You'll learn how to use the portal to build your team, certificates, app IDs, and provisioning profiles, as well as how to distribute your app for testing and to the App Store.

Let's start by looking at the iOS Developer Program.

A.1 The iOS Developer Program

Joining the iOS Developer Program is more than paying some money and "being official." It gets you access into seemingly limitless resources for iOS development. If you're part of another member's team, you'll need to become a member yourself to run apps on devices, distribute your apps through the App Store, access the forums, and so forth.

A.1.1 Enrolling in the developer program

The Apple iOS Developer Program is easy to join. You need to have or create an Apple account, which costs $99, but it doesn't take much to join. If you join the program as a company, you may also need to provide proof of the company's existence (such as articles of incorporation).

Start by going to this site: http://developer.apple.com/programs/start/register/create.php.

When creating an account, you'll have to fill out the usual information such as ID, password, and so on (see figure A.1).

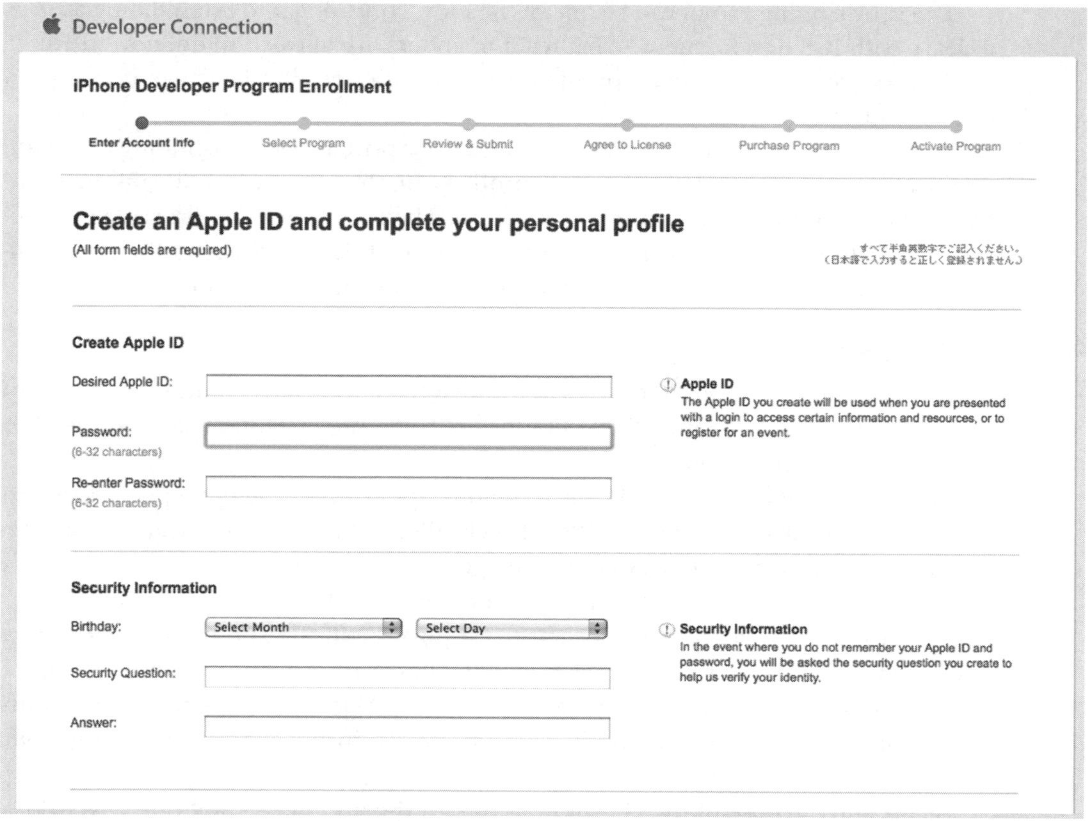

Figure A.1 Creating an Apple account when enrolling in the developer program

A.1.2 Developing while you wait

You won't be able to create everything you need to install the app on your iPhone, but you'll be able to run it in the simulator, which goes a long way. I recommend enrolling in the program as soon as possible to have full access to the resources and functionality of the program and Provisioning Portal.

As mentioned in chapter 1, you can get the SDK without being a member of the program. If you didn't already, join and download the SDK here: http://developer.apple.com/programs/start/register/create.php.

If a week or two has gone by and you still haven't been approved, I recommend calling (800)633-2152. After you're approved, you'll be able to enjoy the wonderful world of creating certificates and provisioning profiles.

A.2 Provisioning Portal

Joining the Developer Program gives you access to the Provisioning Portal. The portal allows you to take care of the your account's administration work necessary for developing apps beyond the code, but it isn't where you develop or distribute your app.

The Provisioning Portal can be one of the most confusing and intimidating aspects to learn with iOS development. What team members are allowed to do, how to create certificates, what a provisioning profile is, and how they're all related can be tough to understand.

In chapter 1, you were introduced to the various portal aspects including the team, certificates, app IDs, and provisioning profiles. In this section, we'll look in more detail at each of these and how to create them. Then you'll use the provisioning profiles to create builds for distribution. By the end of this exercise, you'll have a real-world feel for what's needed to develop and distribute an iPhone app.

A.2.1 Obtaining certificates

Certificates and provisioning profiles are probably the two most confusing aspects of setting up iOS development. Ultimately, they're not a big deal and you don't need to create or change them too often.

Certificates are used by developers of iPhone apps during the build process to sign the apps to be run on an iPhone/iPod Touch. Without a certificate, you can run the app in the simulator, but not a device (see figure A.2).

There are two types of certificates: development and distribution.

The How To tab clearly explains how to create a certificate and the steps necessary to download and install it after it's created. It's a linear process of creating a certificate signing request (CSR) with the Keychain app on your Mac, uploading that and approving it, and then downloading the final certificate. To install the certificate into your keychain, double-click on it.

Again, the purpose of the certificate is to sign the app in the build process to run on an Apple device.

Figure A.2 iOS Developer Program portal certification tab for creating certificates

Figure A.3 Downloading the WWDR intermediate certificate from the iOS developer portal

You'll also need the Worldwide Developer Relations (WWDR) intermediate certificate. You can download this from the certificates that are under the Development tab (see figure A.3).

To install the WWDR certificate, like other certificates you'll create, double-click on the .cer file, which will launch Keychain Access. Select the Login keychain when prompted and click OK.

A.2.2 *Adding devices*

The Devices tab allows you to manage the iPhone/iPod Touch device unique IDs for your account. These are the devices that are allowed to run your apps, whether through the development environment or ad hoc builds, which you'll learn about later.

To add a device to this list, you must first get the unique ID of the device. Erica Sadun has developed a great app for this called Ad Hoc Helper. It emails the device's unique ID to an email address you specify during execution of the app.

If you have access to the device, an easy way to find the unique ID is through iTunes. Connect the device, click on the device name under Devices on the left side, and then click on the displayed serial number. It then toggles to display the unique ID—Identifier (UDID).

Selecting Edit > Copy (or Command-c), copies the ID for pasting (see figure A.4).

Now that you have the device ID, you can click Add Devices and enter a device name and the unique ID you copied from iTunes. Click Submit and you're done (see figure A.5).

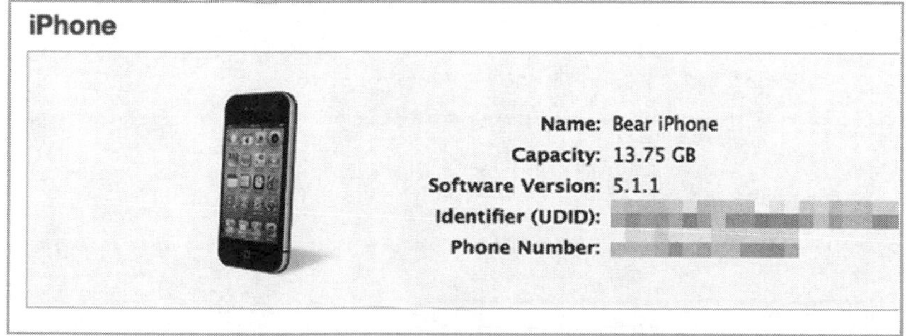

Figure A.4 Using iTunes to find the iPhone/iPod Touch device's unique ID

You can register 70 additional devices.
You can register up to 100 devices per year for development purposes. Any devices added, then later removed, still count towards your maximum number of registered devices per year. Learn more

Device Name	Device ID	Profiles	Actions
Bear i4	990095af9794beabe31ff374b4...	33 (Details)	Edit
Bear iPad	75e3c2a6016637920b2af3fb7a...	32 (Details)	Edit
Bear iPad2	8c0257c32e7cbac51a8920c8fc...	15 (Details)	Edit
Bear iPhone	2da3950f46a2fd177495de9b6e...	36 (Details)	Edit

Figure A.5 iOS Developer Program portal devices tab for adding your iPhone/iPod Touch device

Later, as you want to send people ad hoc builds, you'll need to update your list of devices and add them to the ad hoc provisioning profile.

A.2.3 Creating app IDs

App IDs are used to identify your apps in your provisioning profiles. They're also used in APN and external hardware accessories and can be used to share keychain data between a suite of apps.

To create your app ID, click New App ID. I recommend you create one app ID for each of your apps. Type in a general description of your app, enter the bundle identifier, and click Submit (see figure A.6).

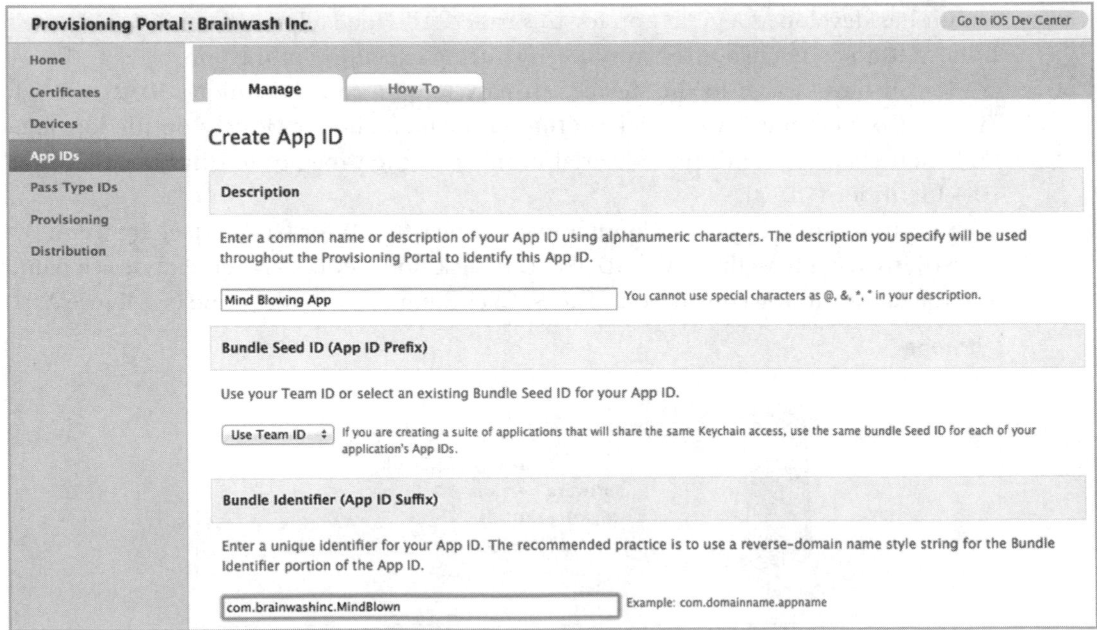

Figure A.6 iOS Developer Program portal app ID tab for creating app IDs

There's nothing to download or install for app IDs. This information is used in the provisioning profile creation.

A.2.4 Provisioning profiles

Provisioning is the other most intimidating area of the portal, but it needn't be. Navigating through the portal means understanding teams, certificates, devices, app IDs, and provisioning profiles. Each of these are different concepts and are mostly technical and unique to iOS development (to a degree).

Like certificates, provisioning profiles are files created on the server and downloaded to your development machine. For development, you need a development profile installed. For distribution, there are two types of profiles—ad hoc and distribution. Ad hoc profiles are used to send builds specifically for certain devices. This is a great way to send out test/demo/beta builds to clients. Distribution profiles are needed for building your app when you're ready to submit your app to the App Store.

To create a development provisioning profile, click the Development tab, click New Profile, enter a profile name (something with "dev" in it works for me), select the certificate you made earlier and the app ID you created, and then any device you want to develop on (see figure A.7).

Click Submit and you're taken back to the Development tab with your new profile pending. Wait a minute, click the Development tab again, and it's probably ready for download.

To create a provisioning profile for distribution, click on the Distribution tab, enter the profile name (something with "dist" in it is helpful), select your app ID, and click Submit.

For in-house distribution, you use an ad hoc profile. Creating an ad hoc profile is similar to creating a development provisioning profile, except when you click the Ad

Figure A.7 iOS Developer Program portal development provisioning profiles creation

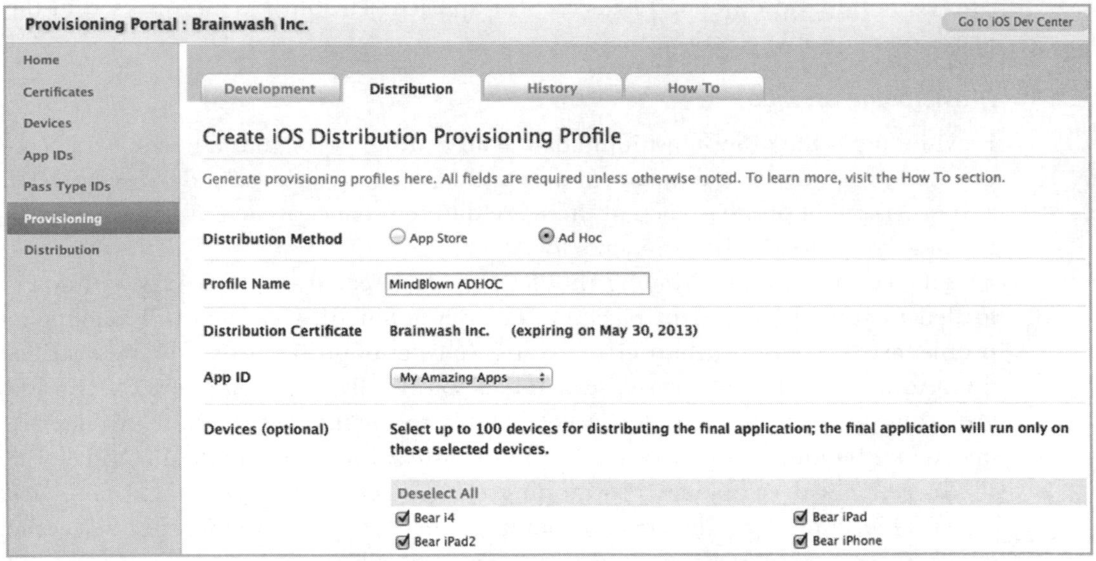

Figure A.8 iOS Developer Program portal distribution provisioning creation is necessary for the App Store.

Hoc Radio button, you must select which device(s) the app is allowed to run on (see figure A.8).

When you download the provisioning profiles, you can install them by dragging them into iTunes and syncing with your device. Xcode does a good job of selecting the appropriate provisioning profile based on your project settings, but we'll get into that later.

From Xcode, you can open the Organizer under the Window menu. The Organizer lets you see the connected device, crash logs, provisioning profiles, and more. If you select Provisioning Profiles on the left, you'll see a list of profiles at the top. To see details of a profile, select one. Among other things, you can see what device(s) it's installed on to confirm that it's installed on your development device (see figure A.9).

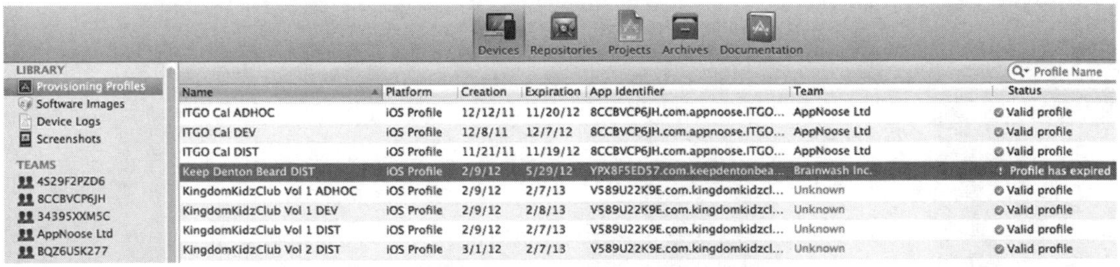

Figure A.9 Provisioning profile as seen in the device using the Xcode Organizer

You can congratulate yourself on becoming familiar with the iOS Provisioning Portal and be confident that you have the necessary knowledge to navigate it.

You've paid your dues (literally) in enrolling and creating your provisioning needs. Now let's create an ad hoc build that can be installed on some devices.

A.3 Distribution configurations and builds

As stated earlier for provisioning profiles, there are two different types of distribution for your app. Everyone knows about apps being in the App Store. That's what is usually seen as "distribution." But ad hoc distribution is another kind. Ad hoc distribution allows you to send the app to select people to run and test on their iPhone.

You already specified your allowed device IDs and created the provisioning profiles. Now you can tell Xcode to use them when creating your ad hoc build and distribution build.

In this section, you'll go through the steps to create your ad hoc and distribution configurations using the appropriate provisioning profiles. Using those configurations, you'll create an ad hoc build and distribution build. You'll also look at how to send (or distribute) and install the ad hoc build. Distribution to the App Store will be covered in the next section.

A.3.1 Creating distribution configurations

Now that you have your certificates and profiles installed, let's set up Xcode to use them. You'll continue with your Hello World project.

Start Xcode and open your Hello World project from before. To the right of that, select Hello World under Project (see figure A.10). In the Configurations area, click the + button to duplicate the release configuration to create ad hoc and distribution configurations.

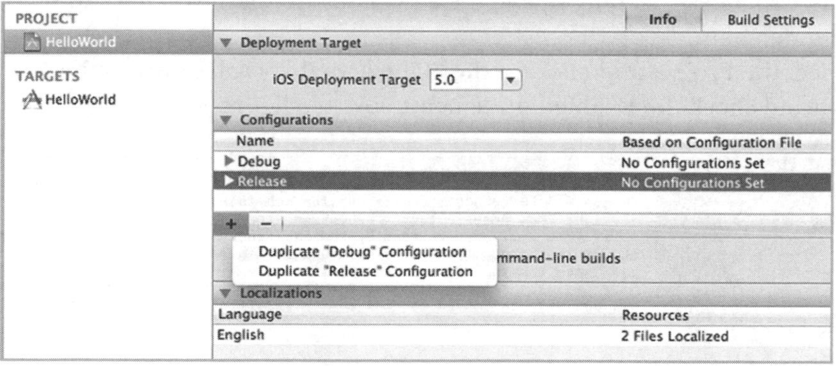

Figure A.10 Editing project configurations in the Xcode project info window

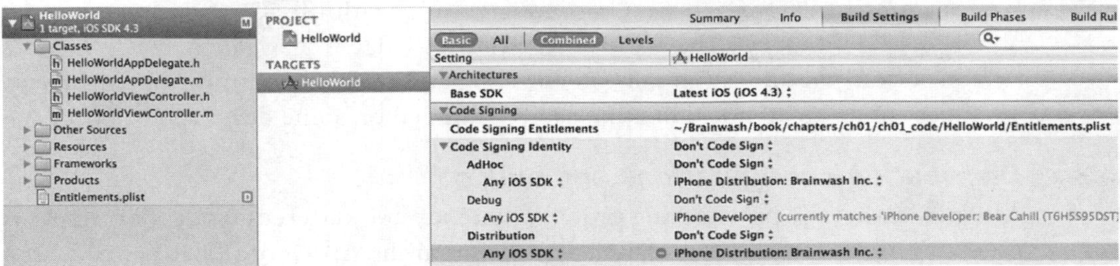

Figure A.11 Xcode info window for Hello World project configurations

Next, the new build configurations need to use the appropriate provisioning profile. Be sure the project is selected on the far left pane and select Hello World under Target to the right of that. Select the Build Settings at the top (see figure A.11).

In the Code Signing Identity field, make sure iOS Developer is displayed (and that your profile details are specified in the gray text) or click on the right value and select the correct profile for each configuration.

Let's run the app on your device to test that you set up the configuration correctly. Connect your iPhone/iPod Touch to your Mac. If you sync first, wait until that's done. On the top left of the Xcode editor window, make sure Device - <OS version> is selected and select Run from the Product menu (see figure A.12).

The app will compile, install on the device, and execute, showing you the same Hello World label right on your device! If you're prompted to allow the code signing, select Allow or Always Allow.

To bring up the Log Monitor, press Command-7 and select the execution (top is most recent/current). This app doesn't produce any output other than the start time, but soon this window will be a good friend.

There's an extra step to enable the ad hoc distribution: you have to set the necessary entitlements.

Select the Project and click on the Summary tab. Scroll down to the Entitlements section and check the Enable Entitlements box (see figure A.13).

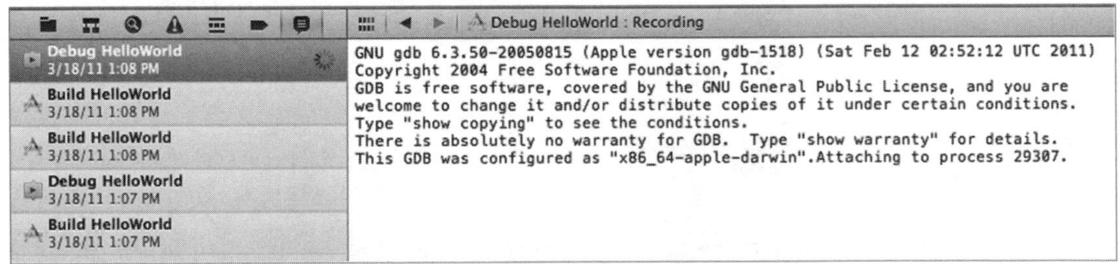

Figure A.12 Xcode log monitor during execution of Hello World on an iOS device

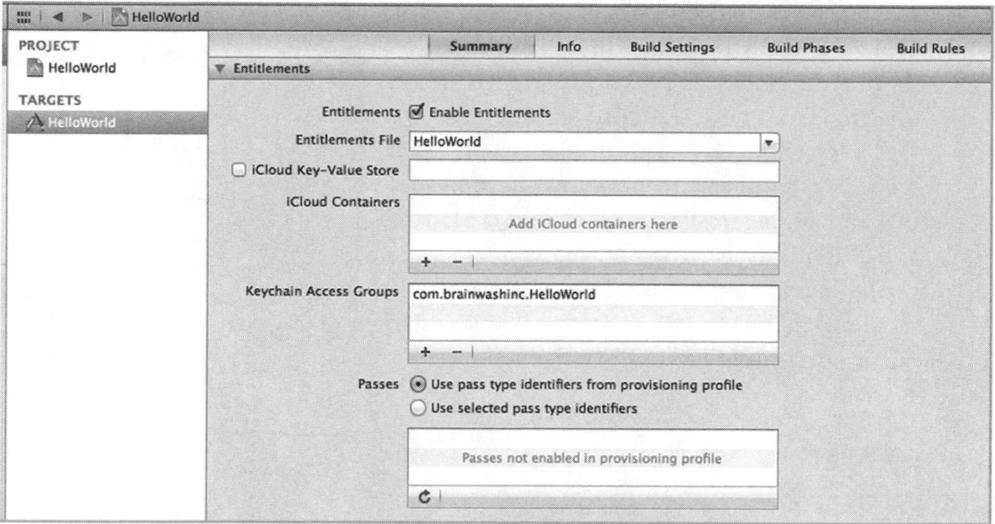

Figure A.13 Creating ad hoc entitlements file in Xcode for a project

Open the Info window again by selecting the Hello World project and Hello World under the Target to the right. Under the Code Signing group, verify that Code Signing Entitlements has the name of the entitlements file you created (see figure A.14).

Select the ad hoc configuration from the configuration drop-down menu. Select Product > Build For... > Build for Archiving. Make sure the device is selected as opposed to a simulator and that the app isn't currently running or this option won't be available. This is a build you can send to someone in your device ID list for them to install on their device.

Again, this person's device ID must be in your list of devices in the program portal. Also, when you add their device, you need to edit your ad hoc provisioning profile and include their device in the list of devices. This will cause the profile to be recreated. Download it again, double-click on it to install, and build using the ad hoc configuration.

I prefer to recreate my ad hoc profile whenever I add a new device. That way I'm already in the portal and can move forward without logging in twice.

With an ad hoc build ready, you can send the app to others. It will only work on the devices you selected when you created the ad hoc profile. After they receive and install the build, they can run the app on their iPhone/iPod Touch.

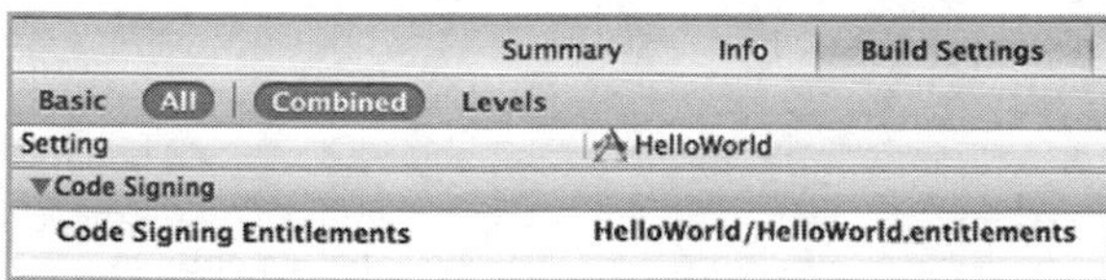

Figure A.14 Setting code signing entitlements for ad hoc build in Xcode target info settings

A.3.2 Installing an ad hoc build

The easiest way to create an ad hoc build to share with others is to select Archive from the Project menu (see figure A.15).

The Organizer will display when the build is complete and give you the options to Validate (against iTunesConnect), Share, and Submit (see figure A.16). Validate will verify that the various settings and required files are valid according to the Apple submission requirements.

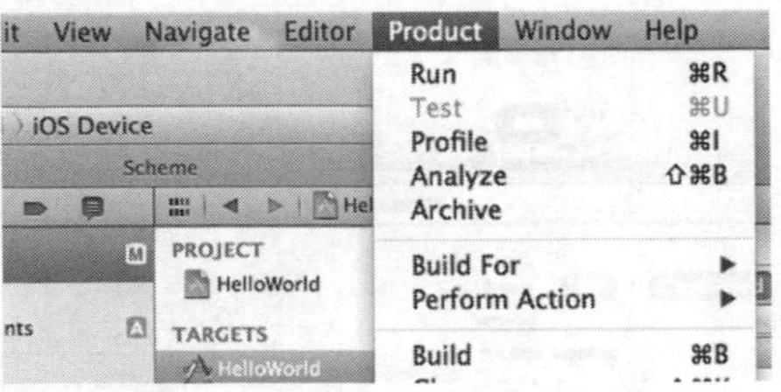

Figure A.15 Ad hoc build and archive to send to others

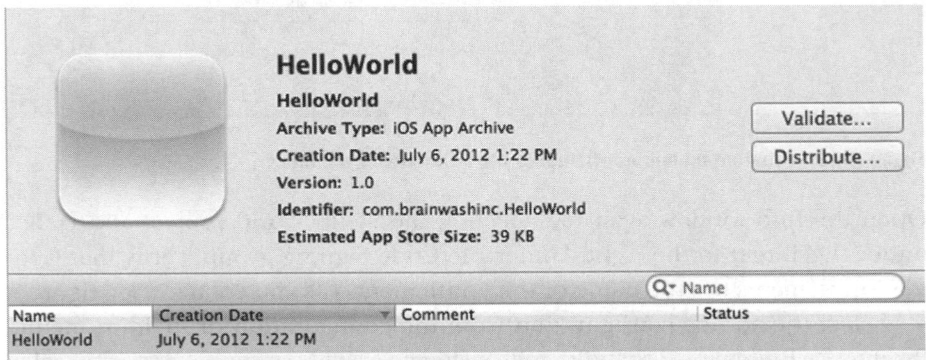

Figure A.16 Ad hoc build and archive organizer options

Distribute allows you to submit the app to Apple for review, distribute an Enterprise or Ad-Hoc app, and more (see figure A.17). Select the identity (app ID) and click Save to Disk. Xcode will create an ipa file that you can now send to users with devices associated with this ad hoc profile.

When the person receives the app file, they can simply drop the two files into their Apps area in iTunes and sync their device. If the user gets an error (like `e8008016`), it usually means that their device ID isn't in the provisioning profile.

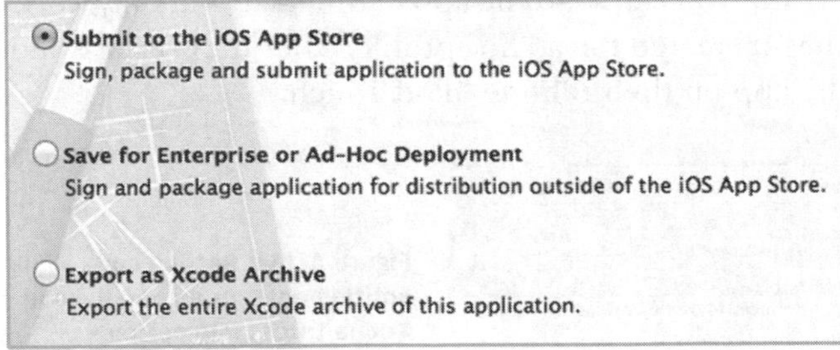

Figure A.17 Ad hoc build and archive organizer distribution options

iTunes won't show an icon for the build unless there's a special version of the icon in the project. This special version needs to be a 512 x 512 png file named iTunes-Artwork (no file extension).

Now that you've seen how to develop and test using the simulator and ad hoc builds, let's look at distributing through the App Store when your app is ready.

A.4 App Store distribution

The goal of developing an iPhone app is to submit it to the App Store for distribution. If you've successfully followed the steps in the previous sections, this section should be simple.

Because you've already set up your distribution provisioning profile and created and tested the app on devices, you're ready!

The Provisioning Portal can be intimidating and confusing, and the same is true for iTunesConnect, which is where you submit your app for review. But I think you'll see that it doesn't have to be difficult. Learning how to do it now will allow you to develop your apps without having to worry about what's to come. Also, with related concepts fresh in your mind, I think learning it now will be easiest.

A.4.1 Files required for distribution

There are a few steps to submit your app to the App Store. Your app is the main item you need to upload, but there are other required items (see table A.1). Other icons and images can be provided to display better on other devices and in other areas of the OS. Details are here: http://mng.bz/v90L.

Table A.1 App Store required files for app submission for distribution

Icon.png	57 x 57 png image for your app
Large icon	1024 x 1024 version of your icon
Default.png	A 640 x 960 image to display while your app is loading
Screenshots	One to five screenshots at 320 x 480 as jpg files
App	Your app zipped up

The specifics of these files are important, so let's look at how to prepare them.

A.4.2 Preparations for App Store Submission

Most of the earlier items are self-explanatory. The screenshots may be taken from your desktop while running the app in the simulator or from your device by pressing the Home and Power buttons simultaneously. Use Command-s in the simulator to take a screenshot. Be sure you selected the Retina display device from the Hardware menu so that your images are the correct dimensions.

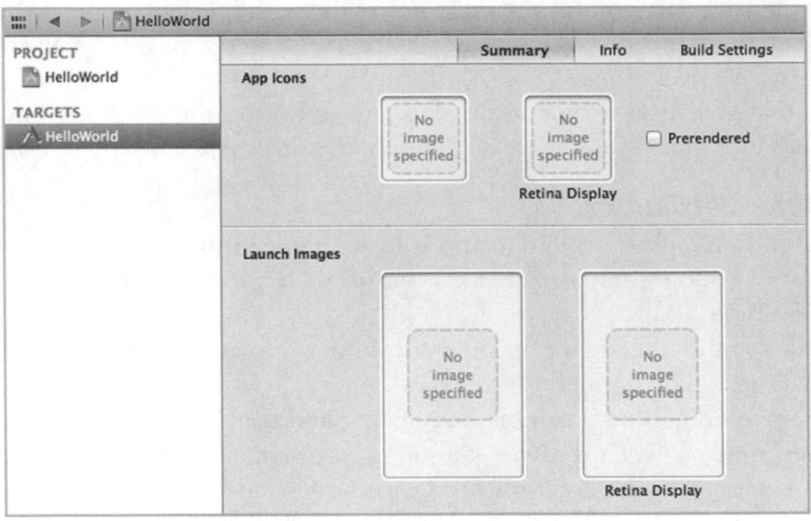

Figure A.18 Add and copy the icon file to the project resources

Drag your 57 x 57 icon file into your icon to your App Icons area in your Target's Summary (see figure A.18). Do the same for the retina icon (114 x 114) and your Splash Screen/Launch Images.

A.4.3 Uploading to the App Store

To create the distribution build, select Archive from the Product menu (make sure your iOS device is selected in the Scheme on the top left). When the Organizer displays your archived build, select Distribute and then Submit to the iOS App Store.

From there you'll be presented with the steps to log in to your iTunes Connect account (see figure A.19) and specify the necessary data to submit/upload the build.

You don't want this app to really be reviewed, so if you submitted it, remove it from the review process. Under the app in iTunesConnect, click Reject Binary. This will remove the app from the review process.

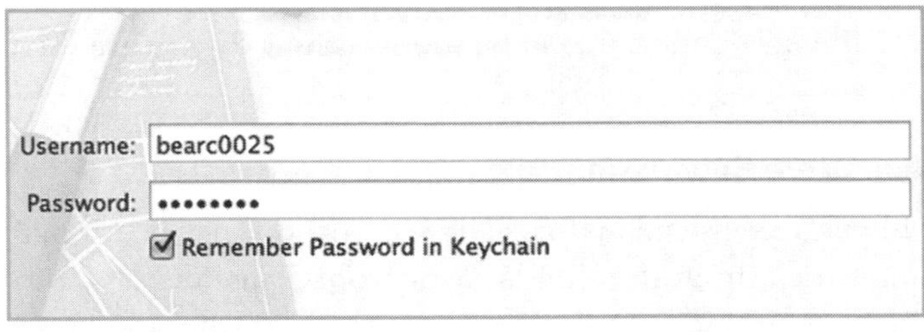

Figure A.19 Log in to iTunes Connect to specify the app being submitted.

A.5 Summary

I can't tell you how I dreaded diving into the Developer Program and more so the Provisioning Profile when I first started developing for the iPhone. I clicked links and buttons on the various pages with caution. At each step, I held my breath. When I submitted an app, I hoped each step would work.

Eventually I got more comfortable and realized how the pieces fit together; I no longer worried or hesitated to load up the sites. Now, I'm surprised when something doesn't work the first time and, when that happens, I can quickly determine the cause and fix it.

In this appendix, you've seen how to navigate the Provisioning Portal. More than that, you've put it to use with an ad hoc build installed on devices and even submitted your first app to the App Store.

These same steps are used for each app you develop. In some cases, you'll need fewer steps because you won't have to set up all of the provisioning needs—you can use the existing ones you already have.

I see the Developer Program as a great resource. I see the Provisioning Portal as a necessary evil. It helps protect Apple, but also prevents nonpaying devices from running apps, which keeps people from having your app without paying for it. While it's not the fun part of developing for iPhone, it's necessary.

index

Symbols

A

D

N

O

V

W

X

Z

RELATED MANNING TITLES

Hello! iOS Development

by Lou Franco and Eitan Mendelowitz

ISBN: 978-1-935182-98-6
300 pages, $29.99
February 2013

iOS 4 in Action

Examples and Solutions for iPhone & iPad

by Jocelyn Harrington, Brandon Trebitowski, Christopher Allen, and Shannon Appelcline

ISBN: 978-1-617290-01-5
504 pages, $44.99
June 2011

Android in Practice

by Charlie Collins, Michael D. Galpin, and Matthias Kaeppler

ISBN: 978-1-935182-92-4
648 pages, $49.99
September 2011

Objective-C Fundamentals

by Christopher K. Fairbairn, Johannes Fahrenkrug, and Collin Ruffenach

ISBN: 978-1-935182-53-5
368 pages, $44.99
September 2011

For ordering information go to www.manning.com